Silk And Scarlet

Henry Hall Dixon

SILK

AND

SCARLET.

BY

THE DRUID,

AUTHOR OF "SADDLE AND SIRLOIN," "SCOTT AND SEBRIGHT," ETC.

REVISED AND RE-EDITED.

WITH STEEL ENGRAVINGS.

LONDON:

FREDERICK WARNE AND CO.

BEDFORD STREET, STRAND.

Engraved by J. B. Hunt, from a Photograph.

DICK CHRISTIAN, ÆT. 70.

"HORSES, BLESS YOU, I'VE KNOWN 'EM GET OUT OF A DITCH AND PUT
THEIR FORE-FEET ON EACH OF MY SHOULDERS, MY COAT'S BEEN ALL
SPLIT UP BY THEM. I BROKE TWO RIBS FROM A DOG CART WHEN I
WAS SEVENTY SIX. I THOUGHT I WUR DONE THAT TIME".

Vide Print in the Parlour at
Barleythorpe.

PREFACE.

AFTER two years of no small labour, I have redeemed the promise I made of writing a companion work to *The Post and the Paddock*. In the racing portion of it, my way was clear enough; but the hunting was fraught with difficulty. It struck me, however, that there was one mode of treating the subject which I might legitimately pursue without exposing myself to the charge of plagiarism, or provoking a fatal comparison with those regular hunting writers, who have learnt their experience in the saddle. In many of the capital books which have appeared on the subject, horses and their riders seem to have monopolized the lion's share of notice, to the exclusion of the hounds. I felt sure that there must be not a few stories of the exploits and breeding of the latter, which had been told often enough over hunting firesides, but had never risen to type estate ; and hence I determined to sally forth, and make a pilgrimage with my note-book among the principal English kennels. As regards both racing and hunting, I cannot speak with sufficient gratitude of the kind assistance I have received from every one (and from none more than the late Will Goodall) to whom I applied, although in nine instances out of ten we had never met or corresponded before.

For the first two chapters I can claim no credit. They are the *verbatim* recitals of the hunting deeds of bygone days in Leicestershire and Northamptonshire, as they appeared to two very different minds ; and as Dick has had such experience as "pilot" across Leicestershire, I deemed it prudent to send him off at score in the first chapter to make a pace, while, in the words of the equally renowned Billy Pierse, "*I toddled behind.*" After spending so many days with Dick in the prosecution of our historic studies, it would have been a sad lack of politeness not to give a print of him. The attitude and expression is exactly that which he assumed when I read him the proof-sheets of his lecture ; and it was, I regret to say, on one of those errands that he incautiously walked, with his right hand in his breeches-pocket, and falling against the kerbstone on a frosty night, laid himself up for nearly the whole winter. Tom Sebright and Tom Rance, as the senior foxhound huntsman and whip of England, also claimed a portrait ; and that of poor Will Goodall is taken from a photograph, which his widow kindly allowed me to copy. Mr. Osbaldeston's well-known figure will be recognised in the sketch from the pencil of Mr. Ambrose Isted ; and the Turf has its representative in Jem Robinson and Dick Stockdale, the latter one of the most devoted lovers of horses, and best-known characters in the whole of the East Riding. His brother Yorkshiremen would indeed be amazed, if they went to an agricultural or a foal show, and did not see Dick leading something into the ring, and making it stand well up.

Unlike *The Post and the Paddock*, which was mainly a reprint from the *Sporting Magazine* to begin with, and gradually swelled into a " Hunting Edition," the present work is, with the exception of eight or nine pages (which I have adopted on the principle of " the man who eloped with his own wife "), entirely original. If it is ever fated to reach a second issue, it will receive not one line in addition ; and it goes to the starting-post with the assurance that it has had a long and steady preparation, and that, if it cannot at least run to the form of its elder brother, its trainer has no excuse to make for it.

GOODWOOD CUP MORNING, 1859.

TABLE OF CONTENTS.

ENGRAVINGS.

SILK AND SCARLET.

CHAPTER I

DICK CHRISTIAN AGAIN.

" A gentleman who practically explains all the above accomplishments,
to the great edification of young horses, and the no less astonish-
ment of weak minds."

DICK CHRISTIAN had practically sounded the
depth of every ditch and brook in Leicestershire,
for more than half a century; but its foxhunters had
never half sounded him in return. They little knew
what a capacity for authorship, which was not destined
to blossom until its seventy-eighth spring, lurked in
that thickset frame and merry twinkling eye; and
until, when a graver task was ended, I sought him
out at Melton last summer, and discussed the chances
of a second Lecture with him, I was nearly as much
in the dark myself. Seated beneath the chestnut
shade of "Norton, by Beningboro'," I found him as
remarkable in his language as he had been when I
gave him his first trial eighteen months before, and
firmer than ever in his hero-worship of Mr. Assheton
Smith, Sir James Musgrave, and Captain White. It
was not for any lack of epistolary stimulants on his
part, that I delayed my visit so long. He fairly
thirsted to be in print once more; and the post had
brought me an admonition to this effect, " You don't

B

know what injury you're doing yourself, delaying my
lecture so long." It seemed to me that we had indulged enough in mere table-talk; and hence I
determined to make a gig survey of Leicestershire
with him, and ask him to point out to me the leading
hunting features in that Waterloo of his existence,
where he had so often fallen and fought again to-
morrow. The season was hardly in character with
the trip. Thorpe Trussells was radiant with dog-
roses, and honeysuckles clustered amid the hedges
of Ashby Pasture; but he assured me that his hunting
recollections were just as vivid, summer or winter,
and soon sketched out a pretty comprehensive journey, through the Belvoir, the Cottesmore, and the
Quorn. Three sunny mornings we sallied merrily on
our way; and although Dick added another tumble
to his Mammoth bead-roll, and the jolting occupation-
roads threatened at intervals to play havoc with my
notes, I found his geography of the most jocular
order, and travelled over his memory as follows.

RIDE THE FIRST.

" What gallant run did brave Meltonians share,
But thou wast 'forward,' or the foremost there?"

Dick gives a
general sketch of
his health.
I'M right glad you've come. What a
many have been asking me when
they're to have this new lecture of mine.
In Essex they were always at me. What fun I've had
down there at Sir Thomas's! We were jumping all day,
doubles, rails, stake and bounds, never off it. Grand
horse that Sir John of his. I was there nigh three
months; but I got a bad cold. The doctor was sent
for to me. He comes, and I tells him my age; he
handles me. *" One of your lungs,"* he says, *" is as
sound as wax, but the other's not quite the thing."*
Then he asks me which side I sleeps on, and I says,

"I used to sleep on my right side, now I goes on my left." "*Ah!*" he says, "*I have it: you're as sound on your left side as any child ; it's a touch of the liver ;*" bad cold, something like the agey. So I come back to Melton.

They've got quite to call me "*The Emperor*" down here. I heard nothing of it till Mr. Kirk, he comes to me at Croxton Races, and he says, "*Why, Dick, you've got a new name. It will be from that lecture of yours.*" One or two of them were on me about it at the cricket match. The Quorn and Cottesmore farmers, on a market day, they give me no peace of my life. They've all got my lecture ; and they learn bits out of it, and keep pitching 'em at me ; I can't walk up the street but one or another begins with me. It's just the same at the meet ; and the gentlemen is quite as fond of the game. The ladies make much of me. They've took to that lecture uncommonly. They say they never just properly know'd before what an owdacious man I'd been.

The effect of his "Post and Paddock" Lecture on society in general;

and on the ladies in particular.

I once jumped a whole flock of sheep near Gadesby, in Mr. Osbaldeston's time. I think we'd found at the Coplow. They had scruddled into a corner, just like that near those pens. The hounds were running like mad. I was leading. I sends my horse at the rails, and clears the sheep, every one of 'em. My horse he hits the top of the rail, and goes clean bang on to his head. The shepherd, he shouts, "*Now hang you, that just sarves you right.*" I says, "So it does, old fellow," and I gathers myself up, and goes on, and we kills the fox at Ragdale. No one would credit it ; it's as true as I've this whip in my hand. Deary me! how horses has rolled on me times and often—squeezed— bones broke—all that sort of thing! If I were to tell all the good runs I've seen, it would fill a ledger. I

He jumps a flock of sheep.

began hunting when I was eight years of age, and I've never missed a season since. I rode second horse for Sir Gilbert. Mr. George Watson, he once said to him, " *You'll kill that boy, riding day after day without stirrups.*" I wasn't hurt a bit in that sheep job. Bless you, I could turn a somersault in them days, when I felt the horse going. I throwed myself clean over his head, and always ketched on my legs; no end of gentlemen saw it. I sold that horse that very day to the Duke of Montrose; he was Marquis of Graham then ; he lodged along with Colonel Powis, where the lawyer lives now.

Recollections of Sysonby Hall. There's Sysonby Hall, first place you comes at. Wellesley Pole, they made him Lord Maryborough, lived there. Lord Maynard lived at it once. Wright was at Sysonby Farm. He was a great man with Lord Plymouth. This was all his land where we are now—(it wasn't Bill Wright, of Uppingham, the dealer ; nothing of the sort) ; he sold Sir Harry a many horses. Lord Plymouth gave him Juniper to travel with, and Breny Hawken, coal-black all over ; wide in his ears ; I broke 'em both, and a sight of trouble they gave me. Captain Ross bid my lord a thousand guineas for Juniper, to run the steeple-chase against Clasher. Blythe of Sysonby Hall, was a very hard-riding man. There's a Wright at this farm now, no relation of the other.

He discusses ages with Mr. Cradock. Now, there's Mr. Cradock ; dash me, but we must have that in. Him and I's hunted the country longest of anybody. No ; blame me, there's Lord Jersey ; I musn't forget him ; and Parson Empson. We met at this very Sir Harry's cover, and he says, " *Well, old boy, how are you ? I forget which is oldest, you or me.*" " *I'll speak presently,*" I says.—" *I was born in March '79, and I think, sir, you would have comed about August '78 ;*" and he says, " *I'll be bound you're right.*" Them were the very words we had, plump before all the gentle-

men at the side of this very cover. That Wright I
was telling you of, this was his farm we're   Goodricke's
driving over. There's a litter of foxes in   Gorse.
it this year. I'm glad of it. They talked of doing
away with it; it's been blank so often. There'll be
some seventeen acres of this cover. When I first
knew those trees round it, they were no higher than
my knee, now they're toppers. We'll pull up at this
gate. There you've just got a proper view of the
covers. Yonder's Ashby Pasture, right on there.
Well, I never did see so much keep in the country.
My eyes! what a crop of peas! You wouldn't like
any farming remarks?

That's " The Great City," just below you—Welby;
some people call it that. See what a funny old
church! There's not half-a-dozen houses in the
parish. Over there's Six Hills. I've known 'em come
from Shoby Scholes, right over all this fine country to
Belvoir. Look, what a nice view you get of that
great church now! That's Goodyer's Gorse, just over
the hill. Old Mr. Goodyer made it. I   The late Mr.
knew him well; he was a terrible keen   Goodyer.
foxhunter; like the stay of Melton at that time.
That's his house where Mr. Coventry is now: where
Sir Harry lived. He made a terrible noise out hunting; he used to enjoy it so; he'd holler the moment
he could; gruff rather, but very good language, only
so noisy. He was a great cock breeder; fight with
anybody. He always rode in yellow breeches, and a
groom's scarlet coat, with great laps, and a white
collar; his hat was as round as a plate; he'd cuff
along uncommon; heavyish man; such a droll good
sort of fellow; he made the gentlemen laugh; he was
particklar noticed for hollering, all in fun; he was a
quiet man enough; it raised his spirits so, but he never
spoiled no hunting.

I used to come here reg'lar to practise in the
season. That's a nice little brook. Many's the time

I've made them hop over it. When I was with Mat
Milton, I've actually been here of a
morning before I could see the fences.
Mat gave me five guineas a week, board and lodging.
I just lived as he did, meat and drink; best as was.
He lent me King Richard, by Dick Andrews. He
was Crockford's horse, and a great favourite for the
Derby, but the lad lamed his leg the night before the
race; he was, no doubt, hired to it. I used to make
all Mat's hunters. Many a thousand times I've been
three hours over these fields before we went out
hunting; two.or three tumbles reg'lar before breakfast. We had sometimes nine horses out; we rode
three half-way to cover, then three were posted for the
other half, and three when we got there; we jumped
'em all the way; for all that, we couldn't get them
ready quick enough. He sold ninety-six horses to
the Melton gentlemen one season I was with him.
It's as true as I'm sitting in this gig alive.

Poor little Matty! I killed him. He
used to cry sadly. Old Matty would
make him follow me. I well nigh drownded him two
or three times. My reg'lar orders were to "*go and
ketch 'em*," and the little chap was never to leave me.
Mat always said that he would lick him, if he stopped;
but he never did, that I heard of; he was a kind-
hearted man, only such a blackguard, and always
bankrupt; never out of that mess. Blame me, he
would get him home after hunting, and nurse him like
a woman. How he did take on if he was ill! he was
such a nice little boy, only fourteen, and never an
ounce above five stone. I was ten stone then; I never
got heavier till I had the small-pox second time, when
I was fifty years of age, just about; wasn't it curious?
I brought him up just as I wur brought up myself.
That was what Matty wanted. I mind when old
George the Third died, he put us both in mourning
alike; he was a loyal sort of fellow, with all his coarse

Marginal notes:
His Mat Milton engagement.

Education of little Matty.

talk; and gave us both new green suits, with black
buttons, to hunt in. Nice little lad! he was quite
broke down with consumption early, and he only came
for a very little bit the next season. A frost come,
and I went with him as far as Northampton; he went
on horseback; he said he'd never see me no more. I
was grieved, just. His father lived where Quarter-
maine does now. At those very owdacious places,
poor little fellow, he used to holler out, " *Where are
you ?*" He couldn't spy me, for them bulfinches; he
didn't know if I wur up or down. We never turned
the horses' heads, but went bang at them. Lucky if
we only got three falls a day. He was so light, he
used to bound up again like a ball. Captain White
and Mr. Maxse, they did so enjoy seeing us at it.
When they got to one of them reg'lar stitchers, they
used to say, " *Here's Dick and Matty coming; they'll
have it.*" They'd served us that way so often, we
know'd what they meant. I was not so forward in
those days, with the lad to mind. When I see them, I
says, " *Matty, here's a rum un on afore us; take fast
hold of his head, and don't fear nothing.*" I always
put him on those I knew to be perfect. Sir James
Musgrave used to back us against the fences. Once I
sees them coming on the road to meet us, I thought
there was something up, and there it was, a great big
stile and steps, and a deep ditch. I hears Sir James
say to Mr. Maxse, " *I'll bet you twenty guineas he
comes over it;*" and my word we won it for him.

We've got pretty well out of this rough On the Turnpike.
travelling now. There's a place we must
have a touch at. Wright's Lodge, it's called. He
was a great man with Sir Harry, bred lots of cocks,
always a good sporting chap, but he never kep a
hunter. Now, we're on the Nottingham road; we'll
go spanging along. There's Scalford Gorse, that was,
just behind Old Hills. Them's the Duke's, mind you,
both of 'em. It's a beautiful country, but not like

Ranksboro'. That's your country. There's a bit of a
Marigold's Mud
Bath. peck I had in this hollow, if it's worth
while putting down. It was in a ditch
full of mud. I was on Marigold, the mare I jumped
down that hill with. I was only schooling of her.
She went right backards, plump in. I claps my hand
on the saddle, and vaults clean over her head. Flat
on her back she lays, and I held her head up, or she'd
have been smothered. Dal! that's the very place.
There was some of them ditching; one of 'em—
Judd—John Judd—that's it—he says, "*I hear some
one a hollering; I'll lay any money it's Christian in
that 'ere ditch.*" They gets cart-ropes, and pulled her
out. The mud was wedged in like mortar from the
pommel to the cantle. It did her good; she never
drops short in a ditch no more. That's Old Hills—
they never miss finding; nice great place. That's the
Holwell Honey Clump, it's a mark for fox-hunters
thirty miles away.

He does the hard-
riding farmers. I had a queer go near here one day in
Matty's time. I had three horses out,
two of 'em placed for me. The first stood still with
me, going through those sheep pens on the right
yonder; the second was close by, and then I tires
it. Two farmers, John Parkes and Jack Perkins
—them were two owdacious boys at that time of
day—had been riding against me like fury, and never
left me. I gets on to my third horse, and rode him
to the end of the run. Matty sold him for 300
guineas ; he wasn't worth a hundred. What luck it
was ! The other horses nicks in so handy that day,
they didn't know but this was the same horse I started
with ; you couldn't tell the three asunder; all of 'em
bays. It's a real fact, I did the changing so sly; be
hanged if they knew. How pleased old Mat was!
He popped it on stiff; but the gentlemen, they'd just
as soon then give two or three hundred as one. Blame
me, the more you asked them, the better they liked it.

This is Kettleby. You see this public, the Sugar
Loaf — it was my walking ground. Gad! it made
me puff up these hills. Many's the The Waste Walk,
time I've done it with three stone of
clothes on my back; going into Melton so beat. I
had a drop of warm gin-and-water in here, and then
off back again. I walked hard for Clinker, not so
much to get off flesh as to keep in wind. I could do
it like nothing then. I often got off 4 or 5lbs. in a
walk. The gentlemen used to be all along this road
before Croxton Park. Captain White was a grand
walker. "*Sharpish work for me, old boy, this morning,*" he used to say when I meets him. They didn't
like that muzzling work. Sir Harry Goodricke and
me was in training three weeks for that match with
Mr. Osbaldeston, which never come off; he'd not have
rode less than thirteen, saddle and all together; stout,
fine-made fellow; always took a deal of exercise, or
he'd have been very lusty.

I've done a good deal of wasting; hot and its sugges-
tions.
weather, hot liquor; heat agin heat, as
long as ever you live; in hot weather gin-and-water,
strong as blazes, as hot as ever you can; I've experienced it. I once kept to nothing but gin and
gingerbread for a whole week to get to my weight.
That steeple-chase come off close against Steeple Chasing.
London. Beecher won on Eliza, and
Jem Mason was second; and Grimaldi beat off. I
rode Caliph again at Ross. I hurt my hand; you
see the mark there to this day. That all comes of
trying a four-pound saddle. I was in dreadful pain,
but they ties it up, and I comes out to ride Bones
for the next race. General Gilbert was the starter.
You see, he knew me so well. So I says to him,
quietly, "General! give us an item." Just as he
drops the flag, I kept a watching of him, and he tips
me the wink, and I jumps off with a thundering good
start. It was twice round, but they never fairly

reached me. One of them, a mare, I forget her name, gets to my knee, but never no farther. They wanted to chair me round the town; but I says, " *I'll have none of that, I'm not a Parliament man, it may do well enough for such likes as them!*" I thought they'd have killed me with drink; every one wanting to stand. An apple's a grand thing to bite when you're very much beat after a race. I had rode those heats for Mr. Lorraine Smith, at Leicester. I wasn't prepared, never knew I was to ride till I got there. I was all but fainting in the weighing-house. There was a doctor or two wanted to be on with brandy-and-water, and all that; but I says, " *Bring me an apple;*" and I bites it and comes round entirely. He didn't write all the Billesdon Coplow song, did Mr. Lorraine Smith. They say Mr. Bethell Cox, of Quorley wrote part ;* he was such a queer old boy, with one hand ; one day he forgets, and he unscrews the false one while he is dancing a quadrille, and it comes off while a lady were holding it ; she were sore afraid, poor thing.

Jem Mason.   I know'd Jem Mason well. He used to be at the Dove House, at Pinner, with Tilbury, when he was a lad. I'll be bound he wouldn't be above fifteen when he first rode up from Stilton there. The whole place was laid out with fences, and a race course. They tell me the railway cuts clean across it now, somewhere nigh the Pinner Station. Tilbury had as many as two hundred hunters at one time. Lots of them came down here; Captain Fairlie's Wing was one of them. He mounted Count Sandor, did Tilbury ; him that Mr. Ferneley drew all those pictures of. I mind Jem first rode The Poet in the St. Alban's Steeple-chase. The boys at Harrow rigged him out, and talked about nothing else for

---

* From inquiries we have made, we believe there is no doubt that Mr. Lowth, son of Robert Lowth, Bishop of London, wrote the whole.

a month. He had to carry three stone dead weight.
The horse stopped at his first fence, but he beat them
in a canter; nineteen on 'em. Old Tilbury and Jem
used to come to Brixworth every year with horses.
Jem jumped Winwick mill-dam one journey, and set
the whole field. The hounds killed four fields on. My
word, Sir Thomas Whichcote regularly did   How Sir T.
him and a lot of hard riders two seasons Whichcote
ago. They run from Colston cover. Jem pounded him
gets first to a high gate, near Buckminster, on Kegworth.
and he gets off to open it; Sir Thomas comes up,
and jumps it clean on Kegworth—him that he bought
at Sir Richard's sale. Sir Thomas says, when the
gentlemen talks of it, " *Precious hard if* 320 *guineas
can't pound somebody.*" It was a deal spoke of. Jem
never did no good with Lottery till he rode him with
Josh Anderson's stag-hounds. He always had a
double-reined snaffle and martingale. I see Jem once
come down here for a match; I don't mean that
Abd-el-kader one. It was Tilbury had the match on,
but the gentleman run back; same ground as Clinker
and Clasher; the horse had to go over the ground. I
had one of Watson of The George's horses then, and
I galloped the ground with him as if we were racing.
Blame me, if he could have licked me; he was not a
horse of much vally, no fashion, but a clipping jumper.
He'se driving a roaring horse trade now, is Jem, in
London.

Yes, I remember Bill Wright of Upping- Affray with Bill
ham: he was a good-hearted chap, but   Wright;
such very vulgar language. Bill and me were always
partickler intimate; boys together in the racing
stables. We once quarrelled out hunting with Lord
Lonsdale! If we didn't get to horse-whipping each
other! We did indeed; for three miles, and straight
across country; cut for cut. It was from Preston
Gorse in the Prior's Coppice country; all the gentlemen shouting " *Well done, Dick!*" " *Well done, Bill!*"

It pleased them uncommonly. We took our fences reg'lar all the time ; if he was first over he stopped for me ; if I had fell he'd have jumped on me ; and blamed if I wouldn't have jumped smack on top of him. We fought back-hand—this way—any way we could cut. Dal! I was as strong as an elephant then ; we pulled our horses slap bang up against each other ; he gives me such tinglers on the back and shoulders ; but I fetches him a clip with the hook-end of my whip on the side of the head—such a settler—and gives him a black eye. Then I says, "*Bill, will you have any* and their Happy *more, I'm ready prepared for you ?*" We Reconciliation. were like brothers almost, after that. It was all a mistake ; he thought I had been finding fault with a grey horse he wanted to sell. It would be six weeks before we spoke. It was Reeve, of the Falcon Inn at Uppingham, brought that about. We had left off at Launde Wood, and I stopped there for gruel. Reeve says, "*What's this between you and Bill? I'll stand a bottle of wine to see you make it up; let me send for him, and see you shake hands in this very parlour ?*" "*Well!*" I says, "*I don't malice him, if he don't malice me.*" So he comes, and we had a glass together, all right. We were the biggest of friends after that, Bill and me. Wright of Sysonby, sold lots of horses Mr. Greene and to Lord Plymouth, for great prices. Mr. Sysonby.   Greene got Sysonby of him before he come of age, and the two could go just. He was nearly as good as "the bay mare ;" (singular thing Mr. Greene never gave her a name) ; but not so great through dirt. Sysonby gave Mr. Smith and Shac-a-bac a rare showing up in the Harboro' country ; it was a strange wild day ; they found in a patch of gorse near Gumley. The wind blew the scent, and the hounds flashed over it. Mr. Smith rides Gadesby first, and then on to Shac-a-bac ; they had an hour and twenty minutes racing all the way. There was only him and Mr. Greene left. All on a sudden Shac-a-bac starts a grunting, and stops; Mr. Greene whips off Sysonby, and says, " *You get on my horse, they're running for their fox.*" On Mr. Smith goes with Sysonby, and then Mr. Greene nicks in with Gadesby, and gets on him and finishes. There they was, at the kill, same horses they'd started on, only riders changed; singular thing, wasn't it ?

Bill Wright was one of what they called The Flying Blue "The Blue Coats ;" nothing stopped 'em ; Coats. such crashers, they'd hardly wait for hounds to get on the scent; long blue coats and gilt buttons. Let me see : give me time; I'll have 'em all. There'll be George Marriot, Jonathan King of Beeby (he bred Tilton and a many first-raters), Wright of Sysonby, Jack Wing, the two Gambles, Jack Fryatt (the Julius Cæsar and Vivaldi man), John Woodcock, Jack Deverill, Bramley of Bushby, Bill Blower of Rotherby ; (I tutored him ; his father gave me many a sovereign for noticing him ; what a sight of money he's made by hunters !) Tomlin of Lye Lodge, Williamson of the Coplow, Sam and Bill Henton of Ragdale, Gamboy Henton of Hoby, Frank Needham, Carver of Ingoldsby—he made nigh 2000 guineas for seven colts out of one mare. I can't think of no more ; Heycock came after these. What a fellow Heycock was to ride ! Dash me, I knew such a break with him and Sir James. He'd just got a new Shropshire horse, had Sir James ; always went there for them if he could ; as like as apples they all were ; a great man for a grey if he could get one—he bought a many of Tom Smart—he'd give three or four hundred, as soon as look at it. So Heycock comes up to Mr. Heycock's him, out hunting, " *How d'ye like your* Recipe. *new horse, Sir James ?*" " *Pretty well,*" Sir James says, " *only he makes me a little nervous ; he hits his timber.*" " *I'll tell you what to do,*" says Heycock. " *Take him out by yourself, quite private, and give him two or three heavy falls over timber ; I always do it.*"

There was such a laugh; he was such a desperate
chap that way. "*God bless me, Mr. Heycock, you
make my hair stand on end.*" Them was Sir James's
very words; and he was a precious hard un too was
Sir James. Sir Charles Knightley teached his noted
black horse Benvolio that way; he sends him like a
gun through two gates, and he jumps the third clean
enough. Heycock rode Clinker in that

The Steeple- great steeple-chase from Noseley Wood
chase from Nose-
ley Wood. to Billesdon Coplow, nearly four miles.
He'd have won if the bridle hadn't come off. He
would have the double bridle changed for a snaffle.
They hadn't taken up holes enough; and when it
come off at a fence, the horse wouldn't let him put it
on again. One horse came from Essex; a cobby-
looking thing; they told him at starting he wouldn't
tell, at the end of three fields, where they'd gone, and
it came out true. King of the Valley gave me a deal
of trouble that day; he was such a great big horse
I couldn't get him up at his fences. We had all an
hour given us to see the ground after we'd weighed
in Mr. Greene's laundry. Bill Wright wouldn't stir,
but sat on with his pipe and porter, and rode as well
as any of us.

Holwell Mouth That's Holwell Mouth—we'll be there
and The Vale. directly; ain't it almost like a punch-
bowl? The Quorn can't come no further than here;
they're a bit jealous of each other, and they're never
done drawing it. It's really in the Duke's Hunt, but
I've seen the Quorn draw it for years and years. The
gentlemen get all along at that side, and some at the
other corner. There's such a spring of water down
there, if you can find it. There's been an old rusty
bowl chained to it this many a year—didn't I tell you
it was first-rate? Clawson Thorns is a great cover—
what a cover it is! That Marigold leap of mine's
close here; people came to see it from Nottingham,
when it got into the paper. Dash me! only to think

it's a plantation now, and they've filled it up from bottom to top. She was a beautiful mare, this Marigold, but very bad to break; she throwed two of my sons, and no end of grooms, but she never got rid of me. Mr. Coke had another bay mare with her; he gave 300 guineas for the pair, at three years old. They were both bred by one farmer at Scalthorpe, just by here. Field Nicholson had them in Lincolnshire, to learn them fencing, but he was too hasty with them; so Mr. Coke sends them to me, and I had a tough fortnight's job of it. Field Nicholson was always a great man with Sir Harry Goodricke; him and Tom Brooke of Croxby first come for a fortnight to Melton together, and stopped at The George. The fences in the Vale are tremendous, when you comes at them—stake and bounds—wide ditches— timber very big, as big again as these 'ere, when you get where the grazing ground is. I once hear a great shooter—a reverend gent—say he fairly stood and trembled before a Vale fence, to think how he could get over. Sometimes they goes right away for Widmerpool—by Broughton, Hickling, and Colston Bassett way—and sometimes they bends short to Piper Hole. That's Wartnaby Stone Pits— The Road to Six good laying—gorse and thorns-like; it's   Hills. been a great meet ever since I can remember. Sir James Musgrave, he was always uncommon fond of the Ranksboro' country, and the Rolleston country; Mr. Osbaldeston, he liked Barkby Holt, and Dalby and Gartree; poor Sir Richard, I think he'd be more for Six Hills and them parts—we'll be at them directly. It's precious hot. Blame me, if you ain't dropping off to sleep! You'd nigh missed Cant's Thorns — that's one of them bye-covers; what a country they have to Harboro', thirty miles right on end! I've ridden in a run from it, and grass all the way. Not half a mile from that's Lord Aylesford's cover: rare things I've seen from that, right away to

Oakham. That's Mundy's Gorse—small, enclosed country, and plenty of foxes. Lord Suffield had such a clipper from here; fourteen miles clean away to Colwick, side of the Trent. See! that's Shoby Scholes—there, on the other side of the trees. There's a reed pond in one part; that's where Tom Sebright put the double on "Perpetual Motion." I think he was a Belvoir fox; he mostly took off that way. I've seen a many good runs from it, and bushels of beaten horses; they so often brought a fox from other places there.

The Six Hills Country. This is the Six Hills country. Dal! there's nothing that's not happened to me in it; the fences are quite jumpable, but most of it's plough. The horses can't stand on above half an hour, if they keep straight on without a check. The fields are small, none of them above ten acres. They're always a jumping; single fence with a ditch; some of them a ditch on both sides; ditches not very wide, but wide enough to throw a horse down. The slower you ride at them the better; they only want a handy horse, a perfect hunter, not a flying horse.

His Huntsman Career. I had a long time with hounds, as whip to Sir Gilbert. I never did much as a huntsman, except once or twice when Abbey was not out. I could tootle a bit. Bedad! you should have heard Sir Richard blow his horn; that was music, I believe you. Old Abbey was a bit of a musician, that way; I couldn't blow much. Jack Davis, of the Rufford, he can make it rally out. I could holler, and speak to a hound pretty well, but I had only a middling voice. I once made a bit of a hit when I had hold of the hounds, just over a road. Lord Lonsdale was out. "*Richard,*" he says (he always spoke that way), "*Richard, that's as fine a cast as I ever saw made; you quite deceived me.*" We brought the fox from Mankrie Wood, close to The Bull at Witham Common, seven or eight miles, slap through Woodwell

Head, right away to Melton Spinney. My horse was so beat, he could just trot—that was all he could do. Blame me, he couldn't walk, and he couldn't gallop; if he offered to walk, he slipped down. Mr. Charles Manners and one Flintham were out, and they went and stopped the hounds. It's truth; I never told a lie in my life, that I know of.

That's a bulfinch, not half a good one His Bulfinch though; not stiff enough through. Come, Meditations. there we have it at last. Them's the bulfinches; them's the stitchers. They're thickest about Ashby Pasture and Barkby Holt. In old times, we used to go slap-bang at them, hollering like fun, to cheer up horses and men. Captain White was a good un at that game. How he would holler, to be sure! Those are rails, just; a horse 'ud want a deal of handling at them; if we didn't get their fore legs high enough, their knees 'ud get below it, and over they goes; their tails often came clean bang into my face; my word, it made you look out sharp. What a one the Captain's Merry Lad was for rails in a corner! he popped over, for all the world like a deer. You see Mundy's Gorse over there, it's got regular earths, and Ella's Gorse beyond it. Walton Thorns' to our left; it's a square cover, all gorse. Now we're on the Foss Road; they call that Thrussington Wolds. It's a long woody cover, not a gorse.

I had a good bit of fun from this cover A Day with in Mr. Hodgson's time. I'll tell you how Marigold. it was. Mr. Coke, he was partickler proud of this Marigold, and he wanted her to do something to be talked about. So I gets a message by his groom that I was to ride her at Six Hills next day. " *You've to wait,*" says the groom, " *whiles Mr. Coke comes.*" I was quite struck what the deuce he meant; I thought her so perfect a mare. So I waits, and up comes Mr. Coke. " *I want you to ride her,*" he says. " *Mind you do your best with her; go into the cover with the*

C

hounds, and never leave them." So in I went; and I'm blamed if he wasn't waiting to see me come out— great dry ditch, and cut and bound hedge. "*Now, that's well done,*" he says; "*go on, and keep with the hounds.*" It was the beautifullest run of an hour and a half; they viewed him the last mile afore they killed him, close by the water-mill in the Navigation by Ratclyffe. Mr. Burbidge, he rides up to me. "*What, Richard, you've had a glass too much, to go that way; you never stopped at gates or nothing, and you beat us all clean out.*" The gentlemen comes up when we had killed, and they says, "*Now, Coke, what do you think of it?*" He says, quite short, "*It's very satisfactory, I think.*" So there was something in it I

Influence of Captain White on his character.

didn't know of. Captain White was up to it. I hears him, about a field behind me, hollering all the way, "*Go along, old fellow! go and ketch him, gentlemen!*" The Captain was always for me; he kept hardening me on. I don't think I'd ever have gone at such fences, but he had such a pleasant way with him; never done hollering at me. I couldn't help going a tickler.

Brooksby.

This Thrussington was a shiny place in Sir Harry's time; capital doings there. They've pulled all the kennels down. They're not much of cooks at that public-house; they cut the ham as thick as my thumb; you didn't make much way with it. Barkby we can't see from here. This is Brooksby; nice place, ain't it? Hay smells prime, don't it? There's land as is land! General Grosvenor lived here, and then Lord Cardigan a bit. It was a great meet in Mr. Meynell's time. They drew Cream Gorse and Ashby Pastures; it was all open like a common; there was no trotting by bridle-roads then.

Lord Lonsdale's Hounds.

Mr. Meynell and Mr. Noel, I mind they once joined in the Ranksboro' country. Noel's had all the best of it: Arthur Abbey hunted them. Mr. Smith and Lord Lonsdale clashed three times, when I was out, and Mr. Smith got the fox every time. Lord Suffield's once crossed Lord Lonsdale's when they were a going from Tilton to Owston Wood; Lambert drew his hounds into a corner of a field, and let 'em pass. Lord Lonsdale's were not so quick in the open, but they had the longest runs. They had a fine wild country, and they were capital killers. They went off latterly; I've seen 'em run tail for a mile. They was never so good after the madness; that would be in 1830. Lambert wasn't so keen. My lord, he built a kennel at Stocking Hall; then he brings them back to Cottesmore, and lived there a many years. He was a grand man for hounds, was his lordship; there are many who think they know, but it's not thinking as will do it.

The oldest gentleman as kept hounds in The Packs of old. this county was that Mr. Noel, of Exton.

The hounds were still kept at Cottesmore. Arthur Abbey was his huntsman; he was a big, heavy man, with a rasping, strong voice. Many a tuppence I've had for taking off his spurs, when he come home from hunting. Lord Gainsborough kept on the hounds as usual after Mr. Noel; and when he dies, Lord Lonsdale (Sir William Lowther as was then) took to them with Philip Payne. Philip was a first-rate little fellow—always swore by Lord Lonsdale's blood. His lordship gives them up to Sir Gilbert for a few years, and then he had 'em back again. The first Mr. Meynell. time I hunted the Quorn country was with Mr. Meynell, in March, 1796. We met at Langton Caudle, tried that and Welham spinneys, Stanton and Glooston woods; found at the Fallow Closes, and killed; then we found in Stockersten Wood, and losses him near Hallaton Fern. What a wonderful man he was to holler! shrill voice, good language. He rode small horses with short-cut tails. Jack

Raven was taller than Mr. Meynell. I don't see any improvement in hounds myself; I don't. The Harboro' country was his fancy. Mr. Meynell gave up in 1800. Jack Shirley was one of his whips. He was an owdacious fellow; big and stout, with a rough voice. He was a great man with Mr. Smith; and Sir Richard, in Lincolnshire.

Another Tumble. We'll get a short cut down here past Cream Gorse. Dal! if I know much about these roads; I've been across these fields thousands of times, too, with the hounds, and out larks with the gentlemen. I scarcely ever fell when I was out larks. I've been fox for the gentlemen all over the country; it didn't signify what part of the country you were in if they wanted to have a lark; be it where it would. There was an assize job at that house; a poor lad got murdered. I don't just see how we'll get out of this field; we must just go back through the gate. What's coming?—

* * * *
* * * *

There's a go! Oh dear! Get to the horse's head! I wish we'd never comed here. I kep on a talking, and you a writing, and we never saw that grip. What a balcher I comes out of the gig! I drove my nose right into the ground: then you tumbles out on top of me, and pins my legs right down. There's above twelve stone of you! I always likes to hitch my legs away, and you fairly held 'em fast. I thought the wheels would be over me. It's all very well—you've done nothing but laugh at me these ten minutes; but your hat's quite as bad knocked in as mine. There's your note-book—I see it come flying over my head; that 'ull be your pencil, in that tuft of grass. Deary me! how Captain White would have laughed, if he had seen us! This pimple's bleeding on my nose; it was in the ground, I don't know how deep. That 'ull only be a graze on my eyebrow; I'm

bleeding badly, though. Just lead the horse, and I'll
get to this pond, and get you to give me a bit of a
rub-down. It's a bad job trying these short cuts,
except you're on a horse ; we must keep it snug when
we gets to Melton.

We'll be right now; I'm for leaving the road no
more. Sing'lar thing, wasn't it, we Ashby Pasture
should have had that tumble together ? and Thorpe Trus-
I'm always in for them things. Barkby sells.
Holt's too far for us to touch at; you can just see it
through yonder, if you stand up ; but it's such a deuce
of a misty day, with all this heat. That line of trees
is Cream Gorse ; now we're straight for Ashby Pasture. Aye! it's quite a wood! People see those
pictures, and they fancy it's a bit of a gorse. Pretty
place this Thorpe Trussells; it looks quite like a
flower-garden now; don't it? How sweet the roses
and honeysuckles smell! Take the reins. I must just
step out, and get a bunch for my old woman; she's
such a one for flowers—the house is chock-full of
them. Mr. Greene, he was wonderful fond of Thorpe
Trussells ; some clipping runs he had from it. I
wasn't in the country when he was master. He
showed 'em some rare sport—never finer, they tell
me—and only a scratch pack to begin with. Tom
Day handled them wonderful. We're at Gartree Hill
now. Mr. Osbaldeston's fox lived here ; he was a
dark-coloured one ; most of the great runs I've seen
have been with them sort. He always came out
reg'lar at one point, and gave 'em ten miles of it
through Leesthorpe, Cold Overton to the right ; they
lost him in Branson Field—Oakham Pastures that was.
They never could make him out ; he must have got into
some drain they didn't know of.

That's Buttermilk Hill, and Burrow Hills over to
the right, where Lord Cardigan and Lord Gardner
had the match I told you of. It's as flat as a race-
course on the other side. Lord Suffield's had a grand

fifty-four minutes over Burrow Hills here, same day
as Lord Waterford lost his Norway wig.   Here's the
The *Clinker* v. Clinker and Clasher ground.   Mind you
Clasher Ground. put this down.   We starts at Dalby
Windmill—Dal! there you've got it at last through
the trees—left Burrow village to the left, under Burrow Hills ; Twyford to the right, over Twyford
Brook ; Marfield to the right, over Marfield Brook ;
John o'Gaunt on the left, and finished on Tilton field-
side—five miles, all swingers the fences.   I should
just like to have one peck at steeple-chasing again.   I
shall be eighty come March ; it 'ud be such a thing as
never was seen, just to say I'd done it.   Three miles,
I could manage that well over a good Leicestershire
country.   I'd get myself into such prime condition.
I'm a bit touched in my wind now for a long run.
That's Squire Hartopp's.   He's a terrible good un to
encourage fox-hunting—just in the heart of it.   He
used to ride uncommon well ; now he don't come out
in scarlet.   We're through Little Dalby now.   That's
the hedge where I took the great jump on Sir James's
horse.   That's Melton, at last: we must keep that
tumble snug, or they'd laugh at us rarely.   I'll be
ready for you at nine in the morning, and then I'll
show you a country, just—the Quorn's nothing to it.

RIDE THE SECOND.

" And still the best nag was reserved for the day,
When Tilton was named as the meet."

Horses for Lei- YOU ought to have looked in at Mr.
cestershire.   Gilmour's horses before you come
away this morning.   The old grey's there yet, him
that I was took on for the *Sporting Magazine.*   He
wants a deal of licking still.   There are only four studs
in the town now.   Those will be some of Mr. Coven-

try's on the road ; he looks like Leicestershire, that
one, long and low. I like to see all four shoes when
they're going along; it shows action. For riding, I
like mares as well as horses. Give me 'em lengthy
and short-legged for Leicestershire; I wouldn't have
'em no bigger than fifteen-three : great rump, hips, and
hocks; fore-legs well afore them, and good shoulders;
thorough-bred if you can get them, but none of your
high short horses. Thorough-bred horses make the
best hunters. I never heard of a great thing yet but
it was done by a thorough-bred horse. Many of these
modern men, they'd tire anything : they Seat on Horse-
don't set at liberty on a horse, as I mean;   back.
they've no proper power on their horse ; a man's body
should be all loose, but he should be firm in his thigh;
you shouldn't be able to see under 'em when you're
behind 'em.

I mind once coming across here with He excites Mr.
hounds. One day I rode slap off a bridge   Maher.
into a field to get to 'em ; this place reminds me of it.
I'd the hounds all to myself, and one of the gentlemen
gave me half a guinea—many's the half-guinea I've
got that way. One day they found at Glaston Gorse;
they were all a trying to beat me. I heard Mr. Maher
say—Paddy Maher, they used to call him—"*Hang
that fellow ! ·he wears that left leg spur, and he catches
them ; it's impossible to beat him: we'll have him yet.*"
Thinks I, if we do but come to a stitcher, I'll get shot
o' you. We comes up to some deer-rails, near Normanton. "Now's my chance," I says, and over I goes.
"*You may go if you like, and be hanged to you ; I shan't
follow you,*" he shouts. Captain White, Colonel
Lowther, and Sir James, none of them would have it ;
Mr. Maher shouted particklar at me all the way. There
was quite a *Haw, haw!* among the gentlemen, when
he out with that last expression. We killed directly
after that. I was riding a horse of my own ; I bought
it from a farmer at Ashwell, here. Sir James gave

me 160 guineas for him, and called him *Christian ;*
he was a brown one, by Vivaldi. I never wore but
one spur, and seldom that. I only want my fingers;
them's the things for ketching 'em up, and making
'em go.

A ride for Sir   Sir James once gave Tom Smart four
James.   hundred guineas for a horse; he could
get through bush fences nicely, but he knee'd the big
uns. He had given him a fall or two, and the hounds
had to meet at Owston Wood ; so he sends to me, to
wait at Burton toll-bar till he comes up. Then he
says, "*I want you to go across country from here to
Owston Wood, and I want to see you go all the way.
You thread this road to Pickwell ; take which side of
the road you like.*" "*Dal ! this is a rum un,*" thinks
I ; so I chose the right side. We went straight between Pickwell and Somerby ; then I takes him over
four high rails, and Sir James would see him come
back ; he was well satisfied then, and he carried him
capital. Lord Lonsdale and all the gentlemen liked
the Owston Wood country best of any ; it's quite
Leicestershire fencing ; like the Harboro' country, very
little plough, good scenting ; quite open country, every
kind of fence. Mr. Moore—he was a great man at the
Old Club—he still would make me use two spurs when
I rode his horses. What an hospitable, charitable man
he was ! He seldom missed a day ; and he could ride
pretty fairly, but not one of those clinkers I've been
telling you of.

Lord Wilton.   Talk about all these men, there's none
     kep up his riding better for thirty years
than Lord Wilton's done. He's quite a front man yet ;
him, and his son, and Captain Lloyd's always there.
He don't ram his horses till hounds settle to their
work ; he always rides perfect horses. If he misses a
good thing, he's sadly riled. There never was a better
groom than that one of his, Goodwin ; pleasant fellow
as need to be, and the best groom-rider as ever come

to Melton. He's well pensioned off now, and got a
house in the park as well.

Now, do stand up and look ! There's Emotions on
a country worth your coming all the way viewing Ranks-
from London just to see. There's your boro'.
country ! A steeple-chase once came off right here
from Burton to Adcock's Lodge, half-way The Gypsey
between Melton and Oakham ; it seems Steeplechase.
only yesterday—the Marquis, in blue, falling at this
very fence, on The Sea. He was nearest on 'em, but he
was half a field behind Mr. Villiers. Poor fellow ! he's
dead now ; he rode Gypsey. I had the doctoring of
that mare's mouth—grinders grown quite sharp, bless
you, sharp as a needle—quite cut holes inside her
mouth. It's a nice place this Adcock's Adcock's Lodge.
Lodge. I mind Sir Harry asking me
where he could get a good bit of bread and cheese
after hunting ; and I says, I know the mistress here,
and she's an uncommon clever woman. Sir Harry
goes in, and the cheese was capital ; and he had his
butter and eggs from her reg'lar as long as he was in
Melton.

There's your country ! not a bad jump that The Whissen-
Whissendine there ; get a little lower down, dine and Ranks-
and it's all one, like a navigation. I never boro'.
seem to have been out of that brook. What fun I've
seen in brooks ! Templeman—aye, "Sim," "Sim," in Lei-
you call him—was down here in Mr. Er- cestershire.
rington's time. He had mounts on some of Lord
Howth's and Mr. Errington's best horses, and he went
like a house afire. Many of these flat riders can't go
a bit. One day he was on The Hare, a pretty little
chestnut, one of Mr. Errington's, and he jumps clean
over two or three of them in Glooston brook ; his mare
jumps a bit short, and he comes on the bank right
across Mr. Gilmour's legs, while he was getting his
horse out. Such fun ! I got in lower Huntsmen in
down. Charles Payne, he's now hunts- embryo.

man to the Pytchley, used to ride second horse for
Mr. Errington, in those days ; Clark, him that hunts
the Duke of Beaufort's, was riding second horse here
same time for a Leicester gentleman ; I can't think on
his name at this moment. Deary me! the many times
I've seen bits of lads in Leicestershire. Some of them
takes good care of themselves, and so gets on ; others
just the contrary.

Sir Richard and   I've seen the gentlemen single them-
Mr. Gilmour.   selves out and ride jealous. I once saw
Mr. Gilmour and Sir Richard have a rare go in the
Vale, when Sir Richard lived at Lincoln. That was
about the first time I remember seeing him in this
country. They come nearly from Jericho to Upper
Broughton—some five miles, over a rare stiff country—
Smite and all. Sir Richard was on a grey that time,
and Mr. Gilmour on Vingt-un ; sometimes they were
close together, then they parted ; really riding bang
to hounds. Mr. Gilmour beat him a field at last, for
all his weight. Mr. Howsen and Mr. Banks Wright,
they were first-raters ; one of them was half-brother to
A Struggle of   Sir Richard. The finest bit of jealousy I
Five.   ever see was from Glaston Pasture to
Ketton Village—five on 'em. Mr. Gilmour on Vingt-un
was first again ; there was Colonel Lowther, Sir James,
Mr. Maxse, and Captain White ; you could have covered them with a sheet nearly all the time, but they
couldn't head him. I was watching them on one of
Sir James Boswell's, the year he went to live at
Somerby. Mr. Moore was out, but he couldn't keep
company. You can't lay it less than seven miles, no
check ; they came up by the Welland Meadows.

Ranksboro' and   There's your country, only just look
Rocart.   round you now! There's Ranksboro'
Gorse! capital good care Lord Gainsboro' takes of
it. Right over there to Tilton and Owston, such a
country ; fences big. One day we only ran from
Ranksboro' to Cold Overton Park, and every horse

had his mouth open, forty or fifty of them. I never could just make it out; the foggy day must have done it; country very deep; not a bit above three miles. As good a thing as I ever rode in from here was in Lord Lonsdale's day: we run him to ground at Collyweston Low Wood, near Wansford, ten miles by the crow, but I warrant we went it sixteen, and a nice spread-eagle we had. Look at Rocart; ain't it a pretty little place? nice brook that for practice; rare little cover: it don't look much like finding now; it's all over white blossoms.

Now we're in Langham. Dal! it's He remembers well I've thought of it. That's the very his Godfather. house where my godfather lived. The very spot; it was always sixpence for me when I see him. His name was Mr. James Jackson Melita Langham; he was a very great cocker; he bred 'em; me and my father used to breed lots of 'em, and get walks for them; almost all greys—duckwings and mealy greys; they was indeed—beautiful cocks; he wouldn't sell a many. He wouldn't sell no hens or spare his eggs to set. My father and him was very thick; he used to sell him a deal of barley, that was the way of it. No relations, but always very friendly; sing'lar, wasn't it, that should have jumped into my mind?

You see that bye-bar there. I never go The Bye-bar to cover but I think of it. When I lived Jump. at Luffenham, I had horses and rode, same as at Melton. The man wouldn't let me through without paying that morning; we were always the best of friends, but the wife had been worriting him, and he turned stupid. I'd never comed a yard on the turnpike-road, but away from Beeby; so I says, "*Be hanged if I'll pay; you may shut the gate;*" so I turns round, and at it I goes, over where the foot people gets through. "*That's paid you,*" I says. "*You sees a jump precious seldom, sticking here for halfpence all day;*" so he laughs, and he says, "*You're quite welcome, I'll never ask you to pay no more !"*—that 'ull be nigh forty years since.

His Butcher **Dal!** things does come to mind so ;
Apprenticeship. the way you puts it. I'll show you where I was put prentice to a butcher ; Mr. Hubbard they called him ; that was the very self-same spot ; many's the sheep I've killed. I cóuld skin a head like winking ; I liked the going to market best ; he had a little blue frock made for me, all trim and nice. One market-day he leaves me at home, and said I should drive the dung-cart. I served him out for that ; blame me, if I didn't. First thing I did was to drive against every gate-post, and I pulls one or two of 'em down. Then I tied the horse and cart to a gate, close by a dung-heap, and took out the greyhounds, and had a good course. When I gets to the horse again, the cart had sunk into the dung and nearly choked it ; so I whips out my knife, and cuts the bridle, and off home to Cottesmore. When Mr. Hubbard comes back, he says, " *Where's my boy ?*" and then he off after me. He wanted me sadly to come back with him ; but I says, " *Sir, your kindness to me is more than I deserve ; it's no use, my mind is set upon horses ;* and has been to this day.

Tricks of Boy- I'd only be thirteen when I went to the
hood. racing stables. Oh, dear ! what monkey tricks I was up to ! When I was at Barham Downs, some mountebanks comes to Canterbury, and the trainer lends me his pony, and away I goes. I thought I could do as they did ; so coming home, I jumps on the saddle, and there I stands ; up comes a postchaise, and I gallops by the side of it all the way home ; the driver and the people inside laughing at me ; one ot them pitched me a shilling. If they sent me anywhere on a pony, I used to ride through all the water I could : I had once well-nigh been drownded. That
A Quid pro Quo. billy-goat job ; that's all in my first lec-
ture ; I just wish you'd seen it ; he ran

about the Park, and went on like anything; reared
up against the trees; then back to the house, and
bang against the front Hall door, and smashed a sight
of glass panes. It was "*Maa, Maa !*" all the time;
such fun to see him. They used to call "*Maa, Maa !*"
after me, in the villages, for many a day. We was
going through North Luffenham with the hounds,
when a blacksmith puts his head out, and tries it on.
Abbey the huntsman, he says to me, "When he comes
that again, just you ask him '*Who hanged the boar ?*'"
He had gone and tied a boar to a post, while he made a
ring for it, and when he came to put it in, it was dead.
That touched him up pretty smart : he called after
me no more. Precious cheeky of me to say it, after
that dung-cart business.

Mr. Hand lived at Barleythorpe here. Mr. Hand's gruel plan.
He was quite a noted man—a rare sport-
ing fellow—two hunters and a hack, and much respected by the gentlemen. When his horses come
home, he first gives them gruel, two pails-full if
they'd drink it ; others never gave the quantity. His
horses always looked well; he never gave over till
hounds did ; he had a chestnut and black for years.
We're getting nigh Oakham now. There was a funny
steeple-chase here, betwixt Mr. Gilmour Mr. Gilmour and Captain Ross's Match.
and Captain Ross. They started here in
the Oakham Road, close to Ashwell.
There was very little difference in weight. Mr.
Gilmour, he was fixed to start between two trees at
the bend here, and he had to jump that fence. Captain Ross had a hundred yards start, and he was set
on the other side yon third fence. Mr. Gilmour was
on that noted Plunder of his; good shaped horse,
went low with his head. The Captain rode Polecat.
I piloted them; it was about three miles. The
Captain he kep a long way ahead till he come to
Burley-lane; then his mare refused the hedge, and
right up the lane with him. Mr. Gilmour, he comes

up, and he never offers to jump the fence, but he rides up the lane to meet him; touch him was half the bet—a hundred touch, and a hundred win. When they met, Captain Ross began to dodge; quite laughable, just like two boys at play; and Mr. Gilmour, he just catches him a tap on the hat with his hunting-whip. Then they started fresh out of the lane, and the Captain won by thirty yards. Plunder ran in that Noseley Wood steeple-chase Field Nicholson won; that were how the other match come on. The Captain was a poor hand across country, without some one to lead him; couldn't make his own running nohow, but go anywhere any one else went; a bold man and a good creature he was too. He gave me 100*l.* when Clinker beat Radical; Captain Douglas was on him that journey; I was pilot for him; it was from Barkby Holt to Billesdon Coplow.

Cover-side Plea- The gentlemen used to be always a santries. gammoning on with me at the covert side, some way or other, blame me; Sir James, and all of them. They'd get me to say something of one or another of them, and then they'd go and say, slap out, " *What d'ye think Dick's been saying of you ?*" or " *your horse ?*" and then there'd be such a laugh. Deary me, what cheerful times them were! Captain White in partikler was always on that way; when he was behind me in a run, I'd hear him; such a laugh he had; " *There goes Dick! down again! Haw, haw! What? down again, Veteran!*" That was his manner exact. " It's nothing when you're used to it," that's what I always gave 'em back again on them occasions; you'll see it at the bottom of one of those pictures, where I'm tumbling. They would still ask me how I felt with a horse on top of me. Gentlemen

Riding Old gets falls very bad; you see they're gene-
Horses. rally on old horses; the old uns fall like a clot; if they get into difficulties, blame me, they won't try to get out; they will do that when they get

to ten years old. They haven't the animation of a young horse; those young uns will still try to struggle themselves right, and they'll not touch you if they can help it. I'll be bound I'd be safer riding twenty young horses, than one old one. When a horse made his start to jump, I always knew if he was going to fall. I prepared myself; if he took off collected at his fence, I could keep him so; if he was falling, I could clap my hands on his withers, and get clear of him, and keep the reins too. These great natural jumpers are desperate dangerous; they won't collect and get out of danger; if people get killed, a hundred to one them great natural jumpers does it; when they're a little pumped down we comes with a smasher, and you gets killed, or goes on by yourself into the next field. I hate larking with horses. I mind Mr. ^{The effects of} Nevill and that chestnut mare of his, ^{Larking.} Verbena (Lord Southampton had her when he was at The Quorn), he thought her the best animal he ever rode. Once I see him jump three gates with her, coming home from hunting, and she stops dead at the fourth, and she was never the same after. I see her, after that, refuse a gate with Dick Burton, when he hunted The Quorn. "*Spur her again, Name!*" I says. Dick never sees me to this day but he hails me with them words before we shake hands. Mr. Nevill spoilt Reindeer just the same way; he was a grand entire horse; and Mr. Coke offered him 500 guineas for him. We were coming from hunting one day, and he says, "*Let's have a lark, it will do Reindeer good.*" I couldn't get him off it nohow; nigh the end of the fourth mile, we comes down together. "There, we've done it now, sir," I says; the very next fence we comes to, a very small one, he stops. I made him have it; but he was a lost horse from that day. No end of trouble with him.

I must have a bit of a peck at this ^{Ralph Holding,} Rarey. I should like to know if he can ^{the Horse-tamer.}

ride them across country, when he has tamed them.
I warrant I did well nigh as much as ever he did, fifty
years ago. They say it's just taking up the front foot;
you knows, so you says nothing; that dodge is as old
as that oak-tree there. The first I ever see attempt
these things was a soldier. He went about with a
brass belt and a horse on it; they called him Ralph
Holding; blessed if I don't think he's living near
Loughboro' now.* Mr. Coke, he asked me to go to a
gentleman who had some horses on the forest, at
Ulverscroft Abbey, near Leicester. There were three
horses there, and he had served them all the same,
and he got them quite quiet. Then I asks Mr. Hill,
of Melton, to send for him; he had got a grey that no
one dare handle. My word, he gets him into a loose
box, and tackles him. The horse come bolt at him as
he opens the half-door. Then he puts his hand into
his waistcoat, and takes out a little box with some
brown powder in it; he wraps some rag round his hand,
puts the powder on it, and goes right up to the horse,
and rubs his hand over the nose and ears, and carries
it right away along the back to his near hind leg; he
lifts it up, and lays the horse's foot on his knee, and
begins hammering and singing "*Law! Law! Jaw!
Jaw!*" a hundred times, and the horse took no more
notice than nothing. I runs in where they were at
dinner, and I says, "*Do come, he's a hollering and
hammering away.*" Mrs. Hill, she was so took with
laughing when she see him, I thought she'd have
fainted clean off. Then he put a halter on to him,
and gets him into a close. He says, "*Lay down,*" and
down he lays, and kept there, till he told him to get
up. Then he stands agin his head, with his finger—
"*One, two, hold your head up;*" he did; "*Lie down;*"
over and over again; no straps, no nothing, but this
powder. He tried to ride him afterwards, but he

---

* "The Emperor" was perfectly correct in his surmise.

when they were hung; I stood on my father's pony,
and looked over his shoulder; I wasn't ten yards off
them. The youngest of them, Bill, father had hired
him to be a shepherd; he had been at our place
only a week before he was took, to settle about
coming. Poor fellow, he cried sadly; his brother
Dick, he was a regular hardened one—you know what
he said about not dying in his shoes: I heard him say
it distinct. He could see Appleton, the village he
lived at, from the gallows, and he turns his face right
towards it, and he says, " *Now, I'll prove my mother a
liar; she always said I'd die in my shoes ;*" them were
his very words; and away he kicks them among the
crowd. I think I see him a-doing it. Father went
quite white, and fairly trembled in his saddle. They
had chains from the waist down between their legs,
and they hung on the gibbet that way. That was a
great plum year, but there was no sale for them round
Oakham; people wouldn't buy them if a fly had been
at them; they had a notion they'd been at the gibbet,
and sucked the flesh. I took no notice of it: I always
ate plums when I could get them. They hung till
they fell down; the good one lasted the longest;
people watched for that. I never heard of any one
finding bits of their bones; I've seen part of their
clothes lying about when we've been drawing the
gorse, but never no bones; they say they're not to be
seen. That green field on the left where the sheep's
feeding, just on this side the windmill, is where they
were hung; that house is where the doctress lady
lives; her that makes the wind pills. I've heard she's
got as many as 150 patients; she takes two or three
days to get once through 'em. I'll just call and speak
to my old friend Tookey, in Oakham here, while the
horse is getting his gruel.

Daniel Lambert and Wilcox. We must have Wilcox, of Luffenham
in; he kept the Fox-and-Hounds; he
was a five-and-twenty stone man, and very reg'lar with

Lord Lonsdale's hounds. He used to ride a grey
horse; there are many pictures of them; he'd be
fifteen-three, and could carry a ton weight, if that
were all. I've seen the old chap go like mad for
twenty minutes; he'd jump, if he was reg'lar put
up, over a turnip hurdle; he looked nearly as
big as Daniel Lambert. I knew Dan, and he
knew me. I met with him at Leicester and Stamford races. We had races twice a day for three days
at Stamford; eleven o'clock, then to the ordinary at
two. He was dressed like a groom, and lived quite
private; he'd hardly be quite at his full growth then;
there'd not be much more than forty stone of him;
he was above fifty latterly. Many's the time I've
talked to him in Stamford cock-pit; he could set 'a
cock uncommon well, for all he could hardly get near
the table, for his bulk; he was a cheery man in company, but shyish of being looked at. I've been
along with Parson Harvey scores of Parson Harvey.
times. I was at Tattersall's, and saw him
buy an unbroke three-year-old colt; he puts on a
halter, and leads it out of the yard himself; then he
says, "*I'll give it back, or I'll ride it back*," and in less
than two hours he did. He just bluffed him, and got
a curb-bridle; all people got round him—quite sur-
prised. They always said there was a touch of the
Old Gentleman about him, he could do anything with
horses; I've known women as could, if they had a
nerve. I've used oil of rhodium and elecampane
scores of times, in a powder, myself; it's Horse Taming
something like two guineas an ounce. Drugs.
Stallion-warts ground make a wonderful powder; it
smells just like Eau-de-Cologne: rub it over their
noses; then wet your finger in your mouth, and rub
it over the roofs of their mouths. I've quieted dozens
that way. Why I've known these things, and taking
up the leg, these sixty years, and people talk about
them in the papers as if they were new. There's not

a dodge I haven't tried. I never used these drugs unless they were very bad; handling them's the thing.

The first Break-ing Effort. The first I ever got a-back of, to break, was a three-year old of Sir Gilbert's. I'd be nigh sixteen then, somewhere about; she'd let no one but an old groom come nigh her in the stall, or anywhere else. He was lunging her one day in the park, when Sir Gilbert, he says, " *Let Dick get on her, and have a try.*" Them words of his was the making of me. A nice job we had; then they straps up her near fore leg; she was as bad as ever; then they on with the bluffs, and gives me a leg up. I fixes myself well, and I says, "Let her leg down;" she didn't move; then I off with the bluffs, and up she goes with all four legs, kicking and plunging. The old groom, he says, " *Sit fast, and I'll hold her at this game till she beats herself;*" then I pets her, and we got quite friendly. I kep on her till we got into the stable, and made much of her. She lets go at me as I was getting off, but trust me I gave her a check for that. I still keeps petting of her, and I got off and on several times with the groom fast hold of her head. I rode her every day, and she became quite a first-rater in Rotten-row, when I went up and down there after Sir Gilbert. I rode six years after him there; Head-groom days at Sir Gilbert's. then he bought Sir William Lowther's hounds, and gave me head over 40 or 50 horses. I was head-groom ten years; the last two we had no hounds; he gave them up when Sir William come to the title. The country used to be much heavier than what it is now; it required stronger and better bred horses; all of them on thorough-breds had the best of it after an hour. It wasn't drained, and the horses wern't above ground half their time. Sir Gilbert used to buy the biggest three-year-old tho-rough-breds he could lay his hands on; he wouldn't stick at 300*l.* for them. If there was any good-looking ones that no one would ride, his London dealer had still orders to send them. One come down, a great fine grey; he'd jumped rap at a chaise in London, right in, bang; got his head and fore legs in, any way. I rode him on a great day, from Tilton. I jumped that fence where Wilkinson the huntsman daren't come; he got the sack for that; Mr. Smith jumped it, and he bought the horse for 200 guineas. When Sir Gilbert gave up the hounds, thirty of them were sold at Tattersall's, and they made all manner of prices, from 250*l.* to 500*l.* After the sale he gives me 100*l.*, for the condition I had put them in; there wasn't one I hadn't broke myself.

Then he puts me in a farm for eight years, and I took to it pretty well; but horses were still my hobby. Sir Gilbert used to send me horses when I was on farming, to ride with hounds, and teach them the way they should go. I couldn't keep off it; I didn't care much for crops, and all that sort of thing, so I sets to riding and training, and I have done that these four-and-forty years reg'lar. I never had but two horses I couldn't get to jump; one of them was a very fine one of Lord Alvanley's, and the other Lord Harborough's; neither of them would go from their hind legs. It was proved that neither of them were right in their backs. I still said it must be so; everything I put them to, they dragged with their hind legs; it's not quite so easy, but if ever I rode a horse at water, I could guess if his back was just the thing. *Dick as an Agriculturist.*

Now about breaking young horses. When they're taken from their dams, *Mode of Breaking.* they should have a nice little head collar, with a rein to it; use him very quietly, and let him play about with the rein in your hand; try every now and then to touch him; but you must take your time. Get a nice carrot, wash it clean, slice it small, and let him smell often at it; he will soon take to it, and then you will be able to take up his leg, and have a look at his feet when you like. They'd be good two years old before I did much in the breaking way with them. The first two winters I always liked to keep them on new sweet hay and bruised corn ; then I put on a nice smooth bit, with a ring in the middle, and a player fixed on it ; the bit should not be bigger than my thumb here, and that ain't a very thick one. It should be four-and-a-half inches, and even in the mouth. The head-stall should not be too long, to let the bit get low in the mouth, or he'll get his tongue above the bit, and he'll never have a mouth all his born days. You must not bear him upright with the bridle rein. Put two round rings on each side *How to put him on the Bit.* of the stall-post, one five, and the other six feet from the ground. Then get two pillar-reins six feet long, with buckles and billets at each end ; buckle the rein to the bottom ring first ; pass it through the top ring, and buckle it to the bridle-bit. The bottom end of the billet-strap should be good eight inches, to take up or let out, not a bit less. That's the way to put a horse on the bit ; it don't punish him ; and it acts with a leverage, so that the horse can play with the bridle-bit, and he'll soon get a good mouth. I've got the exact drawing *The Christian Bridle-bit.* of the bridle-bit at home ; gentlemen send to me for it ; I'd several made this last spring. I draw'd the pattern of it thirty years ago ; it's my own invention ; it hurts no horse's mouth, and they can't run away with you. I can stop a horse, or put him on his hind legs with my finger, better with one of those bits, than many can pulling with their whole fist. I've often a deal of correspondence with gentlemen wanting them. When you've had the roller and straps about him, get the saddle carefully on, and lunge him ; give him his time ; and always use him to go round to the right hand ; then take him back to the stable, and put him on the bit, and get some one to stand by his head, with a rein to the bridle, and then try to get off and on till you're tired. A few days will make him ride; people is always so impatient, and knock them about so. Dal! I should as soon have thought of hitting another man's child.

I never was at Ascot but once in my An Interview life, that would be in that great Zinganee with Royalty. year, I had gone to London to sell a horse to Prince Lieven. When I gets to Ascot, blame me, nearly the first man I sees was Jess Austin, the king's hunting-groom. He come up, and he says, " *You're the very man I've been looking for this long time; I heard you was coming up; the King wants to see you; I'll go and tell him.*" He wouldn't be ten minutes coming back, and he says that I was to go with him the minute the Cup race was run. So I goes with Jess, and I makes my obeisance; and his Majesty he begins first thing quite joky about his stay with Sir Gilbert; he knew I was up to all his tricks with " Old Tot" Hinchley. He remembered the names of every horse I'd put him on; blamed if he didn't! Then he says, " *How well you look, Christian; I want a horse of your own breaking to carry Lord Maryborough with my hounds.*" So I told him that I had one that would suit him; and he says, " *I'm glad of that; there's Lord Maryborough in that stand waiting for you, and you can talk it over with him.*" We conversed slap bang before all the people; some of them knowed me, and they began at me. " *What the devil's up, Dick? are they going to make a baronet of you?*" But I answered them, " *Oh, nothing!*" and away I goes to his lord-ship. So I tells him all about the horse, and that Mr. Marriott, of Welby, bred him. " *Ah!*" he says, " *he must be related to my old friend, George Marriott. I've hunted with George scores of times; he was a very joy-ful merry man.*" He didn't have him after all; he got his off fore leg in a gate, and it filled. Jess Austin came twice to Melton special to see him, and I takes the horse to Windsor, and jumps him over some high timber in the Park, but the leg wasn't just the thing ; so he says, " *I daren't take him,*" and paid me a good sum for expenses. Sir Edward Baker took a fancy to him, and gives me his horse and 100 guineas for him, and rode him many seasons with pleasure. He was only a one-armed man too. I sold his horse for 165 guineas, so I did capital. I first see the King when he was at Normanton ; he wur at Melton in the long frost of '14, lunching with Mr. Berkeley Craven, at the Old Club. Belvoir were his head quarters at that time.

A Triumph of Patience. I'll tell you a bit of a story about Mr. Marriott, of Welby. How strange it should just have jumped into my head ! I had a horse of his in training. One day he comes to see him ; I says, " Mr. Marriott, there's the clergyman of Exton ; his horse has got master him, but you can manage him, I'll warrant ; it's all in your way home." So away we two goes. Mr. Ellicot comes out to meet us. " *How are you and your horses going on, Christian ?*" " Very well," I says ; " I hope you and your family is well." Then he takes us to see the horse ; and he begins, " *I wouldn't take twice as much for him if I could ride him.*" Then Mr. Marriott, he says, " *I like his looks uncommonly ; but if I buy him, and he will go to Leicester when I want to go to Nottingham, what's to be done then ? it will spoil my day's market.*" So Mr. Ellicot says, " *Come, let's go in, it's tea time, and we'll talk it over.*" We had tea and a bottle of wine, and they makes a bargain. Mr. Marriott takes him home ; and the very first time he rides him, he stops dead at a gate. A man come up, and Mr. Marriott shouts to him, " *Here's a shilling for you, my man ; go to my house, and bring me the Leicester newspaper.*" Blame me, but he sat on his back six hours, reading the newspaper. The horse wanted to come back, and tried it on several times, but he

wouldn't let him. Now and then he tries quietly to
get him up to the gate, and about tea time he does it.
He then rode him through, making much of him; he
was such a patient clever man; he'd have sat on him
for a week, and had his victuals and his umbrella sent
him, rather than be beat. That evening he rode him
to Kettleby, Grimstone, Asfordby, and so home, and
opened all the gates on the road. He gave him no
trouble no more; you see as time and good management brings all things to pass.

You want a touch at hunter training. Hunter Training.
When they're taken into the stable, give
'em plenty of air and walking exercise three or four
hours each day; whatever you do, never make them
sweat. Give 'em an ounce of sulphur and half-an-ounce
of nitre in their corn twice a week; for the first month
I like new hay better than old, but it must be the
very best. Give them plenty of walking exercise
up hill, and now and then give them a trot, but not
too much of it. You may increase it by degrees;
then walking over ridge and furrow is a grand thing
to give them action. Action's the thing! if they
haven't got it, they're like a pump without a handle,
blessed if they ain't. The less you gallop hunters
the better; all you want of them is to be in good
condition, and fresh on their legs. It's all very well
galloping race-horses if you like; but no horses should
go very fast or know their best pace, till they're put to
the test. There's many a good horse spoilt by them
tricks. I says, let me have a horse a bit above himself; he's much pleasanter to ride, and better able to
do a right good day's work. Never press a horse very
hard going down hill; it beats them far more than if
they go fast up hill. Becher did it to Vivian in that
great five hundred guinea match with the Marquis on
The Sea; he quite overset his horse; and he'd have
lost if the Marquis hadn't gone wide. I never see
Becher wrong but that time.

Teaching to
Leap.

When I wanted 'em to leap, I always took them to a very low bar, knee high; hold 'em there till you get him on to his hind legs, then let him go; likely as not he'll drop on the bar; take him to it again and again; if he turns a bit nervous, wait with him; when you've got him to go from his hind legs, then start him the same way with water, four feet wide. I was very fond of beginning them with a bit of timber like the body of a tree in a park. They can't get a leg in; if they force themselves against it they pick over; they must spread themselves. When you get him to the fences, begin with small places; first walk him to them; then trot him; you'll soon find you may take him at them any pace you like. It's only confidence he wants; then you may take liberties with him, but do it in good temper, and keep him in the same. He'll soon get confidence for the stitchers. Whatever you do, never go fast at them; don't go too slow or he'll stop; a many horses have been spoilt that way; give him time to get his hind legs under him; if you're too slow they buck, jump short, and don't spread themselves, and then down you both goes. When you takes a horse at his jumps, hold him steady by the head, not pulling him hard; the longer you hold him steady, the further he'll go. A horse doesn't jump the farthest by going over fast at his fences, or water; he wants to get his stride well up to them; he can't go to last long if he'se not kept collected; he'll soon be beat, partickler in deep ground, and ridge and furrow. When I go to try a horse on such like ground, down hill is what I choose: if they have action to do that all right they will make something. That was Sir James's plan— take 'em across ridge and furrow and down hill—I don't care anything about up hill.

Sir R. Sutton's
Cannon Ball.

Some horses is very queer about water. Sir Richard's Cannon Ball—him that he gave a thousand guineas for—he'd always jump water,

and a fence too, if the water was from him. Blame
me! the other way he wouldn't face it at all. I never
used thick bits. Nearly all horses ride better with a
curb than a snaffle ; but mind you never uses too sharp
a one ; they only irritates the horse. I always puts
the hunting curb on the first time with young horses ;
you must let 'em have plenty of liberty to play with
the bridle, but mind as his tongue don't slip under the
bit ; this is the most consequence of anything. Don't
be a-feared when these restive horses bolt against a
hedge, or a wall to try and rub you off ; pull his head
slap against it ; and he'll not try that game twice. It's
nothing when you're used to it. Dal! if them old
words of mine hasn't slipped out. When your horse
refuses his fence, never spur him, or maul him about ;
they doesn't know where they are, and Riding School
comes to no good. They want a bit of   Practice.
riding after all this, to get them into form for a lady
or gentleman. You should have seen the one I made
for Lady Lennard, last year. I trot 'em with the right
leg first, head a little to the left, and quarters to the
right. Then I takes them into some riding-school,
and rides them round and round, right-hand way ;
first walking, then trotting, not too much of it. Pet
him and chat to him a bit, and give him a piece of
carrot with your left hand ; I've had a good ton or
two of carrots about me one time or another. When
you begin to canter him round, get him on to his
hind legs, and go as slow as you possibly can. Be
uncommon quiet with him ; keep him right leg first ;
if he changes, take hold of both your reins level, pull
lightly with your right, and put your left hand forward
on both reins, leaning down as much as required. I
can make 'em walk backwards, and sideways, and
canter the figure of 8, aye ! twenty times running. I
have indeed ; it's truth every word I'm telling you ;
Lord Scarbro' would tell you, if he was alive, poor
man.

Rufford to Wit. Lord Scarbro' engaged me to go to Rufford, when I met him at Bunney Steeple-chases; that 'ud be in '41. I was with him from October to May, reg'lar in the house, all comfortable for fifteen years, and he never gave me one angry word all the time; quite the reverse; everything I did was always right with him. He was a very cheerful man. I rode Skirmisher's grandam when I was there; then his lordship tells me to look out for a horse, and I took such a fancy to Lord Henry's Gardham, when I see him at Ollerton, that I got him to send three mares. She was one of them. I rode her filly to hounds, and I tells his lordship "She's such capital action, and so fast, I warrant she'll breed race-horses." I never rode a nicer; such a beautiful jumper; quite a lady's horse. So his lordship set his mind on Voltigeur, and the old and young mare both goes. This Skirmisher and Sharpshooter—he'll be dead that one—were the foals. I wonder what relations you call them; that licks me. What a strong man Lord Manvers was! he was always very friendly out hunting. I've seen him get to places that wasn't practicable, and he'd get off and smash it down as if it was only a stick to break. Miss Milbanke, what a clipping rider she was with the Rufford! such a seat and hands; I never see her beat

Climbing Burrow Hill. by none of them. That minds me of poor Lady Eleanor Lowther. What a thing I once see her do! She come to the very steepest part of Burrow Hill, close to the hounds; and she says to me, "*Richard! if you will go up here with the hounds, I'll follow you.*" Near the top, hang me if I didn't think she and the horse would be over backwards. I says, "Do, my lady, catch hold of your horse's mane, and lean forwards more." So we gets up safe, and they all went round, and, my word, the gentlemen did stare when they see us.

I've seen many good runs when I was at Lord Scar-

bro's: one of 'em was with The Grove, A Disaster.
from Blythe Whitewater Gorse, and killed
in the Bramley country ; fifty-six minutes. They
went as if they were running in view all the time, but
they never saw the fox till one field off where they
killed. There never was a check or a holler from end
to end. I saw it all the way ; I was on a bay four-
year-old of Mr. Foljambe's. The only horse I ever
killed, was a thorough-bred one of Mr. Foljambe's, he
was by Comus, and he gave 250 guineas for him at
four years old. It was a very bad job, was that. This
was the very horse I got eleven falls from in one day ;
you have that in my other lecture. I had just got
him ; he would jump anything, and a nice horse he
was, up to thirteen stone over any country. It was a
stake and bound hedge, with a wide ditch to you ; he
jumped it beautiful ; there was a stake lay on the
ground, and he lands on one end of it, and the other
tilts up right into his body ; and he dies in two hours.
The late Mr. Frank Foljambe was out that day ; he
was a first-rate man across country, and kept a rare
sort of horse. The Rufford's a particular The Grove and
pleasant hunt for ladies and farmers. Rufford Cracks.
There was more of them in this and the Grove than
any I ever saw ; clipping riders among them ; some
of the Grove farmers has bred the best hunters that
ever went over Leicestershire—Clinker, Clasher, Clipper, Panza, Smasher, Crossbow, and Doctor, both of
them last was Sir Harry's ; they all come from those
parts. That's the Peterboro' train there : we must
look sharp ; we'll see a bit of the Duke's country,
when you come back next month.

RIDE THE THIRD.

"At twelve o'clock they did appear
At Thistleton Gap in Leicestershire."

I 'VE been thinking of a deal of things about Mr. Smith and Sir Harry since I see you. This is the Grantham road; we'll hardly have time to look in at The Road to the Belvoir Kennels. That's Norman's Belvoir. Cover; they often find in these little covers, just before us, and slap away for Freeby Wood, and right over the country for Garthorpe; sometimes Piper Hole way; they do come over this road with a tickler. That's old Squire Norman's farm; he was a great man in' Mr. Goodyer's time. Thorpe Arnold's on our right; that's a new cover they've been making; they'll have many a go over the Quorn country now; that's their object. There's John Bull, you just see the top of the cover; there's a strong brook at the bottom; I've been in a few odd times; it's a tidy jump in some places. Scalford Brook's on the other side of the hill; there's been a many in that. Near that left-hand clump is where the Gorse was. Melton Spinney's to our left on the hill, you can only see the trees. They're never done getting good runs from it. That was a Melton Spinney fox they run up the tree in Croxton Park; he came down like a cat, but they found him next week, same place, and killed him. Will know'd him again by his long white tag. That's part of Norman's cover; they used to call it the Broom Spinney; you say you can't write? we'll pull up at this guide-post. That's Lentils on the left; I remember it thirty years ago, no higher nor that gate. That's Freeby Wood yonder, a very favourite cover, and Waltham Thorns, the two best covers about here. Stonesby Gorse, just beyond them, they like quite as well. Garthorpe Sways will be to

the left, almost close to them. Hickmorton's right
away beyond , I'm the worst fellow in England to
remember hounds' names ; I never took no notice of
them ; no matter to me what they were, as long as they
went fast enough.   This 'ere very cover,   The Freeby
Freeby Wood, I mind Sir James Mus-   Wood Burst.
grave comes up to me ; I was on Red Nose, the very
horse of his I tackled Lord Cardigan with ; he says,
"*Mind you get a good start !*" so I look out pretty
sharp.   There were nearly two hundred with the
Duke's that day ; such a crasher over the Lings to
Croxton Park wall, in sixteen minutes !   I was head
man all the way ; Sir James was on his old grey
Baronet.   Lord Gardner, Mr. Maxse, and Sir Harry
—he was on Limner—were the only ones near me.
Sir Harry shouts to me to open a gate, and I jumps
it and then turns round and laughs ; "*Hang you*," he
shouts, "*that's the way you open gates, is it ?*"   It was
a good five miles ; regular coursing ; severe jumping.
Goosey and me have had much conversation about
that run ; it's talked of to this day after dinner.
That's Piper Hole ; those trees over the hill, it's just
at the top of the Vale.   Mr. Musters run a fox from
Colston Carr to it, when I was with him one day.
Weaver's Lodge and Newton Toll-bar is also great
meets with Will.   I don't know much about his
horses ; I've seen him on a cropped one he thought
a deal to, and Catch-me-who-can ; that's the very
name.   They all say there never was   A Rare Trio.
three such clipping huntsmen in Leicestershire at one time as Will, and Jack Treadwell, and
Mr. Tailby's man—I can't just think what they call
him—Jack Goddard, that's it.   Such ones to go, too ;
none of the gentlemen can overhaul 'em.   I should
like to see them three have a fair go at each other
over that Clinker and Clasher ground.   They'd make
short work of it.   That's a capital cover, Goadby
Gorse, yonder ; Goosey had his biggest run from

there; that's only the top of it; it's a wood cover, perhaps twenty acres; now you catch the top of Holwell Clump there, where we rode last June. That's the gate to Croxton Park. What a go I had there many years ago, one races! thirteen of us, whips and huntsmen of all the three hunts; such proposing of healths! I was always for larking when I was a little fresh, but quite sensible. This is Branston Lings—a sure find; when it gets hollow, they burn it down; half of it you see is burnt now. Those are the Belvoir covers right from this 'ere hollow to Stathern Point; such ding-dong Will has there among the cubs.

The Sproxton Thorns Flyer. That's Sproxton Thorns over our right. I remember as it might be yesterday, we found a fox there with Goosey, and lost him at Greetham, sixteen miles on end; we met next day at Croxton; and the Duke would go to the Thorns again. Two foxes went away, and we settled to the old fox, and went four miles beyond Greetham to Pickworth Wood. I'm sure it was the old un, he didn't go a quarter of a mile out of his line the day before. Mind you put that down; strange, wasn't it?

Belvoir. Here's a pretty scene! what they call Croxton Banks, on your left, all the way along. Several small covers; they run them through; some of them hold a fox. That's the coach-way to Belvoir. The Duke, my word, he's just keeping the game alive. What a deal of conversation I've had with him at the cover-side, one time or another, about hunting! He comes up to me, when I got back from Essex last year, and he says, "*I'm quite glad to see you amongst us again, Dick, it's like old times.*" I says, "*Thank you, my lord, I is hearty and well yet for my years.*" Such a one to go when hounds are running! I see him jump the Park-wall at Croxton, near the entrance-gate; it's nigh six feet, and a tidy drop on the other side. Will Goodall, and none of them, would have it. I was hunting a bit when I come up from Rufford, at Christ-

mas-time, to see the missus. It was as bold as that
Smite job, when Lord Scarbro' come out like a
drownded rat. That's all in my first lecture. Now
you see Belvoir. The kennels are just down in the
bottom, half a mile from the Castle; they were at
Croxton in Mr. Newman's time, and nice old kennels
they were. This weather will make the farmers skip
about. I always think that valley looking particklar
pretty; single trees like. What a lot of Belvoir Visitors.
them there were at Belvoir fifty years
ago; such riders!—Lord Forester, Lord Jersey, Lord
Delamere (Mr. Cholmondeley that was then), Lord
Robert and Lord Charles Manners (them were the
Duke's brothers), Colonel Mellish, and Mr. Assheton
Smith—all riding like devils against each other across
the Vale. John Wing, of Sedgebrook, was one of the
best riders across the Vale, as a farmer, in those days
—tremendious! Him and I's gone together miles; he
was about my age. Mr. Smith was always there. He
once tipped a gate on Lazarus, and came on to his
head; nothing but the peak of his cap saved him.
I've seen those two Mr. Tomlinsons, from Cheshire,
ride wonderful here; there was no beating them. It
put Goosey quite out to see them going as they did.
Wonderful great meet, the Three Queens, up that
road to the right. You can't see the house; it keeps
the name, but it's not a public now. The country's
not very open; it's the hounds and huntsman as
brings them. No bulfinches, but some rattlers when
you get into the Vale. There used to be a nice little
cover, Corston Hills, where the man and the potatoes
are, here; but they've grubbed it up—there's only that
little bit left.

I remember Mr. Newman giving up The Belvoir
the Duke's; it would be in 1805: he had Huntsmen.
'em fourteen seasons. I was out that day. Shawe
had been waiting a whole year for the place after he
left Sir Thomas Mostyn's. Goosey whipped in to

E

Newman and Shawe; he'd be made huntsman in
1816. Will Head was another of Shawe's whips, him
that hunted the Cheshire many years. He was a
great man with Lord Hastings. He's living at Lei-
The Marquis of Hastings. cester now. Poor Lord Hastings, he was
a terrible funny man about his weight—
never out of the scales. If he got above twelve stone,
he was for wanting a new stud; often only one bit of
dry toast and egg in a morning, for fear of putting
hisself up. How he did love hounds, to be sure;
never away from the kennels, and drawing pictures of
Will Head in the Oak Tree. them. Will Head and Will Derry was
great men with him. Will Head had a
chestnut they called Wroxton, and rode him eight
seasons. I never see such queer fore legs; good un
to go, for all that, but bad at a brook; a savage
beggar, never leave you if he could get at you. Once
Will gets took up into an oak-tree at Sheepheads, in
Charnwood Forest. He hung there, and this Wroxton walks right from below him, and stops to look;
there Will hung, but the horse never offered to touch
him. Will thought he'd have eat him that round;
but he was as sensible as a Christian—wouldn't take
no wrong advantage.

Mumford—him that hunted Sir Harry's hounds—
is dead. He was a good kennel-man, but no great
hand across country—no nerve at all. Beers and
Will Derry were his whips. Will hunted them two
seasons, when Mumford was ill. He died, they tell
me, not long back. He'd have told you a deal, if
Shawe, the Huntsman. you had seen him. Shawe was a prime
fellow, quick, and plenty to say for him-
self; never let his hounds lose him for lack of chir-
ruping; and such a ready chap at an answer. He
used to say, "*I don't want whip or horn, but as many
pairs of spurs as you like.*" He was groom to Lord
Moira once. Such an uncommon beautiful voice.
He bred the hounds a deal higher than Mr. Newman

--quite a high man. Goosey always brings the
hounds to cover, and he follows on his hack. Buckle,
the jockey, was often down staying with him to hunt.
He'd a great horse-leather pair of boots he wore; he
left them behind, and Will Head got them. Lord
Forester was master of the hounds seven- Lord Forester
and-twenty seasons; he's just turned and Mr. Grant.
them over to the Duke. Deary me! I wish his father
and Lord Delamere were alive, to read these lectures
of mine. I've known this lord from a boy. When he
first come to Melton, they called him Mr. George
Forester. He was at the Old Club—you've seen the
picture—that's him a-warming the fire; it was Mr.
Grant as did it. Mr. Grant takes a monstrous lot of
beating across country yet, for all his weight. Lord
Forester's never been out of flying things since I've
known him. Such a man for sport—longest days
anywhere! Him and Will didn't think nothing of
finding a fox by moonlight. Will whipped Belvoir Records.
into Goosey some four-and-a-half seasons;
and he took to the hounds in July, 1842. Then
Goosey goes to be kennel-huntsman to Sir Richard,
at Cottesmore. He dies at his cottage at Wools-
thorpe, and they buries him at Knipton; you can't
see it from here. Mr. Newman, he'll be buried at
Waltham. Shawe died at seventy-six, but I don't
know where. He had the hounds eleven seasons, and
Goosey six-and-twenty. Goosey used to keep a
foreign black fox at the kennels. It's stuffed at the
Belvoir Inn now. Last season they kills one hundred
and twelve foxes in one hundred and sixteen days;
season before, one hundred and twenty-four foxes in
one hundred and twenty-three. Capital sport, ain't
it? I know it's correct, I hear it from Will Goodall
myself; Will and I are always uncommon friendly
They've sixty couple of hounds, five days a week;
they run 'em mixed

The fight between Cribb and Molineux ?—to be sure

Cribb v. Moli- I was. Now, that was just first-rate. All
neux.   the magistrates in the county of Rutland were there. It was the Saturday magistrates'
meeting at Oakham; and they all come off to the
fight when they'd done—the whole kit on 'em. They
pulled down hedges, and got their gigs through; no
end of trees broke down. They fought at Crown
Point, near Thistleton Gap. There was such a song
made about it. It's stiffish land, a good deal of
plough. The farmer wanted fifty pounds for his field.
He wouldn't take a cheque—he knew nothing about
them things; wouldn't let 'em fight till he had some
name on it he knew. So Mr. George Marriott come
forward and signed; he was wonderful fond of a bit
of fun. They fought on a stage. I was on horseback
—a mare of my own, I gave Mr. Harper eighty pounds
for her—not ten yards off them; I was crowded in,
and I drawed my legs up and stood a top of the
saddle all the time they were fighting. I'd hard work
to get them down again. There must have been ten
thousand people. I thought at first go off Molineux
would have killed him; he was a reg'lar rusher. Cribb,
he kep drawing away, and fought him all round the
stage; he wanted to blow him. Captain Barclay was
in a carriage close aside of me; and I see him get out,
and go up to Cribb, and tell him after the second round
to alter his fighting. In the third and fourth round,
Cribb had the best of it. I could hear the blows as
plain as a drum; he did punish him then. Cribb had
a place under his eye as big as a goose's egg, and
Gully lanced it for him. They only fought eight
rounds. Barclay had Cribb in Yorkshire to train; he
made him plough, and fill a dung-cart—all the hard
work that ever he could put him to. He was in beautiful condition, fine as a star, just like snow aside a
black man. The black wur fat—that licked him as
much as anything. We ran over the very spot where
the stage was, the day Captain White's Jupiter was

killed; they all remembered it. Captain Barclay
stayed a deal about Melton when Brummell wur down at Belvoir. He was a
great man with "The Beau." You wouldn't have put
'em together, would you? I've known the Captain
drink broth from the kennel-boiler. Once, when he
wur walking those great matches on a road, he met a
regiment of soldiers; they formed into two lines, and
let him pass, they thought so much of him. Such a
real John Bull! He was never done talking of "The
Chicken." He was a miner, or something like that,
from Staffordshire or Dean Forest—blame me! my
memory's so bad for them sort of dates. They
catches him, and brings him up to London. Captain
was down Holborn way, to meet him; he was quite
amazed when he see him get off the coach, all out of
condition; no form at all. He thought he'd been
done, they'd sent up such an account by post; but he
put him on a good tap of porter, and he improved
wonderful. He was always a training of him, walking with him to keep him cheerful. Once two officers
at an inn were for pitching into 'em because they'd
got their breakfast-table; the waiter just whispers
"*Barclay and Chicken,*" and they waits to hear no
more. What curious expressions them fighting men
does use! The Captain once tell me he overhear one
of 'em say, when he wanted a match, "*Why won't you
fight I? I never did aught to offend yer.*" He used to
tell his stories, did the Captain, in quite a deep voice;
singular dry manner with him. Pleasant man, very;
talk about The Chicken for everlasting. It'ull not be
much above four years since he died. He was a
great farmer latterly, somewhere about Aberdeen. A
strange man for droll stories was the Captain; go on
about his fighting dog, Trusty, for a week—all about
how those London men tries to do him. Blame me!
if they didn't rub stuff on the other dog's back; but
Trusty knew more than they did, for all they thinks

themselves so cunning. Dash me! there was no living dodge that dog wasn't up to. He won fifty times. The Chicken took to drinking when he'd won his battles; quite an uncultivated man. He died of consumption very early on. Those London bars killed him.

"Old Short Odds." Old Richards—"Short Odds" they called him—was quite a Mr. Davis at Croxton. What a hatfull of money he won on Mr. Maher's Shugaroo! it was a hundred to five against him. He was a queerish dresser: brown kerseymere breeches, those brown drill gaiters, and a brown coat and spencer—often a whitish one in summer. He had a choice flower in his button-hole reg'lar. He began as a stocking-maker; then he bet at the door of a cock-pit; and on that way. I've met him many a time driving one horse and leading another behind his gig to Newmarket. One of them was a big brown seventeen hands high; he'd change them about on the road. His own corn always went with him in the gig; and such a sight of stockings! They were like money with him. Blame me! if he didn't always want to pay you in stockings. He had a mill he called Bobbers Mill, near Nottingham; he took a good bit of the rent for that in stockings. When they drew bricks for his house, he paid them that way. Such a queer fist he wrote. I've often seen him out at Wartnaby Stone Pits and Shoby Scholes; the gentlemen were at him the moment they see him, to lay them against something. One day I hear them say— "*There's old Richards, if he hasn't come out hunting with an umbrella!*" So he says, "*I'll bet any one of you five hundred you'll not hunt with or without an umbrella when you're my age.*" "*Who's to hold the stakes?*" Captain White says. "*Oh! there'll be some one left when I'm gone; we'll leave it to him.*" He had a chestnut cob latter part of his time; always rode very slow. They tell me, eighteen months before his

death, he galloped through Asfordby full tilt. He
was uncommon partickler about stale bread ; lock it
up in the sideboard till it was a fortnight old, and
take the crust back if he couldn't finish. Not a bit of
a miser either. Made a deal of his money by betting
and buying up plots of ground alongside great pro-
prietors.

The first time I ever see Mr. Smith   Mr. Assheton
was when I lived with Sir Gilbert, at   Smith.
Normanton. He was always along with him or the
Duke; they didn't know much of him in the Quorn
then. One day Lord Sefton's met at Brooksby, going to Ashby Pastures. He drove Jack-a-Lantern six
times at a flight of rails before he could get him over ;
people were all asking who it was. Jack often wouldn't
jump a fence if he offended him ; then he would get
off, and give him a kick and a hit with his fist, and
call for another. He was a rare man with   Fistiana.
his fists ; quite fond of it. Once he had
a round with a carter in Leicester. He said he had
touched his horse, which was tied to some rails, when
he was in the bank. Off he galloped to Quorn, just
as he was ; sent the man 2*l.* by his valet, for turning
on him so well. Then what d'ye think he did ? He
put a beefsteak on his eye, and pulled a night-cap
over it ; gets into his carriage for all the world like a
man going to be hung ; and went out several miles to
dinner, and tells the whole story, and what a brave
chap he'd met. English of him, wasn't it ? That's
your sort. There were a many different tales about
it, but they tell me this at Quorn.

He was his own huntsman all the time   Mr. Smith's great
he wur at Quorn, from 1806 to 1816.   Hunters.
Tom Wingfield had left ; Dick Burton and Jack
Shirley were his whips. I've known him, if he were
at Belvoir, come all the way from Belvoir to Gumley
of a morning, two-and-thirty miles, to cover, and back
again at night. He had horses posted at Melton and

Tilton. Tom Thumb, Robin Hood, Gift—he bought him from Lord Mornington when he was Wellesley Pole—and Lazarus were some of his great Leicestershire horses. Then there'd be Minister, a little chestnut; he used to ride him in the Vale. He'd stop at nothing with him. It was a great speech of his, if he ever saw a horse refuse with his whips—" *Throw your heart over, and your horse will follow.*" He never rode fast at his fences. I've heard him say, scores of times, " *When a man rides at fences a hundred miles* His Style of *an hour, depend upon it he funks.*" He Riding at Fences. got a many falls. He always seemed to ride loose, quite by balance, not sticking with his knees very much. He used to think he was round-chested, like a ball. I've heard him joke, and say that was the reason he never hurt himself falling. He never made nothing of his leaps; he'd turn round in his saddle over the biggest, when he was in the air, to look for his hounds. He always went slantways at his jumps; it's a capital plan. The horse gets his measure better; he can give himself more room: if you put his head quite straight, it's measured for him; if you put him slantish, he measures it for himself. You always see Mr. Greene ride at fences that way. He was just a coming out when Mr. Smith was master, and he put him up to many a clever thing in riding. He'd another dodge, when he rode at timber; he always went slap at the post: he said it made the horse fancy he'd more to do, and put more powder on. His Desperate Nothing ever turned Mr. Smith. If Leaps. we had come near the Coplow, I'd have shown you that big ravine he jumped—twelve feet perpendickler, blame me if it ain't, and twenty-one across; it's been nearly the same these forty years. They had brought their fox nearly a mile and a half from the Coplow, and he went to ground in the very next field. He was riding Guildford, a very hard puller, and go he would. The biggest fence he ever jumped in Leicestershire was a bullock fence and hedge with ditch and back rails near Rolleston, on Jack-a-Lantern. People got up a story that he once jumped a lock on Jack, but it was nothing of the sort. All that family never pulled an ounce ; The Lantern they were all slugs. There was Young Family. Jack, and Charlotte Lantern ; she was a sweet mare, but none of 'em like the old horse, when he was in the humour. Mr. Boultbee, of Tooley, bought Jack for a stallion, but he had a bit of riding out of him. Mr. Smith didn't half like it. Some one asked him if he'd seen Jack take his fences ; and he says, quite angry, " *Hang the fellow! I never thought he had any jumping left in him, or he shouldn't have had him.*" You scarce ever see him with a curb-chain ; if he had one, he'd cover it over with wash-leather. Once he was a great man for snaffle-bridles ; then he turned round, just as he did with the size of his hounds. Latterly he'd ride with curbs with long cheeks—very severe. Small curb chains are the worst things in the world ; they deaden the mouth. The links should be single, and large. I've seen Sir Harry with them like the links of cart-gears. I wonder how many bridles I had made for him ? He always scolded if I told any-body else of them ; he used to say, " *Don't tell 'em, let 'em find out.*"

No man that ever came into Leicestershire could beat Mr. Smith ; I don't care what any of them says. He was always for being away as quick His Style of as possible ; best fox, he says, always Hunting. broke first. He'd get away with three or four couple of hounds ; then they'd come to a check, and the run was spoiled. The whips could never get the others out of cover fast enough for him ; he was always too quick a drawer—drew over his fox scores of times. He was always a bit of a roarer since I knowed him ; no great horn-blower ; he had a bit of flageolet in his horn the last few years he hunted.

When he did get away, you might as well be hanged as go before him ; same way in Hampshire. He was very uncertain. Sometimes he wouldn't lift his hounds at all ; you must lift and lose no time, if you want Hunting Science. runs in Leicestershire, with these big fields. You must get shot of the crowd. Sir Richard was all for making his hounds hunt, and he killed far fewer foxes with these big fields. Science is no manner of use now in a Leicestershire field, except to teach you the run of a fox and where to lift 'em ; same in the Pytchley country. Never leave 'em alone, if you want to get runs and kill foxes. There are ten men go out now where one used to go, and there are a hundred sheep to one to what there were in Mr. Meynell's time ; they all run a fox, and Leicestershire what are you to do ? Mr. Smith was Foxes. wonderful fond of Shankton Holt. I've seen him get away with three foxes from it in one day ; it was a great nursery for them in his day. He liked Staunton Wood and Langton Caudle uncommonly ; he always said the wildest foxes lay there— away directly. Staunton Wood foxes now get no further than Rolleston. There was no cover at Nosely, or Rams-Head, or Rolleston, or Keythorpe in those days. Vowes Gorse was only made in Mr. Osbaldeston's time. Mr. Smith used to say that an hour and a half from Widmerpool to Blackberry Hill, near Belvoir, slap across the Vale, was one of the best he ever had in Leicestershire. He'd be very little above ten stone then ; latterly he'd be much above that, but never above eleven ten. He was a great one for weighing himself—took his machine about with him regular to Wales, and everywhere. They were saying the other day he gained four pounds the fortnight before he died. Mr. Osbaldeston. " The Squire" was the oddest man you ever saw at a cover-side. He would talk for an hour ; then he would half-draw, and talk again, and

often blow his horn when there was no manner of occasion
—always so chaffy. The whips mostly drew the cover
while he was talking. Very keen of the sport, though;
sometimes have two packs out in one day: get away
with his fox like a shot. After that second leg business, he was a bit nervous in a crowd; he wanted a
wide berth. At a fence, it would be, "*Now it's my
turn—don't press!*" If he could get well clear of
them, he went like a bird. He was a rare match-rider
across country; I never see a better at that game.
Mr. Gully used to be a deal down with him at Quorn.
Tom Sebright hunted the hounds when Sebright and
his leg was broke. It was grand to see Dick Burton.
him and Dick Burton swinging them round in their
cast, fifteen miles an hour, over everything. Tom had
such a musical voice! Rode with a loose seat and a
slackish rein, quite on the balance. They was a grand
pair! and Jack Stevens and Dick Sadler come after
them; good uns to go, they were. They're both
dead now. Tom Sebright and Dick How they lost a
Burton were with The Squire at Ather- Fox.
stone. I have heard them laugh about it scores of
times. They once run him to ground, an hour and
twenty minutes, from Hopper Hayes. Then they
dug till eight at night. They thought at last it was a
badger. The Squire, he goes home, and Tom digs
his fox out by moonlight. Blame me! if a hound—
Benedict they called him—doesn't catch him by the
leg, and pulls him slap out of Tom's hands; and away
he slips under their bellies, and gets clean off. They
runs quite a ring. Dick went to stop 'em, and he
tumbles rap over a tree in the middle of a ride. Then
he gets to a gate, and he hears the fox come blowing
up to it; it was quite a frosty night: and he fetches
it such a clip with his whip—he was so mad about
it—and they goes home quite down in the mouth.

Mr. Edge used to live with Mr. Smith Mr. Tom Edge.
when he was there. They were an un-

common silent pair. Mr. Edge very seldom spoke
unless Mr. Smith said something to him; Mr. Smith
never let him have more than a pint of port a day,
he said he'd get too fat. I never saw him less than
eighteen stone yet; he used to pound away on that
great big horse of his, Gayman; queer-looking creature it was; thin neck, large head, raw hips, and a rat
tail; for all the world like a great seventeen hand
dog-horse. You couldn't get your hands between his
front legs, he had always boots on. They had a tre-
mendously good thing from Botany Bay, without
touching the Coplow, and killed a field off the cover
at Schlawson Windmill; thirteen miles in all. Mr.
Smith was riding Gadesby and Mr. Edge was on Gayman. There were only those two, and Mr. Greene on
Sysonby, and Fryatt of Melton, him that had Cannon
Ball, on Hastings, up. Mr. Smith pulls his watch out,
and it was nearly five minutes before any more come
Lord Plymouth's up. Lord Plymouth bought Hastings
Cracks.   from Fryatt, for 300 guineas, next day;
all through that Botany Bay run. Fryatt would have
taken 120 guineas, and been glad of it, going to cover.
His lordship never could ride 'em when he had got
them; that was my job; he could hardly get Hastings over a fence. Fancy and Zigzag were two of
the best he ever had; they were so well-known, the
Melton children called chairs in the nursery after
them; and kep on riding them like mad. Fancy was
a rich brown: he gave 600 gs. for her, to Mr. Peter
Allix. Zigzag was a chestnut, much stouter. A mare
of Lord Rancliffe's, called Shade, was as sweet a thing
as ever I saw; all over a blood bay; I rode her a
steeple-chase at Cheltenham. I broke nearly as
handsome a one, a black un, this year, for Mr. Wright
of Ratcliffe.
Mr. Gurney tak-   Mr. Edge could have licked Mr. Gur-
ing the Water. ney and Sober Robin. They were both
going at one time; it would be same country, and

same week as that Shac-a-bac got that tying up I told you of. They had a tremendious run, and kills near Market Harborough, in the Navigation. Mr. Gurney, he gets off Robin, and he goes and fishes the fox out; then he lies on the bank with his legs up, to get the water out of his boots; and all the gentlemen a laughing at him—such a sight! there was so much of him.

There was quite a do at Rolleston Mr. Smith's last when Mr. Smith come back to have a day in Leicester- day at Shankton Holt; it would be in shire. April, 1840. Dick Burton and Will Cowley come with him. There were twenty-eight couples of hounds, and fourteen horses. Mr. Smith rode Antwerp, and Dick had a grey one called Jim Crow, that day. Antwerp had a deal of hair and skin knocked off in the train, so he got Dick to paint him a bit. There was quite a party at Rolleston to meet him. Prince Ernest came from Deane. I'll be bound there were three thousand on horseback; when the first lot were at Shankton Holt, the tail end weren't out of Rolleston Gates; all so pleased to see him among 'em again. They were looking out of the window, Mr. Smith and the Prince and Mr. Greene, when a fox crossed right in front of them, to Rolleston Wood; he'd got frightened by the noise. Mr. Smith says, " *We'll have him,*" and they went there first to draw, but he had gone on. Then he went to Shankton Holt, but he hardly half-drew it. The top part's the thickest, and he was never in it; he seemed quite nervous for his hounds, the crowd was so great. Mr. Greene goes up to him when he blew his horn on the Carlton side, and tells him he'd not been half through it. He says, "*Never mind! which is the way to Norton Gorse?*" So away he goes with the hounds, across country with Captain White, and Mr. Greene, and Dick Burton, and one or two more, as hard as they could split. Not ten people but thought they were running; it was

good four miles, best pace. Lord Wilton was took in
as well as the rest. He comes up to one of the gentlemen at Norton Gorse, and says, " *You must have
had a capital thing : have you lost or changed ?*" They
didn't find at Norton ; then they were for going to
Glen Gorse ; but part of it was cut ; so they went off
to Hardriggs. I don't know where all the foxes had
got to that day ; none at Nosely Wood, or Staunton
Wood, or Glooston Wood, or Rams Head. Nearly
all the field got tired out and went home. Blame me!
they'd never have found at Vowes Gorse, if it hadn't
been for Mr. Hodgson. He was master of the Quorn
then ; it put him up, all his country being so blank ;
so he wades into the gorse with his jack-boots, and he
whips a fox out himself. It was a hottish day in
April ; and they hadn't very much of a run. Mr.
Smith went to Lincolnshire—Sir Richard was master
then—to bid it good-bye ; they had some grand sport
in the woods there ; killed five foxes and run one to
ground in six days.

His Belvoir Day.　　The old Duke gave him a grand day
　　　　　　　in his country. The hounds slep at
Ropsley Kennels, ten miles from Belvoir ; they'd
vanned them there from Lincolnshire. They first
found a vixen in Ropsley Rice Wood, and it kept
knocking about half an hour ; then it went away for
Hunby, and he lost it one or two fields off another
big wood. Mr. Smith, he was patient as anything
that day ; he casts forward, and he crossed the line of
a disturbed fox ; such a ding right through Ingoldsby,
Osgodby Coppice, Truham Parks Wood, and Nor-
wood, right to Grimsthorpe Oaks. Will Goodall gets
into the wood, and he sees the fox in one of the rides ;
off he slips quite quiet to Mr. Smith, and tells him ;
he was casting across the park. When he brings the
hounds, blame me, if the fox wasn't standing there still,
waiting for him. Mr. Smith come to the spot, and he
sees him too ; it 'ud be nigh four minutes, and he'd

never stirred. I never hear such a thing, and Will
and Dick they tell me the same. Wasn't it sing'lar?
It seemed as he wanted to be ketched. But they
didn't. They sent him round The Oaks very hard for
a quarter of an hour, then away by Grimsthorpe
Castle, through Kickly Wood to Dunsby Wood, then
they got among a lot of fresh foxes, and he had the
hounds stopped. It would be a good twelve miles
they ran altogether. Then he took 'em to Cottesmore, and Lord Lonsdale gave him a capital day from
Owston Wood.

We musn't forget poor Sir Harry. Sir Harry Good-
When he come of age, he hunted with ricke.
Mr. Smith at Lincoln. Mr. Grantham, his uncle, was
there too; Mr. Smith give up the hounds that season,
and Sir Richard took to them; then Sir Harry come
to Leicestershire, in Mr. Osbaldeston's time. Mr.
Holyoake and him first met on the moors; then Sir
Harry come to Ketton, and after that they two took
stables at Melton together, first where Lord Wilton's,
and then where Mr. Coventry's is now. He was a
strong resolute man, but he couldn't ride like Mr.
Holyoake; he was first man at one time, was Mr.
Holyoake, for a twenty minutes' thing; to see him
ride Brilliant—my word—Mr. Ferneley's got such a
picture of him on him, shoving the fox along; a rich
dark chestnut; such a countenance! such an eye! he
had him from Newmarket. It would be seven or
eight years before Sir Harry took the hounds; he
wouldn't do it till the country gentlemen had had a
reg'lar meeting at The George, to offer it to him; they
were right pleased to have him. There was a hare
and a brace of pheasants every year for the farmers
from Clermont; that 'ud be his place in Norfolk; and
so quiet with the stockingers, he had 'em at a word.
"*Now, my good fellows, you've quite as good a right to
see sport as we have; do get back a little and keep
quiet.*" That was the way of him; and he'd give

them a couple of sovereigns to drink; they'd be as mute as mice. He was judge in that great race between Clinker and Radical; Sir Vincent Cotton started them; Captaih Ross and Captain Douglas rode them; I was pilot. There was a deal of talk about a steeple-chase between Sir Harry and The Squire; a thousand a-side; ten miles out of the Cottesmore country, by Barrow Gorse to Cream Gorse; Sir Harry was to have rode Limner (him he bought of Mr. Lynes); he was a wonder of a horse. It got first talked about at Squire Hartopp's, of Little Dalby; Sir Harry and three of his best horses were in training for three weeks; I and my son James were to have ridden with him on Smasher, and another thoroughbred,—in front and behind; Dick Burton and another with the Squire. It got settled a day or two before; the gentlemen thought there'd be a wrangle, so they got it stopped. I think The Squire would have out-rode him. The farmers didn't like it. They can't abide staghounds and harriers, and all that sort of thing. I don't wonder at it; many of their farms is just like gardens. They're good ones for foxes though; that's right enough with them.

His Crack Hunters. Sir Harry was slow at his fences; he crept, seldom jumped a fence clean, made his horses jump in. He got a many horses from that Gould of Swaffham. His estates were near there; The Smasher was among the first lot of horses he bought; he was named right enough, he was a regular smasher; he was a fine owdacious brown horse, and wanted nice hands; rather a queer style with him; he'd get quite under his fence before he jumped; Sir Harry rode him in one of my bridles; nothing could beat him across country. I've seen Sir Harry do 'em just when he got fairly into a run; Lord Plymouth gave 500 guineas for him; his lordship tried it on two years; Sir Harry told him he couldn't ride him, and he wouldn't take no less than his first price. He often mounted Lord Plymouth, did Sir Harry. This Smasher was the only one his lordship ever rode yet with anything like confidence—as I call it. He got lamed with my lord after two seasons, and he gave him his keeper to ride about on. The Doctor wasn't a stout horse ; he always laid down his ears when he come to a fence—I like to see them with their ears pricked—if a horse lays his ears down he's looking behind him ; depend upon it he's been cowed some time. Sir Harry was uncommon fond of a chestnut with white stockings ; a bit of a whistler though. Blamed if I can just think on his name ; he'd be sixteen hands ; all that : he once jumped a brook before he got him, for a thousand guinea bet, and won it too. He dropped under George Beers, and died in the field. ' Markwell whipped in with George, to Will Derry.

Sir Harry had the hounds very little His Mastership. more than two seasons. There was no subscription for covers then ; no nothing. They cost him well on to sixteen thousand altogether. Thrussington kennels took good six of it. He'd be pretty nearly his own architect ; they got crabbed somehow ; and the hounds went back to Quorn. Rent of covers was about six hundred, and lambs and wheat and fowls they'd be nigh three hundred more. Well, it is so. What a deal those foxes did eat ! They ran well too. He tried his hand at importing some. Didn't make much out at that game. They used to hunt six days reg'lar. He was such an active man was Sir Harry, he must have something to do. That was the reason he took to cocking. He didn't care for the fighting. He used to look quite pale and cut up in the pit. The breeding and the feeding was what he liked. Never one galloping off to see them at walk. If there was a bit of a frost, he'd seldom be away from the kennels, or seeing the covers, or the farmers or something. No rest in him. The farmers would

F

do anything for him; quite proud to do so. They were indeed. He quite got round Snow, him that used to live near John O'Gaunt; such a desperate man; he would head the fox times upon times; he was always for sticking me with a pitchfork. I never see anything just so savage before or since. Sir Harry always came from Doncaster races to have some cub-hunting; he had an account sent him reg'lar of it once a week, the moment they began. He took to the hounds after Lord Southampton; they used to hunt right away from Zouch Mill to Bunney; and from Melton to Clipston in Nottinghamshire. It's cut up into three now. In Mr. Meynell's time the company used to be at Loughboro', at The Anchor there. It would be about 1804. The Duke of Rutland published a map of the three hunts; Melton was just the centre, so they came there after that.

Goodricke's Gorse. Aye! it used to be a grand cover in old times; it's Lord Bessborough's ground. I don't know what they'll do with it now. They disturbed a vixen and two cubs this year, with their rabbiting, dug ever so far into the earth. Another time, just before the hounds were coming, some one comes and draws it over-night with terriers. It's a fact; i hear they were properly watched. I don't care what they say. It's truth.—What a one Sir Harry's Nerve. he was for nerve! It would be only the year before his death, a big chestnut run away with with him in Ireland, in a gig. He sticks to him like anything, and drives his head bang against a wall. Out he jumps, and runs thirty yards, and down he goes; couldn't keep on his legs with the shock; it shook him sadly. His second horseman, Harry, told me. Poor fellow, he went quite deranged when his master died; he was so cut up. He used to valet him when his regular man didn't go. Go to the world's end for him if he held up his finger. Blamed if I wouldn't have done the same. He was such a good-tempered man. I see a lad from Melton once follow him when the hounds were running hard from Glen Gorse. His horse rolls right over him at a drop fence; Sir Harry pulls smack up; and he gets off and lets his own horse go. Then he picks him up, and sets him in his saddle all right again; never thought nothing about the hounds. They caught his horse though, and he saw all the run. The year before he took to the hounds, he jumped a great flight of rails into the Spa-field, near the town. The hounds came to a check there; he hit his leg, and was lame good three weeks. That was a sad teazer for him.

What a strong active man Sir Harry was! When he was grouse-shooting in Scotland, he'd tie his clothes on his head, and swim across those streams; never stop at nothing. It was quite a treat for him to fight a horse. He had a black un that nearly beat him though; it was the day he went coursing with old Mr. Marriott, at Edmundthorpe. They killed three of Lord Harboro's hares going; such a game! Mr. Marriott was quite in a way about it when he overtook them; he thought his own lad had been doing it for a spree; Sir Harry took all the blame. They had this horse out with the greyhounds. They were all on him; first Sir Harry, then Mr. Holyoake; but he tired them all out, whipping and spurring him. Mr. Holyoake used to walk behind, and give it him with the whip, when Sir Harry was on; and he carried on this business all day. Mr. Marriott and his son both had a try. He kicked up a rare dust in Rotten Row, and got over the rails, and then Jack Stevens rode him. They got him quite quiet between them, and Lord Plymouth gave a thousand for him. Him and Mr. Edge of Strelley was uncommon intimate. Such clipping pointers Mr. Edge had—liver and white and black and white. Grand doings there *Meltoniana.* used to be at Melton then. Forty gentle-

men always dined at Sir Harry's at Croxton Race
time. There was only one day then. Sir Harry
lived when he first came where Lord Wilton does now.
It wasn't anything like so big a house then. You
took a look at their new stable and them bricks—
clinkers, they call them—before you come off to-day.
You've seen nothing better than that in your journeys,
I'll be bound. Then he shifted to Burton End. Mr.
Maxse and Mr. White lived there before. They christened it " Claret Lodge ;" the name was right enough,
I'll warrant it.

The Gentleman He began a finer style of cooking, did
with the Pistols. Sir Harry, at Melton. His cook very
nigh got shot one night. He was out lateish, and
there was a military gentleman stopping with Sir
Harry ; never done firing pistols. He hears the cook
tap about one o'clock at the pantry window, to be let
in ; and up he gets and lets fly twice over, at him.
Never gave him no time to say who he was. He had
to sit on the granary stairs all night : good for nothing in his profession next morning, and as fierce as
blazes. Durstn't go and tap again for his very life.
I've heard him give the story scores of times. My
word ! he told Sir Harry smack out, that he'd
answer for nothing going right with the dishes if that
gentleman warn't sent off; so Sir Harry gives him a
hint.

His Illness and He always liked to do everything dif-
Death. ferent to other people ; always thought
he knew better ; rather singular that way ; wouldn't
copy no one, or let any one guide him. Once condemned a whole lot of hounds for next to nothing.
He'd have been master yet. What chopping and
changing there's been with them Quorn hounds since.
I never see any one quite so keen of the whole thing
as Sir Harry. So good to his men, and every one, no
matter who, if he only did right. Poor fellow ! he
wouldn't be very much above thirty when he died.

Three-and-thirty would quite fetch him. He saw Lord Plymouth's death in the paper when he was at breakfast at an inn in Liverpool; he'd just sailed over there in his yacht, to bring a friend home to England; he and Lord Plymouth had been together a few days before; that shocked him terribly. That fall I told you of did him no good. Never quite the same man after. It was inflammation that killed him at last; he told the doctors they couldn't salivate him; then he just turns his face to the wall, and dies. I've never been quite happy in my mind about Melton since.

But now Grantham Station was reached at last, and our quaint gig partnership was dissolved. I shut up my note book as the bell rang, and as I watched the game little veteran drive away, I felt a little sad that my pencil was to be put in rest, and that my researches with him into the golden prime of the little hunting metropolis of England had reached their final close.

CHAPTER II.

OLDEN TIMES.

"There's many a lad I've known is dead,
    And many a lass grown old ;
And when the lesson strikes my head,
    My weary heart grows cold."
CAPTAIN MORRIS.

A LTHOUGH the flickering twilight of life may be
stealing upon us, and we can no longer follow
the chase, let us not repine, but rather
revert with pleasure to the rapturous joys
which in bygone days it has afforded us : how, in
glancing over the pack, we have been gratified by the
shining coat, the sparkling eye—sure symptoms of fit-
ness for the fight ;—how, when thrown in, every hound
has been hidden ; how every sprig of gorse has bris-
tled with motion ; how, when viewed away by the
sharp-eyed whipper-in, he stole under the hedge ; how
the huntsman clapped round, and with a few toots of
his horn brought them out in a body ; how, without
tying on the line, they flew to head ; how, when they
got hold of it, they drove it, and, with their heads up,
felt the scent on both sides of the fence ; how, with
hardly a whimper, they turned with him, till at the
end of fifty minutes they threw up ; how the patient
huntsman stood still ; how they made their own cast ;
and how, when they came back on his line, their
tongues doubled and they marked him for their own.
As the old woman in the fable regaled her nostrils
with the redolence of the dregs of the Falernian wine,
so does the old sportsman cheer his flagging spirits

A Retrospect.

by recalling to his mind the days when youth, and strength, and buoyancy gave zest to the delights of the chase.

Amongst the most celebrated packs of former days was that of Lord Spencer's, yclept the *The Old Pytchley* Pytchley. They hunted alternately the *Club Days.* Althorp and Pytchley countries. After having hunted one for about six weeks, they removed to the other kennel, and *vice versâ.* The boundaries of each were as scrupulously observed as if they had belonged to different packs. If they lost or killed on the confines of one country, they never drew for a second fox in the adjoining one, but went back to the one they were hunting at the time; the consequence was they were' continually drawing blanks, neither country being large enough for the length of time they remained in it. Assheton Smith (father of the late T. A. Smith), Doughty and Conyers, Lemon and Bligh, were constant inmates of Pytchley; and the Old Blues, who were for many years quartered at Northampton, were almost identified with the country. They have left an imperishable name, in that they made what is now called "The Blue Covert," near Harrington Wharf. There is an old story, that one morning the whole party went to lunch with Sam Isted, at Ecton. Forgetting the hour of the day, they indulged rather freely in the claret-cup; and on their return they followed Conyers into a deep morass on the edge of Orlingbury Field, and which is called "Conyers' Bog" to this day.

The first huntsman of whom we have *Dick Knight.* any knowledge was Knight, commonly called Mr. Knight, but of whose qualities we have little information. He was succeeded by the illustrious Dick Knight, who hunted the hounds as long as Lord Spencer kept them. His character has been so fully described elsewhere, that we will not dilate upon it. At that time, many of the gentlemen of the .

county hunted ; and when the hounds were at Althorp, their houses were open to their friends residing at a distance, where unbounded hospitality prevailed. When the hounds went to Pytchley, they shut up their houses, and removed there with them ; the ladies accompanying their lords to the old mansion, which, though not affording all the modern luxuries, contained ample space and every social comfort which could be desired. The hounds were never ridden over, which is so much the habit of the present day, but had plenty of room given them. Dick Knight generally took the lead ; and Lord Spencer— who had the finest thoroughbred horses of the day— sitting down in his saddle, followed him whithersoever he might go. It was almost thought a breach of etiquette in any one to go before them. A story is related, that once my lord, who could not hold his horse, was amongst the hounds at a check. Dick, wholly forgetting himself, and overpowered by the enthusiasm of the moment, cried out, "——, *my lord, hold hard !*"

Lord Spencer's Successors. When Lord Spencer, to the great regret of every one, gave up the hounds, they were taken by Mr. Buller, who kept them only the season. Stephen Goodall hunted them ; and owing to his patience, quietness, and thorough knowledge of his work, combined with a good scenting season, they had excellent sport. John Warde came next in succession, and was at the head of affairs about twelve years. He changed the system of dividing the two hunts, and took the old house at Boughton, where he kept the hounds. As far as hunting the country went, it was an improvement ; but it knocked up for a time the old Pytchley meetings in a great degree. When John Warde gave them up, Lord Althorp succeeded him, and Pytchley became itself again. Oh ! what joyous days were those ! Under his lordship's management, the system was completely changed. The hounds were bred lighter and quicker. The men were of the first caste, and the horses as good as money could procure.

Charles King, the huntsman, was about Charles King. five feet ten, and weighed about ten stone, just the proper height and weight to make the most of a horse ; strong enough to hold him together, and not too heavy to oppress him. He had the eye of a lynx, a most intelligent and animated countenance, which lighted up when things went well. His seat and hand were perfect, and when going along he held himself forward in his saddle. He had an innate taste for music, and played a good deal himself, which probably gave him such an ear for a hound's tongue in covert. In fact, as the Yorkshiremen say, he was a bad one to beat ; and ages may elapse before his like be found. His favourite horses were quite thoroughbred. Perhaps the one he liked best was Contingent by Chance, grandam by Highflyer; and the next of his favourites were Boadicea, sister to Sir Charles Knightley's Benvolio by Alexander, and The Swede by Agonistes. He had several other charming hunters ; but these three were out-and-out the cream of his stud.

It is, perhaps, too much the habit of Sport with Lord old sportsmen to hold up the system of Althorp. past days as preferable to those of the present. We are inclined to believe, however, that, in the records of the Pytchley Hunt, such splendid sport was never before known as at that period. His lordship kept a Hunting Journal ; and if it be now among the records of Althorp, it will tell how they found at Purzer's Hill, ran over old Naseby Field, to Hothorp, in fifty minutes ; and how, after a short check, they hunted him over the finest part of Leicestershire, and killed him at Sir H. Halford's, at Wistow : how, at another time, they found him in Crick Osier-bed, ran over Crick and Yelvertoft Field, over Honey Hill, into

Leicestershire, almost without a check ; and how,
after being bothered by sheep, they dropped to hunting, and, coming up to him, killed him in view at
Brunting-Thorpe : how, on another day, they found
him at Crick Gorse, ran over Clay-Coton and Lilburn
Field, under Hemplow Hill, over Cold Ashby Field,
across Naseby Open Field by Sibbertoft, through the
corner of Marston Wood, and killed him in the open,
close to Marston Trussell, in an hour and seventeen
minutes, after one of the most brilliant runs on record ; and again, how, twice in the same year, they
found at Crick, and each time killed him in Badby
Wood. We could recount many other runs of the
highest order, but it might be tedious to those of the
present time to read the narratives of days so long
past.

The Club at Pytchley was at that time in the zenith
Pytchley. of its glory. The mornings afforded un-
mixed pleasure, and nectar crowned the night. Lord
Althorp was a constant attendant ; Frank Forester,
Felton Hervey, Dick Gurney, Hugo Meynell, Charles
Knightley, Peter and Charles Allix, John Cook,
Nethercote and Davey, were generally of the
family party. Scotland sent her tributaries in
those most excellent men, Sir David and James
Baird. The Emerald Isle lent her support also in
Lucas and Bruen ; and Tom Grosvenor and Roberts
were occasionally of the party. George Payne (father
of the present George) often joined the circle, and no
one enjoyed it more. Lord Alvanley now and then
came from Melton, and with him mirth, fun, and
revelry. Frederick Ponsonby sometimes came over,
and also Poyntz, who added life and spirit to the party.
The studs were of the first order, and the riders were
worthy of them. Jealousy was unknown, and sport—
and sport alone—was the object of all. The old
gentleman who stalks over the country with a scythe
in one hand and an hour-glass in the other has made

fearful havoc in the ranks of the Pytchley Hunt;
a few veterans, however, have escaped his grasp.
Amongst those who are gone, we will mention two or
three.

Peter Allix was a first-rate performer, A few Cracks of the Hunt.
and ever where he should be. By his
friends he was familiarly called " Scratch-face :" as, if
a weak place in the fence was not handy, he would
rather take a bulfinch than lose his ground. Felton
Hervey was a beautiful horseman, quiet and gentle,
with undeniable nerves; and was always in the right
place. Frederick Ponsonby, who was more *au fait* at
facing a bayonet than a brook, met with an extraordi-
nary accident. Lord Althorp mounted him on a bay
horse, curiously marked with white spots, which he
bought of Lloyd, of Aston. The hounds were running
quick, and they came to a brook with a high bank on
the opposite side. He put him at it so hard, that he
could not blink it, and literally broke his neck against
the opposite bank. The Colonel was flung on the
other side, holding the rein, which he pulled, thinking
to get him out, when he found he was as dead as a
stone. Sir Thomas Salisbury was a great addition to
the circle; he had ever a smile on his countenance,
and was always in good humour. He did not look
much at the work of hounds, but was a good horseman; and his main object was to get as much as he
could out of his horse without upsetting him. Two
maxims he invariably pursued : one was never to go
over ridge and furrow; and the other never to go into
a field of swedes, which from their holding the wet
caused the ground to be always deep. Of course the
hounds often slipped him, but he trusted to a skirt, or
to their turning to him; but happen what might, he
never abandoned his horse. Roberts was a good
horseman, and a hard rider. His best, a bay horse,
was got by a half-bred stallion, out of a thoroughbred
mare, a hard puller and difficult to ride, but he went

right well. He had a mare which probably was not worth much, as there is an anecdote of Sir Robert Leighton having lost his pocket-book; and when it was found, there was a memorandum in it to the following effect: "To remember not to buy Roberts's mare." We must not forget one of the greatest acquisitions to the hunt, Andrew Barnard (afterwards Sir Andrew); a most cheery one over the country, and the life of the party at the social board. His memory will be fondly cherished as long as there is any one alive who can recollect him.

Captain Jones and his Pilot. Captain Jones, of whom Lord Althorp bought his celebrated horse Midnight, was another of the visitors. He was a good horseman, and a hard rider; but could not go without a pilot, always attaching himself to the man of whose judgment he had the greatest opinion. One day he was following a gentleman, who was in the habit of going slow at his fences, however hard they might be running. After the run he came up to him and said, " Sir, if you will ride so slow at your fences, I really can't help riding over you." The gentleman replied that he was very sorry to hear it, but he had been so long in the habit of it, that he feared he could never break himself of it.

Lucas's Barn. An odd adventure occurred to Lucas. On one of the short days in December, he left his hack at a long distance from the place where they killed him, and soon after he started on his way towards Pytchley, it became pitch dark. He got into a field, out of which he could not find his way; and at length stumbled on a barn, where he and his horse took up their abode for the night. The barn has ever since been called Lucas's Barn. Another day Dick Gurney's Views of the Meltonians. some of the Meltonians came over from the Harborough country, to teach the White Collars how to ride to hounds. They were rather pushy; and some one said to Dick

Gurney, "Why, those Leicestershire men can't turn, can they?" "How the devil should they," says Dick, "when they have a pound of starch in their collars?"

One of the frequent attendants in the field, although he did not come to Pytchley in those days, was Mr. Small, of Clifton, who was one of the neatest of men in his dress, and quite a beau in his way. He had a round-crowned hat, which fitted him like a hunting-cap, a pepper-and-salt coat, leather breeches, beautifully cleaned, which buttoned high above the knee, boots shining like polished ebony, very short tops, and narrow leather boot garters, with small silver buckles. He had two black mares, so much alike that it was difficult to distinguish one from the other. The ears of both were cropped, and he rode both in a martingale, neither of them wanting one. He was as particular about the appearance of his horses as he was about his own. His bits and stirrup-irons were most highly polished; and he had an old-fashioned saddle, the pommel low and back, and the pannels of plush. Whenever his horses travelled, he had stuffed pads to hang on the pillars of the stall, to prevent the hip bones being chafed. Altogether he was the neatest and sprucest man that ever graced the Pytchley hunting field.

The Pytchley Brummell.

We could relate many more anecdotes of those times, but enough is as good as a feast. As everything in this world, however charming, is doomed to decay, so the Old Club, the scene of so much conviviality, harmony, and good fellowship, yielded to the inexorable hand of Fate. Some became old; some became slow; some took to war; some to wives; a general blight prevailed, and Pytchley was no more.

The End of the Old Club.

Turn we now to the Forest, "where William Rufus was by Tyrrell slain." 'Tis said of old people that they recollect events long

Recollections of the New Forest.

past, better than those of recent date. We have picked up fragments from an octogenarian, whose memory is of this caste, and who upwards of fifty years ago frequented the glades of this charming woodland. At no period of history and in no country was the noble science of hunting more eagerly followed or more thoroughly enjoyed. Although old Meynell was not there to aid them with his counsel, his genius pervaded them, and the real love of the chase was inherent in the foresters of those times. Placed in a remote corner of the country, they were little heard of; and but for a few strangers who visited them in the month of April, the world would hardly have known that such a pack as that of the New Forest existed. There were no enclosures to stop or lame the hounds, no sheep to foil the ground, and no hawbuck shepherd to head the fox, but the country was as wild as nature made it. The foxes, the deer, and some wild ponies were its only inhabitants. The old foresters were cast in a rough mould, and had no recourse to the foreign aid of ornament. Skilled as they were in shirking a bog or bobbing their heads under the boughs of an oak, they were out of their element when they got into the open amongst the fences. Facing a brook, or topping a stake-and-bound, was not in their category. Yellow buckskins and brown tops was the only dandyism they aspired to.

The New Foresters. Williams and Harbin were two of the oldest inhabitants of the wild, and they both knew hunting well. Williams was a light weight, and saw as much of the hounds in the course of the year as any of them. Harbin was heavy, and not a first-rate horseman. John Warde used to tell a story, that one day they killed a fox near his house, and he asked him to dine with him. The old Squire said, " I'm all in a muck sweat; but if you will lend me a shirt, I don't mind roughing it for once." " I will lend you one with great pleasure," replied Harbin,

"but I fear mine are not big enough for you round
the collar." "Big enough?" says the Squire; "why,
if they will fit you, they will fit a hog, and it's hard if
they won't me." Pole, yclept Dobbin, was another of
the old set. He loved hunting dearly, but his horses
were not of the first caste. The one he chiefly rode
was an old grey, with a rusty snaffle-bridle, and the
stuffing hanging out of the pannels of the saddle. He
relied on his knowledge of the Forest, and saw a good
deal of sport. He was rough in his attire, and did not
(like Brummell) impregnate the air with otto of roses.

One of the most joyous sportsmen who Mr. Boscawen
came to see the April fun, was Bos- and Admiral Cod-
cawen; a thorough polished gentleman, rington.
of the old *régime*. He was, when young, a captain in
the Horse Grenadiers, a regiment which acted as a
body-guard to George the Third, but which was dis-
banded eighty or ninety years ago. His love of the
chase was extreme, and although advanced in years,
he was as wild as a boy. One day they got away close
to a fox, and ran into him in a quarter of an hour,
without a check. Only three men were there, among
whom was Boscawen. One of them exclaimed, "What
a beautiful thing!" and the other said, "Why, it's a
nothing; my horse had hardly got on his legs."
Boscawen, who was close by him, said, "I do not
know whether your horse had got on his legs, but I
know that mine had just got off his." He bought a
light cat-legged horse of some one at Lyndhurst, and
one morning, as they were going to covert, he asked
Tom Sebright what he thought of him. "Why," says
Tom, "I would rather shoot him nor ride him; he
ain't got legs bigger nor our Hoodman (Woodman)."
Mr. Compton, the master of the hounds, lived at the
Manor House, and had generally some friends with
him in April, and amongst them was the late Admiral
Codrington. He was a good sportsman; and though
a sailor, no landsman could ride better. He had a

beautiful hand, and was a capital judge of pace; and indeed quite a model of a horseman.

Billy Butler the Parson.   Amongst the birds who migrated from their own country, was Billy Butler, from Dorsetshire. He was a lively jovial soul, and loved the sport with all his heart. George the Fourth when Prince of Wales took Mr. Sturt's house at Critchell, and kept a pack of hounds. Billy Butler hunted regularly with him, and was a great favourite. One Saturday after hunting, his Royal Highness said, " Billy, you will dine with me to-morrow ?" " To-morrow, your Royal Highness," replied Billy, " is Sunday, rather a bad day for a parson to dine out, but I shall be very happy to dine with you on Monday." " So you shall, Billy," said the Prince. No man was ever more jealous of a proper respect, or ever resented the breach of it more strongly, but with one so thoroughly *naïf* it was impossible that he could be angry.

A Word on Scent.   To the majority of sportsmen who compose the hunting field it may be difficult to comprehend why they have not sport every day, and they often attribute the want of it to the inefficiency of the hounds, or lack of judgment in the huntsmen. The mystery of scent they do not take into account—a mystery which never has been, and never will be solved. On the mornings which appear the most promising the hounds can't run a yard; whilst in a bitter east wind with a pelting rain they can't go wrong. On the most gaudy day in the autumn, when there is a white frost the fallows generally carry, and rain comes on. In spring a white frost is the harbinger of a fine day, and oftentimes the scent is perfect. When the dewdrops hang on the hedges, when the gossamer floats on the bents, the want of scent may be accounted for. When neither of these causes exist, when it is dry both above and below, and when the atmosphere is clear, it would puzzle the most astute philosopher to tell you why they can't lay hold of it. Hounds when going to covert will almost tell you if there be a scent or not. They will sniff the air and go with their heads up, and show buoyancy of spirits, if they know they can run ; but on the contrary, when it is a bad scent they will hang down their sterns, and seem indifferent as to whether they went on or not. The sure symptom of want of scent is when a hound rolls in going to covert. *Apropos* to this is a story of Jem Butler. One morning when the hounds met at Lamport, his favourite bitch Rosy was rolling near his horse; and the late Mr. Bouverie, who was close to him, heard the following soliloquy : " No galloping ; no fun, Rosy ; Rosy ! thee must hunt to-day !"

In the formation of a pack nothing is so essential as the proper selection of stallion hounds. As a general principle it is not advisable to breed from a young hound. So long as he is in full vigour he may not show vice ; but when he loses his power is the time he will show it, if he has it in him. An honest hound will hang to the line when he has lost the power of running to head. That, in short, is the trial of his worth ; and if he stands that trial you will do well to breed from him. Hounds which are to be hereafter valuable must begin with chasing. There is probably no instance of a good stallion hound who began by hunting. It must have been observed by all men conversant with breeding, how diametrically opposite in character are hounds of the same litter. There was a remarkable instance of it in two hounds bred by John Warde, in 1807. Their names were Alfred and Audrey, by Lee Anthony's Anthony ; the former one of the wildest and most difficult hounds to break, and the latter the deadest hunter from her entry. John Warde used to say, " When those nine-stone skinny fellows are miles ahead, Audrey is my best friend." She toiled along ;

Selection of Stallion Hounds.

G

and when he came up to her and cheered her, she
turned her head and looked back at him, as much as
to say, " Come along, old heavy; I'll take you to
them." Ranter was one of the wildest hounds, and
the most difficult to break, but one of the best of
stallions. Tom Wingfield used to say that he never
had so much trouble with any hound before. Assheton Smith's Champion and Chorister were by him,
and they were the sires of some of the most valuable
hounds in Lord Althorp's pack—a pack which would
go up to the scent without going beyond it, and
thereby would wait upon a fox who never would wait
for them.

The Chase of   Nearly sixty years having elapsed since
Yore.   the few anecdotes we have recorded took
place, we must be excused if we cut short the thread
of our tale. Never was any period more propitious
for the chase. The breeding and management of
hounds was thoroughly understood : men went out to
enjoy hunting, and not to spoil it. The country was
not gridironed by railways, nor did steam engines
impregnate the atmosphere with noxious gas. There
were not two or three men draining in every field. Of
the few sheep there were, the greater part were rotten,
and hung in the brambles of the fences. Hunting
was then at its culminating point. Modern science
has doubtless filled the pockets of the jobber and the
speculator, but it has gone far to destroy the noblest
pursuit which the gods ever bestowed on mortals.
With whatever evil eye the age of feudalism may be
viewed by the present generation, it was the age for
sport. Those were the days " *when nature's dress was
loveliness,*" and which in vain we may sigh for, for the
like will never return.

CHAPTER III.

SILK.

"No more shall he at Doncaster
Each foal and yearling pat ;
Or ride up Goodwood's leafy slopes,
To the trial ground with Nat ;
No more with Kent and Marson
Shall he scan each pet in form ;
Or view their place, as in the race
They sweep past, like the storm."

IF there is any meeting which we Shadows of the
should love to call up with Merlin's Past.
mirror from amid the shadows of the past, we should go
back seventy years, and take a glance at Knavesmire.
The choice with us, for once, would be more for the
sake of the men than the horses. We would fain see
the Prince of Wales, in his blue-coat and tight-fitting
buckskins, cantering on his brown crop-eared cob up
to the door of the Grand Stand ; Peregrine Wentworth
on his grey, with Lenny Jewison, and Cade ready to
go to scale in the "all white" at his side ; Hutchinson
of Overton in a coat dark-green as his colours on the
lists of the day ; and Sir Charles Turner fair and
ruddy, as becomes the knight of the orange banner,
which was so soon to find its worthiest bearers in Bening-
borough and Hambletonian. That meeting, which is
still marked with a white stone in Yorkshire hearts,
was the dawn of a new era for the Turf, which had
known many ups and downs since the Duke of Cumberland's executors had sold off his stud. The names
of "Bolton," "Queensberry," and "Rockingham" had,
it is true, lent lustre to "the sport of kings," but it

was not until the Prince of Wales and "Bedford," "Grosvenor," "Abingdon," "Barrymore," and some ten other equally choice spirits, threw their souls into the cause, that it revived in earnest on Newmarket Heath.

The Warren Hill in '89. "A View of Noblemen's and Gentlemen's trains of Running Horses, with the Grooms and Horses in their full liveries," was the popular print of 1790. The Warren Hill is the scene of the afternoon's revel. Quiet little Newmarket just peeps forth in the hollow, in the centre of that restless panorama, and in the far distance the Ely Minster turrets cut the cloudless sky, and struggle manfully for pre-eminence with Highflyer Hall. In the foreground is the Prince, by the grace of the artist a somewhat slim-looking buck, in a sort of Don Cæsar de Bazan beaver, standing up in his phaeton with four greys, and booking a bet with the shrivelled Duke of Orleans, on horseback at his side. His brother "York" has alighted, and is gaily pointing out to "A lady" (as the key observes), a long sheeted string, which are, West Australian fashion, cutting down the Warren Hill like a scythe, in the direction of King Charles's cupola chair. On the extreme left, the Countess of Barrymore, in the costume of

"Those teacup days of hoop and hood,
And when the patch was worn,"

sits in the phaeton by the side of her eccentric liege lord, (who was so soon to fall lifeless in her arms, as his hand held the reins), and listens to the animated periods of Charles James Fox as he exults in the coming laurels of his Seagull and his Put. John Duke of Bedford is also amid the throng, and so are Haggerston, George Hanger, Wyndham, Captain Grosvenor, and Bullock. That ancient oddity, Colonel Thornton, though not much of a racing-man, has wandered off here as well, and Falconer's Hall, where

his seventy hooded hawks were kept, to complete the
devastation among the Yorkshire Wold game, which
his three 150-guinea guns, " Death, Destruction, and
Fate," were unable to accomplish, is forgotten for the
nonce in the prospect of the forthcoming Grosvenor
Stakes.

During the whole of the new era, Mr. <small>Features of the</small>
Fox was confederate with Lord Foley, <small>New Era.</small>
winning 30,000*l.* at one Spring Meeting alone, and
alike ready to match his horses "cross and jostle,"
over the Beacon, at a moment's notice, or play for a
shilling at teetotum. With him politics and racing
flowed pleasantly on together. He had no more active
canvasser for the buff and blue than Old Tat, in the
Westminster election, and he bought Maid of All-
Work from him when it was over. Tandem did well
for that far-seeing auctioneer, but " Hammer and
Highflyer" was the toast of his heart, and he loved
best to hear it drunk with all the honours by the whole
body of Newmarket jockeys, when he gave his annual
dinner to them at Ely, after the toils of the season.
Eight of the three great races fell to Highflyer's stock,
but at last he wasted away into the exact image of his
three-year-old self; and, although only nineteen, left
470 winners in the Calendar. His owner died soon
after, just as the Turf—to which the rivalry of himself
and O'Kelly, the one buying up Marske and the other
Herod mares for their paddocks, lent no little zest—
once more began slightly to decline. This languor,
however, soon passed away. Highflyer began to live
again in the stud triumphs of Lord Derby's Sir Peter,
and Eclipse in King Fergus, for whom Mr. Hutchinson would have fought to his knees in blood. The very
coal-heavers discussed the merits of the looming
match between Hambletonian and Diamond, quite as
learnedly over their cheese and onions at Mundy's
Coffee House, as their betters, led on by the owners of
Eclipse and Bacchus, amid hazard and faro upstairs ;

and Sir Harry Vane Tempest, who brought the thrilling news in person, at last, to the more aristocratic haunts of the Cocoa Tree, rode the winner in the Park next week, and drew the Prince of two thousand on a prize-fight, almost beneath the gibbet of Jerry Abershaw.

The nineteenth century found Betts and Hilton in office on the Heath; Lord Sackville the best rider at Bibury, and Jonathan Bray the door-keeper at Tattersall's. The Duke of Queensberry's green *vis-à-vis*, with its long-tailed blacks and its shrivelled muff-wearing tenant, was an object of interest to every gazer in the Ring, and eight years more went by before

> "The jockey boys, Newmarket's crew,
> Who know a little 'thing or two,'"

sang mock dirges over that "Star of Piccadilly." Although in obedience to his vow, the Prince's eye was no longer kept in practice at Newmarket, he could still see through a horse like a hoop; but his colts, which ran within the rails of St. James's Park before going up to Aldridge's, did little towards clearing off the seventeen thousand odd, which he incurred with his farrier in seven years.

The Sancho *v.* Pavilion Match at Lewes. In 1804, the great Mellish constellation arose with Sancho and Staveley; and Brighton and all its Steyne joys were made still more delightful on that July afternoon, when he appealed for the second time against the result of the New Claret Stakes, in the three thousand guinea a-side match over Lewes. Sir John Lade, whose cook-bride had once challenged a fair rival to drive four horses eight miles at Newmarket for 500 p.p., sat behind six greys on the royal barouche, and the Colonel followed with his four to match, in charge of the Countess of Barrymore, who might or might not have been cognizant of the fact, that her whip was to act as second to her husband at day-break.

Pavilion, with Sam Chifney up, was the first to canter; and then Buckle, in his white and crimson sleeves, on the lengthy yellow bay Sancho ; but even the knowledge that his owner, who led him down the course, had backed him to win 20,000*l.*, did not dispirit the layers of 6 to 4 on his old Raby conqueror. The result of the first match over Lewes had made them equally wild to back Sancho ; but he had hit his leg at exercise a few days before, and this was the only chance of saving their money. The odds, however, quickly fell to 5 to 1 as Sancho went up to his opponent's quarters in the last mile, and commanded him from that point till his leg gave way within the distance. Such trifles did not weigh very long on a philosophic mind like the Colonel's. He lunched at The Star with the Royal party as calmly as if he had been losing mere three-penny points at whist, and at daybreak was seen entreating Mr. Howarth, who had stripped to the buff to prevent his clothes getting into the wound, to shake hands after one shot, and dress himself once more.

About this culminating period of his The Betting of fortunes Mellish never opened his mouth the Period. under 500*l.* in the Ring, and the southern division caught the betting infection. Even old Elwes was known to eat nothing all day but a piece of crushed pancake, (which had been made at Marcham, two months before, and which he would persist in styling " as good as new,)" and yet to stand 7000*l.* for Lord Abingdon on one match ; and the *Sporting Magazine* could write, two months previous to the Fyldener St. Leger, 1806, " There is little doubt that upwards of one million of guineas has already been laid." The Northern betting, however, was very slack in comparison with Newmarket. The men who clustered on the distance post side of the Stand at York thought 10*l.* a great venture, and an even 50*l.* between Lord Scarbro' and Mr. Garforth on that two-year-old or " Paddy

Land racing," which the latter detested so much till he tasted its sweets with Oiseau and Otter of his cherished Camillus blood, was talked of all over the county. George Sundley, who was once a noted cock-setter, and Michael Brunton, the Richmond druggist, became as nothing when Gully, Ridsdale, and Justice opened their betting-books and "peppered" and backed horses in earnest as well; and even Tommy Swan, the amateur horse-dealer, who was lean, high-shouldered, and would lay against any mortal thing, began to draw off in the face of such rivals, and reseek his quiet parlour in the inn at Bedale.

The betting mart at Doncaster up to Tarrare's year was the long narrow upper-room at the Salutation, and it was there that Jim Bland delivered his portentous offer of " *A hundred to your walking-stick against Theodore !*" Many quite as odd wagers as that were heard on the Stand. A Yorkshire Friend laid the owner of Antonio 10*l.* even, that he couldn't whistle when the horses came in. Mr. Ferguson accordingly commenced when they were at the distance, and right loud and shrill was the note. " *Nay,*" said the crafty layer, " *thou must only whistle when I tell thee,*" and as they swept past with the scarlet in front and Wrangler at his girths, the signal was given, but the lucky lawyer could only make a blow of it. When the new rooms once opened their flower-clad portals, Lord Kennedy was the mightiest hero over their Board of Green Cloth. One evening it was as much as one friend at his side could do to stuff the banknotes into his coat pockets, as he won eight mains at hazard in succession; and when the emulous ardour of the spectators almost foamed into frenzy, a man near the table sold his seat for five guineas !

The Holywell   As the century wore on, Mr. Watt and
Hunt Club.   Mr. Petre began to be names of dread at Doncaster, as Earl Fitzwilliam and Lord Archibald

Hamilton had been before them ; and the Holywell
Hunt, who were among the first to test

"The pure Saxon of that silver style"

from the lips of the then Hon. Mr. Stanley, when he
took the chair as "the Derby colt" at their dinner,
kept the game alive on the Cheshire side as each first
week in October came round.   There was always
something to come away up the Mostyn Mile, where
Birmingham and Touchstone knew such grief, even
when Pryse's Ambo, roarer as he was, could keep up
his charter no more.   But it was not on racing alone
that merry club relied.   Jack Mytton brought greyhounds as well as horses to the scene, and cared little
whether he met Mr. Lloyd of Rhugett, with the Champion and Lunardi, or Mr. Best with his Muslin and
Streamer blood.

No keener critic than the great Dr.   Dr. Bellyse, of
Bellyse of Audlem rode behind the   Audlem.
slipper that day.   A blue dress-coat with gilt buttons,
light coloured kerseys and gaiters, a buff waistcoat,
and a pig-tail just peeping from beneath a conical
low-crowned hat, completed his attire ; while a golden
greyhound, the gift of his friend Lord Combermere,
lent a tasteful finish to his snowy frill.   Never in his
life had he seen either Derby or St. Leger, but his
eyelids knew no rest in the long night of suspense
which followed them.   He was a walking polyglot on
race-horse pedigrees, from the Godolphin Arabian to
Memnon.   The Grafton blood in the South, and Mr.
Garforth's in the North, were both especially dear to
him ; but he would invariably toast General Mina
when he won, and troll forth with double emphasis,
on that evening, all his lodge lays of "a Free and
Accepted Mason," or his famous matrimonial ballad—

"We scold and fight, and both repent
That ding-dong went the bell."

Pre-eminent and assiduous as he was in his profession,

his patients had to show a clean bill of health during the Chester race week, or give up all hope of having him. The Stationers' Almanack was not truer to the year than his yellow gig with his fourteen-one Brown Tommy to the Hop Pole yard at Chester, on that Saturday afternoon. On the Monday he sallied forth to the Hotel Row, and received a hearty annual welcome from all the lovers of " the Turf and the Sod," to whom, from his quiet worth, and his wonderful memory and information on every point, he had become so endeared. Years wrought no change in the dress or figure of this old Cheshire worthy, or quenched his love for either science. The cock-pit began at eleven, and the in-go ended soon after one ; and then before a Grand Stand arose, he was always to be seen, stationed on Tommy, in the middle of the Roodee, to watch what horses were doing all round, and armed with a gigantic umbrella. He held the belief that there were "always so many fools on a race-course," and hence he kept it to shoot out in self-defence, in the faces of the young blades as they galloped recklessly across him from the cords to the river rails.

The Chester Cocking. Cocking was then the chosen amusement of the race mornings, and no one on this point was so great an authority as the Doctor. He spoke, too, out of the fulness of his strange experience, as he had the privilege of all the walks on the Combermere, Shavington, Adderley, Doddington, Peckforton, Beeston, Oulton, and divers other estates in Cheshire, Shropshire, and Wales. In some seasons he sent out a thousand chickens, of which barely one-third would be reared, or fit to produce at an important main. After dinner, on the Saturday of his arrival at Chester, he gave an audience to his feeder, to sound him as to the condition of his cocks, and learn his opinion of the forthcoming main ; and not unfrequently that functionary would arrive with a

couple of bags slung over his shoulder, and the pets
of his fancy remonstrating inside. During the week,
he would over and over again slip away from those
who wanted to talk to him about weights, and watch
his brown-red champions busy in their pens, scratching at a fresh-cut sod, or a spadeful of the purest
gravel, fresh from the bottom of the Dee. Any feeder
who did not furnish these stimulants, at least every
third day, would have held his place on a very frail
tenure. He would have a hundred cocks taken up
from their walks for Chester, in order that his feeder
might select the best, and put them in training from
the Thursday week to the Monday, when the smaller
cocks led off in the five days' main. Two years old
was the favourite period for selection, as they became
greasy at three, and far beyond the 4lb. 10oz. standard; and eggs, sugar-candy water, hot bread and
milk, barley, rue, butter, and rhubarb formed the chief
part of that dainty diet, which few were fated to taste
more than once in their lives.

He inaugurated his career on the sod Different Breeds
with the original white piles, which carried of Game Cocks.
such a wonderful spur that "The Cheshire drop,"
which would occasionally come out in a long battle,
when the odds were twenty to one, was considered as
fatal as the "Chifney rush." These were the cocks
with which the Cholmondeleys, the Egertons, the
Warburtons, the Cottons, and the Raylances fought
all the great county mains; sometimes against each
other, but more frequently against the Mexborough
and Meynell families. The Doctor, however, convinced himself that their constitutions would not stand
the discipline of modern feeders, and at last, by judi-
cious crossing, made his brown and black-reds carry
as good a spur, and bear the most punishing preparation to boot. They were chiefly bred from his old
"cut-combed hen," whose descendants were crossed
with his brown "crow alleys," two of Gilliver's black-

reds, and the Westgarth cock. Six pullets to one cock, and the eggs as closely bred in as he could get them, were two of his leading tenets; the greater part of his chickens were also hatched in April and May, and he used the same stud-birds for about three seasons.

A Peep at the Mains. The old families in Cheshire and the neighbouring counties were as proud of their breed of black-reds or birchen duckwings, as ever Mr. Garforth was of his Marcia or Mr. Pierse of his Tuberose; and Potter and Gilliver (who fed for Mr. Leigh, of Lyme), took rank in the public mind with Robson and Croft. The feeling had struck deep root for years. It had penetrated almost within the sombre walls of York, and quiet burgesses remembered how Mellish and Sir Francis Boynton had fought main after main at Bootham Bar. There was a dim story, too, that Colonel Thornton had matched his best hawk against a game-cock, at Preston or Knutsford, for a thousand guineas a side. Be that curious wager more or less, ten guineas a battle and two hundred the main was the usual standard. At race meetings they often fought one "in-go" by candlelight, amid a perfect Babel of bets; and in the Royal Westminster Pit of yore, no mains were ever fought by day. To such a height had this Roger Ascham passion grown, that although the bye battles were only honoured with common calico, the Derby main bag, with its rich lace, and its needle-embroidered coat of arms, was alone worth the five shillings admission to see. Lord Sefton, Mr. Price of Brynpys, Captain White, and Mr. Bold Haughton, all fought at Chester; while Lord Derby and Mr. Leigh of Lyme, generally reserved their cocks for the Preston and Newton mains. Setting was quite a distinct profession from feeding, and from fifteen to thirty guineas was Porter's and Gum's regular fee for a great main; while George Sundley, Sam Gosling, and Redfern were all in request for minor issues. Gilliver held cocks clumsily in his large hands ; but Owen Probyn of Birmingham, an asthmatic deathlike man, with a long thumb, and nail which he could so deftly use, was esteemed three battles in a main better than any one of his compeers.

It was generally one of the articles that they were "to fight in fair reputed silver spurs," which were, after all, little more than steel thinly washed over, and there was not a more cunning craftsman in this line than Singleton of Ireland, whose countryman lost with Dr. Bellyse the first great contest, of forty-one mains and ten byes, that was ever fought at Chester in the new subscription pit. He then gave it up to Lord Derby and Mr. Bold Haughton, and the two last mains of importance at Chester were between these two, in 1833-34. The Potters were his lordship's feeders for many years, and Roscoe his breeder. His cocks were principally duckwings, but he latterly fought more reds, all of them selected from an enormous number of birds, and always of the finest form and daintiest feather. Neither his lordship nor Dr. Bellyse lived to see their battles royal put an end to by Act of Parliament. The latter died in the January of 1829, nearly six years before the Earl, when he was but one day short of seventy, from a mere casual ailment, in the fullest vigour of body and mind.

Strange, indeed, was the contrast be- The Wrestling tween that crowded pit in St. John-street, Ring at Carlisle. Chester, and the race accompaniments at "Merrie Carlisle" on a September afternoon. A dark and almost breathless ring of ten thousand is gathered under the hill-side, on The Swifts, and George Irving and Weightman—the wrestling champions of the day —are within it. There they stand, with their necks crossed, and their hands swaying between them, watching with the eye of a falcon l..t the other should "get hod," and put it in his fatal cross-buttock. In vain the umpires threaten to blow them out of the ring if they keep up the delicious suspense much longer ; but all in vain. Weightman kens Geordie's, and Geordie kens Weightman's grip too well to let him have him by the waist a half second in advance. Then they smile, raise their heads, shake them at the umpires, and try it on once more. No better luck again ; till at last the bell rings for Canteen to saddle, and confront his Border friend Fair Helen, and Bonassus for the Gold Cup. At the sound their hands close round each other at last with a snap which nothing can unloose this time. Hayton or Bolton Gate must rejoice or wail ere night. Weightman's tall lank frame towers upwards, as he seems to lift the little one almost off his legs, and prepares to fling him into space, but Geordie is busy below. Again and again he stops the dreaded cross-buttock, but the hipe has done its work at last, and the Eden bears to the Solway the long thunder-fledged shout that "Lang John" holds the belt once more. And so the stalwart Cumbrian crow-alleys settle their differences ; and as they hold the plough on their fell sides, or along the rich meadows of the Petcrill, the Gelt, and the Caldew, or herd their Cheviots amid the heather wastes of Bewcastle—near scenes hallowed by Dandy Dinmont and St. Ronan's Well—they may well think with pride, till another Carel Races comes round, of how

> "Chapman was the man
> Who bore away the prize from all
> At the merry sports of Flan ;"

how Jonathan Whitehead "can fling them ony way ;" and how Robert Gordon and Jackson of Kinneyside were still the best cocks in a far nobler main than Chester's.

A Turf Retrospect. But the race-course seems to have faded from our notes, and we have left

the Chester Roodee far behind. The Doge of Venice
and four other Cup winners had alone passed the post,
when the keen eye of its county handicapper was
glazed and dim ; and the poor of Audlem and miles
round knew him no more, to their sorrow. But Jack
Mytton was still great and glorious there with his
Halston, in the same year, too, that the Blacklocks
carried all before them at Doncaster; and that
Voltaire, after defeating Sir Hercules in the St. Leger,
sent down—under Tommy Lye's guidance—his half
brother Laurel, and Fleur-de-Lis in the Cup. Now
Velocipede's erring sinew can be patched up no more ;
and even three St. Legers in succession cannot avail
to keep Mr. Petre in the Racing Calendar. Anon we
have the brothers Chifney era ; and visions of
sanguine Will in the yard at Tattersall's, on Priam's
settling-day, with a table before him and a pyramid
of bank-notes thereon. Their fortune has proved as
fragile as that paper pile ; and then comes Lord
Exeter triumphant with his white-legged Sultans, and
Lord Jersey nicking the blood best with his Cobweb
at last. Mr. Bowes and his "all black" appears on
the scene when Plenipo goes off ; and although the
Sledmere-bred Grey Momus may fail him, a lanky
cast-off Priam foal from Bretby, who trotted up with
her dam to Tattersall's, gives Lord George the weapon
which he has pined for years to wield. Then sets in
the Westminster dynasty, which Touchstone had
begun ; and his lordship twice over draws nigh his
dearly beloved Doncaster, a full week before the races,
right confident that his yellow jacket and black cap
will there achieve what Epsom has denied it. Now
Lanercost and Beeswing end their long Cumberland
and Northumberland rivalry, and Alice Hawthorn is
on every lip. She, too, at last, subsides into a worn-
out mare, out of whom even Bob Heseltine cannot
raise a gallop ; and then Sir Tatton goes forth from
his accustomed wicket, and ere he leads back his

namesake to scale, gives Bill Scott for the last time
that handshake of victory which was to be proudly
felt by many a jockey, year after year, at Doncaster,
but by *him* no more.

The Hero and young Alfred Day contribute not a
few to the thickening honours of the Danebury stable.
Lanercost achieves early stud laurels not inferior to
Reveller and Pot-8-os ; "B. Green" is great for one
short season, and becomes a dissolving view ; and
Surplice—the very month that his late owner, after all
his proud political and turf imaginings, is found stark
and rigid amid the night dews of his own father's
Flood Meadow—gives the cue to three others to break
the double spell.   Then arises the *furore* about Nancy.
Teddington and West Australian—one of them hardly
in bloom, and the other born the very year Velocipede
died—become giants in the land.   Mr. Parr discovers
the great Arabian Night secret of turning old lamps
into new ; and in proof thereof, after smashing "The
Squire's" last hope of a St. Leger with Saucebox,
twice over sends up the listhouse shutters with Weathergage ; and then the rivalry of the Voltigeur and
Dutchman stock is as keenly looked for as when their
sires went out to do battle for Aske and Middleham,
in days which, for hearty racing excitement, their
county will scarcely know again.   Yorkshiremen talk
of them yet on the burning rock of Gibraltar or the
side of the Great Salt Lake.   Well might a traveller
write of a little tailor who had wandered westward :
"Mormonism was the creed of his last.year or two,
but Doncaster Races the creed of his whole life ;
Brigham Young, in his eyes, less than the owner of the
St. Leger winner.   He had seen every St. Leger since
he was five years old, and could recount the names of
all the winners.   He would do a job five per cent.
cheaper for me than for any one else, because I had
seen Voltigeur run the dead heat ; and had I only
seen the Dutchman beaten for the Cup on Friday, I

could have knocked off ten or fifteen more. No ten-year-old saint expressed such grief for the ruined Temple of Nauvoo as he did for Doncaster Church ; and if I mistake not he will see the New Church before the New Temple, and will sit down once more among the old comrades to a raised pie and a tankard of ale."

JOCKEYS.

" With saddle strapped behind his dapper back,
Who canters up the heath on pigmy hack?
'Tis Robinson or Chifney : mark his seat,
How firm and graceful, vigorous yet neat !"

JOHN DAVIS.

IT has been well said of Englishmen generally, that they come honestly by their horsemanship, with Hengist and Horsa for their Saxon founders ; but still it is to Yorkshire that we have to look for the germs of real saddle science. The history of jockeys in fact may be said to commence with its John John Singleton, Singleton, whose register is still in the the Jockey. Church chest of Melbourne near Pocklington, and bears date May 10th, 1715. A rumour that race-horses were trained on those Wolds, which he could see in the distance as he tended cattle on Ross Moor, first excited his ambition to catch and race the shaggy colts which picked up their living around him ; and the correction which he caught in due season from one of the common-owners, determined him to fly to that land of promise, and engage himself to a Mr. Read, on the terms of sleeping in the stable, and eating what he could get. The connexion thus frugally begun, and cemented in its commencement by a mutual love of horses and lack of cash, ended only with death. The needy race-horse owner had his horses better trained and ridden at the village feasts than they had ever been before ; and the lad, if he got no riding fees, made up for his Duke Humphrey fare at home, by taking them out in kind at the booths. His seat and judgment became so famed among the farmers, that . one of them, in the hour of victory, insisted on paying him with a ewe, whose descendants soon swelled into a dozen.

They in their turn were chivalrously sold to pay the fee of Smiling Tom, a half-bred Arab, from the Hampton Court stud, whose produce out of one of Mr. Read's mares won the Subscription Plate at Hambleton, but was beat by " Peggy-Grieves-Me" and two others in a field of sixteen for " The Guineas" next year. Winter was fast approaching, and with only slender funds in either purse to meet it ; but aided by the countenance of a sturdy butcher from Pocklington, who knew the mare, and rode 120 miles to back her, (stabling himself and steed under a haystack by night,) she and John won the Morpeth Plate, and two others at Stockton and Sunderland as well. The stables at Grimsthorpe soon became fraught with winners, and a filly which the Marquis of Rockingham purchased out of them, induced his lordship to offer its good genius the situation of jockey and trainer to himself. Long before he was forty, he had the lion's share of the Yorkshire riding, and henceforth he hailed from Newmarket during the spring, and Thixendale in the summer. Seven years after he had defeated Herod and two others with Bay Malton over the Beacon Course, his half century in the saddle ended ; and he came back permanently to Yorkshire, and was buried in nearly his eightieth year, hard by his first master. No jockey had so many pictures taken of him ; but that which represents him riding his hunter Merry Bachelor, in his gold-laced hat and long coat, and with a brace of greyhounds, on the look-out for a wold hare, at his side, hands down most faithfully the seat and character of this first great Northern Light.

Chifney Senior was just beginning to Sam Chifney, Senior.
prophesy of himself as Singleton resigned
his Rockingham jacket to Kit Scaife. Modesty was
not one of Sam's virtues, and he thus described his
acquirements when only eighteen: "In 1773, I could
ride horses in a better manner in a race to beat others,
than any person I ever knew in my time; and in
1775, I could train horses for running better than any
person I ever yet saw. Riding I learned myself, and
training I learned from Mr. Richard Prince." However, there were few to dissent from the first part of
this eulogy, although they might not give credence to
his notions of riding with a slack rein, lying under the
wind, and "getting a head out of the brisket" when
the spur fell dead elsewhere. Those were days when
jockeys might as fitly have appeared arrayed Esqui-
maux-fashion, as in "peg-tops;" and brown breeches,
with bunches of ties which might have made them
pass muster for "The Driving Club," white stockings,
and short gaiters, encased their nether man. This was
Chifney's and Singleton's wonted attire, but there are
those still alive who remember how the former wore
ruffles and a frill whenever "he took silk" of an afternoon, while love-locks hung on each side from beneath
his jockey cap; and how he would trot up and down
Newmarket at intervals in his drawers, and then by
way of variation do the greater part of his wasting in
bed. Be this as it may, he has left a name, which
losing no lustre in his son's hands, has been trans-
muted into an English proverb, and at which no
modern Rabbi in racing science dare to shoot out
the lip.

Dick Goodisson, who was slightly old The Goodissons.
Sam's senior, found his way from Selby
in Yorkshire to Newmarket, nobody remembers how,
and gradually wound himself into "Old Q.'s" good
graces, by his flash of lightning style at the post. He
was a terrible sloven in his dress, and there were

times when the Duke might have said to him as Mr.
Toots did to the Chicken, " Richard, your expressions
are coarse, and your meaning is obscure !" but they
were only parted once, for three weeks, and then his
Grace was the first to make it up by asking him to
go and see a horse sweat. At one time he used to
go about Newmarket with a leather case in his pocket,
which contained 500*l.* in notes. His reason for bearing so bulky and precious a burden, was that he had
once been unable to cover that amount, when a
tempting bet was offered him in an inn, and " I lost
that" was his constant complaint to the day of his
death. Both his sons, Charles and Tom, were brought
up to the profession. Charles died in his twenty-
seventh year, four seasons before his father ; and Tom,
who was a very safe rider and a fine judge of pace,
won more great races in his principal patron the Duke
of York's life-time, than almost any jockey out.

William Clift. Clift, who died at Newmarket within a
few months of the younger Goodisson,
was also Yorkshire-bred. He first showed himself as
a lad, when he was selected in his shepherd's smock
by a despairing Fitzwilliam tenant, who began to
think that he would have a loose pony at the post in
the sports at Wentworth Park. Eventually he succeeded Peirse and Jackson in the green, and a pension
from his lordship, for twenty years' service, formed
one of the three which he enjoyed till his death.
His cotemporaries used to speak of him as "a wild
uncultivated Indian." It has been handed down that
on one occasion he did not scruple to say to the Duke
of Dorset, who had employed him, and asked him
how he liked his horse, " *Hang me ! you see I won ;
that's enough for you.*" As a jockey none were more
honest, but he punished very severely ; would race
with anything and everything from end to end, and in
fact his science was very much below what might
have been expected from a man in such vast practice.

He thought very little of riding to and from Pigburn each day of the York August, when he was
between sixty and seventy; and ten years after that,
he would walk the twenty-eight miles, from Newmarket to Bury and back, simply to give his legs a
stretch. A man of such physical endurance was invaluable to the London insurers of tickets in the
Irish Lottery; and it used to be said that his absence from Newmarket at intervals during the winter
months, might be accounted for by the fact of his
being sent to Liverpool, and riding with relays of
horses from there to London, the moment he had
ascertained at the pier the number of the tickets which
had been drawn a prize.

Sam Arnull, who died in the February Sam and Bill
Arnull.
of 1800, some years before his elder and
equally lucky brother John, is only remembered as a
quiet still man, who won a great deal for the Prince
of Wales and Lord Foley, and loved a smart groom
and hunters. He was uncle to Bill Arnull who rode
for Lord George Cavendish and the Marquis of Exeter,
and who died when trainer to Lord Lichfield, the very
year before Elis won the St. Leger. Bill was always
considered a very fair finisher, but a bad judge of
pace. Wasting was also a sore burden to him; but
in a moment of enthusiasm it is said that he performed the unrivalled feat of knocking off 7lbs. in one
day, which he accomplished in two walks to Kennett;
Robinson, who had "walked" with him in the morning, going by his side in his plain dress, to encourage
him on in the afternoon. There was no comparison
between them in riding, and it was never more strik-
ingly proved than in the match of Priam and Augustus. In the spring Priam had received 3lbs., and
only won a head at a mile; whereas in October Lord
Chesterfield, without consulting his confederate, not
only gave 16lbs. in a 1000 a-side p.p. match across
the flat, but laid 3000 bye as well. Poor Will could

not leave well alone, so he raised his whip near the finish, and the horse turned to it, and just let Robinson come on the post.

Sam Barnard. The Sam division, which has been so prolific of great jockeys, also furnished another in Sam Barnard, who rode seven-six all his life, and whose constant expression when he had a difficult horse to handle was, "*I never could carry him, no how.*" His horse fell with him at Ascot, and his eyes were so nearly cut out of the sockets, that he eventually went stone blind. Shortly before, he had, singularly enough, ridden and won the Claret Stakes for Sir John Shelley on Comus, without any intimation that he had lost his sight, and on his return to the weighing room he described his whole ride as one marvellous "succession of leaps."

David Jones. He is not the first old jockey whom the same calamity has overtaken, and among them was David Jones, who survived every other witness on the Dan Dawson trial. He began his life as one of the scarlet penny posts, and rode with his horn and saddle-bags between the General Post-office and Hampstead Heath, three times a day. Then followed a stable apprenticeship under old Chifney, and from being a head lad at Newmarket, he rose to be head groom to the Marquis of Westminster and General Grosvenor, and was one of the first two persons that ever slept in Eaton Hall. He sailed next to India and Spain, and was all through the Peninsular war, as head groom to a General of Brigade, and came home, speaking three languages, to train and ride once more. Priam winning the Derby, was about the last image that impressed itself upon his failing retina. Total blindness, and the ruin of the London season by the death of George IV., which left his May Fair lodging-house unlet, broke him down in the same year, and at last the workhouse at Chelsea was his lot. In the summer time we used often to meet him among the

Brompton lanes, led by a little girl, when he had shed
the pauper's grey for a few hours on a holiday, with a
flower in his button-hole "to show 'em I've been in
the country ;" and the year before he died he assured
us that he should like to get a match on, to walk any
man of his age five miles yet.

Such stories he would tell over and over again of
old times. How for instance, in his hunting groom
days, he out-manœuvred the crafty Mat Milton ; how
he "wasted" from Hampton to Hyde Park Corner ;
how his three terriers killed and ate one of Mr.
Grantley Berkeley's best fox-hound whelps at walk ;
how General Grosvenor once despatched him to the
Newmarket turnpike for a bladder of hog's lard, when
his horse's feet had got snow-balled just before a
match ; how Robson the trainer looked, "just for all
the world," like a clergyman, and seldom did more to
a boy than hit him with his black glove ; how Cork
and Tiny knew each other 300 yards off on the Heath,
and instantly desired battle ; how he fed a golden
roan Egyptian on tamarinds off Lisbon, and cantered
him to try his paces between the guns on deck ; how
he spent the anxious night before Waterloo ; how one
master shot himself through the head almost in his
presence ; and how his only hope of " leaving the
house" went for ever when his soldier-son died at
Scutari. At last he fell fainting in the heat on his
way back early in June, from " The Corner" where he
went once a month to receive a small allowance, left
him by the late Mr. Edmund Tattersall, and when we
next saw him he was on his death-bed. He dared not
speak ; and after handing over his scissors and a few
old letters, he would insist on retaining only eighteen-
pence out of the few shillings he had left. When we
pressed him for his reason, he stealthily clutched with
his hand as he lay, to indicate that the other paupers
in the ward, who leant forward and glared savagely in
their beds, or hobbled within ear-shot to catch the

faintest whisper that might pass between us, would, as
he knew from sad experience, rob him the instant he
died, and that he was determined to foil them. All
was over when we next called, but we learnt that
even in his death throes he had been once more with
his string at Hampton Wick, and calling for champagne into the weighing-house, to toast a winner.
That weary chequered story of eight-and-seventy
years was closed at last, and relief, not in-door nor
out-door, had come in a far grander shape, as we
claimed him from the dead-house, and laid him to his
rest on the morning of the longest day.

A Batch of Yorkshiremen. We care not to go very deep into the
old riding chronicles of Yorkshire. They
would date back to Charles Dawson, who, after
running four times in succession on Silvio, second to
Dainty Davy, for the Richmond Cup, won it with him
next year, when Dainty was out of the way, and
christened his training stables after his name. There
was one Leonard Jewison, also, who began in 1761,
and rode for a quarter of a century for Mr. Peregrine
Wentworth, and trained his stud at "The Arras," on
the Wolds near Market Weighton, where the Kipling
Coates four-mile Plate of 10*l*. used to be run, on the
last Thursday in March. This race day was at one
time a great parting reunion for all the coursers and
fox-hunters, as it was the last week of hunting; but
the country is no longer, as then, open and unenclosed
to Malton, and the Plate has now to be decided along
the road. Then there was George Serle, who rode
Ambidexter for the Leger (although the lists of the
day would persist in saying that Shepherd did), and
latterly trained for Sir Mark Sykes, at Marramat, near
Sledmere. Garbutt was one of his lads, and had a
fine seat, but no head; and although very resolute on
rough horses, he was so severe that owners and
trainers hardly liked at last to employ him. John
Kirton wound up his endless Cup victories by "getting

the Guineas," in a court of law; George Herring
proved himself a worthy pupil of "Black Jack"
Lowther, by winning nineteen races running; and
John Cade and Tom Fields, who were born in the
same village as old Singleton, both commenced life by
seeing which could run fastest with the bricks as their
master moulded them. Frank Collinson's Epsom
victory on Pan indirectly led to his death in the very
prime of life, and just when his fine power on a horse
was securing him abundance of mounts, as he slept in
a damp bed along the Great North Road, on his
return, and never looked up again.

About 1807, Shepherd, Jackson, Billy Shepherd and
Pierse, and Ben Smith had all the best of John Jackson.
the Northern riding. Shepherd had most wonderful
knowledge of pace, and though he seldom failed to
make running, was never known to overmark his horse
at four miles. He rode a great deal for Sir Thomas
Gascoyne and the Rev. Henry Goodricke, who ran his
horses in Mr. Gilbert Crompton's name, as well as for
the Duke of Leeds, Sir Mark Sykes, and Mr. Pierse.
The best portrait of him is on the last-named gentleman's Rosette; but after all his hard struggles in the
saddle, he had a still harder one with poverty at
Malton to close. Jackson, who only yielded to Bill
Scott in the number of his Leger victories, had a rare
start with Mr. Hutchinson's stable, which he knew
right well how to use. He had the prettiest seat of
the four; but Billy Pierse, who was the shortest, had
the strongest and truest rush.

On race-evenings Jackson was often excessively
quarrelsome, and it was long a joke against him that
when he bustled out of the inn at Catterick, after
Sykes, the trainer, to pay him off for losing him (as he
considered) Mr. Watts's riding, he encountered, and
had several rounds with a chimney-sweep, who was
going to his morning labour. In the harlequin jacket
on Tramp, Blackrock, and Altisidora, he had a great

time, and he never quite got over the severance, from some very trivial cause. He also rode Filho da Puta in that memorable St. Leger, which worked up a sporting Baronet into such a state of delight, that he thrust his stick through half-a-dozen pier glasses at the Reindeer, and lamented that there were not more at hand. No man was more honest and respectable; but, although he had been able to ride 7st. 7lb. almost to the last, he had but little left when he died. Before he took to his inn at Northallerton, he held the race-course farm, and the horses made the turn just below his front door. On both afternoons he was wont to keep open house for his friends; but his kindness was sadly abused, and scores who scarcely knew him by sight, used to be found deep in his beef and beer.

Ben Smith and Billy Pierse. Ben Smith succeeded his master, John Mangles (who trained and rode for Lord Archibald Hamilton,) and was afterwards regularly engaged for Lord Strathmore and the Duke of Hamilton. It was somewhat remarkable that he never had but two mounts in his life for Mr. Gascoyne, and on each occasion won a St. Leger. His career was a very hazardous one, and in his second bad accident he injured his arm so much that he had to whip underhand ever after. He was of so saving a disposition that it used to be said of him that he would have ridden all night if there had been any one to put him up; and on one occasion candles were tied to the posts at Carlisle, and he rode in a hack race for a half-crown fee! He was the most quiet simple-minded creature that ever trod Yorkshire ground, and never seemed quite awake to the outer world except when he was "up," and then few, save Shepherd, could make play so well for four miles, and still have a run left at last. No one ever heard a coarse word, much less an oath, from his lips, and his neat figure, as he walked down Middleham in his snowy cravat, his single-breasted black surtout, and his delicate cream-coloured breeches and gaiters, did his good dame a world of credit. Occasionally he would ride over to Belle Isle to see Billy Pierse, or "The Governor," as he was always termed; and his absent rejoinder, "*Glad of it, sir! glad of it*," to old Mr. Pierse, when he told him, as was his querulous wont, "*how very poorly*" he felt that morning; and his comment upon a sacred picture, the subject of which is familiar to every child of three, raised many a smile when he was gone.

It is recorded of him that he was never seen in a passion but once. A two-mile race over, Preston—of which Ben, who was on Corregio, made, like every one else, a dead certainty—was the scene of it; and Bill Scott and Pierse, both on horses of Mr. Yates's, composed the field. "*We'll have our wark to beat him, now we're both on*," said Pierse to Scott. "*We mun try and put him out of temper.*" "*No use trying that on*," resumed Bill; "*he's just like a post.*" "*Never mind*," replied Pierse; "*no one has a better chance than thee, Bill; be off, and slip it into him.*" The task just suited Scott, and away he cantered alongside his victim. "*I'll give it you to-day*," he began, with the usual garnish. In vain the gentle Ben tried to parry him with, "*May be! May be I thee's a young man; thee hasn't gotten to the end yet.*" However, flesh and blood could not endure the torrent of abuse which followed, within ear-shot of so many people, and in less than five minutes another conversation ensued near the distance. "*Governor! the old fool's regularly got his mettle up; what are we to do?*" "*Do, Bill!*" replied that functionary; "*go away with Gaudy as hard as ever thee can split; mak him believe all thou's said, and I'll toddle behind.*" And so when they did go, Ben was in such a downright passion at his tormentor, that he followed him every yard of the way. At the end of a mile-and-a-half Gaudy fairly stood still; Bill looked over his

Ben Outwitted by Pierse and Bill Scott.

shoulder as a signal, and on "The Governor" went with Paulowitz. Thus Ben's horse never got a pull from end to end; but after all, he was only beaten a neck. Ben made up his mind from that hour that Scott was "*a sadly forrard young man ;*" but he never seemed to bear him any malice.

Billy Pierse's Riding Dodges. Billy Pierse had a triumph of a similar character against the boys over Richmond. Finding that it was hopeless to beat them on his old horse with all the weight, he conceived the bold idea of making every one of them run away, and before he had got round the top end of the Stand, and half-way down the hill, every horse but his own had the bit in his teeth, and he had only to watch them come back to him one by one, and win as he liked. The flexor muscle of his arm was a wonder of anatomy; he could hold anything breathing with those fat little hands, and finished as strong as a lion. "Kneeing the lads," was another favourite pastime of his, and he tried it on so hard with Mangles at Catterick, that he almost drove him through the hedge on to the Boroughbridge road. A good deal of cross and jostle work was overlooked in those days; but Mangles thought that he might at least have allowed him to stop in the race-course. "*Nation starve thee, Billy!*" he remarked when they had got out of the weighing tent; "*if it wasn't thee I'd complain; thou might have killed yen.*" "*Well! how are yer, old acquentance ?*" was Billy's regular salutation to his friends, who cited his maxims as oracles, and he used to mention it as an unspeakable source of comfort to him, that "*I've done as many as have done me.*" This must be understood in strictly a Yorkshire sense, as owners knew their man too well to insult him, by even hinting their wish that he would, as he phrased it, "do an uncivil thing" for them. He never wearied in talking of Manuella and the great bet of 20,000*l.* to 5*l.*, which the Duke of Cleveland laid him, that he would not win the Derby, Leger, and

Oaks on her. His son was very naturally so nervous at the family prospects, that he could not put the tongue of the buckle into its place as they saddled in the Warren ; and Billy, who was as cool as a salad, suddenly pushed him aside, with " *Get out of the way, thou cur! thou's never been a son of mine,*" and completed the job himself. No one then suspected she was a roarer ; and hence the late Mr. Jacques used to say that on the Derby-day he "*couldn't get within half-a-mile of the mare for the crowd ;*" whereas, when he went to look for her before the Oaks, which she won, "*there was no one round her but Billy and the boy.*"

With the Duke of Cleveland he was quite a racing prime minister, and he would visit him for a month together at Raby, and dine with him every day. He used, however, to say, on his return, " *I never forgot, auld acquentance, that I was Billy Pierse. I was useful, or I wouldn't have been theer.*" He won several races for his Grace on Haphazard, who was found at first to be so bad, that he was ordered to be sold for what he would fetch ; and Billy's sturdy figure, (which knew little diminution of its iron vigour at seventy-four), going up in the pink and black stripes to take him from Sam Wheatley, is hit off to the life in a famous print of the time. He had his last mount on Agricola in the St. Leger of '19 ; and he might have rivalled the ninety years of his father, who fought by the Duke of Cumberland's side, at Culloden, if he had given a second thought to the unusual colour of the bottle of pure colchicum, which was sent him, twenty years after that, by his doctor's assistant. The draught had, however, got far too deeply into his system when the doctor arrived, and found out the fatal error. He maintained all the stern tranquillity of a Mohawk chief when he was told his fate, and simply said once that it was "hard to die before yen's time." Richmond will not willingly forget her brave old burgher.

Bob Johnson.   Bob Johnson was a bold resolute fellow, with rather a rough seat, and not a very first-rate head in a finish. He never rode so well after he fell against a post on Tinwald Downs, from which, now, all traces of a racecourse, and the stone which was put to mark the spot, have altogether departed. There is little doubt that he became flurried and mistook the distance for the winning-post, or else he would not have brought General Chassé, who had tremendous speed, (as those who saw him come through his horses at Newton can best vouch for), but only one run, so far away as the Intake turn in the Leger. Two years after, he pulled off his blue-and-white indignantly in the Round House at Doncaster, saying "*In course thou knows I ride no more,*" as soon as he heard that Mr. Lockwood would not even place Beeswing, when there was not a shadow of doubt among the spectators that she was second. Robert devoted himself henceforth to training her for Cartwright's hand, and making remarkable speeches when she won. He was always for keeping it dark; and hence when any one asked him "*Well, Bob! how's t'aud meer?*" and desired to advise him, they never got more than, "*In course thou knows she's well,—thou can do as thou likes.*" Bobby Hill, who generally valetted her, was alike mysterious, and his invariable reply was "*She's well, mind yer ;—that's all I know.*"

Frank Buckle.   But we must leave the North for a time, and steal back once more to Newmarket, and times when

> "Tho' long by the beaux reduced to disgrace,
> The *Buckle's* the gem and the pride of the race."

Frank was originally apprenticed to a saddler, but showed his contempt for what stable-lads generally term, "the scratching in the book," by running away early on, and leaving his indentures to take care of themselves. When he had worked himself into a good line of Newmarket riding, he determined "to walk in the light of the constitution," which once forbade bull beef to be eaten unless it was baited, and kept up the usage most strenuously on the Mill Hill. Latterly his cattle fancy took a more orthodox turn, and he was wont to employ his York race mornings in buying the primest oxen or cows he could find, and sending them to graze at his farm near Peterborough. During his first residence in that town, he thought nothing of riding the ninety-two miles to Newmarket, for trials, and back at six o'clock to tea. To praise his riding would be to gild gold; but many still stick to it that if they turned him once round after a race he would not remember anything about it, and that, if he was turned round twice, he would forget even what horse he had ridden. His shape and seat were exquisite, albeit he was so small that he came very little beyond Robinson's shoulders, but he always sat remarkably high.

During his thirteen years in Robson's stables, "Our Jim" would promise another Jim Robinson. lad half his plum-pudding on Sunday, to rack up his horse, in order that he might run off to the Heath and watch "Frank" ride. His own maiden race came at last, and Mr. Delmè Radcliffe little dreamt what "a feather" was running second to him on something of Mr. Kit Wilson's. One of his earliest matches was on Conviction against Buckle on Pigmy, in which the latter bolted away forty yards first, and ran out from distress in the cords. "*Don't come that trick over me again, young un!*" said the indignant senior, when they returned to scale, but assigned no reason for his wrath. Matters stood very differently between the two in their great match with Abjer and Ardrossan; the latter of whom was so savage that he tried to tear Robinson out of his saddle. In vain Frank shouted at the post, ,' *Stop, and let me get up to you.*" But "*I can't, he'll worry you; follow me, and I'll wait for you,*" was the answer; and as faith was of course kept, a punishing finish ended in a dead heat. Buckle always whipped overhand, whereas Robinson never did, unless he was vexed with his horse. In this instance he especially rejoiced in his opportunity, as while he was buckling his rein the week before, in the Ditch Stables, when they were about to try, the horse savaged him, and not content with flinging him into a corner, knelt upon him, and would have finished him out of hand if Lords Exeter and Foley and Dick Prince had not rushed to the rescue with their walking-sticks. After being beat in his trial, Ardrossan went home quietly enough, and then he flung his boy into the manger, and bit off his thumb. It was for these double enormities that Robinson paid him off in the dead heat, and the horse never forgave him. Two years after, when he visited Burleigh, Lord Exeter at last prevailed upon him to enter his stable on the assurance that "*we've got him as quiet as a lamb;*" but the instant Ardrossan saw him, he broke his halter, and his visitors were fain to scuttle out forthwith. As years grew on he found a worthy successor at Newmarket in Kesheng, who sent an eminent painter, pots, palette, mahl-stick, and all on to his back among the straw, and then bit off his lad's ear so neatly that he has been christened "Kesheng" unto this day.

Another of these great matches was for five hundred apiece between Dictator and Merlin. Each side had some thirty thousand depending on the result, and each jockey would have almost given his right hand to win. Buckle waited with Dictator on the whip-hand to the bushes, where the apparition of an old woman with an unfurled umbrella made his horse swerve to the left across Merlin's heels. This let Robinson steal two lengths, and lost Buckle the race by a neck, and a thousand pound fee from Mr. Blake into the bargain. The whip race between Mameluke

and Lamplighter also ended in Robinson's favour, and
both horses were so beaten that they could hardly keep
the track. Mr. Gully had stationed himself in the
Abingdon Mile Bottom; and as Robinson—although
beaten fifty yards—found that Lamplighter must come
back on the hill, he called out to him, *"All right!"*
The Ring at the Duke's Stand thought the great book- ·
maker for once in his life fairly bewitched, till they
saw the horse he galloped off to pepper, fairly stand
still, two hundred yards from home. Four years
after Mr. Gully stood on the rails near the Red House
at Doncaster; and in spite of Margrave's dwelling
action, and Birdcatcher seeming a winner to every
other eye, he became the speaker in his turn, and
shouted out, *"I've won!"* in tones which rose to
Robinson's ear above the thunder clatter of the
seventeen.

But to resume. It was on Sam Chifney   Sam Chifney.
rather than on Buckle, that Robinson
principally fashioned his riding. Great as was his
admiration of Frank, he always maintained that he
"hadn't Sam's fiddling;" and true enough Sam's
fingers on the reins, when a horse had a delicate
mouth, went like the feet of a dancer on the tight-
rope. There was no greater treat to Jim than watching them at their dainty work, when he made the running in a trial. *"You might as well look for a rat as
for Chifney!"* and *"First find out what he's doing, and
then beat him;"* were also great sayings of Robinson's,
and Sam unexpectedly took his pipe out of his mouth,
and thus returned the compliment one evening, in the
shape of a rebuke to little Arthur Pavis, who was
boasting that he would as soon ride a match with
Robinson as anybody—*"*You *ride with him! you'd
better go to bed!"* The tone of contempt was such as
poor Job assumed, when some one asked him who was
to ride Melissa against Fandango in the Doncaster
Cup; and just half pointing with his whip over his

I

shoulder to the six-stone-nine skeleton of a "Vicar," in a straw jacket twice too big for him, who sat half crouched on a bench in the weighing house, he answered, "*him.*" Both were dead before the next Cup day came. Sam very seldom spoke at the post or in a race, and if he did it was generally, "*Glimed if I think we can catch them,*" or something with that mysterious prefix, the exact meaning of which nobody ever knew. His left hand whipping was very good, but he was not so quick with either hand as Robinson; and, in fact, the latter, as young John Day said well of him after their Ugly Buck and Minotaur match, "*could punish a horse most in the least time*" of any jockey that perhaps ever rode over Newmarket. Four strokes in the last twenty yards was his way of popping the question, and on one occasion, when riding for the Whip, on Cadland, he fairly frightened Zinganee by gently cracking it at brief intervals within ear-shot, right across the beacon. In fact he had, like Sam, so many dodges, that the jockeys always declared that neither he nor they ever knew when he was beat. In stature Robinson was nearly half a head less than Sam, when the latter chose to get out of his shoulders, but he measured upwards of six inches more round the chest. Wasting was no labour of love, and in consideration of the great exertions they had to make, Jem Bland christened the one "Old" and the other "Young Pincher." Robinson wasted much the better of the two. In his hey-day, he could get from 9st. 10lbs. to 8st. in a month, and although on more than one occasion he was found fainting on a stone-heap near Kennet and brought home in a cart, yet at the time of his sad accident he could ride 8st. 5lbs. easily on a 2lbs. saddle, and a new 4lbs. one had just arrived from town.

Chapple, Croft, and William Edwards.

Jemmy Chapple was another of the patient school, and like Jim and Sam he rarely spoke of racing, and in fact seemed to have no real taste for the profession which he so worthily followed. He was only three weeks, after being transplanted from Hampshire to Neale's stables at Newmarket, before he won his maiden race at Beccles, and then began his quiet but sterling career, in which it has been said with truth, that he never gave a race away. He was seized with spasms of the heart the night he rode Ariosto for the Cambridge-shire, and hardly ever appeared in public again. Croft, whose health did not permit of his riding long, and William Edwards, were contemporaries, and so much alike as boys, that they might have established a mutual " Clearing House," in consequence of the fees which were perpetually paid to the wrong one by mis-take. Will, who was the eldest of his family, came out in 1800, and won the Feather Plate over the last three miles of the beacon on à Fidget colt. The Prince of Wales, who knew as well as any man out what riding ought to be, engaged him for his light weights, and on one occasion he took his celebrated ride from New-market to Doncaster on a three-year-old black mule, resting at Tuxford on his way there, and coming through in one day on his return, while Clift, who had posted his second horse at Wansford, could hardly keep up with him. In 1826, when the Duke of York's health began to decline, and reports reached Windsor that a strong effort was to be made to make Good-wood outshine Ascot, George IV. commenced training and breeding once more, and placed his horses under his charge. Eighteen race-horses, including Fleur-de-Lis, the Colonel, Zinganee, Hindostan, and the best of his own breeding, Sir Harry Beagle, were at "The Palace" at Newmarket, when the King died, and as William IV., after four years' trial, tired of the whole thing, Edwards retired on a 300*l.* pension.

George Edwards, who died about 1850, was a very strong but not nearly so finished a rider as his brother Harry. He never re-

Henry and George Edwards.

covered the shock which his prospects received when his good master the Duke of Orleans was killed from his carriage, and he found himself thrown out of his place and pensionless. His greatest hit for the Duke was picking up Beggarman out of the Goodwood stable, as a 500*l.* cull, and training him to win the Goodwood Cup next year. The Duke of Beaufort employed him to the last, and so did General Peel, who had procured him his place with the Duke of Orleans, and scarcely ever liked to miss his fine judgment in a trial. At times his natural high courage in a race sadly required steadying, but it stood him in rare stead when he got locked in with a mass of horses, and scarcely a man alive could see an opening, much less make one for himself. Harry Edwards rode his first race at Newmarket on Rabbit, against Robinson on Antonia, 6st. 7lbs. each, Ditch-in. He set to very high, and his great length of arm gave him immense leverage, and when he gave a horse one of his jobs, he seemed almost to carry him. This wonderful power was especially apparent in Don John's last race ; when he was opposed to Conolly and Alemdar. There was a long consultation between Lord Chesterfield and John Scott in the Four Mile Stables as to whether he could start, and Harry's veterinary lore was finally invoked. Pulling off his white kid gloves, he passed his hand down his back sinews, and replied, "*He'll pull through, and only just.*" The result proved that he had not drawn his bow at a venture. He could hardly keep him on his legs from the Duke's Stand, and then both his back sinews went so completely, that they were nearly an hour getting him home to Neale's stables.

Old John Day. Perhaps the greatest triumph that John Day, that Hampshire patriarch, ever had, was winning the Oaks on Oxygen for his good old master, the late Duke of Grafton. Every udge of riding who saw it, vowed that he ought to

have been created Lord Danebury in his " all scarlet,"
on the spot. His early life was one of no common toil,
and he had often to ride from race-course to race-
course, on his ponies, with his saddle-bags in front,
nearly 100 miles in the day. He has one boast, a
very proud one for a man who has reached his double
eminence, that he was married in a stable-jacket, and
that for two years after he did not treat himself to a
bottle of wine or a surtout. With the early end of his
bachelorhood came the crisis of his fortunes. It was
then he went to Newmarket, where he was but little
known, and to use his own expressive words, they
"looked cold on me." Still the Duke of Grafton
knew sufficiently what stuff he was made of to put
him up, both in the One and Two Thousand. Buckle
was a great man then, and the young country jockey
thought that it was only hoping against hope to beat
him on a favourite. " *I saw Buckle,*" we have heard
him say, "preparing to go, and it seemed as if something told me that if I went first, I should beat him.
And I did. I got the first run, and I beat him. Then
I won both races for his Grace. He sent for me, and
I came to the door, with my hat in my hand. ' *Come
in, John Day,*' So I did, and I stood on the mat.
' *John Day, I'm going to make you a present for the
manner in which you have ridden my horses this week;
I am about to give you 20l. in bank notes of Messrs.* ——
*bank at Bury St. Edmund's—most highly-respectable
bankers.*' ' Thank you, my lord, for your great kindness.' It was a great present in those times. After
that I got 500l. for winning one race."

The connexion between him and the John Day's Visit
old Duke was never weakened on the to the House of
Duke's side, and but for one instant on Commons.
John's ; and well it might, when his Grace thus broke
on his astonished ears, after a race, with " *You're a
thief, John Day ; you're a thief !*" " *Your Grace, what
have I done to displease you ?*" " *You stole that race !*"

John's thefts after this fashion were perpetual, and, in fact, he was, perhaps, never quite so great as in the colours of Whittlebury. As the blind man said, when, after groping among many colours, he at last felt scarlet, "*It stirs my blood like a trumpet.*" On all occasions he was a very dashing better, and occasionally he was considerably astonished in consequence, and never more so than when he got on Coronation, and found three minutes after, when every eye was on him in his canter, and he dare not hedge, that he ought to have laid the 500*l.* to 200*l.* on his horse, precisely the other way. John's aversion to the name of Ireland was about on a par to that in which he held Gaper, and arose from the firm impression he had of the great amount of man-shooting which goes on there. His great story, about the difference between "paying and receiving," was very characteristic, and pointed a fine moral; and perhaps a better judge of racing and of two-year-olds especially, on whom latterly he was not so hard as he once was, did not exist anywhere. The day he was, perhaps, seen most in his glory by the metropolis, was when after calling at Carlton Terrace, he proceeded through the Hall of William Rufus, with his white cravat and his immortal umbrella, in search of the Premier, in the Commons. The policeman on duty was quite callous to the explanation "*I'm John Day;*" and he had to sit on a stone bench, contemplating the cartoons, and reflecting how his lad had won his trial, till Lord Enfield recognised him, and brought him and the noble owner of Iliona together, the result of which was, that his lordship wrote to the right man that time, and John departed in triumph.

The two Sam Days. His brother Sam had been for some years a dweller near Reading, when he was called from his farm like a second Cincinnatus, to take silk once more; and so industrious was he, that in spite of his bulk he wasted in his second year from 11st. 6lbs.

to 7st. 12lbs., and got into the scale at that weight
for Pyrrhus First, at the Derby. Young Sam was
also a very strong good rider, and more round-
shouldered than any of the family. He had a fall out
hunting with Sir John Mills's hounds, near Parnell
Wood, and died three days after, at Mr. William
Sadler's at Longstock, where he was carried. Strange
to say, three hunting accidents with three very different results, took place in Hampshire on that fatal
morning, as Dick Burton and Councillor Moody had
a severe collision at a fence with Mr. Assheton
Smith's, and Dick's head was cut open so severely
with the flints, that he was unable to come out again
for nearly a year. He saw his hounds kill their fox
as he lay on the ground, and tried to stagger to them,
while the Councillor was stretched under the hedge,
with his face quite black, and Lord Bruce and Mr.
Sidney Herbert beside him, undoing his cravat. He
was carried on a hurdle to a farm-house, and awoke
to find his head shaved, and himself so much recovered that he could walk off.

Young John Day was articled for John Day, Jun.
some time to a veterinary surgeon at
Oxford; and few, when they saw his stout form
tearing week after week across the Ilsley Downs, with
" Jim Morrell" and his merry harriers in the wake of
" a straight-backed un," dreamt that he would rise to
be the eminent eight-stone jockey, with whom few,
even of the cracks, would care to have a race home.
His first winning ride was at Weymouth in 1830, on
Whisk, a mare of Mr. Briggs's. Wasting was with him
always a hard process, and three weeks before the July,
he had 30lbs. to get off for Crucifix. Lord George
presented him with 100*l.* after he won the Criterion,
" *not for winning on her, but for keeping your temper.*"
It was her fault after the three false starts, and she in
fact never forgot the dressing she received from " Old
John," when she had to catch her horses in the false

start for the Chesterfield. Lord George was himself the cause of his losing the match on Ugly Buck against Minotaur, as he stationed himself at the Bushes, and called out "*A thousand to one on Ugly Buck.*" This made John come on too soon, and the result was he won his race at seventy yards, and lost it at twenty ; Jim Robinson, as usual, coming with one of his stealthy rushes on Minotaur, when every one thought he was beaten. For the Old England race with Prologue and Plaudit, all Jim's finesse was of no avail, and as he laughingly observed to John, when they went to scale, "*I don't know which gammoned best, you or the horse.*" The performance was as fine as his brother Alfred's when he was beat three times within the distance on Vivandière, for the Yorkshire Oaks, or when, as *Argus* well said, "The Heath fairly rose at him," when he finished for the One Thousand on the Flea.

Charles Marlow. Marlow was a very nice, but not perhaps a brilliant horseman, with good hands, very patient, and a most resolute mode of riding them out. "A race is never won till you're past the post," was his invariable motto ; and hence he always persevered while there was an ounce of squeezing powder left. Few but him could have brought home the Knight of Avenel in the Port, or landed Elthiron and Phlegethon at Ascot. Still, his style, like his seat, was not firm and close ; and his set-to was so high, that he often seemed to have the horse's head as well as his own in his hands.

Conolly and Pavis. Conolly and Pavis had both immense practice, both being able to ride under 7st. 8lbs., but they were not quite first-class. Conolly was superior to his brother-in-law, sweet-tempered, and a cool steady hand, powerful, and so far a safe rider that he would never throw away a race from trying slight experiments. In style generally we have often heard trainers compare him to

Bartholomew, with a slight preference for the latter. Arthur Pavis could ride six-ten to the last. He was a quick and natty style of man, but flighty and gay in his manner, dreadfully conceited, from having been made so much of, and having had, for so many years, a light-weight monopoly. He won a great many races on very good horses, but he was comparatively weak in the saddle, little dependence could be placed on his judgment in trials, and his death let up a very much better man in Nat. Like Sam Rogers, he never won any of "the three," but he always asserted that George Edwards, who was his brother-in-law, struck Caravan in the Phosphorus Derby, and prevented him winning, an assertion which George, who did not win 10*l.* by the race, as stoutly denied.

If he only kept hold of their heads, Tommy Lye's rare knowledge of pace made him, like Wakefield, most dangerous in heats. This the lads knew right well; and it was always their aim to go fiddling fiercely up to his girths, and if by their gammon they could succeed in frightening him into getting his hand—or, as they phrased it, "his fishing-rod"—up, it was generally all over with him. George Francis, who was a very strong and clever rider, completely broke up his charter in heats; and, "*Come, Mr. Tommy, none of your dodging this journey*," was the answer we have heard him make over and over again, when Tommy came to the post with his knees almost up to the horse's withers, and his left hand dangling down, and begged " *You boys to mind and keep straight, and well out at the turns.*" At last Tommy got so terrified that the two compromised the matter, and arranged to give each other their places when they were beat. Francis was originally engaged by John Scott at Newmarket, through the intervention of Martin Starling, when he was passing through it with a drove; and hence his Malton title of "The Drover." He was consigned to the care of Billy Roughhead, the eccentric old groom who used to travel with Lord Chesterfield's brood mares, and for a bet, wore no hat on his yellow shock for a year; and his way of coaxing his charge to walk with him to Malton was by buying him perpetual tarts on the road, and dwelling on the glories of the Whalebone blood. Johnny Gray was even a generation older than Tommy Lye, and always able to ride 6st. 8lbs. In spite of these small proportions, his friends aver that he got on the betting-room table at Doncaster, and gaily challenged the American Giant to fight, the year when he and Caunt drove tandem through the town, to the great bewilderment of the non-racing burgesses, who thought that, in addition to their other woes, two sons of Anak had descended on them in the flesh. Johnny's last great victory was on Cyprian for the Northumberland Plate, which he afterwards thus described to John Scott in an almost Homeric strain : "*I eased her up the hill; I teased her down the hill; I strode her across the flat; and I beat your flash jockey.*" This description of the struggle was not lost upon society ; and he was reverentially termed by all Malton, "*the head man at Scott's,*" after he had thus beaten Jack Holmes.

Bill Scott.   Bill Scott was a long time learning his business, and was first in Sadler's stables, near Bibury, with his brother John ; and then came northward, in 1811, to Croft at Middleham. His sudden rise seven years afterwards was cotemporary with Comus, whose three-year-old stock foreshadowed their Doncaster prowess by carrying everything before them at Catterick. The betting men collected, as was their wont, in front of Ferguson's inn, and laid 3 to 1 on Lochinvar for the Claret. The Juggler was considered to be such a wretch that Mr. Powlett had given him away ; but as the donee did not think it worth while to send for him till long after the time fixed, he had to return with the halter in his hand ; and as Croft reported that the colt had gone rather better in his last gallop, Bill got orders to dress for him. A deep fall of snow threatened at one time to bring the meeting to a close ; but Mr. Ferguson promptly drove a flock of sheep three or four times round the course, and contrived to satisfy the trainers. Pierse, wide awake as usual, got the "trod," and threw such slush into Bill's eyes that at times he was almost blind. Still he never came till the right moment , and a magnificently ridden race on both sides sent the fielders into ecstasies, and sealed the fame " of the boy in yellow." Bill was then, as ever, a creeper ; fond, as he said, of "making play behind ;" never busy till after the distance ; "*lenient*" in his seat, though not with his whalebone, and rather low and wide in his set-to.

Catterick also was the scene of Temple-   Sim Templeman's maiden win three or four years   man.
after Bill had taken his degree in its oblong meadows. Sim, who was long the stay of old Sykes, first rode Unity, in 1819, at Malton and Grimsby ; but no welcome (1) was printed after his name for two seasons till he scaled-in for Wanton by Woful, on whom he shortly after defeated both Elizabeth and Lottery. Catterick has always been a favourite ground with him, and connected more especially with the chocolate jacket of the Duke of Leeds. It was on one of his shooting excursions to Hornby Castle that he dreamt that he won the Claret Stakes at Catterick on a grey. The next grey (Vèrtumnus), which the Duke bred was accordingly entered ; and although the incident had not been mentioned for many months, the first voice Sim heard, as he rode back to scale, was that of the Duke by the side of the cords, " *Sim! do you remember your dream ?*" It was there, too, that he *thought* he was dreaming, when the Duke slyly handed him *The York Herald*, with his finger on a paragraph, headed " *Novel*

Fox Chase!" and he learnt for the first time how the Holderness had run a fox down his chimney-pot at Burnby during his absence, and broke it up under Will Danby's and Col. Thompson's eyes, in his bachelor bedroom.

The Waiting Game. Sim's luckiest time was when he made his engagement with Sir Thomas Stanley; and then his beloved Battledore not only ran away from his Chester horses, but he won seven out of the nine races he rode that week. Setting aside his great struggle on Buzzard against Harry Edwards on Mercutio at Pontefract, when he was called back dripping wet from the town, to ride over a flooded course, one of his neatest things was on Catherina at Liverpool. General Chassé had been backed by Sir James Boswell for four great races, and won three of them, and this only remained. " *Well! I'll beat you, Sim, with the chestnut to-day,*" said Fobert ; and " *No, not if we run it a hundred yards!*" was Sim's reply. Knowing the General's weakness, neither of his antagonists would make play for him, and they gently cantered till within the distance of home, Lye waiting on Birdlime close at Catherina's quarters. At the critical instant the General lurched ; and as Holmes touched him with his spur, " Sim" just mettled his mare, who was as quick as a cat on her legs, and slipped him two lengths. For all that she only just got home, as the chestnut, having at last something to follow, was catching her every stride. He tried the same game on with Scott, at Doncaster, who dare not set off for fear Coriolanus should bolt. To keep behind till it became a mere question as to which was quickest on their legs was, in fact, "Sim's" only chance on such a bad mare. Bill was so bothered and parched with wasting, that he begged him, out of pity, to leave off walking, and at least to trot by his side ; and so they came amicably over the hill, where their reverie was broken by an officious friend at the rails, who begged to be per-

mitted to bring them both "pipes and something hot."
"*Jack! Jack! I thought you knew' better!*" said Bill,
in, for once, the most crushed tones; and as if to reward him for curbing his tongue, Coriolanus shot away
as straight as an arrow, when he at last ventured to
call upon him.

The names of "Sim" and "Job" have Job Marson and Butler.
so long been connected, that we can
scarcely sever them now. Job's first win was when he
was only fourteen, on Mr. Bell's Cinderella, in 1831,
at Beverley; but it was ten years at least before
Charles XIIth's Goodwood Cup brought him fairly to
his riding. In fact, except in connexion with Mr.
Allen's horses and Humphrey, and the lurching Melbourne on whom he was especially at home, he had
been very little heard of, even in the North; although
Templeman, with all that generosity of feeling which
is the truest sign of talent, never ceased telling the
trainers what a promising lad he was, and terribly
difficult to get rid of when he had anything under
him. He always "liked to see mischief before him,"
and come, next the rails, in the last sixty yards; and
when he did punish, it was much more with his spurs
than his whip. If his phlegmatic nature had to be
specially excited, it was enough to tell him that a
South country jockey, towards whom he never felt in-
wardly very amiable, had said that he was certain to
win; and "*Does 'er? then he wont,*" was invariably the
precursor to one of his finest efforts. Butler's rush
was more electric, but not so strong and steady.
Their seats, too, were different, as Frank leant slightly
forward in his set-to, while Job was as upright as
a dart, and rode a trifle too short for complete
elegance.

In physical power, Marson was the Wasting.
strongest of the two, as he was always
able, from his slight make, to ride eight stone easily;
while Butler ought never to have gone to scale for

some seasons before his death under 8st. 10lbs., and
wore and fretted himself away in getting off the other
3lbs.   Had the Ham and Gratwicke scale superseded
the 8st. 7lb., which just crushes the heart out of many
a jockey, we might, humanly speaking, have had
Frank yet.   His general wasting diet was champagne
and toast; and he would take a pint of the former
directly his walk was over, and have a little gruel and
brandy from a soda-water bottle after each race. With
such severe exercise to contend with, it is only a
matter of wonder that he was able to take his waste
walks so long, and ride so brilliantly to the very close.
Nothing but the deepest love of it could have made
him persevere along day after day ; sometimes scarcely
shedding half a pound down, as the side wind suited
him, to the Bell at Kennet, or the Cock at Dulling-
ham, where cheery Mother Onion of yore used to recount to her muffled visitors the glories of her port
wine and her own Suffolk-bred nags.   It was on one of
the latter, stepping out at the rate of fourteen miles an
hour, that Sam Rogers did much of his wasting towards the close of his career in the saddle, clad in a
coat with a cape that closed over his head into a
Benedictine cowl, to keep the warm atmosphere in.
In the summer of 1858, Johnny Osborne wasted after
a much more primitive fashion, when 7lbs. had to be
got off for his Vedette mount at York.   Starting from
Ownby Paddocks, near Caistor, in a heavy woollen
suit, he walked along with his brother in charge of six
brood mares and three foals.   Gainsboro' was their
point on the first night, Doncaster on the second, and
Leeds on the third, and on the following day they
reached Middleham.

Conduct of Mas-   The race of masters, has, as some good
ters to Jockeys. and true-hearted jockeys know to their
cost, sadly degenerated.   Salaries and presents may
be thrice as large, but all consideration for their feel-
ings seem to be at times utterly forgotten.   Because

his trainer always wants to shift the blame from himself or his horse ; or a *gobemouche* friend who has dropped his money, comes with some sage idea gathered from his *lorgnettes,* to the effect that the horse was brought too soon, we see owners who are said to be models of chivalry in other matters, taking their regular jockeys off in the middle of a season, without a word of explanation. The well-being of racing mainly depends on keeping our jockeys above reproach, and it is difficult for many to hold themselves so if an owner is ready to degrade them at any moment, when he acknowledges the propriety of their conduct in every other way, but only differs with them as to whether a little more could have been made of his horse. Those whose memories can range upwards of a score of years back, will remember how two confederates, one of whom had reasons to wish for a pace, and the other had not, gave their leading jockey in a handicap exactly opposite orders. He naturally obeyed the one who spoke to him last, concluding that the orders were joint ; and the other, who considered himself slighted, not only trampled down every attempt at explanation, but induced his first master to discharge him. The confederacy ended, but the jockey looked up no more. Sporting newspapers were few in those days, and there was no great body of racehorse owners for them to appeal to against so deep a wrong. The thing, however, was done openly enough ; and except in its consequences, it was preferable to the present mode of engaging another jockey, and torturing the old one by slow degrees into sending in his jacket, by giving him the mere dregs of the mounts. A little kind feeling on this head would be worth a host of Turf Reform propositions on others. It is no answer to say that jockeys are private servants. They may be, in one sense ; but still they are virtually subject to an oral and sadly lopsided code of Jockey Club rules, two of which are to the effect, if we re member rightly, that it is purely optional with a master whether he ever relinquishes his claim on their services; and that if they refuse to ride, and want arrears paid up, they must apologize by advertisement, or be warned off the Heath. Hence their claim to far more consideration than they receive.

Race Riding. Would that, on the other hand, we could believe that old racing-men and trainers, who do not love to see regular jockeys obliged to stand down for "Aztecs" and stable-lads, are not too bitter when they shrug up their shoulders at what is often termed "a magnificent finish," and ask " *Where is riding gone to ?*" "There is no patience and quietness," say they, "among the ruck of these lads; they ought to have their legs and arms strapped to their sides; they only use them to maul a horse about in his canter, or upset him in his race." And yet there is scarcely one of the juveniles who does not think that he has forgotten more than Buckle took nearly a life-time to learn, and that his hand is every whit as delicate as "The Old Screw's." When we mark the rare phalanx who went to scale for the Oaks of '44, and think that of those alone, Sam Chifney, Robinson, John Day junior, Chapple, Sam Darling, Frank Butler, and Job Marson will ride no more—we may well, in these latter days, when jockeys are so rife and yet horsemen so rare, full often wish for them back.

TRIALS.

> "Oh! Sutton, Stamford, Woodcock, Larkin!
> Pray look out sharp, or he'll be darking;
> He watched the trials others made,
> And still will follow the same trade;
> And near the Devil's Ditch be seen,
> 'Gliding at moonlight, long and lean.'"

TOMMY PANTON, surnamed "The ^{Newmarket to} Long," is here the theme; and with ^{Wit.} true minstrel's licence, his trainer bones are supposed to moulder near the Ditch Stables. More than eighty years have gone by since he watched the trial horses as they came out with jockeys "up," at twilight or at dawn, to have their question put, and what scores of them have not answered it true! Bronze was beaten so many lengths by Wretch, that she was merely started to make a pace for her in the Oaks, and yet she won easily. Azor had pleased Robson so little, when tried collaterally with Student, that he merely went to Epsom to "valet him;" and yet when Buckle holloaed for an opening, and Robinson pulled his horse almost into the furze to let him up, that 7 to 4 favourite stood still, and was seen no more. Czar Peter and Lady Brough also played ^{Col. Mellish's} havoc with the book of Colonel Mellish, ^{Mistake with} who had backed the Czar after getting his ^{Czar Peter.} measure, that morning for little short of five thousand. Will Edwards' instructions on her ladyship were merely to go along for a mile, and so rigidly were they obeyed, that near the Duke's Stand it was Suffolk to a shepherd's dog on her, as she came on nearly a distance in front, and a regular Ring panic with her. Well might Sir John Shelley ride round and round the mare, as she was unsaddled, as if struggling to pierce the mystery how the Colonel had tried so wildly; while Ben Moss, who rode her ladyship in the trial, absolutely groaned with despair.

K

James and Will Edwards's Trials. Here, too, trainers have made something more than mere "Guesses at Truth." It was across the Flat that Tiny Edwards, the devoted worshipper of Sorcerer, watched from his wall-eyed pony, a trial which convinced him that he had five horses good enough to win the Derby, and one of them that idle Mameluke, whom he had scored down during the winter, when he lay rolling about in the straw-yard, as not worth a brass farthing. Fleur de Lis, The Colonel, and Zinganee were also put together by his son over the T.M.M., as the most suitable ground in its nature to get an exact line for the Goodwood Cup, and after three weeks, seven days of which were spent on the road, they came out the first, second, and third in their old forms to a pound.

Modern Trials at Newmarket. Cooper was never able to try Vulture over the T.Y.C. with anything but the second-hand of his own repeater, but he "tried her very high" with that, and twice over she won. Her pinions were, however, quite clipped at a mile, and she could only get home fourth. Orlando—or "Sandwich," as Colonel Peel facetiously christened him for a few months, after he won The Ham—was only tried seven times in 1843-46. He won both his two-year-old trials, giving weight to a bad lot, and gave 21lbs. successfully to Garryowen, when they were put together on the first of April, next year. However, Ionian had the best of him at evens in their trial, at the Derby distance and weights, some six weeks after; while I'm-not-Aware could only manage the third place with a stone less. That was the last time Ionian ever worsted him, as when they were put together for an Ascot Cup measure, in 1846, over the D.I., he could only finish second at 2st. less. Orlando was in a trying vein that April; and as after having the measure of his D.M. foot taken as well by King Cob and Co., he gave the eight-year-old Garryowen 10lbs., and beat him over that T.Y.C., at which he was once as

great an adept as Oakley. With such proofs of his
form to guide them, they got well on him for the
Ascot Cup ; and as Nat was engaged for Alarm, Jem
Robinson was put up. Unfortunately the bay made
" a merry rascal" of himself at the post, broke his
bridle, and put his jockey down ; and when he did get
off, he jumped the road, and his leg gave way. His
half-brother, Surplice, had been tried high enough in
public before he migrated from Sussex to Newmarket ; but Stockwell, with what the touts guessed
to be nine stone seven, (for who has yet penetrated the
Asiatic mystery of an Exeter trial ?) was seen catching in succession seven or eight who were turned loose
to make play, and only failing to reach little Midas,
with nearly three stone less by a neck.

Wilts has its great Fyfield trial, wherein Teddington
and Storyteller at even weights routed The Ban at
21lbs., and Vatican at 6lbs., as effectually as the
Royalists had done the Roundheads and
Sir William Waller, on Roundaway Down,
two hundred seasons before. The Let-
combe Downs can also take up the tale for Berkshire. It was there that Tom Parr asked Saucebox,
on the Friday before the St. Leger, to be as good as
Scythian, in the Chester Cup, and with Fanny Gray
to make the running, and Mortimer to take it up at
the end of a mile, got an answer in the affirmative,
with five lengths to spare. Here, too, Weathergage
met Melford, three years his senior, and with all his
Worcestershire honours fresh upon him, and made so
light of him at evens, that his party found that the
Goodwood Stakes secret was well worth having, albeit
they had been bound over to lay thirty to one to 200*l.*,
for the possession of it. On we go to Oxfordshire,
and the scene shifts back thrice seven years, to the
ruins of Heythrop and its richly-wooded dells. Starting in one of them, at Painter's signal, just below the
kennels, the mighty Coronation might be seen " suffer-

Fyfield, Ben-
hams, and Hey-
throp.

ing" behind Reliance and Chabron, till, as Jem Hills observes to Jack Goddard, " *They've given him a ring round the top of the park*," and then coming home alone and pulling up at the Chapel so fresh, that every one (bar Jim, who " got beat with Centaur at Petworth"), down to the boiler, becomes firm in their allegiance, and piles crown after crown on to his head.

Danebury.   But Hampshire beckons us back, on a fine October morning, and kicking up hare after hare in our route, we are at last at the summit of Vicar's Cross. Behind us lies Clatford Oak Cuts, the scene of many a rare run, but few so fast as the twenty-two minutes without a check, on grass, from Chislingbury Gorse, straight away to Assheton Copse, in which Mr. Smith on his grey (1), Desperate (William Sadler) (2), and Laura (John Day, junior) (3), were with Mr. Rowdon (who had to bleed his horse), almost the only ones placed. Danebury Hill is on the right, under whose shade Bay Middleton and Crucifix dwelt so long ; and just beneath it is Nockwood, whose fox broke one day the moment Mr. Smith crossed the ditch to draw, and going like a second Themistocles, nine miles to Tedworth, made a spread eagle of nearly two hundred over the Kimpton meadows. They found also in that little fir belt, or Sadler's Plantation, within a stone's throw of the quiet little race-course, which there leaves the valley, and stretches away, dimly marked by white posts, into the wider expanse of Sadler's Down. The Stand railings, within which, on the *Ignoramus* v. *Anton* day, " The Squire," with Tom Sebright, George Carter, and Will Long as his audience, delivered his last great lecture on the Furrier bitches, are put away till another June comes round ; and John Day's black watch-dog, that terror to touts, wanders lazily about the spot, now that his morning patrol with the horses is ended.

On Seven Barrow Farm, in the distance, all is life. A party of coursers,
with Alfred Day on Stonehenge in the midst of them,
are working themselves up into a state of frantic
excitement at twelve minute intervals, and then comes
dulness sublime. John Day bids good-bye to Mr.
Harry Hill (who turns his back contemptuously on
the long-tails, and cares only to catch the up train),
and then, after peering for a space at the edge of the
seeds, goes up to a score of yearlings, whose lads are
cutely contriving to combine both duty and pleasure
for the day. King Tom, Orlando, Andover, Newminster, and Loupgarou have all some high-priced
youngsters in that infant school, which at his bidding
now wends its way home in Indian file up Chattis
Hill. That hill was "Grandfather Day's favourite
gallop." Five-and-thirty years ago it was a mere
mass of juniper bushes, and it was through the paths,
cut with all a backwoodsman's perseverance, that the
old man sent along the thick-winded Luzborough, by
his much-loved Williamson's Ditto, Foxberry, Hougo-
mont, and Escape. Crucifix was never tried, for very
good reasons, after two years old; and Winchester
race-course, at four o'clock on a September morning,
was the venue, when in the presence of Lord George
and Mr. Greville, Dilly and old John met to put
Mango and The Drummer together at 7lbs. "*Beggar
my limbs but we must know the worst,*" was John's
watchword at such a crisis, and three monkeys from
Lord George after the St. Leger, one to Dilly for
training, and the others to John and his son Sam for
trying and riding, proved that he had seen them "spun
out" to some purpose, and that it was not what in
after-years he contemptuously termed, as with his
clear-cut passionless face, he looked on by the Newmarket cords, "*Another of those Danebury pots.*" His
lordship and John must have taken very different
tackle over to Tedworth, or else they could hardly

have persuaded Mr. Smith, in the autumn of his life, that he had a likely Derby colt in Cracker.

Young John Day's Dynasty. Young John's training days may be said to begin with Weatherbit and Old England, the latter of whom lost much of his sluggishness at three years old, and could always get furthest. Weatherbit in his turn could always beat St. Lawrence half a length at the Derby distance, while the Saint had just the best of him at a mile. Mendicant proved himself before the Oaks, two lengths better than the pair at even weights, at a mile over the Houghton Course, whereas Pyrrhus the First could only just manage them at 7lbs. The chestnut was only a second-class horse at best, heavy fleshed, and so big in the girth, that he was obliged to take walking exercise from six to eight before the other horses came out. This was the origin of the report that he had latterly had a mere walking preparation, whereas he was only stopped in his work for a week between the Newmarket Stakes and the Derby, and then went as straight as a line. St. Lawrence was also Cossack's Derby trial horse, and with the Tartar to make the running, was beat by him two lengths, a week before Stockbridge races. Maton was on Cossack, and young John, who steered St. Lawrence at 10st. 4lbs., has never taken part in a trial since. Conyngham, the Two Thousand winner of that memorable Danebury year, tried to give Mathematician 7lbs. before he started for Newmarket, and just failed by a head ; but it was hardly worth while trying Pitsford, as he was never a day alike ; and in fact they thought him most brilliant when he was a yearling. Grecian gave 7lbs. and two years to Equiria over the T.Y.C. before he came out at Stockbridge and Newmarket. Andover showed himself so well, with Hermit in the spring, and took such a steady preparation, that the stable never hedged a penny ; and the style in which he gave Hermit 7lbs., and a half-length beating, in a rough gallop, in which he went on for the last half mile, when Ireland's Eye retired, showed them that they got the public form correctly enough. Aleppo and Roger-thorpe were as near in private as in public. The latter at even weights won the T.Y.C. trial by a neck, and when they met over the old two mile course at York, next year, the 3lbs. which Aleppo received, brought it to a dead heat!

Now we find ourselves in dear old Yorkshire, the week before the St. Leger, Richmond. and more confirmed than ever in our belief, as we rest, carpet bag on shoulder, at many a rustic hostel, that the women fry ham all day, and the men talk about Scott and John Osborne at night. The horses are all at work on Richmond High Moor this morning, as for the first time in our lives we scale the Beacon. Belle Isle lies at our feet, and we insensibly mix up rusty Billy Pierse histories of Oriana, Manuella, Comedy, and Swiss, with Vedette and Ignoramus, those sheeted notables of the present, as we watch Abdale nicking in with them on his pony, in their gallops, and having a tremendous set-to for about fifty yards. Still September has come round without a St. Leger nag for Richmond; and hence the little gap amid the firs, which stands out bleakly against the sky on the distant hills, soon beckons us on our willing way to Middleham.

The Grey Stone, which has seen many Road to Middle-a gallant field sadly "squandered" ere ham. they reached it, and the rich Aske Valley, where we have been reintroduced to Voltigeur, (rolling glorious, muddy, and free, with a subscription already full, in his paddock), that still finer model of a Cup horse, Fandango, and an infant Hospodar—are once more in our lee. Now we are passing Spennithorne church, where beneath a large gravel mound, marked by no tomb-stone, near the chancel, rests all that is mortal of their once great jockey, and we are in Middleham deanery at last. Passing by that gloomy-looking shutter-sealed house, in which he lived and died, and from which he was wont to steal forth for his solitary wastes down Coverdale, that none but a quiet dalesman or two might see him, we find ourselves at the very edge of the moor. It looks at first sight like a mere uneven ridge between two valleys, and we are tempted to say of it, as Mr. Parr did to Tom Dawson, when he had driven right over it to Tupgill, " *Come, tell me where is your training ground ?"*

Scenery and Company on Middleham Moor. The morning was not a favourable one, and the wetness of the summer had made the strings desert the black peat of the high, for the limestone surface of the low moor. Penhill looked down on both in all its cloud-capped majesty, and the wreaths of mist curled lazily along the grouse fells, which tapered away to Carlton Moor Heads; or just lifting the curtain for a moment on the other side, revealed, and then sullenly shrouded, the poet-sung beauties of Wensleydale. It is only ten days from the Leger, and through the driving rain, we can just tell that the lord of the dale is here with his family, to watch The Hadji gallop, and that hero with his tail plaited up, achieves a mile three times in solitary state. But there are other groups besides that. The British Yeoman tout, so called from his delicate attentions to the Champagne winner, is there, and with him, if we mistake not, " The Cooper," *alias* Tub Thumper; while the village schoolmaster, with his white hair just peeping under his little grey cap, stands at ease on his stick, in the happy consciousness that this is Saturday morning, and that the pupils have a whole holiday. Who knows that he may not have another " Early Village Cock," or a " Joe Lovell," in his lot, to astonish the readers of the Sunday papers ? Osborne's and Oates's strings also flit before us, through the mist, all doing good Doncaster work ; and then Fobert and his aide-de-camp

Arthur Briggs emerge, with the pretty Underhand
second in their string, from that little glen on the
right, where Jack Spigot died, and from which 80,000*l.*
in ten years flowed into the Eglinton exchequer. If
" Kitty Brown" had only been in the Middleham
flesh, what rich Spigot Lodge legends he Trials.
could have poured forth, the result of observation
even more intense than a Chaldæan astrologer's. It
is our fate, however, to learn the old Eglinton measures
that morning from far more reliable lips. It seems
that they were on this wise. At two-years-old, Van
Tromp not only beat Eryx at 35lbs. for half-a-mile,
but gave Plaudit, who ran second both for the Cup
and the Derby Handicap, at Liverpool next week, an
honest 10lbs. into the bargain. Next season the mare
and the yearling Dutchman were put together for half-
a-mile at evens, and the flyer won. Defeat, however,
awaited him in his turn, as his half-brother, Mavors,
went two lengths away from him at weight for age,
Knight of Avenel third ; and Lord Eglinton, Sir
David Baird, and Captain Pettat, came down from the
High Moor that day, with the firm ·belief that the
Derby was over. Alas ! for all human calculations ! Exactly a week and a day before the Derby,
he was found to have a leg, and the back sinew gave
way as he flew the road near Tattenham Corner. It
was here, too, that Saunterer proved himself at least
two stone better than Augury ; and that Ellington on
the Thursday before the Derby, gave Gaudy, Panmure, and Preston fully that each, and not only led
from end to end in a mile and three-quarters gallop,
but choked them off by some seventy yards. Well
might Tom Dawson write up to London to take
5000*l.* to 200*l.* more about him for Epsom ; and
stand out 1500*l.* to 500*l.* about him for the Leger,
when he had again seen him cut Panmure to ribbons,
at 3st., within only six days of his Doncaster down-
fall.

Trials at Malton. Langton Wold, where, according to the
Yorkshire belief, Snowball may still be
seen " serving himself" with a phantom hare, met our
eye for the first time the next week. It was under
an almost Italian sky, that we scaled its table land at
last, and trod the little race course, round which
" Black Bill" measured so many Derby and Leger
winners. Malton, rich with its red tile roofs, snugly
nestled in the hollow at our right ; and behind us,

" The waves of shadow went over the wheat,"

as it lingered still uncut on the hills, which marked
where the broken foreground of dell and coppice faded
into the bolder scenery of the wolds. On the left,
across the valley, is Langton Hill, on which more than
one prophet, who was not deceived by the feint of
walking the lot after exercise to the gate into the lane,
has proudly swept the horizon on a trial morning,
with a six-pound-ten opera glass. Above " the turn
for home" peeped the thick green woods of Castle
Howard, amid which Velocipede and his three companions wound their stealthy way at nightfall to
Hambleton, for the trial which was the great chestnut's
crack of doom. There is not a drop of lazy blood on
the Wold this morning. " Tox" with Pearl up, Volta
and nine others from Whitewall are all at work, while
John Scott walks by the side of I'Anson's pony, clasp-
ing his stick behind his back, and looks as if he would
like to be " up and at" the strange outlying pickets,
as they lean in a straggling line against the aged
thorns which flank the gallop. He thinks he sees in
each of them a second Mat Barehead, who was such a
fearful scourge to him in his time; Harry Oxford
and the two Greys have also known " what o'clock it
is," as well as he could tell them, and so has the
mighty Tom of Lancashire, who got the commission
and stuck to it.

And now the word is given for them to cross over

to the long gallop, and each watcher silently steals
away to another watch-tower among the gorse. John
Scott in his phaeton, with Holmes, in his green coat,
and marching as erect as one of the Old Guard in the
van, a friend on horseback at his side, and a lemon-
and-white terrier keeping a sharp look out from the
back seat, complete the Whitewall procession, as it
adjourns for an hour to the tan gallop, whither we care
not to follow them. We would fain linger at the little
red stand, which has thrown out a couple of wings like
cart sheds, and as we muse on old times, we feel
more happy than the little ex-jockey, who hid himself
" in the morning grey" on its leads, and was disturbed in his dream of coming bliss, by the irruption
of that crafty Leadbitter, Jacob the blacksmith, with
the cock-bag.

We can excuse him for trying it on, Bill Scott as a
as a trial, in the zenith of Bill Scott, who   Tryer.
generally rode 8st. 10lbs. in them, would take a man
a life-time to forget. If his language was remarkable
when Mr. Bowes pressed him to say what livery his
lad was to wear, it was still more so when he had a lot
of lads on loose ones to do the work to the turn, and
was lecturing them upon their seat and hand, at the
post. So highly did he think of Nelson's knowledge
. of pace, that he never liked to try without him ; and
although George Izard (who died of consumption
early) seldom rode in public, he was at one time
another essential. Bill's delight was to be right behind
in the middle, to measure his horses to the chains, and
making " White Willie" the ending post in his own
calculations, to send them racing home. We will first
mark Bill on Don John, barely beating George Izard
by a neck in a mile on the Nonplus dam colt, a brilliant, but half-silly son of Velocipede, who was soon
after found dead in his box. Then came the Don's
turn to be defeated as far, by the punchy-looking
Cobham, before the Derby, in which the latter seemed

to be under a spell, and could not go the pace any part of the way. Fortune was never harder on one of her colts. He was called " Scott's chestnut crack" all the spring, and he stood up to be knocked down at the Surrey Union Kennels early in the autumn.

Launcelot, who was a most desperate horse to hold, even in a 3lb. bridle, beat Maroon when their Derby measure was taken in the March of '40; but the order was reversed at Pigburn, in the autumn, and even the ploughed gallop that year could not avail his legs, which went sadly groggy after Epsom. Seven or eight were in the Cotherstone trial, in which Bill contented himself with being third, and sent Nat, who won on Greatheart, back with the firm persuasion that Bretby was to have the Derby at last. Satirist was also beaten very far in his spring trial, simply because he could not help it; but Van Amburgh from the same stable ran a fine winning race home with Marshal Soult; and Bill, on the Duke of Wellington, whom he had for once in his life fancied wrongly, could not stay, even in that weak company. It was all too that Lanercost could do, to get rid of Marshal Soult when they were galloped in their clothes at home before the Chester Cup; but the old brown waked up under Templeman's hand, and ran in a 10lb. better form when the flag went down. Here, too, West Australian deceived them in his first trial, and then showed them through Longbow that Pelion could not win the Derby at 7st. 12lbs.; while Daniel O'Rourke showed his back to the eternal Backbiter; and Impérieuse strode away from Warlock at evens.

Charles XII. *versus* Hetman Platoff. Of all the Pigburn trials none ever exceeded in severity the one between Hetman Platoff and Charles XII. A bad sand-crack which had stopped Charles for a day or two, and proved one of Jacob's greatest farriery triumphs, gave the more compact Hetman slightly the pull in point of condition. For two miles on a sound

course Charles was the best, though Hetman could
have beaten him for speed at a mile and a half; and
the knotty point now was, which was the safest horse
of the two to carry the stable money for the St. Leger.
Ever since his Liverpool victory, Harry Edwards had
pronounced Hetman a wonder, but George Taylor
was in the saddle on that eventful morning, and after
a finish up the Pigburn Hill, in which every ounce was
jobbed or spurred out of them for the time being,
Scott just contrived to win by a head. Alas! that
such a finish should find no record in Weatherby!
Newminster's St. Leger trial at Doncaster was a
widely different affair. The Corporation Steward had
only the office from the landlord of The Salutation,
(where the trainer and jockeys sat out the night,) to
take up the chains by four o'clock, and their party
stole quietly out of their parlour down the meadows
behind to meet the horses in Carr-lane. In their
innocence, they thought it a monstrous good thing if
Newminster could run with Backbiter at 7lbs., whereas
" Sim" had him so far beat at the Red House, that
when they saw but one horse looming through the
mist, they concluded that it must of a surety be the
old one, and that Beeswing's son had been pulled up.

Hambleton was always, from its The Velocipede
springy peat subsoil, a favourite trial Trial.
ground for Whitewall, and they duly repaired to it in
the year of Mundig, *alias* " The Red Cow." It was
there too that Scott on Lady le Gros, and Holmes on
Touchstone, had a measure, and each firmly believed
that the other had been " foxing a bit." Here, too,
Bob Heseltine showed Bill how The Cure could dis-
pose of Alice Hawthorne at weight for age, and by
repeating the exhibition to friend upon friend, caused
old Forth's white hat to be hurled aloft after the St.
Leger instead of his own. It was the scene too of the
-atal breakdown of Velocipede, in the greatest trial
that was ever yet run. George Izard came with the

horses from Malton, eighteen miles, and tried at
Hambleton, at noon.   The day was especially chosen
as being the one after Pontefract races, and before the
touts had time to resume their studies.   Mr. Petre and
Mr. Ridsdale slept at Stapleton over night, and set off
with John Scott and their jockeys in two post-chaises
and four, first thing in the morning to Hambleton.
All of the party, who dashed thirteen miles an hour
up Sutton Bank to meet Izard and his charges, have
gone now, save John Scott and Templeman.   Bill on
the game slow Granby made the running, and was beat
a hundred yards ; Sim on the Colonel, who received
7lbs. from Velocipede, finished fifty before Granby ;
and Mameluke (G. Izard) found that he could not give
anything like 7lbs. and a year to George Nelson and
Velocipede.   Still the morning's deed did not bear
the afternoon's reflection, as the chestnut pulled up
lame in the off fore-leg, and his best days were over.

THE FOREIGN MARKET.

> " 'Mid grim ancestral castles,
>   Where Rhine's dark waters roll,
> Oft have German maidens handled
>   Each young Actæon foal ;
> And the Russians on their dais,
>   As the wassail bowl they pass,
> Carouse to Moscow glories
>   Of the colts by General Chasse."

The King of
Oude's Interpre-
ter on Ascot.
FEW can estimate the intense love of
the Turf and the Chase which
animates foreigners.   Their English
trainers have often told us how they have seen them
quiver with delight when they translated to them,
from " Nimrod," story after story of the hardihood of
Jack Mytton ; and that the news of Hobbie Noble's

sale for 6500 guineas at Warwick made them vow
eternal pilgrimages thenceforth to England in search
of such golden treasure-trove. The horse spirit pene-
trates the bosoms of dusky visitors born under strange
stars ; and the very perspiration stood out in glittering
beads on the features of the valet-interpreter of the
King of Oude, as, after stowing his royal party in
another carriage, he artlessly told us his experiences
of an Ascot Cup day.

This was our conversation.

" *I trust his Majesty has enjoyed the races ?*"

" Oh ! very mush—most beautiful !"

" *Where were you ?*"

" We did come so late by that train ; and we go
into the Queen's Stand below ; but dat was full, and
there was luncheon laid out—*ham !* (and here the excellent Mahometan paused.)

" *His Majesty would like the sight ?*"

" Oh, yes ! But the King, he say to me, ' What for
the people stare so ? Do they take me for wild
beast ?' And I say, ' Oh ! no, your Majesty : it is the
ladies, your Majesty ; they all look at you, because
they *lov* you.' "

" *Who won that last race ?*"

" I cannot tell you—Yes, it was Zi-dam. No, dat
was not de name. Gyd-Zee [" *It would be Zuyder
Zee.*"] " Ah ! dat was it—tank you. It *was* beautiful
race ; I be so pleased. I see him on the left side ; he
make just one great *plonge*, and then he take it in a
minute. That was de race."

" *Did you see this Fisherman and North Lincoln ?*"

" Oh, yes ! dat Fisherman fine big horse. I see
him come forward, and then he in his place. But de
Gyd-Zee, that is de horse ; he win in a minute, and I
do scarce see it. What a beautiful horse, that
Lincoln ! such a sweet white face—we all like him
so. But de Fisherman, he make us larf ; his back just
like a knife—dey give him no hay and corn for a week."

But, alas! at this point the guard saw that some fun was going on, and, no doubt out of respect for royalty, invited him into the break ; and we saw our friend no more.*

Luke Nott and Mr. Kirby. In Russia, at one time, Stuckey and Luke Nott might have made Alexander and his equerries believe that spavins and Roman heads were rather a beauty than otherwise, and that ring-bones and double joints were infallible indications of strength ; but they could not tell Nicholas tales. The royal vendees, when they came out to the front of the palace at Peterhoff to inspect the English arrivals, took the measure of their vendors rather differently in 1845 to what they had done thirty years before. Luke Nott was the spokesman on one of the latter occasions. He had an order for two cows from England, one for a nobleman and the other for the Empress, but the royal cow died on the passage, and the worst had to be led to ᶠthe palace for inspection. " *Why,*" asked the Empress, " *are three teats so large and one so small ?*" " *It's all correct, please your Majesty,*" said the ever-ready Luke, " *three are for the milk, and the little one for the cream.*" " *Indeed !*" was the reply, and nothing more was said ; " *But,*" as Mr. Kirby used to remark, " *I stood fairly trimbling to hear the fellow tell such a wilful lee.*" Many had been sent off to Siberia for less ; and it was all that Mr. Kirby himself could once do, even while he basked in

---

* How different the report of Sunbeam's Goodwood race, as we wrote it down the next month, from the lips of a labourer in a smock, who was sitting within ear-shot of us, with his wife, his six olive-branches, and, of course, the family umbrella, on the sunny slope of the Goodwood Hill. It ran thus :—" There's three gan—yonder they goes ! Yellow's behind 'em—*he ain't fur ;* he'll push it when they get into the straight coorse ! Green and blue is cutting along ! Dang ! yellow's coming up right afore 'em, blowed if he ain't ! They'll have a job with him, mind yer. He's gotten up foremost. Look at that, missis ! Green's lossen all to nothing !" And with that "The Missus" closed his patriarchal mouth by the offer of a very green little apple from her basket.

the royal sunshine, to persuade the Guards that the porter-bottle which burst in his pocket, as he was smuggling it into the palace for one of the princes, was not the prohibited liquor of hated Britain, but " *only frisky beer.*"

In 1853 the palace at Peterhoff was the same, but the actors were changed. Twenty new English horses were being marched round and round, in their scarlet clothing, by the Russian grooms in uniform, in its square; and Mr. Ashton, the English agent, was waiting all anxious to hear what his Majesty would think of The Sheriff by The Provost, for whom 3000 guineas had been refused after he won the July. The Emperor, with Prince Menschikoff at his side, stepped out on the terrace to the instant. Thrice the ring moved round him. "*Very good ! that will do ; but I think I told you, three years ago, I would have no white heels,*" he said, as he challenged a beautiful bay mare. "*She was so good, your Majesty, I daren't leave her,*" replied Mr. Ashton; and "*That may be—it's against the contract !*" told that the stern Imperial ukase against white knew no change. Then The Sheriff was beckoned out of the ring. "*What size, Ashton ?*" "*Two artkeens and four veshiks, your Majesty*" (fifteen-three). A fierce doubting look, almost as daunting as a glance at the sun on a summer's day, was the only reply vouchsafed ; and in two mighty strides "The Emperor of all the Russias" was at his withers. "*Beg pardon, Ashton—he's on short legs !*" And so the bay and the black passed into the royal stables ; and the latter never flinched beneath his royal nineteen stone load at a review. He was the last horse that Nicholas gave orders on, to his army ; and he was led behind him on his funeral-day.

The Emperor's Inspection of The Sheriff.

The white-heel objection has always been a sovereign one with the Russians, and nothing but a white star falls within their creed of

Russian Studs.

perfection; in which neat muscular shoulders, a neck well out, and, above all, a clean jowl, are the cardinal points. There is, in fact, a saying, that "a long swan neck and a beautiful head knock them over at once." There are very few roarers in the country; and the trotting breed, which have nothing to do with the English, did not roar till they were crossed with mares and sires from Holland. The latter are mostly high-steppers, blacks, with drooping quarters, bad middles, fine heads, and lean necks; in fact like very varmint cart-horses. Count Orloff, who was the first of the Russian nobility who devoted his whole mind to it, crossed Symmetry and Trafalgar with Arabs, Persians, and mares of the country, and selected their stock for the stud almost entirely by their trotting action. When the Count died, the Government bought up his stud farm in Crenavoy Varonovitch, and began to breed on a large scale.

Imported English Sires. There are at least twenty or thirty towns in which Government horses stand at a small price; but the choice English sires are stationed at Moscow and Crenavoy. Count Branetski has a very large stud of 700 brood mares, and has spent an immense sum over his hobby of importing Arab stallions. Among his English purchases were Ganymede by Orville, Mahmoud by Sultan, Paramour, Zanoni (*i.e.* Running Rein), Dr. Caius, Joinville, Cardinal Wolsey, and Deerstealer, &c. The Count is a great sportsman, and keeps an English pack of hounds, with Frank Beers, late second whip to the Brocklesby, and son of the renowned George, as his huntsman. He did not think so at first, but he is now convinced that the slowest of his thorough-bred English horses carry him and his men better to hounds than any Arab he can breed. A Government committee of some two hundred or three hundred members examine the sires as they arrive. With the Emperor's chargers and the private gentlemen's horses they do not interfere. Those that are to be advertised are the sole subjects of their surveillance, and they will not allow a roarer under any consideration to be published in circulars or newspapers. Heretic by Muley Moloch was not passed ; and Mr. Ashton had him on his hands for years, simply as a teazer.

Competition in blood sires proved the best ; and hence, when in later years the Government brought over such an infinity of their own, the private owners had to lower their price, and their standard along with it. In the early part of the century, Messrs. Banks and Tomlin had fifteen high-class sires in Moscow ; and while Mr. Jackson had Soothsayer, Leopold, Magistrate, Sovereign, and Antar, Mr. Kirby confronted him with Juggler by Comus, Archibald, and Bourbon. The latter was then sold to a nobleman, and when the Alderman and Fleur-de-Lis, the only pledges that he left behind him, ran so well, the keen old tyke hurried across with a 2500 guinea offer for him. Alas ! the Count was not to be spoken to, except through his steward ; he, good man, would not move in the matter until his dear wife had received two costly shawls ; and after all, the Emperor or his aide-de-camp got hold of the *Racing Calendar*, and would not let him go. We have often sat with the old man, while he told us, race-meeting after race-meeting at York, how he was done out of those shawls. In our last visit, even when his rosary occupied all his thoughts, he looked up at intervals, and dipping back into the past, told that tale once more ; and how he and his favourite jockey, Mark Noble, put a gouty horse into blue clay boots at Ormskirk all night, and won a plate with him next day.

Mr. Walkden came after Mr. Kirby, and an offer of three thousand guineas arrived out from the repentant Mr. Forth for his horse Interpreter, as soon as

Mr. Kirby in Difficulties.

L 2

Lilias (née Babel) had won the Oaks, and Translation run second to Gulnare. The Imperial permit in this case was duly signed, and a van and horses hired to take him overland to Warsaw; but he died of inflammation the night before, and Marcus was left alone. At this time Mr. Walkden held the Government commission for thirty stallions a year for seven years, and in 1827 Mr. Ashton succeeded him.

Old Friends in Russia. The history of our exported sires to Russia is a very chequered one. Middleton and Memnon, the Derby and Leger winners of 1825, both went out, the former along with Birmingham, who got some leggy but very durable stock. Memnon was much more lucky than Middleton; and Elliot, the present Richmond trainer, won some of the best prizes with his son Actor, who was bought to get chargers at the Imperial stud. Allegro, by Orvile, was a great success; but Coronation soon lost caste. The young Squires quite disgraced their great namesake by their softness; Jereed did not get them with constitutions; Ithuriel died after a two years' sojourn of inflammation, and Uriel was sent for immediately. General Chassé's stock were remarkably stout; nearly all chestnuts, and with light manes and tails, and those which did not take after him were bad-coloured bays. Several Russian soldiers lost their legs and arms in attendance on him. No Rarey was found in the whole Russian dominions to quench him, and all that David Saxby could do was to get hold of the rope, which was always attached to him, by the aid of a shepherd's crook. Wanota was another foreigner who often required hooking; but he luckily died young, to the great economy of life and limb. Few have been so much liked in Russia as Zanoni, who was a horse of very great style and beauty. He stood at Moscow two years, and his Magnifique out of Mary, by Waterloo, a twenty-seven-year-old mare, found, as the Galanthuses have done more recently, but few to beat him over this course. He retained a memento of his old Derby days in the broken tusk, on the near side; and he was so shy about his mouth, that to give him physic became almost an impossibility.

It was long a moot question with Nicholas whether he would have Van Tromp. The Voyage of Van Tromp. This goodliest son of Lanercost was following Glen Saddel in a gallop on Middleham High Moor, when some gipsies ran to the wall to peep over. The swarthy apparitions made him stop so suddenly, that his suspensory ligament went, and after Mr. Kirby had had him for two seasons, he offered him to Colonel Schrider for 2000 guineas. The answer was that the Emperor had seen Herring's portrait of him, and did not like his neck; but Mr. Kirby replied that his crest was up now, and the bargain was confirmed. Galanthus and Morgan Rattler, one of the rarest of Lincolnshire hunter sires, went out at the same time, consigned to Prince Galitzin, in a Hull steamer. They were at sea nearly thirty hours, in such a fearful gale, that the captain finding himself overweighted with deck-luggage, was within an ace of throwing all three overboard. The bulwarks were broken in; two horses of minor renown were washed from their stalls against the cabin windows; and a sow farrowed eleven, amid all the wild hubbub beneath Morgan Rattler, before they could put back to port. That devoted horse had been to Germany once before, and kept his sea-legs well; but the two others, in addition to their chafed tails and halter-grazed noses, were most dreadfully distressed. After two days on shore, and having escaped the lot of Judge Advocate, who died of inflammation, and was thrown over in the Cattegat, they reached Moscow in safety. The late Emperor was all for Van Tromp to the last; but, as in England, he has not proved himself the surest foal-getter.

Purchase of
Andover and
Peep-o'-day Boy. Colonel Schrider's next purchases were much less happy in his sovereign's eyes. Andover, for whom he gave two thousand to Sir Tatton, had certainly light back ribs, as many of that tribe have; but still he was to our minds the nicest mover, and best type of a Derby horse that we ever saw by the old "Jersey bay." We remember lingering to the very last, on a Goodwood Cup-day, simply that we might see him once more steal along with Alfred Day, in a walk over. However, his wide ears, his inclination to turn out his toes, and his roaring were fatal to him; but still, despite the latter defect, they kept him for the public in Moscow. Burgundy accompanied him, but soon died; and Freeman, though hardly high class enough to leave Moscow, was received into great favour. Peep-o'-day Boy was principally disliked from his somewhat light fore legs, and the high price which had been paid for him. According to the Russian account, 600 guineas was the first demand, when the Colonel went to visit him at Neasdon. He would not give an answer then; but fairly trembled with delight at seeing a horse just suited to his mind; and when he went to say Yes, the price was raised to 1200 guineas. Another demur shot the price up to 1600 guineas, and the Colonel sent in a fury to fetch him.

Russian Cavalry
Mounts. Hetmann Platoff's ancient objection to greys has gradually lost its force, and one of their crack regiments is mounted on them, while the others have bays or browns. All their chargers are bred from English horses; and when some of the more thoughtful of the Russian officers learnt from the English importers that our horses on the Balaklava day were, perhaps, the lighter-boned of the twain, it may have flashed on them for the first time that the English would not have "*rode us down like sheep,*" if a serf's arm had guided the rein. In the southern parts, the studs for cavalry horses alone

comprise 1000 to 1500 mares each. Strict military discipline is kept up, and all the grooms wear the red collar uniform. The great object is to get the horses as thorough-bred as possible, as the half-breds cannot stand six or seven hours of manœuvring on parade. In the Royal stables alone, in Nicholas's day, there were 600 chargers, and 600 in training, 1200 harness horses, and 1200 in breaking; and these did not include those at Warsaw and Moscow. The chargers were generally in the riding-school for two years before the Emperor mounted them; and if he had marked one for his own when they first entered, he never forgot its name. All the picked chargers were divided between his four sons, when Nicholas died, five or six to each, and after the coronation the whole establishment was diminished. " No more till further orders" was the ukase, and no more have been sent for yet.

It was to select a crack for the French **Sire Purchases** Government that the last legitimist agent, **for the French** M. le Chevalier de Place, came over in **Government.** the July of 1846. Gladiator was his heaviest and most successful purchase, but Lanercost was his first love that year. He became so much smitten with him when Van Tromp had won his maiden race at Liverpool, and was strongly fancied for the Champagne, that he bid Mr. Kirby 3000*l.* for the horse then and there, but he could not be induced to sell. On the Doncaster Monday, the offer was renewed, with a 500*l.* bonus annexed, in case Van Tromp won next day, but Mr. Kirby was still inexorable. Being thus foiled he went off to Dean Hill, in pursuit of Gladiator, and a cheque for 2000*l.* to Colonel Anson transferred to Paris one of the most fortunate bargains they ever made. He was a spiry, muscular, fifteen-two horse, with such an elastic and beautiful trot, that as a park-hack alone, he would at five years old have fetched 200*l.* Worthless, Ionian, Roebuck, and Prime Warden were among the Chevalier's other purchases, and Sting was nearly his last and his cheapest. He started off to Newmarket to see him; but as the horse refused to travel by rail, the two crossed on the road, and he finally followed him back to Tattersall's, and purchased him privately for 600*l.*

Mons. Perrot de Thannberg, the Inspector-General of the Haras, picked up The Baron, the next summer, for ten guineas beyond the one thousand guineas reserve at Mr. Theobald's sale, after some very intricate and curious biddings, which made old Mr. Tattersall think that for once in his life he could not see what was going on. Like Van Tromp, however, the chestnut prize proved rather uncertain at the stud, where he was forthwith priced at 300 francs. Napier, Ion at 450*l.*, and The Emperor, who died very soon after of *coup de soleil,* owing to the reflection on the bricks and sand of the walled yards in which they are so fond of riding their stallions, were further purchases of Mons. de Thannberg's; but he would have Peep-o'-day Boy at no price, and Nunnykirk's drooping back did not please when he had bought him; while Elthiron, Womersley, Hernandez, and Lanercost (fallen some ninety per cent. from his high estate), were the purchases of Mons. Ernest le Roi.

Specimens for the Agricultural School. Caravan had been purchased years before, by the Minister of War, to go to the Military School at Saumur in the South, where he was destined to become a perfect Abraham among troop-horses; and in 1848 the Minister of Agriculture sent over Mons. St. Marie to buy of every kind for the Agricultural School near Versailles. As 120*l.* was his limit for blood mares, he only came within some 40*l.* of the price which Mr. Theobald put on Pocahontas, who was in foal with Stockwell at the time. Having thus narrowly escaped depriving Lord Exeter of his trump card, he bid 1000 guineas for The Baron, but Mr. Theobald would set no price on him. Eventually he departed with a perfect Noah's Ark full of specimens for the pupils. There was nothing—

"To pencil dear, or pen,"

which was not, after that, to be found on their farm. Assault and Cataract represented the blood stock, and two Clevelands, a grey Norfolk trotter, two Suffolk Punches, and a hunting mare of Lord Elcho's, over whom any anatomical professor might have lectured, were the chief residents. Added to these, were specimens from the styes of Lord Radnor, Mr. Pusey, and Fisher Hobbs; Wiseton furnished its shorthorn descendants of old Gold, and game fowl and Dorkings were not forgotten.

The Derby is quite the Frenchman's race, and with a little more Epsom prac- A French Steeplechase. tice, they would become quite as expert Knights of the Foray as those who annually issue from the Grand Stand, and proceed to "draw the hill," about hamper time. Steeplechasing is also their great delight, and it was the one which Captain Peel won on Proceed at Worcester that first stimulated Mons. de Thannberg to establish them at the Haras du Pen, three hundred miles from Paris. The peasants had plenty of brood mares in that province, and it was thought that they would overcome their objection to using our blemished stallions, when they had once seen them jump. A handicap claiming race was accordingly set on foot, and ten or twelve English horses were entered. In their zeal to get a high test, the stiffest of posts and rails were screwed and morticed together, so that nothing short of steam-power could break them; fences were built up with osiers fourteen feet high; a ditch was dammed back till it swelled into a Serbonian bog; and Multum in Parvo, a fifteen-one, Lincolnshire hunter, and Saucy Boy, by Sir Arthur, with heavily repaired hocks, were the only two that got over the ground at all. Saucy Boy had them all so pounded, that his rider, Reay of Repository fame, went back a short space, and dismounted to pick up his whip.

Victories and End of Jem Hill. In spite of these slight set-offs, the plan had the desired effect, as three horses were claimed on the spot, and Multum in Parvo had as many mares sent him as the Government would permit. The peasants were fit to eat him in their frenzy, and carried Jem Hill, the rider, to scale on their shoulders. What Jem considered a still greater triumph was to come, when the Prefect of the Commune insisted on paying the prize in five-franc pieces; and he might well say to Mr. Phillips, as he staggered out of the tent with them on his back, in a horse-cloth, " *Only to think, master, that I should go and win more money than I can carry !*" Next year he won for Mr. Phillips again on The Stoker, when there was as much excitement, and much less to jump; but with that victory came an objection and a wrangle, and so an end of the whole. Jem did not long survive this abrupt eclipse of his French prospects. He was soon after sent in charge of some horses for the King of Sardinia, which he was to deliver at Boulogne. In the darkness, at the London Bridge Quay, he slipped between two steamers moored alongside each other; and no one missed him till a letter arrived to say, that the horses had reached Boulogne by themselves, and with the lip strings not even undone. No clue was discovered, till the very steamer in which he was to have sailed came back from France, and turned the poor fellow up from among the mud with her paddles, as he lay unnoticed, close by the quay.

An Interview with Dick Stockdale and Maroon. The Belgians have but little taste for blood horses; their Haras at Terverin, seven miles out of Brussels, and once the country seat of the Prince of Orange, has gone to sad

DICK STOCKDALE.

decay, and their ideas range very little beyond half-bred French and Norman horses. Maroon was purchased for 1000 guineas; but they hardly gave him ten mares; thus missing the chance of scores of pairs of those slashing whole coloured, coaching bays, which he has sown broadcast in Yorkshire, and the first of which became Her Majesty's for 400 guineas.

The Belgian Chamber of Deputies would have quailed with remorse if they could have only heard the words of his jolly old guardian, Dick Stockdale, when beaming in every feature with delight, he pointed out his " crimson bay" to us for the first time, on a September morning, as he drew himself up to his full height, amid a troop of Driffield prize-Cochins on a little knoll in his paddock at Skerne. There he stood, looking almost as fresh in his twenty-first summer, as when all Yorkshire lamented that Holmes had not thrown his orders to the wind, or that his reins had not been soaped on the Leger-day. Dick dwelt, with emphasis, and outstretched hand, upon his excellent temper, his teeth, and his legs, and after taking a rapid retrospect of their six seasons, impressively wound up with allowing that "*he has but one fault—he's just a little bit too big for Sir Tatton Sykes.*"

THE GODOLPHIN ARABIAN.

"'Midst cringing serfs, and trembling hinds forlorn,
Dwindles the offspring of the 'Desert Born ;'
But here it thrives unrivalled ; far more fleet
Our steeds than those which Yemen's barley eat."

The Godolphin
Arabian

THE antecedents of this Knight of the Wonderful Crest are quite beyond our ken. A treatise might doubtless be written, not only proving to demonstration that his dam could fulfil the requirements of the Koran, and hide her rider with her tail, but settling the very position of the palm tree under which he was foaled in the star-light, or of the tent-door at which children's tiny fingers first fed him with crusts on the slopes of Lebanon. It is enough for us to learn that he measured fourteen and a half; that he was originally given by a Mr. Coke, to the proprietor of the St. James's Coffee-house, and that he died honourably under the shadow of the Gogmagog Hills in 1753. The sire-list, eight years after his death, contained at least fifteen of his sons, one of which, "The Gower Stallion" is described therein as having "bone enough to carry eighteen stone a hunting." Few of them seem to have possessed so much early promise as Spanking Roger, whose dam was by the Duke of Rutland's Cyprus Arabian. He, however, fell dead in a trial, and although the note to his "Portraiture" remarks "that he was a horse of size and beauty ;" it candidly adds, "the latter of which received a considerable addition from a heat of temper in his nature, which was rather too great to be rightly consistent with the advantage of running." Mr. Gladstone, or the most highly tried clerk in the Circumlocution Office, could not have sketched a hard puller more ably.

Calendar Advertisements.

To write attractive notices of their horses for the advertisement sheet of Mr

Reginald Heber (who combined "mild *York River* Tobacco, finest *Durham* Mustard, and right *Woodstock* gloves," with the *Racing Calendar* business), was quite a literary exercitation, with the owners of that day. They are for the most part decisive in their meaning, but wild in their grammar. Dormouse, for instance, " has strength in proportion, and a shape that promises to have been a racer, but was lamed at a year old, therefore not trained, though he walks upright;" while Newcomb's Arabian was " more like the Godolphin, than ever a horse was seen." The Bell-Size Arabian had " his unexceptionable pedigree and certificates lodged in the hands of Mr. *Skeet*, at the *Victualling Office;*" while the owner of the black brown, from Damascus, scorns the idea of his having any mixture of Turcoman or Barb in his veins, and invites inspection of the same " certified on Stamp Paper at Smeaton near Northalarton." " He was bred," says that document, " by the Arab who is Sheick or Chief of Aeria, noted for his breed of horses, and, when a foal, presented to the Bashaw of Damascus, and given by him to a rich *Turk* merchant at *Aleppo*, with whom the Bashaw had great Dealings in Money Affairs."

History says little of Old Cade, except Match'em and that he was a worthy inheritor of the Snap. honours, which, in a stable sense, "*gleamed upon Godolphin's breast*," and that his most renowned son Match'em could command a fifty-pound fee when he was seven-and-twenty. It used to be a boast among the touts, that they could tell a Match'em in the dark, from the way he laid his legs to the ground, and " Snap for speed and Match'em for truth and daylight" was quite a paddock axiom. From a union of the latter and a Snap mare, Conductor sprang. It was a peculiarity of the Snap tribe, that the colts uniformly ran well, but seldom got a winner ; while this order of nature was just reversed in the fillies, who showed a good deal of temper. Sir Peter Teazle was out of one of them, and they received honourable mention in the epitaph which the wits of the coffee-houses wrote upon their sire, who was by Snip and never beaten. It ran thus—

"Died at his seat at West Wratting, Cambridgeshire, aged 27 years, Cuthbert Snap, Esq., who has left a numerous progeny ; he had many favourite daughters, among whom was Angelica, married early to Tartar Herod, Esq., by whom she had Charles Evergreen, Esq."

The Trumpator line. Trumpator was the produce of Conductor and a mare by the speedy Squirrel, who is said to have died in a fish-cart on the Western Road. The aged bones of his grandson found a much more glorious resting place at the end of the Clermont Course, and Paynator, Sorcerer, and Penelope kept up the honour of their line. The former was a fifteen-two horse, very like his sire, but hardly so lengthy ; and his stock had remarkably good legs and neat muscular heads. Dr. Syntax, who was out of a Beningboro' mare, had both these attributes in the highest degree, and those who remembered Match'em were always struck with the likeness between the two. " Doctor," as they fondly termed him in the North, was a remarkable horse to look at ; scarcely fifteen

Doctor Syntax. hands, very broad at the base of the nose, with open nostrils, an eye as full and bright as a hawk's, a high, drooping rump, and on the side view rather short-quartered. He was quite a mouse in his colour, and remarkably short in his coat, on which a slight canter would bring out all the veins, so that he seemed covered with net-work, as if by magic. His smallness as a yearling determined Mr. Riddell to have him cut as a hack for his son, and Mr. Crowther, the then great northern veterinary surgeon, was sent for. He was actually cast for the purpose, but luckily the day came out so hot that it was decided not to operate. Just then John Lonsdale the trainer, looked in, and took such a fancy to the little patient, that he determined to try and get him out of Mr. Crowther's hand on the morrow; but it was only with the greatest difficulty that Mr. Riddell would grant the reprieve, and let him go back with John to Tupgill.

From a two-year-old, he could never bear whip or spur, and Bob Johnson could always get every ounce out of him by merely stroking and talking to him. He fell in his maiden race as a two-year-old at Catterick, and went down again quite exhaused just beyond the post when Little Driver pressed him hard in his last, which was for the Richmond Cup. His practice during his ten seasons was principally among Gold Cups, and confined to Lancaster, Preston, and Richmond. Making running was his forte, and as John Jackson used to say, if any of the others " *warn't up till mark, Doctor 'd find oot complaint afore he'd gotten a mile.*" Still, like his daughter Beeswing, he did not care to have more than eight-eleven on his back. The Lancashire men ran to meet him, the moment John Lonsdale was seen leading him, year after year, on to the Preston Course, with as much enthusiasm as they were wont in later years to cluster round Cerito on a Waterloo Cup day. He stood at Brompton-on-Swale for a short time along with Whisker and Memnon, while Octavian was at Oran; but his last five seasons were spent at William Edwards's Newmarket Paddocks. His stock, the Doctor to wit, were generally somewhat light and shelly. Black Doctor kept up this under-sized family type to the full, in spite of the strains of Lottery and Voltaire, and barring his legs he deserved to become the very Abraham of English cobs.

Gallopade and Ralph (who had a strong dash of Altisidora) were both good Beeswing. horses; and Beeswing was the most noted of "Doctor's" daughters. This pride of Northumberland, who could hardly make fifteen-two, always ran big, and

had the sweetest head in the world. Her hips and
ribs were capital; but still she was rather light-boned,
which might have been owing, in a measure, to her not
having been kept very well as a foal. With all his
varied lore, Mr. Orde had not gleaned that bone and
muscle must originally go in at the mouth, and hence
he did not, from a notion that it would make her too
gross, allow her corn till she was a pretty well advanced yearling. She never hit except to Touchstone,
who did not seem the horse to correct her somewhat
upright shoulders, and Nunnykirk and Newminster,
the best of her sons, were both beautiful movers. The
walk from Warrington to Chester in her sixth visit to
Touchstone was too much for her, and she fairly tot-
tered into her box at the Eaton Paddocks, on the
evening of the second day. After that, she only got
up once, to take a little gruel, and then died, quite
worn out with fatigue, and the weight of a brown
Dutchman colt, which was not due for two months.
There was no mark of violence upon her, but the flesh
came away in flakes from the backbone, as if from a
thing too long kept, and her mane was sent as a relic
by post to Mr. Orde.

Interview with   She was a most tremendous kicker in
Bob Johnson her stall, which was indented five feet
about Ascot. from the ground; but she showed no
vice at the post, and beyond pulling hard at first, she
was a delightful mare to ride. The sprightly style in
which she led her horses round the Stand turn in the
Cup, hugging the rails so as not to throw one inch of
ground away, was one of our earliest and pleasantest
recollections of Doncaster, and it was after she had
given The Shadow a hopeless stern chase in 1841, that
Mr. Orde resting his hand on the betting-room table,
had again returned thanks for her, and repeated for
the hundredth time "*my mare is the property of the
people of Northumberland,*" that his most memorable
scene came off with Bob Johnson. Everybody pressed

him so much when he had concluded, to take the mare to Ascot next year, that, although not exactly liking his errand, he proceeded to the Turf Tavern, to sound Bob on the matter. Colonel Crawfurd and Mr. Powlett volunteered to accompany him, and having drawn the bar in vain, they proceeded to his bedroom. Mr. Powlett shook him into consciousness, as he snored over the glories of the day, and at last he extracted a " *Whose thoo?*". " Bob," said that gentleman, " we've come to speak to you about Beeswing.' " *But what have thou t'it do wid meer t'neit. What's come noo for? Gan thee ways back, and come i't' morning if thoo wants ought,*" was all *he* could extract in addition. " Now, Robert," mildly interposed Mr. Orde, " we've been at the Rooms, and a great many of the gentlemen wish us to take the mare South for the Ascot Cup." Bob stared wildly at his visitors, and then recovering his presence of mind, let out as follows :—" " *Well, then thoo'll just tak her thee sel; I sant gan wid her. Thou'rt just a silly old fule to think of sic a thing; let the Sooth come t'it North if they want to be beat; not we gan to them.*" Remonstrance was hopeless, as Bob's head went resolutely on to his pillow once more, and his heart refused to melt. It was no use begging him to refrain from strong language, so the trio retired, leaving Mr. Orde not a little discomfited, and the others in a roar. He had, however, to yield his point; and although the Vase was just missed, the Ascot Cup came to Nunnykirk, as a memorial of that interview.

Bob was always a very abstemious Bob Johnson's man, but two glasses got into his head. Singing Powers. It was on one of these occasions that he mounted the table behind the Grand Stand at Newcastle to return thanks, after the mare had beaten Lanercost and The Young'un for the Cup; but he did not get on very fluently, and Mr. Orde soon pulled him forcibly down by the coat-tails, and went on with the running in his

M

most brilliant vein. At home, when Bob was a good
deal elated with winning, it did not require much persuasion to get him to sing; and if left to himself, he
invariably struck up the old Cumberland ditty :—

> " If ye ax wheer oi comes fra,
> I'll say the Fell side ;
> Where feyther and mither,
> And honest folk bide ;
> My sweetheart, God bless her,
> She thowt nin like me ;
> For when we shuk hands,
> The tear gushed fra her ee."

He threw such expression into his song, as he proceeded (wringing his hands, and pressing them drama-
tically on his stomach), to describe how Margery
Jackson, the old miser-woman of the Warwick Bridge
road, hired him, and almost starved him to death ;
and how the Carlisle fellows hung and skinned
" Cwolly," the companion of his fortunes—

> " For shoon to their feet,"

—that he was offered a very considerable sum to sing
it on the stage in character.

Jack Spigot and Beeswing's dam was a lame mare by
the Ardrossans. Ardrossan, who was an immense horse,
with a crest almost equal to the Godolphin's himself,
and grandsire to St. Giles and Bloomsbury through
Arcot Lass. Bob Johnson won his maiden race on
her at Doncaster, and she never ran again, as she
slipped her stifle-joint coming home, and became a
cripple for life. Her half-brother, Jack Spigot, came
there the next year, and won the St. Leger ; but he
took such a dislike to Bill Scott, that never after that
would he suffer him to come into the stable, and he
was quite furious, if he even heard his voice. He was
a very beautiful foal, but his dam, a sister to Bourbon,
for whom Mr. Powlett gave a small sum, after she had
been blind and barren for years, took such a perpetual
galloping fit in the paddock, that she almost knocked

him off his legs. He accordingly got a tenant to allow his mare to bring up the colt, and it grew so under its new treatment, that Mr. Powlett wanted to call it "Jack Faucet" after the farmer. To this the latter objected on the ground that it "*was certain to win t'Leger, and then they'll all be hooting and shooting after me.*" "Well, John," said Mr. Powlett, "a faucet's nothing without a spigot," and Spigot was substituted accordingly.

Sorcerer, who was five years younger than Paynator, was the other founder of the Trumpator tribe. He was a black-brown, of about sixteen-one, and not only inherited Squirrel's turn of speed himself, but transmitted a fatal heritage of unsoundness to his stock. His son, Smolensko, showed great breeding, but his Derby year was as Clift said of Cedric's, "all wheelers and no leaders." He was marked with a paint brush on the shoulder for a heriot (as Tumbler and a bull—The Briar—were, at Cobham, in 1858), and his case was cited by Lord Cranworth in the Lords, as being one of unusual hardship. Bourbon might have done much for Sorcerer, as the dams of Fleur-de-Lis and the Alderman were the only mares that were sent to him in his only season in England. Smolensko's son, Jerry, was a black of remarkable size and substance, and inherited a good deal of the Orvile coarseness, through his dam; but Jericho died not many seasons after his celebrated Ascot "revival," and the other Jerries did not flourish in Lord Glasgow's hands.

Nutwith and Gameboy have had the principal keeping of the Tomboy by Jerry honours, but as the former's fee kept him to all intents and purposes hermetically sealed at Burghley, it is difficult to say what he might have achieved. Considering his very limited sphere, he did well; and Knight of Kars bears the strongest marks of his lineage. As he became inseparably connected with Lord

M 2

Exeter, it is rather a remarkable coincidence, that his lordship refused to purchase him as a two-year-old. Mr. Herring had been at Tupgill, painting that portrait of Beeswing which Mr. Orde never lived to see, and was so much struck with his smart look and his light, nice style of going, that he called on Lord Exeter the first moment he could on his return to London, and told him that there was a St. Leger colt which was exactly his style. His lordship replied that he had so many horses at present that he was a seller rather than a buyer; and as Harry Hill did not care to give twelve hundred on the outside chance, Captain Wrather was induced to hold on. Gameboy was small, and full of quality; but his thoroughbreds were too often weeds, and his half-breds giants. A great many of them were also pigeon-toed, which was always the Tomboy fault. Tomboy himself was at one time quite invincible at Doncaster; but the St. Leger honours, which were denied to his son Fancyboy, fell nine years latter on his grandson Saucebox.

The Story of Saucebox. When his dam, Priscilla Tomboy, died, this little fellow had his milk from a teapot, and if William Stebbings had not, more from a mere whim than anything else, told his brother Harry (who died before the race), that he might, if he liked, put in two more in his name, the day would have been Rifleman's. Although he was only fourteen-two, and had been beaten seven times, Mr. Parr got smitten with that beautiful dish-nose head and muscular back, and bid 150*l.* for him at Reading. This was fifty short of his figure, and mite as he was, he pulled off three races, and came up to Tattersall's in the winter with the rest of Josh Arnold's stud. Mr. Parr still felt a sneaking fondness for him, and told a friend to "*buy me Saucebox, for a hundred if you can.*" However, that energetic proxy went nodding on, till he got him for 155 guineas, and the Benhams air agreed with him so well that he took a start, and measured fifteen hands before midwinter.

His misfortunes began a week after Christmas, as his boy suddenly found him walk lame in the Park, where some hedge thorns had been lying about, and on getting off to feel, broke one short into his off fore fetlock. No one could discover its whereabouts, and the leg swelled to such an extent that he was not out of his box for six weeks. After a severe blister he went pretty sound again, but he never seemed to get actually rid of the thorn till he won the Lincoln Handicap. It was supposed that the gathering burst from the exertion, as the leg grew fine from that hour. He had round but not high action, which in deep ground became perfectly dead. Aldcroft liked his style of running in the Ebor Handicap so much, that he begged to ride him in the Great Yorkshire; and Mr. Parr was so convinced, from what he saw of the race up to the distance, that he had the foot of Rifleman, that he did not hesitate to back him at long odds for the St. Leger, in spite of his fourth place. He had also a notion that he did not relish the sharp twisted snaffle in which he was ridden at York; and when he had telegraphed to his London agent for the smoothest bit he could send, he found, when he got upon him in his exercise at Derby the next Tuesday, that he went quite gaily up to it. His confidence was increased by hearing Nat take the odds to two or three sovereigns about him on the Stand.

"*It's not often you see me bet*," said he, when some of his friends demanded to know what was up; "*but this little gentleman took a deal of catching at York.*" And so having scored his twelfth victory, he went back to Benhams for his final polish, and did strong work until nine days before the St. Leger. Three days' walking exercise, and then a gentle gallop, preceded his Friday's trial, and on that evening Mr. Parr went up to London, and got on to win six thousand more, at forties and fifties to one. It was not decided until two o'clock in the afternoon, that Wells, and not Clements, who rode in the trial, was to have the St. Leger mount, and the orders were simply, "*Don't be second! draw back to the last at the foot of the hill if the pace is good, and then come on the outside, halfway up the distance.* Lady Tatton could not make a pace, and therefore the result was achieved in a different way; but the running of her ladyship proved that Rifleman was far below his York form. After Doncaster, Saucebox was never so good again, and his leg filled so much when he had won the Old Berkshire Hunt Stake at Abingdon, next year, that they dare not train him on, and sold him to the French Government for 550*l.* Such were the varied fortunes of "the little cade-lamb" of Hambleton.

The Descendants of Comus. After this little Tomboy episode we must hie back once more to Sorcerer, and follow his blood, which, thanks to a strong corrective in the shape of a Sir Peter cross, has flourished for some fifty years in the Comus line.

Comus. This chestnut, who belonged to Mr. Kit Wilson, of Ledstone Hall, and was marked all over with white and black spots, was rather a grand and even horse, and ran third for the Derby. He went blind from a fever; and it is rather remarkable that Sorcerer and Phantom, also left Sir John Shelley's stable in the same plight. His eyes were as white as eggs, but although Sir Tatton Sykes used him freely for six seasons, until he was rising eight-and-twenty, he only got him one blind foal. He filled the Sledmere pastures with dozens of white-legged chestnuts; but Sir Tatton never had anything by him nearly so perfect as Grey Momus. Mr. Bowe gave five hundred for the grey, as a yearling, with a contingency of fifty for his first win; and he was so much liked at Danebury, that even when his brother Grey Milton was only a foal, they wanted to make a prospective bargain of a thousand for him, if alive at two years old. The bird-in-the-hand style of dealing was, however, more to Sir Tatton's taste, and when he put the ultimatum to them, of paying five hundred guineas down for his foal, or running the risk of his terms two years hence, they would not leave him, and got hit for their fancy. The dam of these greys was a short-legged Cervantes mare, and the last of her race produced twins in 1858, to Rifleman. They are the only twins that were ever reared at Sledmere; and the colt which did its best to baffle Snarry's long deferred hope, by driving its sister from the milk, was even in its very foal-hood the most perfect fac-simile of its sire, when he was in training, that the eye of man could conceive.

Comus's first season was by far his most brilliant one. Only seventeen mares were sent to him at Mr. Kit Wilson's, and sixteen colts and one filly were the harvest. All Mr. Henry Pierse's mares were among them, and his Rosette and sister to Rosette bred Reveller and Ranter, the first and second for the St. Leger; while The Marshal, another of the Comuses in Croft's stable, was third. Only four Comuses were in this race; and in Theodore's year only three started, and beat everything but him. It was with Runt by Reveller, that Mr. Parr drew his first winnings at Haverfordwest; and the blood at one time promised to achieve great things with its mares; but Lucetta's descendants, save and excepting the brilliant but eccentric Phlegon, were unworthy of her, whatever she was sent to. As a general thing, she either missed or they died as foals. Ascot had a good deal of coarseness about him, and so had his son Fernhill, who was rather an ungenerous horse himself, and got all of his stock, that we have seen, save and excepting Gorsehill, of a decidedly common stamp.

Humphrey Clinker was the biggest of the Comuses, and though he did prophesy of himself pretty loudly as he came up the cords, he was, like his son Melbourne, remarkably fast. Old trainers all agree in speaking of him as a golden yellow bay, "and as splendid a horse as ever was seen." In a lucky hour he was crossed with a Cervantes mare, and Melbourne, the greatest hero of all the Comiad, was the produce. Mr. Watts was always an enthusiast for Cervantes, who was a horse of great symmetry, and a fine filly getter; and hence his mare Nitocris was Melbourne's first love. Their filly foal was not a bad one to look at, but her knees failed her early in John Day's stable.

Melbourne. It was the sight of Melbourne's knees, a point in which many of his stock are deficient, that made Mr. Sidney Herbert decline him, when he was offered to him along with two other Humphrey Clinker yearlings at Carnaby, in the August of '35. He gave 250 guineas a-piece for his companions, which belonged to Mr. Robinson senior, and as the son considered that his own colt was as good as either, and declined to take a halfpenny less, he kept him, and became his own trainer—first at Hambleton, and then in a field near his farm. Hesseltine also had him, and then Job Marson for six weeks at Beverley; and what with diabetes, and such a vagrant education, it is only a miracle that he performed so well. He was desperately knuckle-knee'd from a foal, and few horses were ever seen with so thin a crest, or such length from the shoulder point to the hip. A fall from Escalade at the Cawston Paddocks was fatal to him, and it was all they could do after several weeks of care to coax him the three miles to the station. When we saw him in September, he was wasted to a shadow, his gaunt dusty neck seemed a rood long, and he had a painful stringhalt to boot. Speaking out of the fulness of his two seasons' experience of him, Dick Stockdale assured us that "he was always a most vulgar uncultivated horse," and the lop-eared Patty Primrose by Margrave was anything but a flower of loveliness.

Her owner, Stables, had some theory about " taking a real fancy," which con- The Horse Sir Tatton Sykes. sisted in leading his mare round and round the horse, and as Dick humoured him for a quarter of an hour, he might well in after-years attribute the fulfilment of his prophecy, " *I'm certain to have winner of t'Leger,*" to the unfettered working of the charm. However, he had to sell the mare, when she was in foal, for eighteen pounds; and when one of the ugliest and coarsest little creatures that ever breathed Yorkshire air came to yearling estate, it had such fine ribs and gaskins that Bill Scott, who was a wonderful judge of young stock, and made up his mind at a glance, gave a hundred for it. He had a good deal of trouble with its christening. First he called it " Tibthorpe," from the farm where it was dropped. Then it became " Jack Robson;" but as his friend Jack contradicted him about something one day, he withdrew the honour, and placed the colt in the Baronetage at once as " Sir Tatton Sykes." As in duty bound, Sir Tatton came over to see it'; and on his remarking, " *Dear me! Mr. Scott, how his head grows!*" Bill fervently responded, " *Look at his hocks!* · *Those will take him up the hill on the Surrey side!*" And so they would have done to a certainty if Bill hadn't got off so badly to begin with, and then made matters worse by almost stopping his horse to give the starter a bit of his mind. Doncaster put things to rights, and after the real Sir Tatton had led him back to scale, he made an appointment for " five to-morrow morning, sir," with Mr. Herring, to be painted at his namesake's side.

The Melbourne blood nicked well with the Touchstone in West Australian, but Melbourne. it sometimes happened that when he was put to Touchstone mares, he got them, as in the case of Sortie, too long. Blanche of Middlebie, who was so bred, was by far the lengthiest foal we ever handled, but her growth took a different turn. Cannobie, who was out of a short little Hornsea mare, inherited his fine length, and so did Oakball, Canezou, and Tasmania. This characteristic was invariably to be found in his stayers, but his blood hit best for speed when he got them rather short. Prime Minister, for instance, was a flyer, in the days when five thousand would not tempt Mr. Halford to resign his hopes at "The Isthmian Games;" Blink Bonny from the peculiar droop in her quarters always looked as if she had been cut short, and Brocket had not quite enough length for his general frame. Montenegro is the last foal that can be traced to him, and as it was led out on the Royal Sale day, and fell for 610 guineas to Admiral Rous's nod, we thought that there had seldom been a nobler close to a great stud career.

The knob in this colt's throat was only the effects of the Hampton Court water; but still it was not nearly so marked as Wrestler's two years before. By some mysterious law of nature, the Hampton knobs form just under the jowl, and unlike Miss Letty's celebrated one, they do not prove perpetual, but gradually move down, till they merge in the chest. Melbourne himself shared the fate of Lord Brougham, who had his necrology published in some of the daily papers so far back as '37, when he was reported as killed from his carriage near Penrith. They had decided to shoot the old horse in February, and promised one of his legs for a keepsake to go into Lincolnshire; but he rallied, and got a reprieve till May 4th. Long before he failed, he had done quite enough for his fame, or else his scores of winners, beginning with Sir Tatton Sykes at Newmarket, speak through the pages of Weatherby in vain.

THE BYERLY TURK.

'Twas here, in Jersey's colours,
That he viewed his favourite bay,
E'en ere he reached the Bushes
Vanquish Elis and John Day ;
'Twas here the dam of Surplice,
Through light or heavy ground,
The "sky-blue" bore triumphantly,
'Neath many an extra pound."

MR. GOODWIN, in his Table of The Herods.
Thorough Bred Pedigrees, fixed
the advent of this horse at 1689; and seventy years
later, we find Herod, the hero of his line, with both
Barb and Arab blood in his veins. Weak fore-legs,
which were a constitutional failing with him, made
him resign the post for the paddock very early in the
day. He flourished there under considerable disad-
vantages as to keep and care in Sir John Moore's
hands, but ere he had reached his sixth grass, both
Highflyer and Woodpecker were in his foal-list.
Those renowned brood mares, Tuberose and Faith,
were also by him ; and the latter, who was the dam
of Marcia, kept up an unbroken line of greys for forty
years, and foaled to Remembrancer when she was
twenty-seven. Marcia, like her half-sister Vesta, was
one of the gamest of this rare grey blood, and so light
in hand, that, as her trainer Joe Ackroyd used to say,
she "wouldn't pull a duck off her nest." Her son,
Otho by St. Paul, reckoned Merlin and Doctor
Syntax among his Cup victims at Doncaster and
Richmond; and Trajan, a son of Vesta and Delpini,
was long remembered in Sir Mark Sykes's hunt, as
much by his rare stock, as the style in which he carried Tom Carter through many a long day.

The speedy and lasting particles in Sir Peter Teazle.
Herod's nature seem in a measure to
have severed, and to have descended in a remarkable

degree through Woodpecker to Buzzard, and through Highflyer to Sir Peter. Highflyer was bred by Lord Bolingbroke, who gradually became embarrassed, and glad to fly to " The Corner" for a little succour; and Mr. Tattersall, whose red waistcoat and blue coat have quite faded out of living recollection, must have leant on that hooked " lucky stick," (which was never absent from his hand when he made a bargain,) at Lichfield, on the day he saw him run for the King's Plate, and decided to give two thousand five hundred for him. " The stain of old Prunella," his daughter, rose, as time rolled on, into the dignity of a proverb, and the Snap cross brought him early into note, with his son Sir Peter, whom no money could part from Knowsley. He was a rare weight carrier, and won the Derby in a year when O'Kelly was second for both events with an Eclipse, a disappointment over which the Highflyer division chuckled not a little. His most daring effort was to give Dash two stone and a-half over the Beacon, but he got pricked in shoeing three days before the race, and had to be stopped in his work.

He stood at Knowsley while Pot-8-o's was at Eaton, and his stock, like himself, were nearly all fine rich browns. They had great constitutions, but required such strong work for the post, that comparatively few were brought there. Sir Solomon was one of the stoutest of them, and with John Shepherd to measure for him, won against Cockfighter the best four-mile race that was ever run over Doncaster. The pace told its tale as the four-year-old Chance disposed of the two in succession, at the same distance, on the Friday of the same week. Sir Peter's daughters generally bred well, and the cross between one of them and her sire, resulted in an excellent Yorkshire whip's horse. Storey, his old groom, was quite a character; and a legend still lingers at Knowsley, that when he was told that the Prince of Wales had come to the paddock, he sturdily replied, " *Then he may wait until I've done my dinner.*" The portrait of this Downright Shippen is preserved in the picture in the Knowsley dining-room, which is now matched by Longbow and his groom, from Mr. Harry Hall's hand, and a plain flat stone near the boxes, with the simple words " *Sir Peter,*" marks where his favourite lies.

Four eminent sires kept up his charter, to wit, Sir Paul, Walton, Haphazard, and   Sir Peter's Sons. Stamford. The two latter resulted from that cross with Eclipse mares, which was then thought the acmé of paddock prowess ; but the compact little Stamford, who had more quality and less heaviness than the majority of the breed, only preserved the family honours in tail female, and the dams of Mameluke, Beiram, Actæon, and Emilius were all by him. The Haphazards were soon forgotten in spite of the fine cross with Mrs. Barnet by Waxy, from which Filho da Puta sprang ; but after him the blood grew jady with Betsy Bedlam, who fretted and jumped about like a crazy thing when she was out of the stable ; while Colwick, who never really loved a distance, and was bred very closely in through his Sir Oliver dam, got nothing worth speaking of except Attila. In fact, but for Sleight of Hand, whose mares have dotted the Sledmere pastures with several chestnut winners, the Haphazard blood, of which Gambler and Figaro were good specimens, has virtually vanished. Poor Bill Scott invariably coupled Attila with Magistrate, as having tried them higher than anything they ever had at Whitewall. Attila looked almost too pretty to be very good, and when in condition as a sire, he was, like Sultan, one of the most " mouldy" that painter ever glanced at, and Bessy Bedlam was a beautiful little brown mare, rather tucked up, but wonderful in her two-year-old days.

Filho da Puta went very wide behind,   Filho da Puta. and his blood is still to be found mingled with Venison's in Royal Ravenhill, whose dark brown hunters and coachers make dealers prick up their ears. Filho was full sixteen hands, and as good as he was good-looking. He failed in his great match with Sir Joshua owing to his rearing suddenly at the post, and losing some lengths which he never could quite make up. They offered to run it over again for twice the sum, but the Sir Joshua party would not have it. Jackson, who had been rather ill-used in not having the mount, told Goodisson on the first opportunity, in rather a caustic strain, that he was afraid of his horse, and Tom calmly responded that he did not like the job. Tom was a very fine rider, and so abstemious that he would trudge all day with his gun to bag a lark, and eat nothing else for dinner. He rode rather too long, and on one occasion his horse flung him at the post, and when he gathered himself up he simply said—" *There's for you ! that's the grand jockey, Tom Goodisson : if it had been a horsedealer's cad, he'd never have been flung that way,*" and on he got again. Arnull rode Sir Joshua in his match, and as Marshall (who once interpreted "full canonicals" to mean "your hood and body clothes" when an Oxonian went to sit to him) kept him nearly a whole day in full costume on a saddle, "niggling away all the time at one eye," he could hardly be got to face an easel again.

Haphazard. Haphazard himself was a gay nag-looking horse, with a low back and very fine action, but never a great favourite with, nor a great catch for, Lord Lowther. Billy Pierse thought that he had hardly been on a truer four-mile horse than him and Agonistes, both of the same age, and both of them by Sir Peter, and companions in the Raby stable. His finest race on Haphazard was against Marcia and Buckle, for the Great Subscription Plate at York, when he won half a head, though many thought it a wrong decision, and Marcia receiving 3lbs. avenged herself on Agonistes, over the same four-mile course. To prevent all misconception, Marcia and Haphazard met next year for the same Subscription Plate, and Haphazard won a much slower run race; Orvile, who was two years their junior, being last. Sir Paul's were of a much stouter stamp, and his son Paulowitz had another stain of Highflyer in the third cross, a mode of breeding which many good judges adopt with nearly every first-class blood except Selim's. Cain was the produce of Paulowitz and a Paynator mare, and through his son Ion and Ellen Middleton, the finest of the Bay Middleton mares, we have the beautifully topped but rather too leggy Wild Dayrell.

Sir John Shelley bought the clever but cobby-looking Walton when he was Walton. beaten for the Craven Stakes by Aniseed, in the year that old Eleanor was third. He was awkward to ride, and Buckle said of him that he was "always on his head for the first mile." His stock had no great character about them; but although he had only seven mares his first season, Phantom, a winner of the Derby (out of Julia, sister to Eleanor), Vandyke Junior, and Rainbow, who beat Phantom for the Claret Stakes, were among his lucky hits. Bay Middleton, Ishmael, and Voltaire were out of Phantom mares; and George IV. was latterly as fond of his son Waterloo as he had been in his younger days of the Trumpators and Gohannas. His favourite Maria was by Waterloo; and trainers used to say of her, that "it would take twice round the Ascot Cup Course, best pace, before she would blow out a rush-light." It was one of the peculiarities of the blood, that it always bred in-and-in very well, and among other instances Cedric, "the little chestnut buggy horse" who won the Derby, and Ivanhoe, who was nearly the best of his year, were both by Phantom out of a Walton mare. Hence many of the best judges at that time began to think that sire to daugh-

ter, and son to dam, with one cross out, in regular
rotation, was the real touchstone of breeding science.
Walton's most distinguished son, Partisan, who ran
fourth and last in his maiden race to Bourbon,
strained back to Highflyer through his dam Parasol
by Pot-8-o's out of Prunella.   On the Turf he was a
very fair performer, especially in matches, for which
the Grafton stable took his measure pretty accurately
by trying with Whisker.   Trainers used to say of
him that he was the finest actioned horse that ever
went over Newmarket, and after proving the sire of
Venison, Mameluke, Gladiator, and Glaucus, he was
eventually sold for 165 guineas.

Glaucus.   Glaucus, the incidents of whose Ascot
Cup day form one of the liveliest pictures
in Mr. Willis's "Pencillings by the Way," followed
his American admirer early across the Atlantic ; but
Mr. Harvey Combe clung most fondly to his blood in
The Nob, who remained for many years under Will
Todd's guardianship at Cobham Park.   He was, in
fact, so determined to keep it in his hands, that he
put the old horse at a price which few owners of a
thoroughbred mare chose to pay, and when he was
offered sixteen hundred for Trouncer to go to Ireland,
before he ran for the Ascot Cup, and half as much
after he broke down so badly, he would not listen to
either offer.   To use his own words—" I'd sooner see
his hoof on my sideboard than his hoof-prints in any
one else's paddock ;" and accordingly ordered him to
be led at once to the kennels, and handed over to the
Royal boiler.   He was the first foal of Premature,
who was herself foaled, as her name indicates, not
only long before her time, but five or six days before
the close of one December, and she was such a
miserable little object that it was some years before
he even cared to look at her.   After losing three out
of her five fillies in 1846-51, he became most anxious
to have one out of her every year, by The Nob or

Alarm, but she rancorously persisted in breeding him five colts in succession.

Gladiator would have given Bay Mid- Gladiator.
dleton more to do for the Derby, if he
had not sprung a curb at the Spread Eagle at Snares-
brook, a month before, in days too when the solvent
touch of iodine was not thought of in such emergen-
cies. Mundig had been similarly afflicted there before
his Derby, and a few weeks previous to that he had
been borne up in his stall, "dead weak" from inflammation. When Gladiator had been in work again, he
was tried with Ebberston at nine pounds, and knocked
him as completely out of time by six lengths, as he
did in the race itself, where he was almost stopped
after running a few yards, as Bill Scott did not believe
that it could be a start.

Sweetmeat was far away Gladiator's Sweetmeat.
best son ; and although he bore no traces
of it, except in requiring a great amount of work, in
which poor Tasker (who was the first to get on his
back) invariably rode him, he was full of Blacklock
blood. Major Yarborough always maintained that his
dam was as truly by Voltaire as his grandam was by
Blacklock, seeing that she broke to Starch before she
went to Voltaire, and came to the latter's stint to a
day. War Eagle's double connexion with the blood
was much more singular, as his dam was by Voltaire,
and his great grandam was Voltaire's own dam.
After Sweetmeat's fore-leg gave way, Mr. Cookson
purchased him for three hundred, and sold him for
eight hundred guineas. He was a taking horse, with
no very great length or bone, a clever straight head
and neck, and rather heavy in the shoulders, a fault
which may have communicated that tight shoulder
action to so many of his stock. In Comfit, the sweetest filly we ever saw by him, it was painfully percep-
tible, and the same fault runs through many of the
Annandales. He went blind soon after he came to

N

Nesham Hall, and save and except Watchdog, in a race
at Salisbury in 1858, and the colt who was seized with
a panic from the salute of a vessel as it crossed the
Mersey to Lucas's, we remember no case more sudden.
The first eye seemed to go in a day ; the pupil was as
red as beef in the morning, and then the lid and the
ball wasted to half their size, and the fellow one followed suit in ten days. He was always rather a
curious and fitful getter, as regards size, though he
seldom failed to give them a fine turn of speed, and a
dislike to a distance. His colts were generally too
big, and unable to stand strong preparations, but his
fillies very nearly won three Oaks in succession. Like
Bay Middleton, he was essentially a filly getter, and
they are now exceedingly valuable.

Venison.   A gamer or more gentlemanly little
horse than Venison never cantered down
the cords ; and cross him as you chose, nearly all his
stock came small with grey hairs in their coat, a taper-
ing head, and a beautiful deer-like eye. This lack of
size came through his grandam Jerboa, of the Gohanna blood. He was rather a lurching long-actioned
goer himself, and wanted a great deal of assistance.
His turf finish was right worthy of him. He carried
9st. 6lb. at Stockbridge, and broke down about three-
quarters of a mile from home ; but he only faltered for
about twenty yards, and, thanks to the careful nursing
of young John Day, finished the last of the four, with
his head at the winner's girths. The blood hit well
with that of Emilius, both in Fallow Buck and Buck-
thorn ; but handsome and true as the latter was, both
in shape and running, the old temper showed itself,
and they were not sorry to get rid of him at Eaton,
though Backbiter was a poor enough substitute. No
owner need despair of a colt fining down in his points,
if they remember what a "dangerous countryman"
Rattle by Fallow Buck looked on the Derby day, and
what a handsome hero he was when he ran second for

the Cambridgeshire and Cesarewitch eighteen months afterwards.

The Alarms have preserved the staying properties of the family, and a trifle of the temper as well. The. point about him which most struck the eye was his wonderful hips, which might belong to a massive steer. Kingston (for whom the Americans offered 5300*l.* in '58), filled out so much, that we could hardly catch a trace of the original gay-heart, who used to come dancing, Bay Middleton fashion, into the enclosure with Nat or Bob Basham in the orange, and Harry Stebbings' hand on the rein. Barring Orlando, there was, we think, no stud horse quite so beautiful, nor worthier to woo Virago and Mowerina. Jockeys were always fond of him, and Job Marson used to say that he was "quite an armchair."

We have heard of horses, one of Mr. Mare's, out of Breastgirth, for instance,   Cruiser. who left the turf for the Circus; but we never knew any before Cruiser, whose stock were winning while he was nightly lying down at a word among the sawdust. Rattlebone, who is out of Wicket, a shortlegged Stumps mare, as white in her coat and sweetlooking as the whole of her beautiful race, solved the problem at last. Cruiser's temper did not show itself very much at Danebury. In the Criterion he certainly ran somewhat unkindly, and Rogers, who won on Para, backed him at long shots for the Derby, from feeling sure that he could have done much better if he liked. Still John Day had only to hit him two or three times, when he was with him ; but he suspected enough to give the man who took him to Rawcliffe an ineffectual warning, as to not taking his halter off when he got him into a stable, or, as sure as fate, there would be a mess. At Rawcliffe again, they say that "Argus" must have braced himself for his *Post feuilleton* by a series of pork-chop suppers, when he

described certain scenes with that bay Nana Sahib, at
their establishment, than which—

> " Mat Lewis never borrowed
> Any horrors half so horrid"

—so vividly, that Mr. Rarey was induced to beard
him in his den, at Greywell, and soon heard the jingle
of the guinea at the Round-house, for his pains.

The Woodpecker Line. And so, leaving Highflyer, we must
essay to trace the second great branch
of the Herod genealogical tree, through Woodpecker.
He was himself a large coarse horse, with wide lop
ears, almost like a prize rabbit, which descended in a
marked way to his stock. Through him, Petworth
quite " out-Heroded Herod" in its breeding in-and-in.
A grey and a chestnut Skim were both by him, out of
a Herod mare ; and the former was the dam of Grey
Skim, by Gohanna, who was out of a Herod mare as
well. Then again Golumpus was by Gohanna, dam
by Woodpecker, till the stud-grooms were almost as
much puzzled, as dabblers in the Herd Book with the
seventy " Duchesses." Woodpecker's greatest hit was
with Buzzard, who was out of a mare by Dux ; and
the blood of this great unknown was destined to flow
in the veins of the most wonderful leash of brothers
that ever sought glory in the Stud Book.

Castrel, Rubens, and Selim. Their dam was a grand-daughter of
Eclipse through Alexander, but she was
such a mere weed to the eye, that the Duke of
Queensberry could not get five-and-twenty pounds for
her, and therefore he did not think that he had done
any very munificent act, when he gave her away to
his Newmarket surgeon. Her success at Buzzard's
paddocks seems almost fabulous, as her filly, Bronze,
who was also by him, won the Oaks. Castrel, the
eldest of the three brothers, was a magnificent chestnut
of sixteen hands high, and with great quality ; and
but for his roaring, there were few better on the Turf.

Eventually he came into that " Hospital for Decayed Cracks," as Parson Harvey's Sloane-street stables were termed. After that, he stood at " The Royells," in Cheshire, where he was not very lucky, and he was rising twenty-tree, and at Mr. Lechmere Charlton's, near Ludlow, when he got Pantaloon. This chestnut, who was very profusely marked with black spots, was on a very large scale, with a heavy neck and most beautiful legs ; and John Scott used to be one of his most devoted admirers. He was rather proud and odd with strangers, and was a wonderfully cheap bargain for Lord Westminster at six hundred guineas, which would never have been given but for the strong entreaties of Nutting, the then stud-groom. His blood nicked reverse ways with Touchstone's, in the case of Phryne and Ghuznee (the very model of a useful, short-legged mare) ; and in fact whenever it has come together, and with that of no other horse so well. The dashing family speed came out through him in Sleight-of-Hand, and his son, Odd Trick, whose great up-standing quarters sent him like a minié ball up the Cambridgeshire hill, albeit his middle is so little in keeping with them. He is the speediest Mr. Parr ever trained, and the sixty guineas which he gave for him as a yearling, at Sir Tatton's sale, returned with usury in the shape of twenty thousand in bets, none of which was got on at less than thirties to one.

Merlin was, after all, the best racer by Castrel, and Lord Foley gave two thousand guineas for him at two years old. His remembrance of the slings, in the days when he broke his leg running with Tiresias, made such a fury of him, that grooms and breeders grew alike frightened, and Lamplighter and his son, Phosphorus, did not keep the lamp of his fame alive. The broken leg eventually became the best, but the accident produced a most remarkable species of stringhalt ; and he was wont to lift each leg, and shake them tremulously for some seconds in succession, when he was led out with iron rods on each side. Tyler, the groom at Riddlesworth, was the only man who dare go up to him, armed with an immense stick; and one unhappy day, when another of the grooms, whom the horse especially hated, was called for, all that was known about him was that he had been seen going into the box. "*Mercy on us!*" said Tyler, "*he's a dead man; that's the moan I heard as I passed there, ten minutes since.*" And sure enough the horse was kneeling on him, and fairly wallowing in his blood. Both his ears were torn off, and his side was so lacerated that they declared they could see the heart beat. He only lived two hours after he was got away, and Mr. Thornhill settled a handsome pension on his widow. Even when the horse was being painted, he yapped as if he would devour both painter and easel, till his head and breast were all covered with foam.

Rubens had less appearance to recommend him than Castrel, and was a heavy-topped fleshy horse, of sixteen hands, and only fit for a flash of speed. The Prince sold him for a thousand to Lord Darlington, on condition that Clift said he was sound, and the astute peer not only saved the forfeits in two matches, but won twelve thousand, and was offered treble the purchase money for him. Alas! it was always the fate of George Guelph to run counter to political economists by buying in the dearest, and selling in the cheapest market. He did not get a great amount of stock in England, but Defence, Recovery, Coronation, and Ascot were all out of his daughters, some of which were also very successful, both as runners and breeders, in the Duke of Grafton's hands, and his only son of caste was the aptly-named Peter Lely.

The Selims.   Selim was given by the Prince to Colonel Leigh, when his horses were sold. He was full of quality, and so majestic altogether, that no one would have suspected him to be the workman

he was at all distances. Still there was a certain
softness lingering somewhere in the tribe; and it came
out in the Sultans and Langars, although the cross
with Williamson's Ditto and Walton in each instance
was as orthodox as it could be. Langar was a flash
Arab-style of horse about his forehand; and both his
sons, Epirus and Elis, were out of mares by Sir Oliver,
who had a long run and a high reputation for speed,
in Cheshire. The flying white-legged Vulture, by
Langar, lives in the Orlandoes; and the roach-backed
Virago, his great-granddaughter, is the flower, so far,
of the Epirus and Pyrrhus the First line.

The Sultan branch of Selim is a much   Sultan.
more famous one; but it is fast wearing
out on the male side. His forehand, which breeders
used as a simile, was just the thing to catch foreigners;
and hence a story went the round of the clubs that a
noble Russ wanted to barter two thousand acres and
seventy-eight peasants for him! Half a neck was the
fiat against him in the Derby, where Soothsayer's best
son, Tiresias, never let himself be headed. There
would have been no Sandbeck rejoicings in honour of
Tarrare, if "Crocky's white nose" had not broken
down on the Saturday before the St. Leger. He
could hardly be got into Mr. Mawe's stables at Belle
Vue; and some few, who stood heaviest on him, raced
off in chaises with bribed drivers to beat the news to
Sheffield and Nottingham, and try to save a little of
their money. He was sold after that to Mr. Bouverie
and then to Lord Exeter, and had a tremendous
first season. A Stamford and two Phantom mares
bore him, in course of time, Beiram, Ishmael, and Bay
Middleton. The former, along with Galata, that
tucked up but speediest of Burghley mares, and Green-
mantle, made "the narrow blue stripes" a spectre to
trainers for four or five seasons; and if Lord Exeter
had stuck to Beiram instead of Sultan after that, and
not used two crosses of the blood, there seems a strong

probability that he would have held his own much
longer. There was a toughness about the Beirams,
Ilex, and Midas, which could bring them home in a
strong-run race over the Ditch-in, while the Sultans
and Sultanas would be running with their mouths open
long before the Turn of the Lands. Augustus was
rather a brilliant member of the family, but he fought
sadly in his gallop; and Ishmael was the founder of a
fine stamp of jumpers, though none of them have been
equal to Burgundy, as far as build went. The latter
was just the lengthy, short-legged sort of sire that
farmers require. Augur is a grandson of Ishmael,
through Nickname; and although his stock have perhaps no great liberty about them, they are, if not
quick enough to train, dark chestnut fourteen-stone
hunters, ready to keep up the jumping charter.

Glencoe.   Of all the countless Sultans he had
through his hands, Tiny Edwards most
loved Glencoe, a low-backed chestnut with great
speed, and the rare Tramp staying power about him.
His ends were very fine, and Robinson used to look
like a man seated in a valley. It was not, however,
as the pantomimes have it, "The Valley of Calm
Delight," when Plenipo was at hand, and poor
Conolly's good-natured drawling tones were heard
about a length behind, "*Now, Master Jemmy, I'm
here; I can come when I'm wanted.*" He was sold to
a Mr. Richards, of George Town, Kentucky, and died
in the August of '57, in his twenty-seventh year.
With all his ancient pluck, he stood up against spas-
modic colic and lung fever for ten days; and kept on
his feet the last three, till he fell and died quite
exhausted with bleeding at the nose. His picture,
"one of Troye's best efforts in anatomy and colour-
ing," was quite an object of interest at the United
States Fair at Louisville; and if his son, Pryor, had
not died here, they looked forward to getting him to
supply his place in "the Blue Grass Region."

Long before Lord Jersey sent his Middleton.
Cobweb to Sultan, he had no common
Epsom luck with the Web by Waxy blood. Web's
son, the chestnut Middleton by Phantom, had won
the only race he ever ran for ; but that was the
Derby, in which Actæon was beaten and Cain fell.
After that, he bolted away with Sam Barnard, who
thought he was going to Bury, and played the deuce
with everybody and everything. When he was first
broken he shambled and rolled so in his action, and
seemed so utterly unable to walk, that Lord Jersey
and Edwards thought there was not a hope for him.
He was of a Suffolk Punch stamp ; a bigger-boned
horse, and with nothing like the liberty of Bay Middleton. Like Plenipo, a T.Y.C. was his *forte*, and,
owing to his weight, he did not care to carry himself
much farther ; but for that distance Robinson always
thought him better than Bay Middleton. For speed,
trial horses were no good to him ; and he could have
trotted past the post in the Derby. They only laid
seven to four against him at starting, little knowing
the perils he had escaped that morning. His lad had
been got at ; and when he was entrusted with a bucket
of water to plait his mane, he allowed him to drink it
off, and there was nothing but the sponge when Ransome, who was then the head lad, came in. The cul-
prit vowed that he had thrown the rest down the sink ;
but the evidence of guilt was so clear, that at first
Edwards thought it was all over. However, his spirits
revived when he had walked the horse four miles from
Mickleham to The Warren ; but he looked so barrel-
like at the post, that Lord Jersey remarked that he
must have had more water than they knew of. Still
Edwards stuck to it that he was throwing off his food
as he rode with him to the course ; and that, "*even
with five gallons inside, nothing could touch him.*" And
so it happily proved, and Lord Jersey's and the Duke
of Wellington's coachmen were said to have won

considerably above a thousand each. Edwards had learnt from his experience of the Web family, that they could always run big. He was wont to say of them—" *They're as fat as pigs: if I work them two days together, they're lame; and if their bellies brush the ground, they're so good they'll get through.*" Nearly all the Cobwebs had navicular disease, which she inherited from Soothsayer; but still she imparted to them, as a counterpoise, that clear-winded Arab attribute which came to her through Phantom from Sir Charles Bunbury's smart Whiskey tribe. Web and her daughter, Filagree, had each thrown an Epsom winner to Phantom; and it now became the granddaughter's turn to cap them both with Bay Middleton.

Bay Middleton. This distinguished horse was a most frantic subject to begin with; and became so bad, that when Lord Jersey met Robinson by chance in London, in the February of his Derby year, he begged him, as an especial favour, to go back and ride him. Jim accordingly booked himself by "The Magnet," and knocked up Edwards immediately on his arrival. He put his night-capped head forth from his lattice, and said—" *Oh, dear! I'm so glad you've come. He's bolted with everybody. We'll gallop at the Cambridge Gap in the morning.*" Before mounting, Robinson had some fearful admonitions from "Paddy Carey," as the head boy was called. He asked him to stick to his head for a minute, till he was settled in the saddle; but—" *My flesh! I'd better hold the hack—we'll be all killed together,*" was his prompt counter-proposition, and he let him go almost before Jim had time to lick his fingers.

In his first canter, he went very uneasily, as the martingale was far too short, and tearing at the girths. " My Flesh " was then called to let it out or take it off; and when, by a series of nervous dashes, he had succeeded in partially doing the latter, the horse trod upon it and broke it, and feeling his head loose at last, went off like a gun-shot. Edwards in vain tried to lead him on Sepoy; but he had no notion of following anything, and dashed up the hill right across the Cambridge turnpike into The Links. This was his first essay; but Robinson gradually brought him under; and when a few horses had been pulled up, to teach him to leave them on the long hill, he went away from Muezzin, at 13lbs., in a match, with his ears pricked. He was not a quick beginner, and at half a mile many would have scrambled away from him; but whatever distance the race or the sweat might be (for they never tried him), Robinson never heard him blow. He was rather short in his back ribs, and weak in his loins; but his brisket, thighs, and hocks were as good as they could be, and his plump hind-quarters (in which the Cowls follow him), his wicked style of head, and his arched neck, which was so beautifully set in from the withers, may be traced in many of his descendants, especially in the mares. It is a rule which holds good 999 times out of a thousand, that the length of the head multiplied by three gives the length of the horse, and we believe that in Bay Middleton the measure answered exactly. Lord Jersey remarked on the length of his head, when Mr. Herring was painting the bay after the Derby, but—"Yes, my lord, if he hadn't had so long a head you would not have had so long a horse," was the reply. His shoulders were thin, and well laid back, and good ones to correct Touchstone's with. None of his sons really resembled him to our mind, except Ruby, and he only did so when he was drawn quite fine for the Ascot meeting, and then the likeness struck no one more than Lord Jersey himself.

The old horse was ill all the summer Graves of Bay of '56, and died on November 3rd of the Middleton and following year. His heels had been very Crucifix. bad, and kept in perpetual turnip poultices, and for the last three or four days he lay down and tossed in great pain. Matter seemed to come from every part of him, including his eyes; and the mysterious off fore-foot enlarged considerably, but there was no *post mortem* upon it. He was buried within ten yards of his stable door; and but a few days after they had to dig down to him, as Lord Jersey sent to beg the near forefoot. His old mate Crucifix, who just sur-vived him a year, is now buried beside him inside the rustic paling of a small flower plot; and John and Alfred Day have each planted a cedar to their me-mory. The spot was all blooming with hollyhocks when we passed it in October '58, to take another glance at old Crucifix. There she stood, quite wasted and listless, under the wall of a loose box, with withers as sharp as a knife. She had kept in pretty blooming condition till her wonted Stockbridge race levée was over, and then she began to fail very fast. Since Chalice, in 1852, she had bred no foal, and always broke at the end of a fortnight. Her great peculiarity was the narrowness of her chest; and hence, in her training, she perpetually suffered from speedy cut.

Her legs went within a week after the Oaks race, but the secret never fairly oozed out, till the Saturday before the St. Leger. Looking thinner than she was in her "sky-blue and white cap" days, and with her great hips and deep brisket more prominently marked than ever, she seemed like the last turf relic of Lord George, whose heart was at one time never far from the Danebury paddocks. He spent no less than fifteen hundred over them in three years in bone-dust alone, and spread some of it himself with his coat off, while John Day junior wheeled the barrow. A neigh-bouring parson espied him at his labours, and said that he could "*blow off such top-dressing with my pocket-handkerchief.*" Of course some one was kind enough to repeat it to his lordship; and at a dinner party in the neighbourhood shortly after, he told with

great glee how The Church had been touting him
through the hedge, and, little thinking that the very
man sat right opposite him, asked the lady of the
house, " *Who is this parson* * * * ?"

The Selim and Defence blood suited
well in Andover, who only wanted a little Andover.
closer ribbing up to make him look the workman he
was. Still he was a very nice topped horse, and it
was quite a treat to get a bird's-eye view of him from
a grand stand. His stock disappointed us, as they
had his failure of back-rib, which was aggravated by
their length, and lacked general style and quality.
He had also a strong dash of eccentricity at times;
and was once extracted by Snarry from the chimney
of an old brewhouse, up which he had made a well-
meant effort to become a climbing-boy.

As to the infancy of Bay Middleton's
other Derby winning son, the Flying The Flying Dutchman.
Dutchman, we know very little, except that he was
born on Feb. 27th. " *He was always a good doer,*"
said his early guardian, Coverdale, to us, as we
strolled out from Redcar to leave a card on Barbelle;
" *but as for Van, I never could glutton him. Zuyder
Zee,*" he added, " *I could frighten into a mouse-hole, but
he got master of the man somehow on his road to Fobert's.*" Old Barbelle herself had been sent to Ashgill,
who had been sold not long before at an auction for
40*l.*; and within a few minutes of our visit she had
been separated from her Pottinger filly, and the two
were indulging in a succession of answering cheers.
She was standing, after her bereavement, in a cart-
stable, separated by a rail from a black pony; and as
she looked more of the light-necked, drooping quartered hack than the brood mare, we could hardly have
thought that such virtue as three "thousand guinea
yearlings," two of them St. Leger winners, had come
out of her. Her head is rather plain and long, but
there is nothing particular to find fault with her feet,

though her sire, Sandbeck, was rather mulish that way; and so was his son, Redshank. The Dutchman's did not get him through dirt; and we have heard it stated (and as flatly contradicted), by men whose judgment we should be sorry to question, that his doubtful Derby performance was perhaps more owing to a lack of knee-action than anything else. If a horse does not bend his knee well, in nine cases out of ten the Epsom hill puts him wrong, as he cannot lie away so far at first, and trust to his horse's coming back to him, as in the St. Leger.

THE DARLEY ARABIAN.

" To talk with him of other days,
    Seemed converse with Old Time ;
He remembered feats of Banbury,
    And Mellish in their prime :
Hambletonian and *Diamond*
    Seemed but yestreen ; from his lips
Fell tales of young Bay Malton,
    And the colts got by Eclipse."

Eclipse's Origin. LEAVING this renowned Arab, Bartlett Childers, and Squirt amid the olive-tinted haze of time, we come to "Marske, dam by Blacklegs," who is always drawn as standing among the rocks on the sea-coast, in honour of the mansion from which he was named. Mr. Tattersall, who was quite a literary ferret in these matters, and was never beaten except over "The Ratcatcher's Mare," left it as his Scrap Book opinion that—to judge from colour, style, and everything else—Shakspeare, and not Marske, was the sire of Eclipse. "Shakspeare," he observes, "was a chestnut with a white face and legs, and a good runner, whereas Marske was a bad colour and small." He was sold to a farmer after the Duke of Cumberland's death, and stood for a long time at half-a-guinea; but the Earl of Abingdon, in 1776, asked 200 guineas for his services, when he was rising twenty-seven, and he commanded a hundred when he died. Wahtever Mr. Tattersall may have thought privately, he was keen enough to buy Marske mares to cross with Highflyer; while O'Kelly looked out like a falcon for Herod ones. These two proud owner rivals were widely different in temperament. The Englishman only trained once, and let others take the risk; while the Irishman matched everything. Eclipse's stock were all light-fleshed, active, and excitable, and could be got ready to run at very short notice. Those who put mares to him felt quite certain that the foals would be after this type, and chestnuts with white legs and faces to boot.

He died of nephritic colic at Ca- His Funeral and nons, in Middlesex, in 1789, whither he Epitaph. had been drawn in a van. Ale and cake was given at his funeral; and Mons. Vial de Saintbell made his fame as an anatomist by dissecting him. His heart scaled-in at 13lbs., which was 8lbs. less than Mr. Davis's equally immortal Hermit; and O'Kelly chivalrously hired a poet to fling his last defiance at Highflyer and his owner. One verse, which aims at being the most biting, runs thus—

> " True, o'er the tomb in which this favourite lies,
> No vaunting boast appears of lineage good ;
> Yet the Turf Register's bright page defies
> The race of Herod to show better blood."

Fifteen years before, Mr. O'Kelly's grey colt, Horizon, scored the first race to his credit at Abingdon, at two years old ; and in the twenty-three succeeding years, 344 of his winners made 518,000*l.*, an enormous sum for those cautious days.

The direct Eclipse lines of Alexander, The Young Mercury, and Joe Andrews have been Eclipses.

small in comparison with those of King Fergus and
Pot-8-o's.   Alexander was an immense chestnut, and
the sire of Boadicea the grandam of Touchstone.
His stock were much liked for their size ; the colts
being often strongly-whited chestnuts, and the mares,
which were remarkably good, for the most part
browns, full of speed and quality, and with very fine
expression about the head and throat.   The Mer-
curies first came out in all their strength and stout-
ness with Gohanna, who was, like Waxy, out of a
Herod mare, and the twain ran the memorable race
for the Derby in what has always been termed the
Pot-8-o's year.   Seven out of the thirteen were by
that chestnut, and but for the Petworth pet dividing
them, they would have made up the first three.   No
two horses were more widely different to look at than
Gohanna and Waxy, although their forms were as
near at 3lbs. as Scythian and Champagne's were at
evens for a mile.   High quality, so to speak, came
into English blood-stock very much with Waxy,
whereas Gohanna was a plain hunter style of horse
to look at.   He was put to all kinds of mares, and
got great power on a short leg, and if they exceeded
fifteen one, it was beyond the average.   They had
broad foreheads, small noses, and a very prominent
eye, and were uniformly speedy and staying.   Election was one of the smallest and most delicate of his
sons, and very different from the hardy Golumpus,
for whom, before Catton had made him a name, there
was no Salutation bidder.

The Cattons.   Orville's blood united with Catton's
immediately in Mulatto, and one degree
off in Slane.   In appearance the Cattons generally
followed Gohanna, but Mulatto had much more style,
and was more round and plump, and with the most
blood-like head and neck.   Catton was a very firm well-
seasoned horse, and took punishment from Sammy
King, in his races, like a hero.   Few lines of blood

have done more for Yorkshire. Racing, hunting, or coaching, in fact nothing came amiss to his stock; and in the days when George Clark was in his glory at Barnby Moor, the upholder of "the blue jacket and white hat line" on the Great North Road, while Scrooby patronized the black, he got an almost fabulous price for two colts, by his son Akarius, out of Highflyer Coach mares. Like all Lord Fitzwilliam's horses in Scaife's day, Mulatto was very badly broken. Clift used to say of him, and in fact of every one of them, "*Here's a pretty brute! I never get on one but I've a chance of getting my neck broke; no mouth, no nothing; I've to make all.*" Welbeck, on the contrary, was quite as remarkable for the height to which it carried its breaking. The late Duke of Portland used to say that a horse should not go on to a race-course till it could face anything. Hence, in order to complete their education, they were marched over and over again past a drum and fife band, with a flag, in the park, and so many screws of powder were let off on the corn bin, that at last they would hardly put their heads out of the manger for a pistol report.

Mulatto will long be memorable as the winner of that Doncaster Cup race, when Fleur-de-Lis, Memnon, Actæon, Longwaist, and Tarrare went down before the green banner of Wentworth; and his fame is still bright in the Stud-book as the sire of Martha Lynn, the dam of Voltigeur, and Morsel, the dam of The Cure. Old Martha, by no means a handsome, was rather a deep than a broad mare, with fine hips and hocks, and somewhat drooping quarters, a muscular neck, and ribs well arched. Morsel, who looked very little above fourteen and a-half, was sold at a Mr. Thomlinson's sale in Cumberland as a two-year-old for fifty guineas by Mr. Wetherell, the celebrated auctioneer, to himself. He sent her to Physician, whose smart two-year-olds

Mulatto and his Daughters.

O

were then making him all the rage, and sold her for seventy-five guineas only two months before she foaled The Cure. It might truly be said of her that she "marched a queen," and although The Cure had that peculiarity that every muscle in his body seemed in movement when he walked, he never had quite her majesty. As Maroon was in a hunter and harness sphere, the male line of Mulatto virtually ended with Old England, the sire of Defiance. At Sir Joseph Hawley's sale the latter went into Mr. Parr's hands for thirty-eight guineas, where he prospered not a little. It was always a matter of difficulty to get him away from his horses, as, like his father, he had a strong touch of temper and sluggishness, and hence Mr. Parr could so seldom get him ridden to his mind, that he not unfrequently donned his own puce and white. His forehand was good and somewhat massive, but he fell off behind the saddle. Still we thought that we never saw two such good horses of their stamp in one man's hands as when he and Weather-gage were led about at the back of the Northampton course, before they had won their races; and it was a strange reflection that they had only cost about 200 guineas the pair!

Joe and Dick Andrews. Joe Andrews was beaten under his original title of "Dennis-Oh!" by Faith for the great Subscription at York, the day after John Shepherd made his first appearance in silk for a Give and Take Plate, in which 6st. 5lb. 4oz. was allotted for his hamper. He stood for some time in the West of England, and his hunters were thought very high-class, but he died in obscurity many years before his son, Dick Andrews, made his blood famous with Altisidora (who was a chestnut, with a good deal of The Princess character about her), and the renowned Tramp. Dick was rather a narrow horse, with a long, lean, and expressive head, and showed great bottom and breeding. Tramp inherited the former quality from him, and through his Gohanna dam came the broad Petworth forehead.

Tramp was a nice level horse of fifteen- Tramp. two, long and low, and perhaps somewhat straight in his back, and "carried his flag" in a coaching style, which pleased the East Riding amazingly. Of all his sons, Tyke, the conqueror of his half-brother Zinganee for the Fitzwilliam Stakes, was, barring his colour, the most complete resemblance to him. He was himself a wonderful four-mile horse, and the Subscription Purse at York in 1814, when Sir Mark Sykes's Prime Minister just beat him, produced the most betting and excitement that Knavesmire had ever known, except perhaps on the Voltigeur and Dutchman day. They ran the old four-mile course, Jackson forcing the pace with Tramp round the Bason turn, and the echoes of "*Now, Tramp! Now, Minister!*" which rent the air, as John Shepherd went up and headed him coming back by the wood, linger vividly in the ears of the Yorkshire patriarchs yet. His stock had all a knack of jumping, and the only thing against them was a strong inclination to be vicious. Zinganee had the sourest of eyes, but there was no harm in him, whereas St. Giles would stop and kick furiously at exercise, and if he had not his muzzle on, would try to tear his lad out of the saddle; and his grandsons, Inheritor and Zohrab, were in a milder way quite as troublesome at exercise and saddling. Until he had Blacklock, Mr. Watt could never bear to keep a stallion, and hence he parted with Tramp for 300*l.*, and his groom used to bring him very proudly to Driffield on market days, and boast that *his* horse was "shod with four Gold Cups." His new owners kept him two years, and then sold him for fourteen hundred. At last he became blind, and so broken-winded that it was quite painful to hear him sigh. Still breeders were not afraid of him, and although he would not

O 2

notice St. Giles's dam, they were shut up in a loose box all night, and a chestnut Derby winner was the result. Next year Isaac Sadler was so determined to have a Tramp, that the same plan was pursued with his mare Defiance; and Dangerous, another Derby winner, rewarded him as well.

Liverpool. A cross between Tramp and a Whisker mare produced Liverpool, who was bred by Mr. Watt. That fine old Yorkshire worthy was the first to espy him in his morning rambles, as he was dropped in the Dove-Cote Paddock; and away he hurried to tell Robert Elrington, assuring him, while the suppressed twinkle of his eye told a very different tale, "*It's the worst foal you ever saw in your life.*" Although his loins at three years old made many think - that he was a weak horse, they gave up their ideas on that head when they had seen or heard of his race with Consol at Preston. Eventually he passed from Crutch Robinson's into the Duke of Cleveland's hands, and so to Mr. Ramshay's of Naworth Barns, for a couple of hundred. His forelegs were rather too light to· please the Cumberland farmers, and added to this he was a trifle ragged in his hips and thick in his jowl.

The British Yeoman was certainly the handsomest son Liverpool ever got, and like him he was remarkably clean hocked. His promising Derby chance was quite destroyed by a most peculiar seizure. On the setting on of his off arm there came a soft swelling about the size and thickness of a large dish, and another to match above the hock on that side. It looked as if he had been stung by an adder; and the faculty had not agreed as to the nature of the swelling when it disappeared again. He was accompanied on many of his Cumberland journeys by the celebrated little Highland Laddie. This renowned teazer was originally sold after running in a pony gig for 21*l.* 14*s.*, at the rate of 6*d.* per pound, and was purchased for 100 guineas by Mr. Starkey when he won the Pony Sire prize at Chester. As a getter ot race-horses, " The Yeoman " had but very little scope ; and high as his hunter name so deservedly stands, there would have been but very few to touch him it he had been less indiscriminate in his favours.

The dams of Wee Willie and Lanercost Death of Liver-
were almost the only blood mares that   pool.
came to Liverpool at Naworth his first season, and Lanercost was in verity his first begotten, and from a mare who had been bought from Lord Egremont by one of his Cockermouth tenants for something under fifteen pounds. In 1844, the old horse was sold for two thousand to the French Government, but he died before he was delivered. He had narrowly escaped, along with

> " The slight and slender jasmine tree,
> That blooms on my Border tower,"

being burnt alive amid the ruins of Naworth Castle, only to meet a less glorious fate. During the confusion which ensued for the next two or three weeks, he was left to incompetent hands to physic, and his gut was so much torn by their previous back raking, that the glyster passed into his bowels, and he died in most fearful pain.

In spite of this misfortune with him, Mr.   Lanercost.
Ramshay did well with his sons Naworth,
Moss Trooper, and Broadwath, and still better with Lanercost, whom he bought as a yearling for 120 guineas, from the owner of his dam, Otis. He was an enormous feeder, and became so thick and fat that he was sent off to Tom Dawson's to do gentle work at Middleham, all his two-year-old season. The coarse head and neck, the latter of which assumed a ewe shape in many of his stock, were all there then ; and slug as he was, he could always, as if in anticipation of Ascot, make the liveliest resistance if any medicine was to be put down him. When they first

tried it, he went right on end, and struck his head into the plaster ceiling of his box ; and a little egg-shaped indentation which still tells of " Lanercost, his mark," had much more interest for us in our Northern wanderings than Belt Willie's armour in the old Banquet Hall. Among modern horses, Lord Zetland's Tros, in every point but length, most strongly resembled him, although there was no earthly affinity. Harry Edwards took to the flannels again, and " got him out" gloriously in the Newcastle St. Leger, and then he passed into Mr. Ramsay's hands for 1500*l.* It was in the once famous green and yellow of Barnton that he accomplished his best feat of giving Hetman Platoff, who was as fresh as he was stale, eleven pounds for his year, and beating him for the Cambridgeshire. Never were two horses greater opposites. Hetman, as the stable-boys say, " might have been ridden with a woman's garter ;" whereas Lanercost, like his particular friend Melbourne, always had his head on his jockey's arms, and would make a race with a donkey.

To judge from the amount of persuasion he required to move him, he was nearly as thick-skinned as Brunswick, who used to go six miles and wear thick double hoods and quarter pieces, &c., whenever he had to sweat. The last vision we had of Lanercost, in his racing days, was crawling round the turn for home at Ascot, and his action quite gave us that impression, which had more than once flashed across Templeman, that his back was broken. Still, Mr. Kirby was not the man to give him up when there was a shilling to be made, and despatched him to Liverpool a month after for the Cup. The poison was, however, still lurking in his system, and he broke out into such a black sweat the day before, that he was sent home to Yorkshire, and the Turf knew its great modern four-miler no more. He had all the requisites of a racer— fine arched loins and a beautiful back, and with the best of legs, if they had not been afflicted with corns.

Mr. Kirby was amazingly fond of him. He would stand with his hands in his drab breeches-pockets, looking at him day after day with visitors, and then out would come his " *There! it's my opinion—and I've seen a many horses in my time—but I never seed one, tak him altogether, that pleased me mair than Lanercost.*" A pause regularly ensued, only to be thus broken again in the same monotonous tone—"*And thou'll recollect, I had old Orvile.*"

His first year's stud essays with Van Tromp, War Eagle, and Ellerdale were his best; but it was gradually found that his stock did not ripen early, and were not nearly smart enough for two-year-old races, and such a discovery is now-a-days fatal to a horse. Thirty years before, he would have been invaluable. Mr. Kirby moreover did not show his wonted tact as to limiting, and hence many of them came small; and instead of making an annuity out of him for a series of years, he was glad, after five or six, to let him to Lord Exeter and the Hampton Paddocks. His son Loupgarou, who was at the latter establishment one season, heaped coals of fire on their head for tiring of him so soon by beating their crack Orlando cleverly in the next sale average with the 710-guinea Hecate. The backs of the Van Tromps were rather narrow and doubtful, and the Yorkshiremen "didn't like the sample" at all when Ivan first walked into the York enclosure. For magnificence, however, Vandermulin had scarcely a peer, although he was more of a foreigner's horse; and Zeta was the best-looking and gamest Van Tromp mare that was ever out. We shall not easily forget her in two Doncaster finishes, two years running.

Lottery was a very blood-like horse, not very strong behind, but still the best of Tramp's sons, if his temper had not been such a fearful bane. He was drilled by Jem Garbutt in a fallow field in Holderness, and though the spirit was

The Sons of Lanercost.

Lottery.

nearly galloped out of him, it was never subdued. He would lie down and roll when he couldn't get his jockey off, and Mr. Watt was so afraid of further mischief, that he wanted to shoot him. After that he was sold to Mr. Whittaker for four hundred; but one morning he came so savagely at Shepherd, that he dismounted, and turned his hack loose to divert his attention, and the two galloped off Langton Wold back to their stables together. He was fully sixteen hands, and his best race was when he was only beaten half a head by Mercutio, who we believe died on his way home after his Doncaster Cup win. He was first favourite for the St. Leger at 2 to 1; but the flat-footed Will Wheatley turned his toes out and put his spurs into "Tinker" in vain. He had not digested an oat properly for some days before, and was beaten quite easily. The Carpenter was a fine slashing horse by him, and Inheritor was remarkably well built; but he had bad feet and always scrambled a good deal at starting, though he was game to the backbone when he did begin. Zohrab was also a sticker, and after making every one give him a wide berth, both in the saddling ring or at the post, he would summon his energies for one last kick royal, and away. Weight was not a thing he objected to, but he was very long in his stride, and required much holding together. Like Inheritor, he was quite the hunter, and in fact nearly all the Lotteries had a strong Chase as well as Turf stamp about them. His principal son, Sheet Anchor, was quite the rage in Yorkshire at one time, in consequence of his having won the Colt Sapling at York Spring, when quite unprepared. There could be no other reason, as he was heavy shouldered and common, and never filled up over the quarters; in short, a mere magnified colt. After an enormous amount of chances, he in his turn begot Weatherbit, who was the only horse that Mendicant ever hit to, and certainly Beadsman takes completely after her in his points. Weatherbit himself was rather light-girthed, and we did not just fancy the setting on of his neck, but his hind-quarters might be moulded from; and we remember, in fact, nothing in horse-flesh that we ever liked better.

The sturdy little broad nostrilled The Story of Weathergage is as unlike his sire as horse Weathergage. can be. The way in which he came to Benhams is rather curious. Mr. Parr had seen Clothworker done up for the night, and was pondering, cigar in mouth, over his Cup chances, at the little Croxton inn, when Sly arrived, and began saying that such a rare-bred horse from Newmarket had only been beaten a neck for the Selling Stakes at Northampton the week before, and that his trainer had had orders not to take him home. As he gradually unwound the pedigree by Weatherbit out of Miss Letty by Priam, Mr. Parr was all attention; and finding that Armstrong had claimed and taken him back to the place from whence he came, he wrote to say that he would come and look at him as soon as he got to Newmarket, as he wanted a companion for Bardolph. When he went to his stables, and heard that he only asked sixty guineas for such an apparently sound improving horse, he fully thought The Admiral had found out something wrong, and would not close with the offer till he had seen him canter on the Lime Kilns hill. Mizen took him out for exercise the first time, and complained "that his joints snocks;" but all that was forgotten when, with two stone more on, he made such an example of Bardolph and Wells, in their gallop the next day, that Mr. Parr, who was on Selina, was fain to roar to them to pull up before they got among the crowd near the Duke's stand. "Tiny" might well say to Mr. Parr, in the stable that evening, that he "could win the Newmarket Handicap far enough if I was on that one," pointing to the stall of the once despised bay.

Bardolph's defeat did not trouble Mr. Parr much, as

he felt sure he had got a treasure, and he was convinced of the fact when he very soon found him to be
a stone better than the six-year-old Clothworker at
the Derby distance; and able to give Tame a good
lump of weight over the T.Y.C. In short, he liked
him so much that but for his being not a little inte-
rested in Hobbie Noble's success, it was his intention
to have taken a Derby mount upon him, as he had
done upon Sponge four years before. Instead of this,
he rode him for the Aristocratic Handicap at Bath, in
which Justice, a three thousand and not a thirty-guinea
cast off from the Bedford stable, was a bad fourth to
him. Then misfortune descended, and he knocked his
hoof about so much by casting a shoe, that he had to
be kept in damp swabs all day, and be walked about,
hour after hour, on the dewy grass at night. With
this gentle encouragement, it grew sufficiently to bear
a shoe three weeks before Goodwood; but even with
that short preparation, he beat the six-year-old Melford so easily at seven stone each, with nearly a stone
in hand, that they would not hedge a penny.

His action was very short, and he had a peculiar power
of propelling himself with his fore-legs. He could not
bear to have his head confined, and his Queen's Plate
race the next year with Deerhound at Northampton
was very nearly lost from Marlow riding him by mistake in a martingale. He had also a very one-sided
mouth, and would hang to the left when he first came
to Benhams, the moment the rider dropped his hand;
and hence Mr. Parr trotted him for months across
plough and fallow with his head at liberty, and would
never once indulge him by turning that way. The Goodwood Stakes course suited him in this respect, as the
first mile was all to the left, and Wells had the strictest
injunctions to keep his whip in his left hand for fear of
accidents.

Strange as it may seem, they had tried him nearly
a score of times at Newmarket, and liked him less.

each time, and they would not have it when Mr. Parr privately told them before the race how good he believed him to be. The Admiral, however, avowed candidly that he had been far too much prejudiced, or he would have taken advantage of this warning voice from Benhams. Then came the great *coup* for the Cesarewitch, on which several of the ring dons so completely overlaid their books against him, that Mr. Parr, who had got on at fifties, laid off about six thousand of it in a ten minutes' walk between his lodgings and the Rooms. In fact, he was fairly beset, and never paid so dearly for a little exercise before or since. Mr. Megson bought the horse after that for twenty-five hundred, and they thought him, from his Salisbury running at the beginning of his four-year-old season, a still better horse than he had ever been ; but the Northampton race overset him, and he never won again. Kingston smashed him and Teddington up together for The Whip, and the horse at whose name ancient listers still turn pale, passed through Mr. Blenkiron's hands to the French Government, and it seems left to Mandrake to raise up seed to the house of Weatherbit.

The King Fergus line was full of   The Sons of Herod blood, as Hambletonian was out   King Fergus. of a Highflyer, and Beningboro' out of a Herod mare. The latter, for whom 3500 guineas was refused; was a horse of very great stamp, and the living image of Herod himself. He died at Middleham, full of years and stud-honours, and was buried under a mulberry tree in front of Mr. Dinsdale's house. His son Orvile dipped into the Herod blood again, and inherited his deep saucer eyes from his Highflyer dam.

Orvile was the first of Beningboro's get   Orvile. that ever started ; and William Edwards always declared that while Selim was the speediest, he was the best for all lengths that he ever rode. His lungs and courage were quite inexhaustible. As

a proof of this, he ran a four-mile trial with Haphazard at Lewes, even weights, at four o'clock in the
morning, and gave him such a tying up at the end of
three miles that Sam Chifney did not persevere, and
reported so decidedly as to his horse's loss of form,
that he started in public no more. The King's Plate
was run that afternoon, and William Edwards again
handed his horse home first after a most punishing
race with Walton.

He was a very difficult horse to ride, and so inani-
mate and dead-skinned that nothing but a whip that
would curl well round him could make any impression
whatever. His stock were generally large, plain, and
brown, and many of them had rather cart-horse heads.
There was a great deal of the coach-horse about him,
and he stood very much over with one knee, and his
son Don Juan, who was put to Cleveland mares near
Catterick Bridge, got some of the best coaching stock
that ever went to a Yorkshire fair. From a cross
between him and a Highflyer mare, which made three
close stains of Herod in succession, came Scud, the
handsome sire of a handsome race ; but this too close
breeding may have borne fruits in Actæon, whose
head and neck were most brilliant, and whose stock
mostly cut up soft. Through his other son Muley, of
Underley renown, Orvile at one time bid fair to be
very famous ; but while Alice Hawthorn and Wasp
have bred pretty well, Galaor seems the stopping
point in the branch of it which was represented by
the great leggy Muley Moloch ; while Moresco's
descends through Taurus and John o'Gaunt to the
lengthy handsome Hungerford. Taurus was a rank
roarer, but he could almost fly over the T.Y.C., and it
was all that Camarine (who liked any distance from the
T.Y.C., where even Crutch was no use to her, up to six
miles) could do to put him in difficulties by the time
they had travelled over two miles of the Beacon, in
the race which was a finisher for both of them.

Andrew was another of Orvile's sons, and it was
to him that Belvoir owed Cadland, its only Derby
winner, and through his son Prime Warden came the
industrious Clothworker. Sam Darling Clothworker.
claimed him when he had won a Selling
Stakes at Shrewsbury, and Mr. Parr offered him fifty
pounds for his bargain, but did not get hold of him
for some time after. His peculiarity was that he must
start last and catch his horses one by one, if there
were thirty of them. If any of the rear ones could
come again, and clatter up to his girths, he was such
a cur that he would never try after. Jockey after
jockey begged in vain to be allowed to come through
with him, as they knew he was anything but fast; but
his owner never consented, for fear of letting out the
secret. Mr. Parr sold him at Stamford for four hundred, after Weathergage had made such an example
of him, and put the money on his horse for the
Goodwood Stakes, at forties to one; and he was
eventually killed on a little race-course in Devonshire,
where he had descended, like the once great St.
Bennett, among the leather-flappers.

Orvile's best son, Emilius, inherited Last Days of
his plain head, but was not so coarse. Emilius.
He was a muscular, compact horse, with a great chest
and arms, on short legs, and peculiarly straight hind
ones. Add to this a great middle piece and good
back ribs, with a muscular neck, not too long, and
rather inclined to arch. He looked, in fact, quite as
much a hunter as a blood-horse; and some very
excellent ones he got too, at Riddlesworth, where
latterly he had very few blood-mares at fifty guineas.
Mr. Thornhill's executors let him when the Riddlesworth stud was broken up, and he died soon after the
close of his first season at Easby Abbey. His stock,
after he went North, were all rather small; and the
youngest of them was England's Glory, out of Prairie
Bird, though really his last inamorata (for there never

was such a Don Giovanni) was a piebald pony. He
was perfectly well till just before his death, which was
caused by some one giving him a feed of whole oats,
which he was unable to masticate ; and they buried
him near some loose boxes in a paddock which the
Abbot of the White Canons of Easby surveyed of
yore from his study window. A stone that had once
been the crosiered tomb of a cardinal, but had
gradually mingled with the ruins, and then served as
threshold to the box where Weatherbit now stands,
is built into the wall to mark the spot ; and thus,
to a certain extent, Buckle's last Derby winner is
canonized.

Easby Abbey.   For a picturesque combination of ruins
and blood stock, commend us to that
Swaledale Valley where he moulders, on a summer's
afternoon. We had begun, like veritable racing
pilgrims, at the Catterick Grand Stand, which seems
to have been crossed in and in, till all trace of the
original house has gone, and it has become a venerable
brick balcony, doing duty as a granary for fifty-one
weeks in the year. And so we leave that little
meadow course, with its lofty line of ash and elm, its
haystacks, and its hurdles ; and pleasant thoughts
arise of "the chocolate of Hornby," ready for all
comers, and of Sir Tatton in his prime, winning a
pipe of port on Sunley, and cheered as he rides
back to scale by scores of foxhunters, who were right
proud to

> "Let Uckerby boast of the feats of the Raby,
> And Ravenscar tell what the Hurworth have done,"

—as we saunter, scorning the rail, through the
ponderous urn-topped gates, down the river-side to
Richmond. It boots not, when we reach the ruins of
Easby, that Royaldus, High Constable of Richmond,
is buried there. We wonder much more who one
"Fuller, of Newmarket, aged 83," can be ; and we

would rather see the ring under the chapel wall,
where Emilius, Birdcatcher, Teddington, and Longbow have all been lunged in their time, than the good
St. Agatha herself.

A troop of brood mares are wandering near those
ivy-clad patches of walls, which still stand as ancient
landmarks. Mrs. Taft, of Cesarewitch memory,
stands hard by the Abbot's Elm, beneath which the
hunting exploits of "The Curtail Prior of Fountain,"
must have been talked over by the friars in the days
when Robin Hood, heedless of the sheriff of the
county, twanged the yew in many a Yorkshire and
Sherwood glade. Lady Johns and Sweetheart are
holding mysterious converse with The Belle beneath
the crumbling Catherine-wheel of the refectory, whose
mullions have been eaten by mild decay and left it
hanging by balance. Gipsy Queen has ensconced
herself in the massive cart shed, the top of which
once did duty as a Record Office; while her foal,
Curse Royal, is racing round like a lunatic within
some hurdles near the cloisters, as if unable to endure
the thought of the hopeless half-forfeits which its
"man in boots" racing talent has incurred for Mr.
Jaques. Old Comedy, who would hit to anything,
and whom Billy Pierse swore by as the fastest two-
year-old he ever had, till exposure in grass paddocks
made her a rank roarer, has long since passed away,
and she lies at the turn of the walk in the Abbey
Wood hard by her daughter, Burletta and Augur's
dam. Only one living trace of her is in sight, and
that a chestnut Mildew yearling, which is trying to
emulate its great-grandam's good name, and enliven-
ing the good folk of Richmond in their afternoon's
walk by its playful efforts in the ring.

But we must not linger too long at the $_{\text{Sons of Emilius.}}$
grave of Emilius. The Bizarre line of
Orville stopped with Rat-trap, who is remembered, if
for nothing else, by that most punishing of races

which he ran with Mango at Ascot; and Emilius's line has not gone on in very regular order. Recovery and his pretty race fell into disrepute. Euclid died; Plenipo made no stud name; and good as Priam's mares were, he can only be worthily traced in the male line through Chesterfield to the Hero. Priam was a mare-looking horse, and so delicate a feeder that William Chifney used to say that he could tell to a handful of oats what he would eat in a week. His head and neck were light, and his hair feathered from his ears to the collar-place (if it be not sacrilege to speak of a collar in connexion with him) in a most eccentric style. He drooped rather on his hind pasterns, and stood on a remarkably straight hind leg, although nothing to compare, in this respect, with Landscape, who might have had two sets of fore-legs to look at. Lord Jersey had the offer of him as a yearling, but declined it, from an idea that he would put out ringbones.

American Purchases. He was, along with Trustee, Margrave, and St. Giles, one of those high-priced purchases which the Americans made from our turfites in 1833-36. Such was the rage for him, that he not only had a hundred mares at fifty each, his first season, but it was said that "one leg of him" alone was sold for 5000*l.* However, the end came at last; and Messrs. Tattersall were told, the year before he died, that he was now stone-blind, and that they might have him for two hundred if they liked.

The Hero at Danebury. The Hero has got nearly all his thorough-bred stock as small as Rogerthorpe, who was only trained because the learned friend to whom he was offered preferred a half-bred to a thorough-bred hack for his daughter, and received the Goodwood Cup he won in lieu. Theon, by far the best living son of Emilius, was sold along with Wasp and the rest at Raby, when the racing glories of the pink and black stripes ended. He had more quality than any of the family, and he never looked so beautiful as when, although rising twenty, he stood in a fiery fret, with every vein out like the tendrils of a vine, for twelve long hours, on the first day of the Salisbury Royal. His blood mare chances were few, but he invariably got his hunters as good as they could be, and with more size and substance than himself. In fact, it is very much the secret of breeding not to use too big a sire. Middle-sized ones have oftener quality to give back, and get goodness as well as size; whereas big ones too often get their big stock three-cornered, and sadly apt to run soft.

The cross of Emilius and Fleur de Lis Fleur de Lis. came to nothing at first, though it was so much thought of that three hundred sovereigns was bid for the foal if it lived three days. It turned out to be a very mean bay colt, with hardly stamina enough to keep it alive for twenty-four hours. The mare herself was bought when a foal by Sir Matthew White Ridley, from the Rev. Christopher Sykes. In a race she would not bear hurrying, but required to wait, in front if possible. She would not run without a very strong preparation, and was about sixteen hands, on a light leg, with rare shoulders, deep fore ribs, wide hips, and a great deal more action in her hind quarters than her fore, which rather stopped her at a hill, but gave her endless propulsion on the flat.

The Pompey line of Emilius has so far Nancy. stopped short with Nancy, as he has of late had scarcely any blood mares. Nancy fed well and did well all 1851, but she received what was virtually her finishing stroke in the autumn of that year, as she took a gallop on Knavesmire. Going round the Middlethorpe turn, she slipped on a spot where the cattle had trodden down the grass, and sprained her off hind leg so severely, that she never stood a good preparation again. Her great power was from her

P

thighs to her hocks ; but on her visit to Eglinton Park, to run for Lord Glasgow's Three Hundred Sovereigns Plate, she nearly lost the use of those and every other limb, by being thirteen hours in her railway box. To make matters worse, when she arrived in Edinburgh, it was nearly one in the morning and there was no stable to be had ; and if an enthusiastic Scot had not met the luckless trio, and vowed, the moment he heard the name, that if he hadn't had a vacant stall, she should have gone into his best parlour all night, she would have passed the night in the street, along with old Job and his son Frank. Luckily, she grew better with rest ; and although her action was so very short on the morning of the race, that the visitors at Eglinton Castle made it a certainty for her half-brother Hippolytus, careful riding and the 3lb. allowance just got her through. Her great peculiarity, to our eye, was the peculiarly graceful droop of her quarters, in which Saunterer a good deal resembles her. However, until we espied Troy, or rather Grand Mistress, in the sale ring at Doncaster, in 1858, we never met with anything that reminded us of her as a whole. Nancy was difficult to train, and furnished another proof that when mares can once be got into form they are more effective than horses, but that, while the latter will often get back their form, mares when they have once lost it, hardly ever will.

Hambletonian. Leaving the Beningboro' branch of King Fergus's succession, we come to the Hambletonian one. This mighty bay was out of a Highflyer mare, and he and his opponent Diamond were, on the sire's side, two degrees from Eclipse and two from Herod respectively. It was the saying of the day, that the Eclipses were speedy and jady, and the Herods hard and stout ; and there was a talk of matching the two over again at Bibury, 500 guineas a-side at eight stone each ; Mr. Delmé Radcliffe to ride Hambletonian, and Lord Sackville, Diamond. It eventually ended in nothing, and Diamond was made quite a lion of in Dublin, when he passed through it, to his new home, while Hambletonian's paddocks at Middleham became the most fashionable in the North. Shuttle and Hambletonian, both of them Sir Harry Vane Tempest's, were there together, but the Shuttles had such vile tempers that few cared to use him. Hambletonian did not get size so much as speed, and his stock were principally browns. He was a fine and lengthy, but rather a blotchy-skinned horse, a trait which both Stubbs and Sartorius have brought out in their pictures of him.

Camillus and Whitelock were his choicest sons, and Mr. Garforth made a Camillus. most unlooked for hit with the former, who was half-brother to his Marcia and Marciana. He was a grey horse, from a chestnut strain, and became quite white rather early. His make and quality were very fine, and he got many very good grey and chestnut hunters when he was in Sir Mark Sykes's hands. In his training days Mr. Garforth went to see his string at Whitewall, where old Job Marson was head lad to Joe Ackroyd, and heard a bitter complaint from the latter, that the grey couldn't make his hack gallop. Still he did not like to throw him up without one more trial, and it was accordingly settled that he was to go for a Plate at Malton. He stopped for one more plunge at the post, and got thrown an immense way. Jem Garbutt was not the boy to spare him, and at him he went, hand and heel, till he got within the distance post. By some mistake the flag was not dropped in time, or he would have been bowled out, and seizing his opportunity at last, he went in and won the other two heats. He was put to a mere pony mare by Ruler, and the low light-fleshed Oiseau was the result.

Mr. Garforth began to think " that the parson's new plan" had not spoilt the Oiseau. breeding so much as he expected, when he saw him come right away as a two-year-old, from two St. Leger winners, Octavian and Ashton, in the mile-and-a-half Fitzwilliam Stakes, and sold him into Ireland forthwith for a thousand guineas. His temper got completely ruined there by being run three times in one week on the Curragh, when he was quite out of form; and when he came back he was "for noise and row unequalled." Red Hart used to be bad enough at Walmgate Bar, and chase his own quarters round and round till he could hardly be seen for vapour; and Wanderer so nearly ate off his breast in one of his absent fits at Petworth, that he had to wear a cradle for the rest of his days; but they were sucking doves by the side of Oiseau, or "Oyster" as the tykes called him. He was never easy for one moment, and would stand and listen with his head on one side as if for the muffled tread of some ghostly tormentor. Heavy chains were put on his legs, to keep him from kicking himself to pieces, and thus unable to sate his rage on others, he at last turned savagely on to himself at midnight, and tore his own bowels out. He left a son of a very different mould in the elegant little Rowton; but the Revolutions were true to their sire, and fairly killed themselves with temper in breaking for the hunting field.

Whitelock. Whitelock was the other great channel of the Hambletonian blood. Mr. Sylvester Reed bought him from Sir Mark Sykes, and used him as a country stallion, but there was nothing in his appearance which warranted his becoming so celebrated through Blacklock. His only performances were good enough, as he won a Sixty Pound Plate at Knutsford, and lost the Cup after a dead heat with the Cheshire mare Duchess. Still, Mr. Watt always declared that he had a white feather in him somewhere, which must come out sooner or later; and it was this conviction that made him "never take a real fancy" to Blacklock.

Canezou when she arrived in from Pigburn to meet Surplice, attracted a Blacklock. larger *posse comitatus* than any Sheriff of the County ever summoned; but still the High Street of Doncaster was never in such a flutter as when Blacklock walked up it in 1817, distinguished from the rest of Sykes's string by a complete set of oilskin clothing. Discussion rose high among the Yorkshiremen as to his merits. Some would have it he was a great ugly beast, and others that he was the finest they ever saw. There was, however, no difference of opinion when he had galloped on the Moor, and certainly never did horse deserve so thoroughly to win. Nothing but Sykes's over anxiety prevented it. His orders to Jackson were " to look oot for me at the distance, and I'll tell you what to do." Amid the clatter of eighteen horses and the many-headed multitude all " *Blacklocking,*" it was a wonder that he could make himself heard by Jackson, but he unfortunately did, and " *Pull till 'em, John ; pull till 'em ; thoo hast it all thee own way,*" were his words, which unfortunately fell on Bob Johnson's ear as well. Bob was not usually very leery, but he immediately pulled Ebor quite wide, in order that Jackson, who was busy watching Ben Smith on Restless, next the rails, might not see him so readily, and then snapped him on the post. Jackson always owed Sykes a grudge for this, and his happiness was complete when after making all the running on Theodore and defeating horse after horse, he at last saw Muta, as he peeped under his shoulder, get her head up to his boots, and then change legs and disappear. Oddly enough, he would not have been on Theodore that day if Mr. Petre had not seen him a little " cut" opposite the Betting Rooms, the night before, and thought that if that was his Doncaster game, he would only give him the worst of his mounts next day.

Mr. Moss wanted Mr. Reed to buy Blacklock's Sons. Blacklock, but he " dare not venture on his fore-legs," as his fetlocks and pasterns almost formed a straight line. He was a great black-brown, with a stride which required half-a-mile to settle itself in, a head like a half moon, with eyes quite in his cheeks, and quarters and shoulders as fine as horse could wear. Perhaps to the eye he might be rather light in the fore ribs, though the tape told a different tale, and the hocks of his stock generally stood well away from them, a formation which requires great strength in the loin to support. The hunting field was quite as much their sphere as the race-course. The Cambridgeshire men still remember how well John Ward got to his hounds for seven seasons on Forester, and there must have been nearly a thousand of his grandsons, by the hollow-backed Belzoni, one time or another, at the cover side. Mr. Watt gave forty pounds for him as a two-year-old, and after his great racing career he broke through his rule, and kept him for the stud. The result was not encouraging, as his legs frightened breeders away; but Mr. Kirby took him for a season at a hundred, and cleared eight hundred per cent. by his bargain. Mr. Watt then had him back for three seasons, and was beginning the fourth with him, when he died. He had only been racked up five minutes, when a helper came running breathless after Elrington, and gasped out "*Blacklock's dying!*" He had fallen on his side, and never stirred again, and his heart was found to be sloughed. Two fillies dated from that morning, a chestnut filly, out of Sister to Bubastes, and Felix, by him or Langar; but Lady Laura, from whom he had just been led in, had no foal.

His son, Robin Hood, was virtually trained in his old paddock, as he did little else than canter round it, and then walked to Doncaster, where, after being beaten by Laurel in the Cup, he walked on to Lincoln, and won a seventy-pound plate. Cock Robin was the smallest that Blacklock ever got, and very little beyond

fourteen-three; but as good a little one as ever stepped.
Unhappily, on pulling up in a race he fell on his head
and knees, with Templeman, and put both fetlocks
out of joint. He was taken home on a sledge, and
won again next year; but he had to be cast to be
fired, and in the struggle he broke his back.

The Great Lawn near the Old Hall is The Great Lawn
the necropolis of Blacklock and the other at Bishop
Bishop Burton worthies, and an oak tree Burton.
grows from the breast of each. Blacklock and Muta's
wave close together; and two much larger ones, side
by side, testify to the memory of Mandane and
Altisidora. Blacklock was taken up at the end of
six years, and put together by an anatomist. Mr.
Watt paid 10*l.* for a skeleton rider, who yapped his
teeth when a string was pulled; and the spectral pair
were exhibited at the agricultural meeting at Beverley.
Muta was taken up as well, for the sake of her
shoulder, which had set the Pharmacopœia at defiance; and hence the only tenanted grave of that
trio to the left is marked by a mere sapling, which
blooms for Nitocris out of Manuella, the last of the
old blood. Her near hind hock was so swelled with
farcy that the leg gradually became a burden to her.
It was the doing of a stable lad; and although no one
could ever discover the exact spot, there was evidence
that he had struck her with a fork, out of revenge for
not being allowed to go to Newmarket with her. It
swelled so much that she had to be brought back
when she had got as far as Doncaster, and she never
could run again. She was the dam of Birthday by
Assault, the last that Mr. Watt ever bred; and soon
after its birth, he gave orders that she should be shot
at eight o'clock in the morning to a moment, and
opened his dressing-room window to hear the report.
Birthday was brought up on sugar and milk, and is
now a remarkably fine mare. He never saw her after
she was a foal; and when Scott came to settle about

training her he called out after him once more from
the landing, to tell him not to break her down, and
wrote next day to change his mind about sending
her altogether.   In vain did Mr. Martinson, in his
Nancy zenith, offer him five hundred guineas for her,
and she was never trained.

He might well be proud of his blood, as his Mandane, a splendid mare, who wasted almost to a
skeleton before she died, bred Manuella and Altisidora to Dick Andrews, and Lottery to Tramp, while
Liverpool was out of her Whisker Daughter.   Few
breeders could show such results from their endless
searching of hearts and pedigrees.   Manuella, like her
dam, was very handsome ; and all the Altisidora mares
bred well.   After Altisidora's death in the Great Lawn
ditch, the yearling fillies which ran with the mares and
foals were always brought in at night ; and it was to
their being a good deal coddled in small paddocks,
which had neither sufficient space nor ground variation
to give them action, that many attributed the gradual
decline of the harlequin in the return lists.   It must
have been more from this cause than from their being
taken in at night from the Dove Cote or Great Lawn
that the decline is traceable, as the best breeders all
say that six hours a day is enough for any yearling to
be out, and that they should never be allowed to tire
themselves.

Mr. Watt perhaps spoilt his stock most by his undue
love for Cerberus.   He rode many wide chestnut
mares by him, who inherited his lack of size ; and he
was, in fact, anything but a worthy cross to follow
Tramp and Dick Andrews.   Manuella's son, Bel-
shazzar, was the Blacklock for whom he had the greatest fancy, although he was most undeniably soft.   He
had sold him to Mr. Allen ; but when his Cara won
the Two Thousand, he determined not to be separated
from him, and sent off an agent post-haste to redeem
him from the foreigners, who had just got him.   They

had, however, seen the report of Newmarket as well, and a three thousand offer fell dead on their ears. Neither money nor labour stopped him if he set his mind upon a thing ; and in his heyday he would have hacks posted, and ride to his trainer, Sykes's, at Malton, twenty-five miles before breakfast, to see his lot gallop. Such was his love for them that if he had been two or three months from home, he would take a lantern the moment he got out of his carriage, and not rest till he had been all round among "the old blood."

But we must bid it a long good-night, The Blacklocks. and hie back to the four perpetuators of the Blacklock tribe—Buzzard, Brutandorf, Voltaire, and Velocipede. No blood in the stud-book is better-winded or runs better when full of flesh, which shows that the internal conformation is good, and ought to be perpetuated. Their aptitude for a distance displays itself in a muscular neck, without which few horses ever yet stayed ; and they have also great depth from the withers to the shoulder-points, and an immense roundness of rib in making the curve from the spine.

Voltigeur and Fandango have all these Voltigeur. grand characteristics ; and it is not im-probable that if the former had always been allowed to run some stones heavier, he would never, in his earlier days at least, have been beaten. Robert Hill's notion always was, that when Voltigeur's neck was reduced, he would be fittest to run ; but the horse being of an iron constitution, he could not accomplish his object (even by the aid of two hoods all summer, and Radulphus, Castanette, and St. Ann perpetually at him) for a season and a-half ; and he lived long enough to see the neck and strength of his pet leave him together, and neither Atkinson nor John Scott could put flesh on him again.

His sire Voltaire, for whom the Duke of Cleveland

gave two thousand, was suspected to be a bit of a coward and was a little too peacocky to please some eyes. He had a remarkably fine barrel, and a ring-bone on the off fore-foot ; and some of his carriage-horses were as good and lofty as they could be for their purpose. Martha Lynn and Eulogy were the only blood mares he had in his last season (1847), and Vortex and Euphony were the foals. As Charles XIIth's stock have quite disappeared after the failures of that splendid first batch at Doncaster in 1846, whose looks seemed to give quite a stimulus to breeding, and make owners dissatisfied with the puny average of their yearlings, his fame all hinges so far on the Martha Lynn cross. Barnton is, like Melbourne, a coarse-headed, lengthy, rough style of horse, good for any kind of small light mares ; in fact, just the horse to stop gaps when a breeder cannot quite see his way. He is deep in the rib, and rather narrow like the mare, whereas Voltigeur has more of the Blacklock round-ness of rib.

Voltigeur was originally sent up as a yearling to Doncaster ; but as the two hundred *bonâ fide* bid came a hundred short of the reserve, he was sent back to Hart until after the Catterick meeting of the next year, and then came to Aske, where Boone broke him. He got an over-reach the day before he left Hart, and he very nearly gave himself another while running for the Derby. Nearly all his stock are whole-coloured browns, with very springy pasterns, and that thickness of neck which renders them—as in Vedette's and Skirmisher's two and three-year-old days—rather uneven to the eye. Vedette's action was very beau-tiful, and became nearer the ground in his third season ; but up to the very last day George Abdale had him, he could never exactly make out where he was lame.

The Race of Owners for Nat. Semiseria was the quickest of Voltaire's stock that was ever trained ; and she proved it in a very decisive way over Richmond, when she beat The Cure from "the Grey Stone in." Her greatest feat of speed was, however, at Newmarket, in her match with Queen of the Gipsies. It was made at the Rooms over-night : and then, like the rival attorneys of old, when they raced, as the legend goes, to Garrow's chambers, it became a question who could get Nat, as both had him in their eye when they fixed the weights. Mr. Jaques slipped up town first, and, finding he had gone to bed, flung some gravel up at his window. In a minute or two, Nat's solemn night-capped head was seen from behind the blind ; and as business was evidently meant, he opened the window to inquire the cause. "Nat, I want you for a match to-morrow." "*What's the weight?*" "Seven stone nine." "*Then I can do it, sir. Good night!*" was the whole of the colloquy ; and Nat resought his couch. He had scarcely pillowed his head when the gravel battery was heard to open once more with redoubled force, and again he was on the floor. This time it was Mr. O'Brien, almost breathless with haste ; and Mr. Jaques, ensconced in the shadow of a wall hardly fifty yards off, heard these "Voices of the Night." "Nat, I want you for a match to-morrow." "*What for?*" "The Queen of the Gipsies." "*Against what?*" "Semiseria." "*I'm engaged!*" and down went the window. Great was the dismay of "The Traverser" on finding himself thus beaten by Yorkshire, when he thought he had managed it so nicely ; but Nat had vanished, and he had only the stars to consult on the matter. In short, turf history can afford no parallel to it except in the case of an eminent bill discounter, when after having had his mare so specially prepared for a great spring handicap, he learnt for the first time, a season or two subsequently, from the lips of a "young friend" (who did not know his *nom de course*), that the fact of his having specially sent "my horse to knock that fellow's mare heels over head" was the reason why the painful word "*fell*" was affixed to her name.

In the morning, however, Mr. O'Brien got it his own way; and as Cartwright was very anxious to ride Semiseria, on whom he had been fourth in the Cambridgeshire, Mr. Jacques consented to give Nat up. His commissioner, the late Mr. Dykes, spluttered so dreadfully that all the offers against her were snapped up before he could get out his "*I-I-I'll take you.*" Hence he had to operate for himself; and thinking it a rare good thing, 1000 to 300 was the last bet he laid on her. Both jockeys had orders to come through the half mile; and as neither got a pull from end to end, a tremendous finish just ended in favour of the Northern mare by a head. They thought her glandered in the winter, and she was put into a box at John Scott's by herself; but it proved a false alarm, and she was brought out fresh enough to run away with Nat in the next Chester Cup. Mildew, her second foal, was a very handsome and promising colt; and he left everything half-way in his trial at Richmond, and beat Lady Evelyn at evens before the Derby, for which Mr. Jaques stood to win 175,000*l.* on him. Still he was only fifth to Voltigeur, and became so lame after his St. Leger canter that Marlow brought him back to the enclosure.

The Semi-Franc Farce. Semiseria's first foal, Semi-Franc by St. Francis, was barely fourteen hands, and not only ran in a big pasture all summer, but was there still when Mr. Jaques went to Doncaster, ready to pay forfeit for him in the North of England Produce Stakes. However, when he got there, he met Lord Glasgow, who asked after the little horse; adding, "*Belus is in such a state, that if yours is only living I'll guarantee him winning.*" A messenger was accordingly despatched to Easby; and a nice job they had, with lanterns, to find "the pony" on the fearfully wet evening of the Dutchman's Leger day. He

was walked to the rail, and groomed all the way in
the railway-box, to get him a trifle into order. Then
arose another difficulty, as to who was to ride him.
Nat, who remembered his jump on the Iron Duke
at Manchester that May, quite disdained the job, and
told Winteringham that he "wasn't going to have any
harlequin tricks played off on *him.*" One, if not two
more declined, under the impression that they were
going to appear in the "comic countryman" line ; and
at last John Sharp consented to try, if they would give
him twenty pounds, win or lose. The sum was accordingly promised ; and the horse gave him plenty
to do, as he was all over the course up to the hill.
Going down the hill, John obeyed his orders to
the letter, and set him off at his best pace, about
fourteen miles an hour, which soon brought Belus to
a dead stop. At first the ring thought it was coining
money to lay 100 to one on Belus , and then they
rubbed their eyes, and never could exactly make out
how the horses seemed to change places, as if by magic.
Poor Frank Butler's very last Doncaster ride, on Grey-
leg, who had been fetched from Newmarket on the
Friday morning, was equally absurd ; and the St.
Leger course in both instances was happily got over
in something under fifteen minutes ! After his victory,
Semi-Franc retired from public life ; and Semiseria
became the property of the Prince of Orange for five
hundred guineas.

Buzzard was a very nice brown bay, the property
of Mr. Lambton. He was too near for a Blacklock,
and wore a leather cap, in his races, over his blind
eye.

Brutandorf, who was by Blacklock out   Brutandorf.
of a Pot-8-o's mare, was a sad pheasant ;
and Bill Scott warmly vowed, when he got off him,
after the St. Leger, that when he called on him, "the
great mucky beggar rolled his tail, and would have no
more of it." He was a gluttonous, thick-fleshed horse

and very shabby and peculiar behind the saddle, although he filled up there as a stallion. His stock generally did well in their two-year-old season, and one of them, Bounce, ran the four-year-old Emancipation to a head, and was obliged to be entered as a three. His coachers were wonderfully fine, and, like Touchstone, he was never known to get a chestnut. He was so idle at one time that a thirty-six hour day would not have sufficed him; but Dick Stockdale went at him with a cudgel after the fashion of the Arabs, with such hearty good will, that, on emerging from the stable, his face was quite maroon with his exertions, and the process had not to be repeated. Arctic, out of a cart-mare by Old Noseley, was the best of his half-bred nags, and was sold for 80*l.* to Mr. Sidney Herbert, who let a farmer have him, under the impression that he had got a bad bargain; but the new owner begged to send his horse, some months after, to gallop with Percy's lot; and made such an example of them, that they were fain to get him back at a good ransom.

Physician. Among Brutandorf's sons were Physician and Hetman Platoff. The former was a short round horse, and as complete a nag stepper as ever answered to a saddling-bell. At two years old his smart little fillies (of whom Maria Day was the sweetest and the best), could slip away from almost anything, but the second season generally found them out. The Cure, although he did not inherit size on either side, had quite enough of it himself, and a good deal of quality and length to boot; but he required to be very plump, to look his best. He was neglected for a long time, and got rather buried in Scotland, till the dam of Warlock brought him out with Lambton. He got them small, and this is the case with his half-breds as well as thoroughbreds. Underhand is elegance itself, but he is only fifteen hands, while El Hakim at four years old was

still less. The largest and perhaps the best was M.D.;
but he was delicate as a two-year-old, and only just
coming, when the season was over. He was bought
on the St. Leger day; and Mr. Parr was so determined to have him, that with all his high Saucebox
hopes, he waited to bid for him when scarcely four
others were left with Mr. Tattersall. Being the only
bidder he got him at his reserve price, 120 guineas, and
Apathy for 100 guineas. The one was sold, after
winning a race or two, for a thousand guineas; and
the other looked quite as dangerous as Blink Bonny,
when his leg gave way after crossing the road.
Templeman had been unusually anxious about
his mount, and he lived in Benhams for three weeks
before, in order that he might ride the horse at
exercise.

Hetman Platoff was out of a Comus mare, and
though stout enough himself under killing weights,
his stock, save and except Cossack, were seldom fond
of a distance. Cossack was suspected of the same
malady, but his running for the Cesarewitch as a
three-year-old, under 8st. 6lbs., and his Goodwood
Cup finish with Nancy, told a different tale. In
their heads many of his stock go quite back to
Blacklock, but they have rather prick ears, and it
is just a doubt in our minds whether they are not
rather overtopped.

In respect of this short prick ear, they   Velocipede.
bore no small resemblance to Velocipede,
the greatest of the line, whose plate encircling his
portrait may well be the first that meets the eye, as
you enter John Scott's yard at Whitewall. This king
among horses had a rough, vulgar, Roman head, with
a white blaze, and a flesh-coloured nose, which he
transmitted to all his stock, the great majority of
which took after him in colour and marks. His
Juniper dam, half-sister to Camarine, the great mare
of the South, was not more than fifteen hands, but

his own standard was just above sixteen, and Quiver was by far the smallest thing he ever got. Mr. Ridsdale gave eight hundred guineas for his brother George IV. as a yearling, but he turned out a most sorry bargain ; and a mere foil for his elder brother. His finest daughter, Queen of Trumps, was a bad beginner ; and if you watched her gallop, she went lame first with one leg and then with the other, till you became convinced that she was " lame all round." One small knot on Velocipede's off fore-leg, half-way between the knee and the fetlock, pressed on the inner tendon, and made him the magnificent cripple he was, and oddly enough, as if to knock over all theories, his whole chestnut leg was the one affected. After his fatal trial Scott and George Izard hardly left him for three weeks, night or day, and George never ceased applying lotions to it, as the last hope of getting him round. He would let them do it as he lay, but the mischief was too deeply seated, and there was no more dependence to be placed on the sinew, though the heart was never found to falter.

Velocipede's Stud Days and Death. When he went first to the stud, he was stationed at Ainderby, which seems on a clear day to nestle beneath the range of the Hambleton hills, and " commanded the whole country " for two seasons. The village were not unmindful of the high honour of his stay, and his portrait still creaks mournfully on the ale-house sign. And well they might be, as a four-thousand offer from the foreigners was promptly refused. Eventually he passed out of Mr. Armytage's hands into Dr. Hobson's, and stood at the Shadwell Lane Paddocks near Leeds. John Scott often came over to see him, and "*Ah! if I had only such a four-year-old as you, with sound legs, I could break the world,*" fell more than once on his groom Berridge's ear, when the two old friends met in the box. His last public appearance, so to speak, was at Doncaster in 1846, whither he accompanied some

Melbourne and Sheet Anchor yearlings of his owner's, "just to let the world have another look at him." And what audiences he had, too, as he paced in the ring near the Pond, or convoyed his young friends down the lime avenue, back to the Rockingham! Even Bill Scott in his Jim Crow hat, which had two wheat ears in that morning, stepped off the causeway as he was going out to waste (with his two aide-de-camps, lay and clerical, behind him) just to give him greeting. It was none less hearty than his elder brother's, and forcible as usual. "*You old beggar! if I'd you a three-year-old, I'd straight them all if I can't on my own horse; but I think I can with him.*"

Two years afterwards he quitted Yorkshire, and took a four days' journey to his owner's farm at Corney Hall in Cumberland, and there in 1850 he came to his end. Dropsy had set in, with chronic disease of the lungs, and his respiration became so difficult, that he could be heard all over the yard. Non-civilization has been described as being ten miles from a lemon; and here was the dying crack, twenty-one miles from a vet. His body filled, and he became so unsightly and oppressed that he dare not lie down, for fear of not being able to get up again, and propped himself against the wall, as well as he could, refusing all corn for three weeks. His last foal, however, dated from a fortnight before his death, and was a big white-legged chestnut, who ran in a gig at Whitehaven. Matters became so bad, that the groom determined to kill him on his own account, and he led him out to a hill just overlooking the Irish Channel, where he had dug his grave in the sand; but his heart misgave him, and he could not handle his gun. A tailor was accordingly summoned from a neighbouring farm-house, and he soon broke the thread of life, with as little remorse as he would a cat's, and the mighty heart and little prick ears were still. Berridge issued from behind his wall,

at the report; and ere his old favourite was tumbled
into his grave, curiosity determined him, to probe his
malady to the source.   Taking out his gully, he ripped
open his chest, and nearly half-a-dozen pailfuls of
yellow fluid, between water and oil, came away. And
so the great chestnut champion, father of Queen of
Trumps, and grandfather of Canezou, died at last, in
his twenty-sixth year.

The Sons of   The stud fame of Pot-8-o's, a chestnut
Pot-8-o's.   son of Eclipse, was by no means doubtful or chequered, and began in 1793, with Waxy,
who was out of Maria by Herod.   The story went
that it was originally intended to call his sire "Potatoes," and the idea struck one of the lads as so
ludicrous, when Lord Abingdon first told his trainer
of it, in the stable, that he burst out a laughing.   His
lordship good humouredly took up a piece of chalk,
and said, " I'll give you a crown, my boy, if you can
spell the word on the corn-bin." He wrote the
"*Pot-8-o's*" accordingly, and although some stuck to
the Pot-oooooooo, the lad's version was latterly
adopted. Waxy, the idol of his trainer Robson's
heart, was a very beautiful, one-eyed, lengthy style of
horse, with a great deal of the Arab in his look.   His
quality was superb, and with him, so to speak, it came
in the highest degree into English blood stock.   He
in his turn was put to Penelope by Trumpator, out of
Prunella by Highflyer, and this union of the Darley,
Byerley, and Godolphin strains was crowned by the
births of Whalebone and Whisker at the Duke of
Grafton's paddocks, at Euston, in the days when his
brother, Lord Henry Fitzroy, was in command, in
1809-18. Waxy's stock won the Derby four times,
thrice for the Duke of Grafton, and the Oaks three
times ; and with Whisker and Minuet, His Grace
fairly swept the Epsom board.

Whisker.   In those days the Northern and
          Southern breeds were kept very dis-

tinct, and the rich bay Whisker was the first of the
Southern cracks who was sent North, and pitched his
tent near Catterick. The racing circuits too had little
to do with each other ; and there must have been a
very great end in view, to tempt the horses off the
one to Epsom, or off the other, across the Trent to
York or Doncaster. Many Northern men never came
farther south than Newmarket, which they reached by
a weary post, or jolt with their saddle-bags, through
the fens of Lincolnshire and the Isle Ely ; and one of
them, a Mr. Cornforth, who performed that journey
regularly three times a year, for nearly half a century,
had not even once the curiosity to ride on to London.
When they did get Whisker there, the Yorkshire and
Durham men, led by the Duke of Cleveland, dipped
pretty deeply into him ; and he left The Colonel for
Mr. Petre, Memnon for Mr. Watt, and Emma for Mr.
Bowes. Whisker was as near perfection in look as
anything could be, with the exception of being a little
calf-knee'd ; and he seemed equally likely to get a racer,
hunter, machiner, or hack. If a departed horse-dealer
had seen him he would have once more dictated to
his daughter as she sat, pen in hand, " The shadow of
him on the vall is vorth all the money I axes ; he can
pick up his fut and go and catch a bird."

The Duke of Leeds loved his blood even more than
Shuttle's, and Tom Pierse and his father Billy Pierse
thought Swiss (who was out of a Shuttle mare, and
savaged his boy so severely in the Belle Isle paddock,
that his leg had to be taken off), one of the very best
two-year-olds he ever trained. The Whisker blood
has descended through The Colonel and Chatham in
the male line, to Woolwich, who, considering his jady
sire and Actæon dam, was a perfect wonder for a
distance ; and through Economist, to Harkaway and
King Tom. It was always Mr. Herring's habit to
submit his St. Leger sketch of St. Leger winners to
His Majesty through Jack Ratford. When The

Colonel was sent in he received a special enquiry
back with the sketch, to ask if he had flattered him
at all, and when he returned, as answer, that he had
not, the King never rested till he bought him.
" *Buy, buy* " (like the " *Run, run* " of Lord Berners to
his trainer when he came, over night, to beg that
Phosphorus might not start for the Derby)—was all
the commission he would deign give. At the royal
sale Mr. Tattersall thought it such a shame that
the French should get him for a thousand guineas
that he bid fifty guineas more and bought him for his
own stud farm. Setting aside Emma, the Whisker
mares have always been out of the common way.
Liverpool, Tearaway, Euclid, Knight of the Whistle,
The Era, Mango, Cotherstone, Meteor, Mowerina,
Mundig, and Theon are all out of them ; and his
daughter Catherina, who ran for 171 races, was at the
stud in the thirtieth year of her age.

The Sons of   Whalebone was as shabby to the eye
Whalebone.   as old Prunella herself. He had rather a
Turkish pony look, and was broad and strong, with a
shortish neck. His own feet grew very pumiced, and
his mares lost their speed early. Unlike Whisker,
it is on his sons that he has to rely; and Camel,
Waverley, Sir Hercules, Defence, and Stumps, in
each of whom respectively his blood has united with
Selim, Sir Peter, Wanderer, Rubens, and Delpini,
have proved it quite as elastic as his name. There
are scarcely any Stumps mares left, and we met with
almost the last of this lily-white clan at Sir Tatton's
and Mr. Parr's, last year. Save and except a beautiful Shorthorn heifer, made up for show, we know of
nothing quite so beautiful in nature, or so effective in
a painter's fore-ground. The line of Defence, who
was rather thick and cobby-looking, has to trust to
its mares now, from which Hero, Old England,
Andover, Turnus, and Pyrrhus the First sprang.
Waverley, whose head and neck helped off rather

light fore-legs, most probably begot Don John, who showed not a little temper in his stall at John Scott's, where he had a see-saw style of trying to get on to your toes, and then putting you below the manger, which Henry Bradley, who stuck to him through all his training, was obliged perpetually to guard against. He was a creeping goer, with great propelling power, playful at exercise, and had two big spavins at last. It is said that in America he got sadly neglected, scarcely going out for exercise for weeks together, and died not many months after his arrival.

His price was two hundred; but he was dear at that, as he did not leave a single "colt" (the name they give to fillies as well as colts there) behind him. Waverley's other son, The Saddler, out of a Castrel mare, still lives in Footstool; and the odd-looking Mortimer by Fitzallen by The Saddler, who ran forty times before Mr. Parr got him for 200*l.*, would have hit Mr. Davis for 27,000*l.* if he had only got through for the Chester Cup. He was a sluggish style of horse, and Fordham, who could then ride under five stone, could hardly spur him. The Provost was also by The Saddler, but there is little to remind us of him save a few mares. Hybla, the dam of Mincemeat and Kettledrum, is a fine specimen of them; her hind-legs are beautiful, but her fore ones are rather nipped in at the elbows, as both The Provost's and Tomboy's were.

But among The Saddlers, we must not forget the rare old Inheritress. She was   Inheritress.
a big little one, with good ribs, a straight head and neck, and a tail rather high set on. Her original price was a hundred and fifty, and perhaps her finest race was with Sweetmeat at York. Nat got the best of the fifty yards of very deep ground near the distance, and that just settled the matter by a head. Horses generally run well on particular courses. Rataplan liked a little country one; Ellerdale delighted in

York, and Fisherman in Chester, but it was no matter
to Inheritress where she ran, provided it was not Newmarket. The dead expanse of the heath seemed
quite to scare her, and she stood and trembled at the
post till the spurs and a couple of strokes from Sim's
whalebone, which he was sadly loth to inflict on such
a pet, roused her from her dreamy state, although it
could not stir her heart. In after years, Birdcatcher
quite hated her. It was the first time he had ever
shown such daintiness, and when he could be got to
notice her, it was not only a case of "Strangers with-
draw," but even the groom was obliged to retire, and
apply his eye to the key-hole. As might have been
expected, the produce was wretched enough. Touchstone had also a great objection to young mares; and
Assault not merely disliked (for that trait is common
enough), but used to regard it as a perfect insult when
any, be the age what it might, were brought to him,
with satin coats or smelling of the stable. In fact, he
cut up so rough with his groom, when one of Lord
Glasgow's came to him straight from the racing
stables, that the former was fain to save himself and
her from being worried alive, by tying him up as
quick as he could, and producing some highly artistic
efforts in light and shade, with glazing from a friendly
dung-heap, which quite satisfied the little connoisseur's
eye.

Sir Hercules. We need the tongue of old Forth,
seated in his white hat on a summer
evening, under the pleasant shade of his trees at
Mitchel Grove, to tell the story of Sir Hercules and
his stock aright. There was none that the old man
clung to so fondly; and he spoke of his son Hyllus,
whom he sadly wanted to buy back from the Messrs.
Litchwald after he went abroad, as the horse of his
heart, and vowed that he would never have been
beaten, if he could have had a race run exactly to suit
him. The failure of Sting preyed on him to the last

he said, " I had never called on nature too much, and yet he went wrong, I couldn't tell how." There were few horses in his long career that he had studied so closely. Jaques was the last he fancied, and he gave him away to Mr. Parr, with an injunction to run him for the Goodwood Cup, but he dislocated a pastern in his preparation. With all his acuteness, he was a man of very great prejudice, and seemed often to speak of training a horse to win a great race, without any reference to the field he might have to meet. He turned very nervous during Foig-a-Ballagh's St. Leger, when some one told him that Harry Bell was only lying third or fourth below the distance. " Confound the fellow," we heard him say, " I told him to come along, we'll be beat for want of a pace." Ireland has had the best of Sir Hercules, and both Birdcatcher and Foig-a-Ballagh were out of a Bob Booty dam.

Birdcatcher, who was a hard-puller, and very fretful and difficult to train, would stay a long course; but his stock, who invariably carry the Sir Hercules crest in the shape of a few grey hairs at the root of the tail, rather inherit his fine dash of speed, than his staying powers. He stood over a good amount of ground, but he seldom got any thing so long as himself. All his stock were very taking and gay as yearlings, though rather short, on long legs, a little drooping behind, but with capital back couplings. He invariably got them bright golden chestnuts; and if one happens to be a bay, it has a good allowance of white about it. Mr. Jaques paid as high as 800*l.* for him one season, when he earned 1750 guineas, and got Saunterer and Augury for his hirer as well. After trying so long for a crack, he unluckily parted with the pair for 50 guineas each, by auction, as foals at York, and John Osborne, who loved the blood nearly as much as the late Mr. Stephenson, refused, it was said, a thousand guineas for Augury. At Newmarket in 1852, he had only six

blood mares, but Habena and Warlock did not make
Mr. Disney regret the change from Easby, where he
then returned for four seasons more. Owing to a
whim of Mr. Disney's, his turf career was very short,
but unusually brilliant. He gave Harkaway 20lbs.
for his year, in a mile, and was only beaten a head;
and he left his horses outside the distance in the mile
and three-quarters Peel Cup, and was never pulled up
till he had gone a mile further. In fact, as the lad
said—"*I had to clap into him to stop him.*" His
hunters have always been nearly mature jumpers to
begin with; and on the turf, in 1841-58, he had 318
winners of 685½ races, making 110,568*l.* in all. One
fact, and a very important one, remains to be added,
that he has realized for his owner, at the stud, no less
than 7737*l.* 15*s.*

A cross with an Economist mare first brought him
into especial notice with the slim, neat, and savage
Baron. Pocahontas's Birdcatcher filly, Ayacanora,
was rather slight and small in the bone; but she put
her own substance on to her sons Stockwell and
Rataplan. Both these horses began to fine very much
after four years old, up to which point they were unusually coarse; but Stockwell's stock, as far as we
have seen, show great quality and finish as yearlings,
and neither his nor Rataplan's, as a general thing, have
quite the bone or size we expected, while Rataplan's
have his peculiar short drop on the quarter. Harlock
believed Stockwell to be as good as ever he had been,
when he was put out of training, and he was always
much the more resolute horse of the two.

Rataplan.   Once in form, Rataplan could keep
there, and did not require much work.
He liked hard ground; and his game, when the pace
was strong, was to lie well away. Weight was as little
to him as it was to Longbow, and his performance for
the Manchester Cup under 9st. 8lbs. was decidedly his
best. It was quite a sight to see Prince stroking and

talking to him, as they followed the leaders; but in a hard struggle home, he was rather ungenerous, unless he had quite the best of it, and that small picket ear and narrowness between the eyes made him much too cute and suspicious. People may talk about an intelligent head, but horses may be often too cute in that organ. He did not come quite so often as Fisherman, as the latter only walked for a couple of days, then took long gallops for two more, and was all ripe and ready for another start with " *Garge*," who was never to be seen awaiting the arrival of Mr. Parr, on the railway-platform, in "a state of sanguine despondency" about *him.* Fisherman became Mr. Parr's for five hundred at two-years-old. He did not win once in his six starts that season, but his new owner argued that if such a great leggy frame could " act" at all then, he must do wonders as he grew down.

The Chanticleers have always been Birdcatcher's Stock. short, and at one time they were thought rather bad-hearted as well. They are, however, a kind which require patience; often pretty good as two-year-olds, but still oftener improved by keeping. In fact, the whiter they get, the better they get; and we never saw any animal undergo such a thorough change in his looks as Lord Alfred did, between two and four. Hurworth, who was bought for 1500 guineas, and sold the year after for fifteen, was out of a Hetman Platoff mare; and so were Knight of St. George and Daniel O'Rourke, the lengthiest and most compact of the Birdcatcher family. The former cannot be above fifteen hands; but Daniel, who was only fourteen-three when he won the Derby, is now barely half an inch below fifteen-two; and all his wild Malton tricks are gone. He gets his foals of a darker chestnut than the Birdcatchers generally are, and all with backs and legs of iron. His own legs are perfection this way, and as you look down his back, it seems as cloven as a ram's. He reminded us most of a sort of lesser edition of Pantaloon, and has none of that bulky grossness which so many stallions arrive at in the course of a couple of seasons. Womersley, who united so well at Sledmere, with the blood of " Sleight" (as Snarry terms him), was out of a Touchstone mare. He could stay remarkably well, as nearly all his stock have done, and Peck always attributed his difficulties with him to a lump forming between his thighs, which seemed like a callous boil, and interfered so much with his action as to render it almost impossible to train him.

None of the Birdcatcher stock have, however, stayed better than Yellow Jack, who had a good stain of Liverpool blood to help him, and he did what horse has never yet done, and hardly ever will again—stand a strong preparation and run second for the Two Thousand, Chester Cup, and Derby. His legs were never equal in substance to his top; but as trainers say, " they never break their legs if they're good enough." Considering his price he was wonderfully lucky, when we consider the fate of the 1800-guinea Lord of the Hills ; and the 1010-guinea Voivoide. His sale seemed to take every one by surprise in 1854, but Chantrey by Touchstone had been bought in for a thousand guineas only seven years before, the cautious Mr. Gully giving the last *bonâ fide* bid of 980 guineas. Warlock was as delicate as horse could be in his training days, and very short and jumped up in his first two seasons; but still there is something very corky about him now, and if he had only been a chestnut, he was the truest type of what Birdcatcher almost invariably gets.

Touchstone.   " The cart-horse quartered Camel" can fairly challenge Sir Hercules for the Whalebone wreath, with the two own brothers, Touch-stone and Launcelot. They were pretty nearly struck from the same die, but the latter was perhaps the biggest of the two, and did not show so much quality.

The curious growth of Camel's quarters was owing to his having reared and fallen back as a yearling, and another fall of a different kind made him eventually useless. Touchstone was hardly fifteen two, and the roots of his ears were quite his coarsest part. He was alike good for speed and staying; and galloped wide behind as many stayers do, but he wanted very fine riding, and would swerve if his jockey raised his whip. Calloway tried to dodge him, by changing his whip hand behind his back, as he followed Usury up the Mostyn mile; but the horse saw the movement, and was across the mare's track in an instant. Long gentle sweats were his mode of doing work, and one of John Scott's most elaborate recollections is, the way in which he staved off from him a threatened attack of black jaundice. His mares were generally low in the shoulder, and somewhat flat-sided, and hence in both these points the Blacklock blood was a corrective.

The short-shouldered Caravan was Caravan. another of Camel's sons, but he was an idol with no one but Isaac Day; who in spite of some undue prejudices, which would make him stick season after season to a cripple (one of which never lay down for three years), he had few equals either in training a racer, or riding some of those hunters for whom price was no object, over the stone walls of the Heythrop and Vale of White Horse. Had Lord George lived there is no doubt that he would have trained for him ; and "No relation, but always the best of friends," used to be his constant answer when any one asked him if he wasn't own brother to John Day. " *You* didn't win," was his only reply to Pavis, when he saw him after Caravan's Derby, and he never believed that anything ought to have beaten him. In fact, years after old grey Isaac had skimmed over the dirt at Shrewsbury, while Caravan laboured behind him up to his hocks, he would be seen unconsciously nodding his

head and repeating to himself as he sat, "*Isaac beat Caravan—Isaac beat Caravan*," as if he could never completely master the fact.   His highest ambition was to
win the Chester Cup, and he always said that it was
the worst day of his life when Caravan beat Harkaway
over that course, as the handicappers would give him a
chance no more.   In the Houghton Meeting of '41 he
was in his greatest force with Tamburini and Vulcan,
the latter of whom the other Days, who had charge of
him between the meetings, did not consider good
enough to beat old Wardan, much less their Melody.
The party dropped fifteen thousand on Melody;
as in fact they knew of everything in the race but
Vulcan, whose jockey was simply ordered to lie in
front.

Orlando.   It would be strange if Touchstone had
                been able to counteract all the softness of
Vulture in Orlando, whose own action, which is very
straight from his fore legs, did not give us a great
notion that he was a stayer, and certainly as a general
thing his stock are fondest of a mile.   We never tired
of looking at him, as he stood at ease in his box,
resting his near hind foot, and showing the rich
folds of that beautiful muscular neck, as he turned
his high-bred forehead round, and looked with that
fine but dim eye at his visitors.   He was rather light
in his fore ribs, and short from the withers to the
shoulder point; but still there was little to find fault
with in his shoulders, although they may, perhaps,
have been a trifle upright.   Teddington was remarkable in every way, and, in fact, he has always been a
paradox to us in training, though he has proved beyond
doubt already that he is a very clever filly getter.   We
never saw anything more fit and beautiful when he
came out to meet Stockwell for the championship in
the Ascot Cup; and nothing more miserable four
months after, when Taylor sent him off after his
Cesarewitch defeat, on his last solitary and fatal walk,

to the four mile stables, for the Whip. His shoulders were short, and yet he was able to get up a hill ; and he turned his toes out, and yet he got well down a hill. The quickest horses invariably turn their toes out (in fact if they are broad-chested, there is no chance of getting speed without it) and there was a good deal of truth in the retort of Col. Peel's lad to a betting man as he was leading Fantastic to the Heath, *" Turn his toes out, indeed ; he'll make you turn your toes out before he's done with you."* With Teddington, if we remember rightly, it was the near one that went most out, and with Wild Dayrell the off one.

It was to Eaton that old Emma, five times over, took her eight days' journey from Streatlam, through Kirby Stephen and Warrington ; and Cotherstone and Mowerina, the dam of West Australian, were the best rewards of her toil. Seven years before, she had thrown her first Derby winner Mundig, to the game coarse Catton, who was great even in an age of four milers, and would run every yard of the way. The chestnut was the biggest and thickest she ever had, slovenly in his style, and with very great hips. Emma herself was a chestnut, low and long, and half-an-inch under fifteen-two, but not so big in her limbs as the dappled-bay Gibside Fairy. She died in her twenty-seventh year, quite worn out. At night she had taken her mash as usual, and then she had struggled to the door, where she lay stretched out and cold, with her head on the threshold, when Isaac Walker came in the morning. Her form still flourishes in the Cotherstone banner, which Mr. Herring painted for Mr. Bowes after the Derby of that year. Cotherstone himself is in the centre compartment with Bill Scott up; while Whalebone, Camel, and Touchstone on one side, and Whisker, Gibside Fairy, and Emma on the other, gracefully encircle him, with the Streatlam coat of arms. America also

The Streatlam Paddocks.

got its most beautiful importation in her eldest Cat-
ton-begot son Trustee, who ran third for the Derby,
and passed into the Duke of Cleveland's hands. She
has no monument, but they still point out where
Queen Mab, the daughter of O'Kelly's Tartar mare,
who was said to have foaled her when she was thirty-
six, lies under a thorn-tree, near the house, along with
Remembrancer and Pipator.

Four Derby winners, and one of them a breaker of
the double spell, left Walker's hands in eighteen years,
and their portraits, by Mr. Harry Hall, each within a
horse-plate, hang in pairs on two of the boxes. The
paddocks themselves are shaded by high holly hedges,
which John Smith planted ; and there is nothing to
disturb the quiet of the yearlings, save when a mighty
cock-pheasant rises, startled from the neighbouring
brake, and comes whirring through. Six brood mares
were in an outlying paddock, headed by Mowerina,
the remnant of old Emma's race, and who bore the
last foal to Bay Middleton. John Scott's dream that
she was to go to Bay Middleton, and breed a winner
of the Derby, came to nought, as the little bay colt,
although full of promise, died before its time. She
was a great contrast in size to the Flapper, and was
rather a light unpretending mare ; slow in her racing
days, and able to go for a week, till her legs failed.
It was in order to get a little of his coarse bone, that,
in a lucky hour, it was decided to send her to Melbourne, and thence came the real " Lord of Langley-
dale," in the shape of West Australian. He was born
on April 24th, (eighteen days earlier in the year than
Cotherstone), whereas Daniel O'Rourke, in spite of his
small stature, was foaled as early as January 7th. The
" West " had very bad distemper towards the close of
the year, and wasted to a mere sickly frame-work of
skin and bone. It was quite a grapple for life or death
with him for months ; but the spring grass sent him
along, and he looked behind him no more.

And so the tide of luck and fashion Conclusion. in thorough-breds has ebbed and flowed for many a long year. The yearlings by Waxy, Whalebone, Tramp, Reveller, Emilius, Dr. Syntax, Sultan, and Velocipede, have all held sway in their turn; and then the stars of Touchstone, Venison, Birdcatcher, Orlando, and Melbourne arose, and shone with a still steadier light. It was not, how‑ ever, until two-year-old racing began to come in earnest, at Lord George's beck, that breeders looked to public, and not to private sales, and gradually, in self-defence, forced their yearlings to two-year-old estate by their second autumn. Men of the old school might well fancy it a dream, as they strolled down to the Salutation, and saw Hunting Horn or Touchwood brought out to the hammer. The dispersion of the Hampton Court stud in '37 gave a slight fillip to prices; but still three hundred guineas continued to be thought a capital bidding clencher; and it was only when the rivalry of Messrs. Crawfurd, Merry and Padwick had made the "yellow jack" so prevalent, that every breeder, big and little, considered that he had an especial mission to rear a thousand-guinea yearling.

And so at last, from post and paddock, we must pass on to hound and horn. Although we have lin‑ gered so fondly over the hosts of turf worthies and their riders, who have come forth year after year at the sound of the saddling-bell, we must still have left scores of pleasant incidents of man and horse untold. We never pass into the yard at Tattersall's without thinking, with all an author's envy, of the rich bits of character which have been dropped there, with no pen to "fix them," when the "portly York ruled in the touting dominions," and the eighteen or twenty sterling bookmakers clustered in that little room on the left, whose portals old Jonathan Bray guarded with such fidelity and valour. Three of the figures in that Newmarket match picture which Mr. Tattersall hung over the fire-place, just as he received it from the Prince Regent, were headless stumps; but there was head enough to spare in the assembly on which it looked down. "Knockings out" have lost much of their pristine vigour; a great horse now takes generally about two days to go; and there is none of the grandeur which attached to the process when those ancient heroes of metallic renown appeared upon the scene, and dealt their smashing blows.

When Ogden's day was over, "Jerry Cloves," who lost so heavily in his namesake's year, Crockford, Gully, and Tanfield, all went to the fore, with their twenty thousand to ten thousand books on the Derby; but the two Epsom events, the St. Leger, the Oatlands, the Chester Cup, and the Ascot Stakes were almost the only races which they cared to notice at The Corner. Right cautious point-dealers they were too; and 20 to 1 was the very outside they would lay against either Priam or Emilius for The Derby, when they were only colts in breaking. Crockford always wrote with his left hand, and was not so bold a better as Tanfield, of whom the saying went that "he wanted all St. James'-street to himself" when he condescended to walk down it. Peter and Dan Cloves, who were large coal-merchants, also followed in their uncle's footsteps; but they had none of his dash and daring, and were just as quiet as Jim Bland was noisy. The latter could neither read nor write, though his second wife so far instructed him in the *literæ humaniores* as to enable him to sign cheques. He could never make a note of a bet; but when he got home the list was read over to him, and no Crocker or Jedediah Buxton could have recounted more exactly what he had been doing at the betting-post. Bob Steward, of the Navy Office, was also esteemed cool and courageous; and so was Mr. Justice, though he seldom made more than a five thousand book. The Derby, Oaks, and St. Leger contented Highton's book-yearnings; and " Goose " Davis never made one at all, but laid it on hot and thick against the favourites. This was also Crutch Robinson's line; and he very seldom descended on to London from his much-loved Staley Bridge, except for the Derby and Oaks week. It would have been well for Will Ridsdale if he had been as wise; but he would try his hand in a half-and-half way, and his lop-sided book fairly beat him in the long run. And so, as the years drew on, the old betting-giants died out, save and except Mr. Gully; the younger generation adjourned to the new Subscription Rooms, and the number of bookmakers became multiplied by ten.

We would fain, too, follow the fortunes of that coach-and-four which rattled over the stones each Friday before Doncaster from "The Corner" along the Great North Road, with Richard Tattersall, Charles Mathews, Young the tragedian, and three or four of those bookmakers as its merry freight; and be content even with reporting their "Table Talk" on Mameluke, Velocipede, Rowton, or Priam, when they reached the half-way hostel at Alconbury Hill. Alas! *"Doncaster in four hours"* has supplanted this pleasant old custom. It has gone for ever with four-mile races and Portland Plates, where Lord Bathurst's pig-tail and the Duke of Grafton's umbrella have gone before it; the Kents no longer saddle some two-and-twenty for the Duke and Lord George, on a Ham Stakes afternoon; and boy-handicaps and "milk fever" are the characteristics of an altered time. Still, with all its faults and failings, the Arab will weary of his mare and the Kaffir of his lance before an Englishman becomes quite indifferent to "a true and correct list." National instinct makes him love to be within ear-shot of that cry at least once or twice in a summer, and none other can lure a hundred and fifty thousand, with

R

one heart and one pulse, to Epsom Downs and Doncaster Moor. Twelve years have gone by since "John Davis" became its Tyrtæus in "The Ring." He spoke proudly then of

> "The sport which Grafton loves,
> Which Spencer, Portland, Albemarle approves ;
> Which kings have fostered, and a country's pride,
> Protest who may, will never cast aside"—

and who is there to gainsay him ?

CHAPTER IV.

SCARLET.

> "Each season has its joys, 'tis true,
> And none should wisdom spurn ;
> But those who nature rightly view,
> Enjoy them in their turn ;
> The angler, racer, courser, shot—
> As each to each is borne,—
> But the season of seasons, is it not
> When the huntsman winds his horn ?"

RAMBLE THE FIRST.

Prophets of Evil.

WHEN great authorities assure us that fox-hunting is nothing more or less than "a number of horsemen riding furiously after a nasty smell," and cheerfully append their decision that "the whole thing must soon come to an end," it requires more than ordinary faith and elasticity to write upon the subject, with such words of doom in the air. Still the recollection of the scores of quiet evenings which we have spent, note-book in hand, not only with Dick Christian, but in certain snug little Nimrod shrines, from Durham to Dorset-

shire, will somehow inspire the hope that there may
be, in ages to come,

"Once more a view-holloa from old Oulton Lowe,"

and that, although Will Goodall, on "my good little
Emperor," can cheer them no more, the lineal
descendants of Yarborough Rallywood may still
challenge in Melton Spinney.

Hunting men will, doubtless, feel the scent sneer
most acutely, and for them there is no help; but we
are bound to quote in defence of the hounds the
hypothesis of the late Hartley Coleridge, that "what
seems to us merely a disagreeable smell, is perhaps to
their canine organs a most beautiful poem." Beautiful as it may be, both masters and huntsmen have
so far been unable to discover, even approximately,
the laws on which that "poem" is constructed. Earl
Fitzhardinge, after half a century in the scarlet, con-
fessed that he had learnt nothing, except in a practical
point of view, beyond what the pages of Somerville
had told him when a boy. If that was the testimony
of one who loved to walk a fox to death, and give his
cheery "*Well done. Now, that's beautiful!*" as one
of the "old Corbet sort," after minutes of puzzling,
struck the scent at last; others, less enthusiastic, may
leave the delicate scent problem to some future Isaac
Newton of the hunting field.

Will Goodall said in the last letter, Scent in Diffe-
dated April 8th, we ever received from rent Countries.
him, "I can't say that I have observed any very odd
peculiarity of scent in any part of our country; as
with a N.E. wind, and a rising glass, they will run
over any part of it, and catch their fox; but with a
west wind, which has been piercing nearly the whole
of this blessed season, we have never had a week's
good scenting weather." No one living speaks with
more authority than Mr. Farquharson, and he gives
us, as the result of his observation, that "there is no

criterion by which scent can be properly estimated."
" I have known," he adds, " a burning scent when
apparently there should have been none; and *vice
versâ*, I have known a great lack of it under the most
propitious prospects. I have seen hounds fly in a
strong *westerly* wind, which is supposed to be the
most unfavourable for scent, and I have seen them
run in all weathers and winds. There are, however,
some rules which may be considered as regulating
more or less the scent. For instance, when the quicksilver is low, the atmosphere is generally disturbed,
and in that case, if not altogether a lack of scent, it
is so fluctuating and *catching* that it varies almost
momentarily. On the contrary, however, I have
always found that when the quicksilver is steady and
settled the scent is good. The condition of hounds
has a good deal to do with their noses. Dorsetshire
cannot be called a good scenting country in a moist
season; the hills and woodlands, however, hold a
fair scent, and I was able to place my hounds so as
to suit the weather. The last season of my having
hounds, I think, was the worst I can recollect for
scent."

The Puckeridge is nearly all on the plough, and
carries no great scent, and its huntsmen generally like
to force the foxes into Essex. The Ainsty is very
uncertain, and the Hurworth is good in wet, but bad
in dry, as the clay gets as hard as a brick yard. In
the Burton country, scent is not so good as it used to
be; and the Southwold is best on the Tothill and
Greenfield side, and near the Tower on the Moor.
When the High Wold Brocklesbury country is dry it
fails; in fact, " the more rain the better, both for it
and the marshes, and up to our knees and hocks in
mud, we go best." The Berkeley country, on the
contrary, is best when dry; and the Cotswold Hills
hold a scent better than the Vale; but the latter
country knows no medium, and Harry Ayris always

loved most to have it very wet or very dry. In the Heythrop, the scent serves best in wet; and the Oxford side of the country, to wit, the Northaston side, which includes Acton's Barton and Ditchley Wood, is the worst. The Beaufort country is superior to the Heythrop, as it is richer land, and has more grass. Its Wilts side is better scenting, as the Tetbury one requires rain much oftener.

The Grafton country is first rate, as it has so much grass land; and the Oakley is pretty fair. The Pytchley country is generally favourable to scent, with the exception of the northern part adjoining Bedfordshire, and Badby Wood, which is notoriously the worst scenting covert in the hunt. Woodhay is the best side of the Craven country, and the Tedworth is very moderate as a whole, especially on Salisbury Plain, where the sheep make matters still worse. Still the Pewsey Vale is good, and so are Roist Woods and Savernake Forest; but they all want wet. In the Quorn country, the Six Hills and Forest side is capital, and the foxes wilder. In Cheshire the scent differs very little in any part; but in Shropshire, whenever there is scent on the Haughmond Hill, there is none in the valley; and the reverse holds good as well. The Woore side of North Staffordshire and the Market Drayton side, where they join Sir Watkin, is the best; Bishop's Burnt Woods is favourable to scent generally; but Jurymanton Old Park, near Trentham, which is full of young oaks, on a gravelly soil, holds very little except in wet. The Cheshire side of Sir Watkin's country is chiefly grass, and holds a rare scent; while the Shropshire ride is just the reverse, and, without rain at least once a week, the sport is most doubtful. The Old Berkshire shows most sport in a dry season. Becket, Coleshill, Buscot, and Farringdon parts are generally good after Christmas, but the scent in its woods is always remarkably variable. In Tar Wood, they sometimes cannot run a

yard, and yet at other times kill their brace of foxes
without a check; and in Cokethorpe again, we have
known them run all day with scarcely any scent, till
the fog rose in an October evening, and then account
for him in twenty minutes. On Appleton Common
they can carry a head in any weather, while Tubney
Wood, just over the next ditch, is the worst scenting
wood in the world.

Nimrod the Second. The first great practical hunter we
have traces of in England, is "the brave
Burrington," and we only hit on him in a 1733
"Essay on Hunting." The author of it "presumes on
pardon from the loquacious world, if among so many
treatises, vindications, replies, journals, craftsmen, hyp-
doctors, and lay preachers, the press be borrowed a
day or two for a plain essay on the innocent recrea-
tion of us country squires." A fox, it is true, lies
curled up at the end of his Essay; but he runs hare
throughout. Burrington is evidently the Dagon of
his idolatry. It was he, and he alone, who by his
marvellous knowledge of roads and morasses, caused
"the celerity of the march of the Prince of Orange;"
and such was his iron vigour years after he had passed
his grand climacteric, that his eulogist is tempted
triumphantly to inquire, "How many Beaux, Flats,
and Spit-Frog Commission officers would he not at
that age have driven to market with his single hunting pole?"

Early Fox-hunters. Henry Fielding had, it is true, made
Reynard "drop his bushy tail" in a hunt-
ing song before 1750; still it was sound orthodoxy in
that age to hunt what first came to hand; and it was
not until some twenty years later, when old Cooper
was seen cheering Bluecap and Wanton in their five
hundred a-side match against two of Mr. Meynell's
hounds over Newmarket, that the line of demarcation
between hare and fox began to grow sharp and clear.
The Tarporley Hunt proclaimed their allegiance in

1769, and their red saddle-cloth was bound with green instead of blue, as a token. Earl Fitzwilliam had begun the year before, with Will Dean and a few hounds from the Dean of Peterborough, and then Meynell became more and more famous as the century drew to a close. "Marlborough," "Devonshire," "Thanet," "Spencer," "Arlington," Hewlins, Sheldon, Beckford, Monson, Simon Steward, Barnes, and Townshend were but lesser lights at his side; and it was years before "the race of Rutland and the nose of Yarborough" was a received axiom of kennel creed. There was Lady Salisbury, too, the *Lady Salisbury.* most renowned Diana of her day, with her dwarf fox-hounds and her sky-blue uniform, with black collars, lappels, and jockey-caps. Enthusiastic penmen were found in Herts to write up to the *Sporting Magazine* the triumphs of the lady of Hatfield, when she had run her fox to earth, after two hours and a-half at Baldock. "Out of a field of fourscore," says one in the March of '95, "her ladyship soon gave honest Daniel the go-by ; pressed Mr. Hale neck and neck, soon blowed the whipper-in, and continued indeed, throughout the whole of the chase, to be nearest the brush."

Lord Barrymore's eccentricities shone *Lord Barrymore* out as brightly in his hunting appoint- *and Colonel* ments as in everything else. The hunt- *Thornton.* ing field of Louis XIV., at Fontainbleau, was his model, and his four Africans in scarlet and silver, and with French horns, on which they wound blasts loud enough to startle every out-lying stag from his lair, kept him in music all day. The Barrymore fashion did not wholly die out with the old century, but it jumped with the humour of none save Colonel Thornton to adhere to it. He cared far more to see the Yorkshire woldsmen gaze in wonderment at his motley cavalcade, as it wound its way to Foxhunter's Hall, than for any sport he had when he got there.

Fourteen servants with hawks on their wrists, ten hunters, principally by his Jupiter, a pack of stag hounds and lap-dog beagles, and a brace of wolves, against which the farmers soon levelled a round-robin, formed the advanced guard. Two brace of pointers, and thrice as many greyhounds, headed by Major, in rich buff and blue sheets, with armorial bearings, followed in their train ; and his three eighty-guinea guns, and a box full of the plover's head feathers, with which alone he would condescend to fish, rumbled behind in the wagon.

Mr. Meynell.   Unfortunately for us, the writers of the period were much more anxious to note down such mere embroidery of sport, than to follow the sterling career of Mr. Meynell at Quorn. It pleased them better to tell how Merkin was sold for four hogsheads of claret and two couple of puppies, and how a bevy of sportsmen in consequence knew

> " Only from the hollow cask,
> How the waning night grew old,"

than how Jack Raven got his hounds away from Langton Caudle, or Glooston Wood. In 1795, it is true we find a slight notification to the effect that " Mr. Meynell recommenced his campaign in the Leicestershire Furzes ;" and further that " Sir Henry Featherstone had thirty hunters daily exercised in body clothing, near Loughboro' ;" but after that, all became so dark and drear, that we abandoned the search in despair, and determined on seeking out some living oracle, who could furnish the missing links with the past.

Our Search for   On making inquiry, we found that Tom
Tom Wingfield   Wingfield, the patriarch of huntsmen, was
the Elder.   alive, hard by the resting-place of his old master ; and before the week was out, we were at Ashbourne. To find him after that, although we knew that he was within three miles of the town, was no

easy task. The venerable ostler at the inn where
Mr. Meynell Ingram's hounds stay all night when
they come into the country, and who ought to be
quite a gazetteer on such points, vowed that he had
not seen his face, or heard his name for "twelve years
gone Christmas;" while the barber was "only new
come," and knew nothing. A jolly young butcher
was acquainted with such a man, both by sight and
name, but then warming with his subject, and coming
out of his beefy bower, he fairly laughed to scorn
the notion that the Thomas Wingfield he meant
had ever been a huntsman. He knew better, that
he did; it couldn't be that man at all we were
wanting. He, however, referred us to an adjacent
cobbler, and we asked him in that disbelieving
butcher's presence, by way of fixing the identity,
whether this old man had only one eye. The question was unfortunate, but it settled the point, as when
he looked up and answered in the affirmative, we saw,
to our sorrow, that he had only one himself. And so
toiling away up that memorable ascent, "down which"
in political memory

> "Romantic Ashbourne I glides
> The Derby dilly, with its six insides,"

we reached the road-side residence of old Tom at
last.

For a man of nearly eighty-four, he carries head
bravely. It is just thirty years since he laid aside his
horn, on Sir Thomas Mostyn resigning his hounds to
Mr. Drake; but still, with his wiry ten stone frame,
black surtout and stockings, and drab breeches, he
looked quite the ancient martinet of the kennel. We
fully unfolded our mission, and it is no fault of ours
that his features are not preserved herewith in a
wood-cut, but the ice of prejudice was too strong
for us; and though he at first consented, he backed
out on reflection. Modern hunting matters seemed

to have no charm for him. He was anxious, however, to know if Mr. Drake had taken to his
father's country; and when we informed him that he
was half through his second season, it turned out that
he had written, sixteen months before, to a relative,
requesting an answer on the point; but as he was
"the best man in the world to keep a secret," the
question might have been unanswered for years, if we
had not called in.

Meynelliana. And so we slipped with Tom into the
past, and had about an hour and five
minutes without a single check. He quite remembered the Meynell family keeping harriers, and following them with poles; but the real dawn of his
fox-hunting life was when Mr. Meynell sent for him
at ten for Quorn. There could not have been very
much of him at that date, as he not only had to ride
behind his new master with false stirrups in Hyde
Park, on account of the inconvenient shortness of his
legs, but that mighty Nimrod led him, on their very
first interview, from his study to the meat safe, and
after tying a piece of cord round his waist and thighs,
suspended him to a steel-yard, and weighed him,
a trifle under four stone. As he waxed in size and
years, the kitchen became a luckless spot to him. In
a fit of cupboard love, he went to ask the cook, Fanny
Screeton, for an apple, and as he "paused for a reply"
on the threshold, a fellow-servant shot an arrow from
one of the children's bows at him, and his eye was
irretrievably ruined. Still, he made one do double
duty, and right ably too. Lord Stamford had hounds
in those days at Bradgate Park, and Tom was specially selected by Mr. Meynell, and, to use his own
words, "placed as an ensign on John's Hill," to see
what hounds were leading when they joined packs to
draw Swithland Wood. His report was not particularly gratifying to Quorn, as he placed three of Lord
Stamford's first, and two of Mr. Meynell's second ;

then came one of Lord Stamford's, then three of Mr. Meynell's, and he cared to count no longer. Before very long he was made the hard-riding Jack Raven's second whip, while Joe Harrison was first. Joe had his work set him in the kennel, while Tom kept to the stables, and beyond the fact that Mr. Meynell bred very much from Lord Monson, and that the hounds were "a lot of coarse close hunters," he cared to say little for them.

With the Bradley Wood fox, on the contrary, he expressed the very deepest sympathy. The Bradley Wood Fox. It was his wont to break instantly at the end of the wood, towards Ashbourne, and they as regularly lost him at the end of a mile. At last they discovered that he ran the top of a hedge, and Mr. Meynell had five couple of hounds posted at that point. He accordingly went away the next time straight for the Peak of Derbyshire, and was lost near Hopton. Mr. Meynell had gone home early, and as Raven brought the hounds back to the kennel about four o'clock, he opened his dressing-room window, and ordered him to throw them into Bradley Wood once more, as he had just seen the hunted fox steal back. As to "the country people's story about a fox crossing the road before the hearse as they brought him from London," he "didn't believe a word of it ;" but this he did know, that "Mr. Meynell never killed a fox unhandsome, only that once."

We had next a turn at Lord Sefton, who put, according to Tom, much more fashion on the horses and the men at Quorn. Lord Sefton's Mastership. The green collar was kept, but the white metal buttons yielded to gilt with the Sefton crest. Two huntsmen then came on the scene, but his lordship did not choose to discharge Stephen Goodall, who had just had such a wonderful season with his hounds in Oxfordshire ; and hence it was amicably arranged that Jack Raven should be head in the kennel, and take

the cream of the country two out of the four days, and
that the heavy-weight should go into the woodlands.
His lordship bought Mr. Meynell's fifty couple, and
as Stephen had to pack up his household gods, Tom
was sent in his place to Combe Abbey to bring the
Oxfordshire fifty couple to Quorn.   They passed
through Leicester on the Good Friday of 1800, just as
the people were going into church, and Tom said to the
boiler, who was the whip that journey, " *Jack, we
shouldn't be here.*"   Lord Sefton cared very little for
hounds, but his stud was superb, and he never had
less than three horses out in a day.   Gooseberry,
Moseley, and a grey from Cheshire, which was said to
be the finest in England—all did him yeoman's service under such a crushing hamper; but Loadstone
carried him farther than any of them, and once went
so far as not to come to a dead stop till good five
minutes over the hour.   They had run from Brooksby
through Rotherby to Widmerpool, and had their fox
dead beat, after a sharp six miles, when a fresh one
jumped up from a hedge-row; and across the Vale of
Belvoir to Blackberry Hill, where it was found dead
next day at the mouth of an earth.   Half a mile from
that point, the hounds could make nothing of it, and
his lordship and Loadstone only just got to Langar.
Lord Sefton in his turn sold Quorn to Lord Foley;
but it was during the five years' mastership of the
former, that Jack Raven died, and Tom got his pro-
motion as first whip, while George Raven was made
second.

Mr. Assheton   In 1806, Mr. Assheton Smith became
Smith.   king of Quorn in his turn, and Tom rose
to the dignity of kennel huntsman, while the redoubt-
able Jack Shirley, who had never been with hounds .
before, burst on to the world from Oxfordshire as
second whip.   The pack had become sadly uneven in
Lord Foley's hands, the bitches averaging generally
from eighteen to twenty-one inches, and the dog

hounds about twenty-four. Tom never fell in very kindly with Mr. Smith's kennel notions, especially about large hounds, of which Cerberus by Charon, a very noisy one, of twenty-five inches, bred by and given to him by Lord Althorp, was the beginner. Hence he had some sore trials in this respect ; and never, perhaps, attached sufficient importance to the precept, "that speech was given us to conceal our thoughts," at least when Mr. Smith was in his drafting vein. "This Chuworth" (as he still speaks of Mr. Musters, from early instinct) often asked him why some of his favourites were seen no more, and his invariable reply was, " Because they wouldn't go into the smeuse when they were wanted to draw; that's all I know." After eight seasons Tom departed, to be kennel huntsman to "the Squire," in Nottinghamshire, where he stayed one season, and entered twelve of a litter out of Brevity before he passed on to Sir Thomas Mostyn.

Sir Thomas had principally made his pack by sending his bitches to Quorn ; and Gayman, Hermit, Ranter, and Sultan were the hounds of theirs which he most used. Hermit by Justice, from a daughter of Lictor's, got some wonderful gorse drawers, but these Hermits turned out badly ; and nine couple (including Lucifer, Lashwood, Lazarus, and Lictor, by Sultan) were entered from Lady, who at once made and marred the pack. The passion of Mr. Griff Lloyd for Lucifer was only equalled by his hunting appetite for pork-pie and purl ; and Sir Thomas himself was not one whit less attached to Lady, who ran

> " Up stairs, and down stairs,
> And in my lady's chamber,"

exactly as she chose. Still it was a general opinion, that if he had not hearkened to the parson so much as he did, in consideration of their old school-boy friendship, he would have had a much better pack of hounds latterly. Lady's picture continues to be the

best kennel-nursery one we have; and her Cleopatra
Needle monument, ten feet high, but bearing no in-
scription, is still standing in the middle of a field
close by what once were the old Bainton kennels.

Lexicon, one of the hounds in the Duke of Rutland's
pack, goes back to her; but the muteness has not
descended to him.   They were not only short of
tongue when Tom Wingfield got hold of them, but
far too quick for a bad scent, and it was mere chance
whether they had a day's sport at all.   In fact, every
hunting man who saw them, used to confirm Tom's
caustic comments, that "it was principally *our* opinion
whether it was a fox or not; *they* didn't know what
they were running half their time."   During the next
thirteen seasons, they got back their tongue by breeding from the Duke of Beaufort; but still they had
hardly enough to satisfy Mr. Drake, and he selected,
among others, stallion hounds from Mr. Warde's in the
Craven country, which were even suspected of having
too much.   It was a remarkable fact, that in Stephen
Goodall's and Ben Foote's day, they would always
pack with the Duke of Beaufort's (when they clashed
in the Heythrop country) and Lord Althorp's, but
never with the Duke of Grafton's.   In this they showed
their judgment, as the latter were as wild in the open
as they were effective in the woodlands.   Still Tom
Rose sometimes had very fine things with them, and
it was at the end of one of them that he exultingly
shouted, "I'd give five pounds to have Mr. Lloyd
here.   What *will* he say of our *fat bullocks* now ?"

Mr. Griff Lloyd.   Few men knew better about the work
of hounds than "the Parson;" and he was
sure to get to the end of every run somehow or other;
but not content with being field-master, he constituted
himself a sort of standing counsel to the huntsman.
He would never go to covert or to dinner except on
horseback, and he did not care if he rode five-and-
twenty miles to either.   So faithfully did he stick to

Sir Thomas's, that he never but once honoured Jem Hills with his company. "*Hark to the Parson!*" said George Carter, who was out that day; and well he might, as he was not in his best of humours. However, he only saw a twenty-five minutes' thing, and went home at twelve, thereby just missing a brilliant one hour and five minutes from Tackley Heath. At times he was very wild in the field, and liked to slip away with a couple of hounds, till he and Tom Wingfield got to an explanation on the point at Geddington Low Pastures. No one seems to remember how he agreed with "The great Mr. Shaw," who had ridden after Lord Moira, and then hunted his beagles in Derbyshire three days a week; but a scene between him and old Stephen Goodall at Cottesford Heath set the country dinner tables in a roar.

The hounds were in cover nearly an hour, and none of them spoke but Caroline, and she only at five minutes intervals. Stephen, who was always a perfect Job, kept cheering her each time, till at last Griff lost all patience, and dashing down one of the rides, roared "*Why don't you hold your tongue, Stephen, and come away? It's only a polecat.*" There was a deep pause, and from the depths of the wood came Stephen's rejoinder, "*Patience and water gruel, Mr. Lloyd, is both good things—have at 'em Caroline!*" and at that moment the fox was viewed away, and a capital run of an hour brought him to hand. "*This is a very fine polecat, Mr. Lloyd,*" said Stephen, as he held it triumphantly aloft, and the Parson growled out, that "We must all be mistaken sometimes."

<small>Stephen Goodall's Polecat.</small>

In spite of the weight, old Stephen had a most wonderful power of getting to hounds, and when the renowned "Ben Foote, of the Craven," was the first whip, he had only to cast the hounds twice in the season. He seemed to drop on them out of a balloon; and on the second occasion,

<small>Stephen Goodall.</small>

although it was a very fast thing of four miles, without a check, from Reeves Gorse to Fringford Hill, Stephen was just coming into the field on his white Trinket as Ben swung them round. This horse, and the chestnut Ragman were prime favourites, but neither of them carried him like King Charles. Sir Thomas bought his horse from Charles Warde, who found him quite a jade when he squeezed him at the end of the first quarter of an hour ; whereas Stephen, by holding him together, and never asking him to go beyond a certain pace, could get along with him over the best country. He was a fine goer, but did not look up to a great weight. Nothing could induce his rider to go to scale; but Mr. Harrison (who made up, with Sir Thomas, Lord Jersey, and Sir Henry Peyton, the hard-riding corps of the hunt) lured him by stratagem on to a patent weighing-chair, and saw with his own eyes the pointer standing at nineteen-four. Stephen found out that he had been done ; and as Ragman sent him over his head into a pond that afternoon, when they were going to an outlying fixture, and the bacon dripped on to his head with the heat of the public-house fire, which was lighted to rough-dry him, he retired prematurely to rest, growling that he had never gone through such a day in his life. He rode two holes shorter on the right side, and was niggling so perpetually at his horses with his short-necked spurs, that the grey contracted quite an enormous white mark, and the chestnut a black one to match.

Leviathan as he was, his knowledge of hounds and hunting was quite in accordance with his weight. The price of draft hounds has seldom been known to be so high as when Charles X. bought 150 of the biggest hounds he could in 1824-26 ; but such was Stephen's fame as a breeder and breaker, that he could always command as much as fifteen guineas a couple for his in the home market. He loved to stoop them to hare with the couples on, but never ran them in view, and

he was so very relentless on the subject of riot, that
at one time he kept a buck-rabbit, who was carried
into the kennels every morning, and became such a
veteran at the business, that it went hopping about
and nibbling the sterns of the culprits, while the whips
laid on lustily, and cried " *Ware hare! Coom, young
men, get your whips,*" became a regular morning salute;
but one of them rebelled at last so stoutly, and said
he would resign rather than do it, that the boiler ate
the rabbit, and ended the system. In his fourteen-
stone days Stephen hunted a pack in Mr. Corbet's
Shropshire country, and it was then that the old dog
jumped a park wall, and killed his fox by himself in
that memorable style, which still makes the Shropshire
roof-trees ring again in response to " *One cheer more
for the blood of old Trojan.*"

Tom Moody and Tom Sebright's Tom Moody.
father were his whips; but although he
was a very great rider, there was no hunting talent
about the former to justify the hero-worship which
song writers and painters have accorded to him. He
was a little eight-stone man, sweet tempered, but decidedly dirty, and would as soon as not keep on his
boots at a stretch, from Monday till Saturday. His
whole existence centered on hunting, and as he
could not read a word, his spare summer time
was devoted to fishing. He never scrupled to
give up his money to Mrs. Goodall when he was
sober, and beg to have it by only a shilling at a time;
but he had, like poor Tom Flint, "always a pain in
his chest" as he called it, going to covert, which did
not admit of the cold water cure; and his gigantic
horn which was filled with ale, not once, but a hundred times too often, was soon the only relic of him
above ground.

And so we leave the great first whip of Mr. Ferneley's
the eighteenth, and pass on to the still Quorn Hunt Pic-
greater master of the nineteenth century, ture.

S

whom we left at Quorn, with Jack Shirley and Dick
Burton, who came to him at fifteen, as his aides-de-
camp. Save Dick and the venerable painter himself,
every one of the fifteen whom Mr. Ferneley grouped
in the celebrated picture, which he executed for Lord
Plymouth, have dropped one by one into their graves.
Barkby Holt in the spring time of 1815 is the meet,
and the eye stretches away on the extreme right past
the church at Hungerton and Quenby Hall, to the fir-
clad Billesdon Coplow. " *Le Grand Chasseur Smit,*"
as the Parisians termed him when he went over after
the Peace, stands in the centre, by the side of his light
chestnut Gift, of which Dick Burton holds the rein,
and talks to Mr. Mills on his iron-grey ; while his
fidus Achates Tom Edge chimes in at intervals from
the back of that bony Gayman, whom so many were
wont to term "the skeleton cart-horse." Mr. Paris is
in the back-ground on the brown, for whom Lord
Alvanley gave notes untold ; and Lord Plymouth
stands leaning over Fancy, as if, although she did cost
him six hundred, he is glad to interpose her as a
barrier between himself and Lord Aylesford, when he
sees that his lordship's Beelzebub, the most vicious of
his race, has got his ears back for a round with somebody. Oxfordshire has sent its representative in Mr.
Bradshaw ; and Lord Dartmouth on his best grey
almost obscures the figure of Gamboy Henton, than
whom no better " blue coat" ever went to the fore in
" a blazing hour." On the left, Mr. Mayler, who soon
after died in the hunting field, only presents a back
view, as he sits on his brown, and attentively scans
Gift and his rider. John Moore, the father of the Old
Club in *Nimrod's* day, has got among the hounds and
servants, who are as well mounted as their master.
Jack Shirley looks down at his pets from the back of
Young Jack-'o-Lantern ; Will Beck, who was afterwards with Mr. Musters, is up on the dark chestnut
Minster, so terrible in the Vale of Belvoir; and

young Will Burton is lingering on the outside before
he takes his master's hack home, just to see the throw
off. He weighed only six stone four when he was
fifteen, and died not many months after, of consumption, at Quorn. Mr. Smith had his picture painted,
and he was wont to say, as he looked at it, year after
year, in his room at Tedworth, that he would have
given ten thousand to save him.

Will is represented holding some Mr. Smith's
couples, and the dark grey Manager Hound Fancies.
looks up wistfully in his face. This was one of the
twenty-five inch hounds by whom Mr. Smith swore,
and he was so much too fast for the rest of the pack,
that although they buckled a shot-belt round his neck,
and filled him three parts full of boiled lights, he still
defied them and their handicaps. Tom Wingfield
hated him, and if he could see him drop back into the
second flight with an afternoon fox, he never forgot to
mention it. When Mr. Smith bought Lord Foley's,
he liked them small, and bred almost entirely from
the best, with the exception of using a son of the
Fitzwilliam Collier, and going occasionally to Mr.
Musters, whose pack he purchased in 1814, for a
change of blood, and killed a brace of foxes with them
on the Forest, the first day they went out. Lord
Lonsdale's and Lord Althorp's he never sent to, and
"the great calves" was the only title he bestowed on
the Pytchley, when they were in John Warde's hands.
Glorious John returned the compliment with com-
pound interest, when he spoke of "the egg suckers,"
and the "picket-noses" of Quorn, and used a personal
simile of undoubted breadth, when he described to a
circle of friends at Tattersall's exactly what a hound's
nose ought to be. There was hardly a dog-hound at
Quorn much beyond twenty-three when Mr. Smith
chanced to clash with Lord Lonsdale's in Launde
Wood, and Jack Shirley counted twelve of Lord
Lonsdale's first away. Many thought that Mr. Smith's

hounds naturally refused to go to a strange cry; but their master's idea was, that owing to their smaller size, they were unable to jump over the long green briars, which were too close to admit of creeping, and his troubled spirit knew no rest till the bitch standard had been raised to as much over twenty-three as he could get it, and his dogs to as near twenty-five as possible.

It was thus that the Manager dynasty came in; but the neighbouring hunts did not bow to it, and Lord Althorp stuck to the twenty-three and a-half Champion by Meynell's Ranter and Pontiff, and had some fifteen litters of whelps by them one season. The short-legged Pontiff was then the pick of the pack, albeit he was a trifle throaty, and hardly able to go the pace, and his picture still hangs in the ante-room at Tedworth, along with the little half-faced Dairymaid. Tigress also nestled very near Mr. Smith's heart, although she was a confirmed hare-hunter, and scarcely ever came home with them. His love of large hounds did not desert him in Lincolnshire, and the only complaint he had against the county was, that the banks in the coverts rather let his hounds' toes down early, by the stress it put on to them in jumping. However near it might be to cub-hunting, he would allow no "singing" in his kennels, which were situated just below the Middle Station, in Lincoln, where Mr. Chaplin's hunters now stand.

Mr. Smith's Tedworth Pack. When he passed on from his beloved Langton and Wragby Woods to Penton in Hampshire, where he lived till his father's death, we find him again breeding very extensively for size from two brothers Rifleman and Reginald by Sir Richard Sutton's Trimmer. With George Carter came sixty couple of the Grafton hounds, of which no less than thirty were of the good old Goodwood badger pye. Carter had used Mr. Osbaldeston's Ferryman, Ranter, and Royalist by Ranter, as well as Mr. Drake's Sultan,

Regent, and Hampden, very extensively during his Whittlebury Forest campaigns. The brothers, Rochester, Rioter, and Richmond, were all by Ranter, and part of the Grafton pack; and the blood of Hazard conferred a rare Benefit on Tedworth. Sensitive by Mr. Smith's Racer came with Carter, as well as Saffron and Goneril, and there were soon none that he loved better to draw for visitors. He would vow too that Watchman by Vine Larkspur was "without a fault, till he was ten years old;" and he once assured Joe Maiden that Nigel (a grandson of Harrogate), who got nearly all his stock rather cream-coloured, was the best he ever had. He also delighted in his one-eyed Collier, and his Royalist by Fitzhardinge Rockwood, who goes back their Commoner.

Time gradually brought new favourites, Bertram and and none greater than Bertram. This Nelson. silver grey son of the tan Belvoir Bertram was drafted by Will Goodall for being twenty-four and a-half; and as Mr. Smith was still strong in the old Manager faith, and liked his work, he had at one time no less than five-and-twenty couple by him in the kennel. He was lent at seven years old to Lord Portsmouth in rather high condition, and died suddenly on the bench after a day's hunting. Nelson by Belvoir Rustic was the hound which knew him best to the last, and he always singled him out among the pack. When he hunted his own hounds, they would wind him three hundred yards off, and no Burton or Carter could stop them, and he wouldn't have them stopped. At Penton they would dash off in a body the moment they were out of kennel, and wait at the front door, whether they had heard his wonted voice at his bed-room window or not. His intimacy with Nelson was not much cemented in the field, but began when he brought him in the railway carriage from London. He was a gift from Lord Forester; but as he was rather delicate in his constitution, and light below the knee, they did not breed from him, and if Mrs. Smith had lived he was to have been kept in a kennel near the house.

His Last Great Runs.   The last great run Mr. Smith was in, was one of an hour and forty minutes, from Ham Ashley to Hungerford, and he was so pleased with the chestnut he rode, that he gave Mr. Sam Reeves one hundred and seventy-five guineas for him. He christened him from the covert where they found, and ranked him ever after with the Amport, Rochelle, and Ayston, of his Hampshire affections. The last named was perhaps the best of the three, and on one occasion when he tripped on the road to covert, and Mr. Pierrepoint said, "*If I were you, Tom, I'd ride that horse no more,*" he replied, "*If I were going to ride for my life I'd ride him and no other ;*" and he did so for several seasons. His last hunting gallop was on Shamrock in the October of 1856, three miles in twenty minutes from Sinicote Park to Siding Cut, and he crossed the downs as gaily as a boy. The cover side knew him no more after the October of '57, when he just cantered up to Wilbury, on his chestnut hack Blemish, to see his hounds draw ; and he was on her, at the door of his covered conservatory rides, facing over Wilbury Liberty, when he took his last look at his hounds. Carter got his orders to bring the choicest of the 1858 entry, and he and Will Bryce arrived at the usual rendezvous with five couple of bitches by the Fitzwilliam Hardwicke and Hermit. He looked at them a short time, and said, "*Well! they're as beautiful as they can be ;*" bade both his men good bye, and they saw him no more. That June he was in Rotten Row and at Tattersall's as usual on Blemish, and when he rode into the Ring there one morning, and found Mr. Rarey driving his Zebra round it, he made his servant bring his horse along-side ; and quite gloried in showing the celebrated American how nimbly he could still change horses in a run without dismounting. Such was the last public episode in the old fox-hunter's life, and in a few weeks he suddenly took to his bed in Wales, and died after only two days of illness, or rather great weakness. What was once a summer temple at the top of a long beech-shaded vista in his garden, is now his resting-place. Thousands, whose lot it was to labour to pro-duce his wealth, and for whose happiness and well-being he effected so much in return, will long cling fondly to his memory. Still in the eye of the world, which knew little of these things, it was foxhunting which lent such an intense earnestness to his life, and looking back at him only in that point of view, none will be found to dispute, that however hasty both in temper and action he might be in the field or on the flags, he was the mightiest hunter that ever "rode across Belvoir's sweet Vale," or wore a horn at his saddle-bow.

Those were right pleasant days in Early Days in Dorsetshire, when the Prince of Wales Dorsetshire. lived at Moor Critchell, and wore the scarlet coat and white cloth waistcoat uniform of the H. H. His pack of rabbit beagles, seven couple of which could ride to the meet in a couple of panniers, were his delight on bye days, and he had a heartier hand-shake for none than Parson Butler. The coverside would not have looked itself without this eccentric cassock, and his half-sheared terrier, Impey, who was as great a foe to badgers as he was to foxes. He was never beaten but once, on the day when Ben Foote, then a mere boy, was run away with by Traveller (who had been purchased out of a light coach), in a rare five-and-forty minute thing from Frampton to Cerne. "Urging," like a second Mazeppa, "on his wild career," through the village, Ben caught a glimpse of something jumping up at a window from the inside, and when he got back to them, and found that they had come to a twenty minutes' check, they vowed that he had been dreaming in his flight. However, the Parson seeing a fresh chance of distinction for his terrier, stuck up for the lad ; and as it turned out that the fox had got into the house, Impey, assisted by Stormer, the best hound in the pack, eventually drew him from his position under the stairs. This was in October, and he proved to be only a cub.

Mr. Farquharson. Jem Treadwell was but a lad of six, playing about with his younger brother Charles in the pleasant Oxfordshire village of Stoke Talmage, when his future master bade adieu to the quadrangle of Christ Church, and commenced at two-and-twenty as a master of hounds. Scorning harriers as a start, he flung himself boldly into the fox-hunting breach, set up two kennels, and hunted, at his own expense, all Dorsetshire and part of Somersetshire, six days a week from the outset, with thirty horses and ninety couple of hounds. His first meet was in the autumn of 1806 at Bondsley, a very extensive gorse belonging to Mr. Beckford in the Houghton part of the country. This fox-hunting Nestor was not slow to impart to the young leader of the white collars countless wrinkles about hounds and his new country, which he had once hunted himself; and as fifty-two seasons proved, he had found an apt disciple. Mr. Farquharson bought his first pack from Mr. Wyndham of Dinton, and a clever lot they were, the bitches being about twenty-one inches, and the dog-hounds twenty-three ; and his kennel was further strengthened by purchases from the Duke of Bridge-water and Lord Petre, and drafts from the Duke of Richmond. The style of Mr. Wyndham's continued unaltered for many seasons, except that the bitches' standard was raised an inch ; and it was not till much later that the eye of " The Meynell of the West " loved to rest upon a five-and-twenty inch hound. Since then he has kept a large and a small pack, but Jem Treadwell quite shared his weakness for the large, which always went into the Vale, and thought that

they not only "streamed away more," but uniformly
gave a better account of their foxes, be the fences big
or little. Thirteen hundred and forty-four brace were
brought to hand by Jem in his twenty-one seasons ;
but the eighty-seven brace of his 1842-43 season were
never equalled, as far too many rabbit traps got set in
later years, among the short oaks and hazels of Cranbourne Chase, which was once the great Dorsetshire
nursery. Foxes were so rife in the country at one
time, in Ben Jennings's (who came to Mr. Farquharson,
at the beginning of his second season, from Mr. Conyers) and Sol Baker's day, that seven were dug out
of one hole at Downey Cliff, and of the four which
were alive, one was quietly turned out on Blandford
race-course next day, and was killed after going for
forty minutes, racing pace, within three miles of the
old rock. Mr. Nichol had always a very high opinion
of Ben, and he used to say that if it had pleased Pro-
vidence to make a fox of him originally, he would
have picked any other man in England to be hunted
by.

There was a good deal of New Forest
Justice blood in the kennel during the
first part of the thirty seasons for which
Ben was in office, as although Justice, and his son
Jasper had been sold by Mr. Wyndham to Mr. Nichol
the year before Mr. Farquharson bought the pack, the
latter sent bitches to both, Justice especially, for some
seasons, and the puppies, which were generally yellow
and white, turned out remarkably well. When Treadwell came in '37, the dog hounds were generally twenty-
four inches, and he brought with him thirty-two couple
of Mr. Codrington's old hounds, which he had hunted
one season for Mr. Hall in the Blackmore Vale. Reveller was the best of the pack, but he was not big
enough to breed from, and the effort to keep up the
Collier sort was principally made through Richmond.
However, from some peculiarity of climate, Eastbury

*Mr. Farquhar-
son's Kennel
Blood.*

was quite a City of the Plague. The bitches missed, and out of five-and-forty couple of puppies, fully half died of distemper or yellows, before they were sent to walk, and it was a good year indeed which saw nine couple put forward. Luckily there were plenty of good drafts to be had. Trickster and Castor, whose stock, with their fine power and slight lack of length, looked quite of a family, lent no little strength to the Puckeridge drafts, as also did the Trusties with their dark sandy bodies and light-coloured heads; and when Mr. Smith returned to his earlier standard, George Carter always found Mr. Farquharson ready for the large drafts, which were full of Rockwood and Ranter blood. George's old Yardley Chase experiences with Mr. Grantley Berkeley had taught him the value of the Rockwood strain, and he did not forget it when he was at the Duke of Grafton's. The bitches were the best, and as they were remarkably tough and lengthy, they crossed well with the upstanding and rather short Ranters. Mr. Farquharson had Rochester, Rioter, Roderick, and Richmond all black and white Ranter brothers, among which Rochester had the most power, and went straight through a covert if there was no fox. The beautiful grey-backed Rarity from Rakish by Assheton Smith's Conqueror, and who gets her wonderful deer-like neck from her sire Roderick, showed well for Tedworth at the sale; and Rampish, another daughter of Rakish, and Autocrat were equally fine specimens of a cross with the Beaufort Falstaff and Rufus. Adelaide, the dam of that twenty-four-and-a-half inch *Autocrat* of the kennel goes back to Horlock's Lounger and Foljambe's Albion; and all Dorsetshire used to call out for her dam Rival, when they came to a check on the road.

Road-hitting. The talent of road-hitting descends like many others; and Will Goodall had a striking instance of it in Goblin by Harold, both of

whom would fling their tongues when none of the
other "Belvoir black tans" would own to it. Still,
however remarkable Rival might have been in this
respect, the greatest natural wonder of Mr. Farquharson's pack was his Splendour, who resolutely refused
for three years to leave the huntsman's heels, and then
felt what a pickpocket would style "the uncontrol-
lable impulse." Jezebel by Beaufort Harasser equally
withstood all Joe Maiden's endearments till long after
Christmas; and yet, when he was casting wide near
Bewerton, in the Woore country, on a very stormy day,
he saw her suddenly go and feel for the line of scent by
herself through a large herd of cattle, and then speak
to it through a meuse at last. Vanquisher also baffled
Kit Naylor for one season and a cub hunting, and
then suddenly spoke to it on a flagged footpath, of
all places, as he was casting down a lane; but still
Dorsetshire Splendour has quite the palm for obstinacy
as yet.

Mr. Farquharson was fondest of Short Mr. Farquhar-
and Clifton Woods, and Melcombe Park son's Stud.
in the Vale; but his greatest runs during the last
twenty years have been from Uddens and the Decoy
Pond near Kingston Lacey. The former was eleven
miles without a check, fast across the Heath, slower
from Charlbury Hill through Chettle Wood, and then
a brilliant finish from scent to view over the Downs
to Thickthorn Hill. On the second day they had
sixteen miles of it, plough and down; and he hung
very little either in Badbury Rings or the Chettle
Wood Covers, but crossed the Downs by Long
Critchell, through Oakley Wood, and past Woody-
ates Inn to Pentridge Hill, where Mr. Farquharson,
on Champion, was among the few left to see Jem get
off Poplin and give the "Whaw Hoop!" Poplin was
an Irish mare, and left several colts—Spectre, Will-o'-
the-Wisp, &c., by Hobgoblin (whose blood goes back
through Annette to Phantom), as her legacy to the

stud. Cadiz, the sire of Hobgoblin, was a bay by
Ebor, and would have done enough for Eastbury even
if he had only got The Pony out of a pony mare.
This wonderful fourteen-two animal carried Treadwell, who was about twelve-four with his saddle,
through nearly three hundred runs in their eight
seasons ; and be it a cramped or a flying country, she
only gave him one fall. It was, however, on Murphy
(another Irish horse) that he made his celebrated
fourteen-feet drop in the Buckland country. Mr.
Farquharson also sent several mares to Sir Hercules,
when Mr. Sydney Herbert had him in the neighbourhood ; and his rare jumping blood is still represented
in the Langton paddock by Testator out of Variety,
who was an own brother to Mabel, Darling, Kathleen,
and Fancy, the four picked mares of the stud. It
was on one of the two last, or Botanist, that Mr.
Farquharson was latterly seen at the coverside.

Mr. Farquhar-   A kick from one of them unfortunately
son's Last Public prevented him from sharing in the closing
Day.   weeks of his glorious career as master;
and hence we missed him from among the white
collars and the staunch century of farmers who
showed up in obedience to the last announcement of
" Mr. Farquharson's Hounds " at Hyde. We could
not bear to lose this great closing day, but it proved
dull enough, even without seeing a future Dorsetshire
master carried pale and bleeding from the field.
There were two foxes in Newfoundland, and they
went flashing away with one over the bogs, and bent
to the right along the bold heather platforms by
Heffleton Wood, and so to ground. " Treadwell on
The Pony," and looking the very incarnation of one
of those calm, passionless huntsmen who might have
made an Ironside swear that the sport was orthodox,
then held them along the edge of some wheat, to cut
off the line of the second fox; and when they disappeared over a heather ridge, to try again we

departed. This was April 28th; but we heard of the pair for the last time on May morning, when, cold and stormy as it was, the big pack met at the kennel, and drew in the Chace. They found a dog-fox, and killed him in a spinney at the high end of Stubhampton; and as if to make a good end, they broke him up, brush and all, and thus Eastbury was deprived of his last trophy.

We had still one more visit to pay to Dorsetshire, and on the morning of the sale we left the train, about 2 A.M., at Wimborne Minster.

A Morning's Walk.

> " Low on the sand, and loud on the stone,
> The last wheel echoed away,"

as the Blandford mail-bags were hurried off through the mist; and after lingering a little near the church porch till the clock struck three, and then making a wild shot in the darkness at one of the three cross roads, we pointed, as we hoped, from previous hunting map studies, for the Eastbury kennels. We felt no remorse for the beds we left behind us, as it would have required more than Spartan self-control at that hour for any Wimborne publican to arise and let us in, and they were never put to the test. A walk on an early summer morning, just as the bridal chuckle of the blackbirds begins to open in every spinney, and the weasels are never done crossing the road and keeping you in stone practice, is peculiarly exhilarating. However, nature had no more charms after halfpast four; and having once tried the same thing near Godalming, as a boy, for the sake of cub-hunting with Colonel Wyndham's hounds, we can publicly assure the owner of a hay-field abutting on the fifth milestone out of Blandford that he was the unconscious donor of a most charming slumber. The sound of a peal of church-bells came floating up the river, and awoke us at last; and shaking off sleep and the hay seeds, we strode gaily on our way.

The Eastbury Kennels. Blandford did not present any signs of unusual life. One or two masters of hounds might be seen "stealing away" from the "Crown" in the direction of Eastbury, by eight o'clock, to have a quiet hour on the flags before the country stream set in; but scarcely another soul passed us in the next five miles. The first three were along a dusty road; and it was not a little refreshing to find ourselves on the Pimperne Downs at last, and Percy's string of five, with "C" and "O" on their sheets, quietly returning from exercise, the leading object in the foreground. Autocrat, in hound and not in horse shape, was in our thoughts that day; and leaving them to wend their way inside the hedge to their stables, which stand by the roadside some half-mile nearer Blandford, we struck across the downs to the left. Passing "the Bushes," we soon struck into the deeply-wooded recesses of Eastbury Park, amid a troop of browsing Devons, and some young hunting stock, which at once told the tale of the "old chestnut blood." Hard by the kennels the whole of the seventeen puppies (eleven of them brother and sister Autocrats) had politely stretched themselves out for immediate inspection on a straw-spread surface beneath an ash tree, and lay there dreaming and curling themselves into many a fantastic group, over which Frank Grant or Landseer might have lingered with delight.

As the lots were looked over, they were passed through into the adjoining paddock; and many a Dorsetshire man gazed with bitter regret at this grand pack as they "packed" for the last time under a large white thorn. Oft had "The Thorn" been trolled at a Dorsetshire fireside in their honour, and now, alas! but six short hours, and no blast from Treadwell could summon his favourites more.

Five minutes' walk brought us to the house, a fine grey stone structure, with a broad square tower and a massive ivy-clad gateway. The days of portcullisses

and moats had long passed away before Sir John
Vanbrugh numbered Eastbury Park House among
his triumphs. A natural wall of laurel, laburnum, and
lime trees flanks the stable-yard on one side, and joins
on with that belt of plantation which encircles the
park, and amid which, undisturbed by traps and
strychnine, many a gallant fox-cub has been reared
in its day. The house itself—near whose back-dooi
three or four hogsheads of old and pale ale had begun
to know no rest from pilgrims before noon—is only a
solitary left wing; and the remainder of it, which
passed through three or four families into Mr. Farquharson's hands, has long since disappeared. The
deserted wine-cellar, with its prostrate door, its rusty
gratings, and its mouldering ceiling, under whose now-
battered and led-coloured rose many a stoup of Burgundy or Canary must have been drained dry, alone
remains to testify to the hard-drinking spirits, who of
yore wound the *reveillée* for the roe-hunt from Grange
or Houghton Woods, and killed the yellow-breasted
marten for the hem of the robes of their dames or
ladye loves in the pleasant purlieus of Cranbourne
Chase.

We care not to go into the details of that day. *The
Life* has already told how the Dorsetshire men sat
cheering on the wall, and ejaculating "*Hyde for ever !*"
as Mr. Radclyffe formed the new pack; how they
assured Mr. Arkwright publicly, when he bought the
Banker lot, that he "*wouldn't leave a mouse in covert ;*"
how they conjured Mr. Scratton "*to mind and take
care of Rosamond—she's an uncommon good bitch—
I know her well ;*" and how that gentleman was seen
to obey the mandate by taking her tenderly back to
Essex with his own hands. Mr. Osbaldeston strolled
up in the afternoon, to see the horses sold; and old
Percy was there, looking over the lots in the stable,
and recalling many a recollection, as we sat on the
corn-bin together, of the triumphs of the "red and

black cap" of Langton. With him to train, and
Sawyer, and then Conolly, to ride, it was perpetually
seen in front at Salisbury, Weymouth, and elsewhere
in the " south countrie." Grey Marquis, Presentiment,
Garus, and Black-and-all-Black alone won with it
eighty times ; and the last became such a hero in the
Dorsetshire peasants' eyes, that even now they would
as soon strike a horse with a twig of hornbeam as
believe that their black knight could not have
vanquished Eclipse himself. And so the great hunting era of Eastbury passed away on that pleasant
June afternoon. The cry of another pack is heard in
Coker Wood and Badbury Rings ; but still, long after
the present century is numbered with the past, a pleasant
tradition will linger round Dorsetshire firesides, of how
a former squire of Langton took to hounds when a
mere college stripling, and how even his fifty-second
and last season found him with a heart as young, and
a cheer as shrill as ever.

Mr. Codrington. South Wilts claims its notice, for Mr.
Codrington's sake. It was he who en-
tered Jem Treadwell, to fox in 1818 ; and when his
whip, Tom Snooks, next season, blooded an O.B.H.
lad of nine, who contrived to get well up on his pony,
when they killed at Stone's Heath, near Powder Hill,
he little thought that he was entering a future M.F.H.
of that very country, and that the brush Tom presented, and the moustache he so artistically painted,
would produce such glorious after-fruits at Tubney.
Mr. Codrington was a peculiarly quiet man with
hounds ; and as Jem phrases it, " No rating—no
whipcord—make them hunt through anything."
Grovely and Great Ridge were his pet covers in
South Wilts ; and he hunted them once a week regularly, and sometimes twice, till the foxes learnt to
fly the instant they heard his horn. He was fond of
walking round and round a gorse with his hounds at
his heels, and then drawing into a meuse ; and like

Mr. Musters, he never cared to have more than fifteen or sixteen couple of hounds in the woodlands, as he said they did not run so much from fox to fox.

He rode about eighteen stone on his Downalong; and when all the field were pounded one day near Westbury, he got through a great double on him, no one ever knew how, and laughed heartily at them when they killed near Earl Stoke. Dark tan hounds with smutty faces were his fancy; and he had not only a good deal of the Grafton Bondsman blood, but got the old grey dog himself from The Duke in Tom Rose's time. His stock were generally from 23½ to 24 inches, grey headed, and rather fond of hare; but they did not stand over so much ground as the Cryers. Wanton, the dam of Collier by Cryer, was a very fine own sister to the celebrated Beaufort Wellington and Waterloo, and came to Mr. Codrington unentered. Bruiser also was one of a draft from the Cheshire, and strained Back through their Bangor and Bruiser to old Gulliver. The Bruisers were generally dark black tans, great drawers, and remarkably steady; while Collier was a light, airy style of hound, and both a great hunter and chacer. Mr. Codrington's pack were principally by him, when he parted with them in 1826, and let Mr. Foljambe have the pick of the dog-hounds for four hundred guineas; but they did not prosper at Grove, where old Collier also ended his days. The Beaufort Justice sort was one he much fancied, and hence he borrowed old Jason by New Forest Justice from Badminton. He was big, black-bodied, and of great power, and got his dog-hounds very clever during the short time he lived.

But ere we get among his descendants Mr. Nichol of at Badminton we must pause at the New the New Forest. Forest, that hunting ground of the Justice, who has for half a century or more perpetuated its fame in kennel history. He was a son of Jasper, who was by the Egremont Justice (a very first-class hound), and

T

came in a draft to Mr. Compton. Jasper still lives in
Marshall's picture which was engraved in 1803, and
represents Tom Sebright's father in his scarlet and
green collar, gazing most affectionately at him over
the half-door. Lord Egremont's Justice sort were
generally about twenty-four inches, and very thick
headed, and the cross between them and the Fitzwilliam draughts produced lighter and more airy
hounds, and losing the original head. Twelve were
entered in one litter by Justice from Lightning; and
Colonel Wyndham and his brother divided them.
The Colonel also got a very good cross between the
Rutland Chanticleer and his Richmond and Fitzwilliam blood, and when the brothers gave up, they
sold twenty-five couple of bitches (fifteen of them
spayed) to Sir Henry Oxendon in Kent, but the
latter squared out and got so much flesh over the
muscles, that no work could keep them poor.

Justice's grandsons, Justice, Jason, and Jerker were
all very great in the New Forest in 1815. Neither of
the last two had the substance of Justice, who was of
immense bone, and as Mr. Nichol was wont to say of
him "as big as a deer." This eccentric master used
to go to Sir Thomas Mostyn's kennel for a cross, and
loved his Wrangler and Fleecer right well; but it
was through Sir Thomas's Justice (by the New Forest
·Justice from his own Hopeful), who went there as an
unentered draft in 1812, that the Justice blood was
first introduced at Badminton. Philip Payne's draft
came to Mr. Nichol for years, but both his hound-
breeding and hunting, well as he understood them,
were conducted on a very rough principle; and
digging a whole afternoon, fifteen feet after a fox
with his black tan terriers, was the style of thing he
liked best. This, however, was of rare occurrence, as
the foxes used to breed in the morasses among the
alder-stools, and lay curled up there till the hounds,
who soon got as black as ink, drew right up to them;

and then jumped down in view, without any head of earths to fly to. The New Forest plantations are now so grown, that the pleasure of seeing the find is gone, but the bogs still keep up their charter, and when one of the late Lord Alford's horses ran away with him, he only stopped him by running him into one of them near the Doos of Badgery, and christened him after its name. However, the pace of the Pytchley one day stopped him for ever, and he died in the field near Misterton.

In all its other features, there is little New Forest change in the Forest since Parson Gilpin Scenery. roamed with his sketch-book through its glades on the long summer days, and rigidly pulled down the blinds of his carriage, as his coachman, in drab with a cocked hat, drove him to Church on a Sunday, that he might read over his manuscript sermon in peace. We could not help joining in the old man's enthusiasm, as we saw the hounds draw close by Lyndhurst, on our way to Mr. Farquharson's last meet. No wonder there was no find that day among such posies of "stinking primroses and violets," which seemed to cluster at the feet of the woodmen as they sat on the prostrate white trunks of the oaks they were barking. As we occasionally viewed a scarlet coat or hound flashing across those glorious green vistas, beautiful enough in their graceful livery of spring, to bring a "Capability Brown" on to his knees, we grudged sadly that the old glories of Lyndhurst—when the Prince kept his hunting court at the King's House, and other hunts sent their keenest of the keen, to join the party at the Crown and kill a May fox—should have faded, and that a few most melancholy hunting pictures, and a fox's head, which had been painted blue, scores of times, along with the stable-door, should be now the only signs that once merry hostel could make.

Many curious stories are told of the scenes between

T 2

Mr. Nichol and his whip Joe Peckham; how they quarrelled about the number of horns of ale Joe ought reasonably to drink out hunting, and how the latter fled for his life to a magistrate "to swear the peace" after his master had found him standing on his saddle, and loading his pocket with cob-nuts, instead of watching to see the vixen come across the riding in cub-hunting time. Lord Kintore bought his fifty-five couples for a thousand guineas in 1828, but fifteen couple had the kennel lameness and mange; and long before the end of their second season only seventeen couple were in work. What with these, his own, and the Southwold, his Lordship had 104 couple in kennel when he hunted the Old Berkshire and Vale of White Horse countries, and what between their two kennels at Wadley and Cricklade, and five days a-week, John Walker, with Joe Grant and Tom Snooks as his whips, had a hardish time of it.

Badminton.　　It was a lucky chance which led the fifth Duke of Beaufort to try for a fox with his coarse stag-hounds of many colours in Silk Wood, on his way home from hunting. After that, the kennels at Netherhaven, Wilts, soon lacked their tenants; and the deer disappeared from those paddocks near Oldbury on the Hill (where Philip Payne is buried and Will Long lives), beneath the talismanic influence of the pad, which the chaplain of the Somerset family hung upon his bell-pull. Silk Wood has been true to its destiny ever since, and one season, under Mr. Holford's fostering care, there were no less than nine litters in it and his other covers. With such a nursery of 150 acres to swell the list, the present Duke might well calculate that after cub-hunting he had nearly three hundred brace of foxes in his country. Will Long once opened it early in the cub-hunting with forty-nine and a-half couple, and the cry for an hour and a quarter delighted the sixth Duke beyond measure. The seventh would as

soon have seen one of his men with his whip in the
left hand, as anything under twenty couple out; and
if it had been his fate to drop once more among the
scenes of his private pupil days, and catch Joe Maiden
dusting a fox with sixty couple on Delamere Forest,
he would have been all the better pleased.

When Philip Payne came from Che- Philip Payne's
shire to Badminton, he took a strong Era.
fancy to Diligent of the badger-pye Abelard blood,
which was well represented in the kennel, and crossed
her with Nectar whom he borrowed for old acquain-
tance sake from Cheshire. This Nectar was a black
tan with long features, coarse neck, and dewlap, all
marking his old Talbot origin; but it was not so much
for that as for his rare legs and feet that Philip followed him. The Badminton Nectar had the big neck
and long features of his race, and was a coarse, heavy
hound, "who knew nothing about tiring." At walk
he persecuted the hares day and night, but never
showed any unsteadiness with a fox. He ran for
eleven seasons, and even when he was past all use in
every way, he rode twice a year to the Heythrop
kennels, on the baggage-waggon, for a treat, and
wandered about with a perfect ticket of leave into the
kitchen, or wherever he liked to go. The greatest
care was required in breeding between him and Dorimont by Denmark, as they were so closely allied in
blood, through Diligent. Dorimont himself was a
hound with a very short head, and Raffle and Boxer
were two of the best hounds by him. Will Long still
speaks fondly of the style in which the former hunted
a fox half a mile for him along the top of a wall, and
the latter would invariably find three foxes out of
four by his resolution in going through gorse. As a
general thing the Dorimonts ran badger, and the
Duncans (whose sire was also by Denmark) nearly all
yellow pye.

No hounds could ever have too much bone for

Philip, and taking his notions from Earl Lonsdale, whom he swore by, and remembering the Gainsborough hounds whom they had bred so freely from at Cottesmore, he never liked anything under twenty-four inches. He also did away with the heavy shoulders he found in the kennel, and brought in more length and liberty; while Will Long in his turn gave them more fashion, and better fore-hands. Although Philip made very free with both, he liked Abelard better than Justice. He was below his standard, but still a very first flight hound, and got his stock very quick and airy. His daughter Diligent was from Jessamine, a daughter of Actress, a thick-marked Yarborough bitch, who first showed herself out cub-hunting. The seventh Duke, who was rather dainty on these points, did not like her half-face, and hence she was never worked in public again, and died in kennel. She also bred Danger to the original Danger, but he went early to the stud, as he was disabled by a cart-wheel. Still he did his best to avenge himself, as he seized the wheel and clung to it, dragging his broken limb, so that Philip might well say he should have a chance after that.

Dalliance, the dam of Dorimont, was a combination of the blood of this hero in Ruby (a daughter of Belvoir Relish), and Sir Thomas Mostyn's Lictor. It was, as we have before observed, from Bainton that the Justice sort came to Badminton. The Justice who introduced it, was a coarse-necked heavy built hound, of a light hare-pye colour, which came out in his stock, one of whom, Jericho, carried it to the Old Surrey. He worked seven seasons, and ran in the second flight, as most hounds that kill foxes do. Joiner and Jupiter were two of his best sons; but the former's career was cut short early, in front of Glimpton House. Some small plan sticks were put into the ground to indicate a new walk, and one of them ran into his heart, and Philip and Will heard " his beautiful tongue like a bell " no more. Jason and Jessie were two more of the Justices, from Lovely by Mostyn's Lazarus, and Jessamine was the result of her cross with Waterloo, Both Waterloo and Wellington were by Assheton Smith's Collier from Gladsome, whom Philip Payne entered in 1811. She went back through Royster and Vernon's Ranter to the great Yarborough Ranter, and hence it was no wonder that Mr. Codrington always vowed that his Colliers had the rarest blood in England in their veins.

When Will Long, after whipping in Will Long. for eighteen seasons, commenced his huntsman's career in 1826, he went to Brocklesby on his first voyage of kennel discovery, but although he found them rather under the size he had expected, he sent Dalliance down to their Fairplay. Hence sprang Freeman, who, after doing the kennel some good service, went in the spring of 1835, with twenty-five couple of entered hounds, to the Heythrop. Four hundred and fifty guineas was their price, and Lord Southampton paid a thousand for the forty-five couple, twenty of them unentered, which he had from Badminton in 1850. Soon after he began, Will bred his lordship's celebrated Hazard, and took him to Quorn, where Dick Burton entered him in 1828. He was by Harbinger, of Lord Lonsdale's blood, from Purity by Nectar, and was one of the two or three hounds Lord Southampton retained when he left Quorn; as, although his lordship did not take to the Grafton country for a time, he bred a litter or two of puppies every year, and gave them away.

The Duke of Grafton and Mr. Drake Hector. sent bitches to Hazard, and his principal son was Drake's Hector, a name that huntsmen will never cease to venerate, as he did good without exception to every kennel that used him. He was a very powerful broad-chested, and rather light-coloured hound, with a very sensible head, and short on the leg. The latter feature was to be seen in all his stock, who were remarkable as line hunters, and as sound and hard fox-hounds as ever went out. Lord Mostyn had him for a time, and so had Sir Watkin Wynne and Mr. Selby Lowndes, and he was put away in 1848, at the North Staffordshire kennels. His son Hermit was from Fitzwilliam Goldfinch by Yarborough Ganymede, and through crossing him with the Dorimont blood, those illustrious brothers Remus and Rufus arose, from whom nine and a half couple of the present Badminton pack are descended. Each of them for four seasons had about five couple of the best Badminton bitches; and the Belvoir, Berkeley, Rutland, and Brocklesby kennels used them both a good deal, but Will Goodall's fancy was more for Rufus. Potentate, a grandson of Remus, also went to Belvoir, with whose kennel he was connected on the side of his dam Whimsy, by Wildman. He was a handsome style of hound, and a very quick, hard runner, but without any great substance, and got his stock bigger that himself, and the bitches invariably bigger than the dogs. Like Sir Richard's Prompter, he was so resolute that the whip was always obliged to hold him when they were baying the fox, and even then he would hardly be denied without punishment.

The Fitzwilliam Marmion was not very successful in introducing the Monarch blood; he was a close hunter and a capital finder, but required to be crossed with very hard running bitches. The Fitzwilliam Finder did far more for Badminton through Freeman from Drake's Oppidan; and it was the second of their two Flyers, father and son, of the Rutland Collier blood, who got the Fitzwilliam Feudal. Warwickshire Tarquin also left his mark on the kennel in the shape of Trojan from Beaufort Gratitude. There was

never a much better sort, and Will fancied it so much,
that he took especial pains twice over to get Trojan
sound, when he was lamed in the stifle. Flyer,
Warlock, and Prior were the stallion hounds that
Clark selected from Badminton the first year (1853),
that he came to Tubney, and as the Vale of White
Horse is now virtually a Tubney removed, we may
pass to the head-quarters of the old Berkshire at
once.

After Mr. Morrell's entry at Jim Tred- Mr. Morrell's
well's hand, his hunting fancy was Hounds.
fostered to the full during his Eton holidays, by constant practice with his father's harriers. The pack
originally consisted of fourteen couple of the old
Southern breed, and on one occasion they adopted
currant jelly tastes of a higher order, and had a buck
turned down before them in the presence of half
Oxford, on the very Headington Hill, where Mr.
Morrell's house now stands, looking down on the grey
forest of church and college pinnacles. In 1835 he
took the harriers in hand himself, and hunted them for
eleven seasons in the country round Oxford, and on
Ilsley Downs. Latterly they had immense sport, and
not a few of the hardest riding sons of Alma Mater
date their earliest chase experiences from the hunting
lectures and cheery gallops they had with him after
the " straight-backed uns." The pack was principally
kept up by drafts from Mr. Drake's, the Heythrop,
and the Blackmore Vale (Mr. Yeatman's), and consisted at last of twenty-two couple of small fox-hound
bitches, and Hannibal, who had a strong touch of the
harrier about him, and never failed to set the ladies
right at a pinch. In the spring of 1848, Mr. Morrell
took from Mr. Morland that old Berkshire country,
which Lord Kintore and John Walker had made so
famous. Tradition says that five horns are now rust-
ing at the bottom of Rosey Brook (in which Henry
Harris, to his great delight, got a roll his last season),

but we care not to enquire whether theirs were of the number.*

Foxes had become sadly short; but in Mr. Morland's last season, John Jones had drawn Buscot no less than twenty-one times, and found them as good there as in Mr. Pryse Pryse's day. The services of "Jack" were in due course transferred to Mr. Morrell, and twenty-four couple of his old favourites came along with him to the Tubney kennels. Mr. Morland's blood ran back a good deal to Drake's Marksman, Wyndham's Warrior, and Osbaldeston's Merryman. The crosses of Assheton Smith and Wyndham blood in Saffron and Fairy, and Traveller and Rarity, were very strong; and Mr. Morrell was rewarded for his allegiance to Morland's Warrior of the Old Berkshire Whirlwind sort, by the entry of Foreman from Faithful, a great finder; while Horlock's Statesman did him no small service with Famous and Filagree from old Friendly. In his first summer he entered three-and-twenty couple, taking half Mr. Drake's draft, with Mr. A. Thompson, who then hunted the Atherstone; and casting one's eye down the sire line alone, in that pleasant-looking thin scarlet octavo, which records the Tubney history of his ten seasons, we find a strong infusion, during John Jones's day, of Drake's Bobadil and Duster, as well as the Southampton Truant and Archer sort; while Clark's era is marked by a leaning to the Fitzhardinge and Beaufort kennels.

The reigns of these huntsmen are embodied by

---

* Scotland can tell an anecdote of John and his old master, when the former hunted the Fife. John had missed his second horse, and Charlotte, the mare on which Mr. Grant painted him, had fallen quite beaten at a fence out of a wheat-field, after thirty minutes with a second fox. "*What for Charlotte, now, John?*" called his lordship. "*One hundred and thirty, my lord.*" "*What! is that the lowest? she'll get up no more.*" "*No less, my lord.*" "*But the mare'll die.*" "*No she wont, my lord.*" "*Well, I'll have her, dead or alive!*" And after lying twenty minutes, up she got again; and that was the way John parted with Charlotte.

Goode of Oxford, in two capital paint- John Jones and
ings, which grace the Headington Hill   Tom Clark.
library, amid countless heavy-weight carriers, and the
Hercules and Sunderland families. The first in date
has been engraved as a companion to the Heythrop
one, and we seem for years to have never walked up
the High-Street of Oxford, without seeing the pair in
the print-sellers' windows, flanking " Lord Hardinge
and his staff, on the field of Sobraon." John Jones is
on Columbine, and his first whip Will Borrow on
Etonian. Will has been laid to rest in Tubney church-
yard, and his entire grey Buckland (who showed The
Queen's the way over Berkshire, when they came to
Buckland and Beckett) has earned a monument in
Marcham Park ; while Jim Stacey is still as fresh as
he was on the Wood Hill day. It was then that
Jones told him to get forward (after they sunk the
Vale and had a long check) to the head of earths at
Woodhill ; and he took one of his celebrated four-
milers, and beating the fox by about thrice the length
of his boots, had the pleasure of seeing him broken-up
at Land Farm, seventeen miles from Milton Hall
where he was found. Tom Clark, whose taste for
hunting first came on him from seeing Mr. Mure's
hounds cross Newmarket Heath with their fox, when
he was a cotemporary with Nat in Cooper's stables, is
on the chestnut ROB ROY in the second picture ;
while Joe Orchin (who subsequently hunted the
Hambleton until deafness overcame him) is ready for
action on the elegant Sir Warwick, and Will Maiden,
the present Old Berkshire first whip, on Ladybird.
In both of them we miss the master ; but Mr. Grant
has supplied the want in that admirable picture of
him upon his white horse Memnon, (whom he rode for
nine seasons), with Rutland, Musical, and Foreman at
his side.

The latter is a combination of the Foreman and
blood of Warrior and Assheton Smith's Sunderland.

Saffron. Mr. Morrell bought Saffron from George Carter, and he was a wonderful favourite in the Old Berkshire for his quickness, and perseverance in his cast. Eleven of his stock were entered, and it was his son Sportsman, a descendant through Sophy, of Ducie's Bertram and Horlock's Baby, whom Clark before the sale expressed his rapturous desire to "follow across the Channel with a couple of bitches;" and strangely enough he was in the four-couple lot for which Mons. de Bourxie gave 200 guineas. Sportsman had a tremendous drive with him, and must always have something to do, and even when he had been fired in his stifle, he would be with them if he carried his leg. The more direct blood of Assheton Smith's Saffron by Belvoir Splendour from Parasol, (who accompanied George Carter to Tidworth) came strongly into the kennel through his son Sunderland, whose dam Gratitude was of Heythrop Gulliver and Yarborough Gambler extraction. Sunderland was remarkably stout, and always at home twenty minutes first after the hardest day, if he was not watched. He broke his leg as a puppy; but luckily he was out at walk with a surgeon, who very soon brought matters about. He was a rich light tan, with a beautiful head and shoulders, and in these points very much resembled his half-brother Warwickshire Saffron, from whom they bred a good deal at Badminton. Nearly all his stock, of whom Mr. Morrell entered sixteen, might be known by their rich tan smutty faces and peculiarly broad intelligent foreheads; but many of them died of hereditary kidney disease, which killed the old dog in his sixth season. Saffron and Splendour, his half-brothers, were both very good: the former had a beautiful style of flinging and threading his cover with his head up; and Splendour, who went to Ireland, was also an especial finder, and with a much more beautiful and ringing tongue, than either. The Old Berkshire still have Stickler (from Susan by Foljambe's

Stormer), who was Sunderland's best son, and of the same colour.

In 1851, the year succeeding Sunder- Cup Puppies.
land and Foreman (who were beaten for
the Cup by Dorimont by Drake's Duster), Bobadil by
Bobadil from Favourite, and Freeman by Sportsman
from Friendly, were esteemed remarkable entries;
but Rutland and Trumpeter were bracketed for the
Cup. Rutland was nearly twenty-six inches, and one
of seven (including Ruthful and Relish), from Sunderland's dam, and by Belvoir Royal, who had been
sojourning at Mr. Drake's, after being exchanged for
Duster, and then went on to Wynnstay. Belvoir
Royal was an airy hound, somewhat light of bone, but
got his stock very clever. He was also rather a
cripple, and had narrowly escaped being cut in two by
Will Goodall's horse at a fence, which made him very
nervous. John Walker used to say of him that he
never saw any hound so frightened to death of doing
anything wrong; and he finally departed to Co. Kil-
dare. His brother Rustic, who went to the Cheshire
and did no good, was best in his work, but had rather
bad pasterns, and got his stock plainer; while Raglan
was as straight as an arrow himself, but got his stock
rather crooked. Both of them came in the evening of
their days to the North Staffordshire kennels, and
were there put away.

Trumpeter, who attended Clark to Trumpeter.
Badminton, was a white, and very low-
scented hound, and of Fitzwilliam Flasher and Drake's
Grasper descent. He was somewhat throaty, and was
bred from rather for his qualities than his look; as
he always ran to head and could sound his own trumpet into the bargain, whatever pace they were going.
Lord Dacre used his sire, the Puckeridge Trickster,
who pleased Dick Simpson not a little, as he would
draw on ahead, and get to the wind side of him, and
speak minutes before anything else. Sylvia, from a

Sunderland bitch, and Toilet and Trinket from Relish were capital daughters of Trumpeter's, and so was Tawdry, who was found working neck and shoulders up to her fox in a rabbit-hole, the very first day she was taken out.

In 1852 a few were entered by Badsworth Waterloo, by old Whynot, by Ducie's Vagabond. In his undergraduate days Mr. Henley Greaves took a great fancy to Vagabond, and got him from Joe Thompson, and drove him in his gig from Oxford to Badsworth, but he proved to be quite worn out. The Whynots and the Lubins were always great lines of blood at Badsworth; the former were black-and-tan, and had more dash, while the Lubins were sound good badger pyes, and claimed kindred with the Duke of Buccleugh's Lexicon. The half-faced Fleecer was of this year; he was a rare roadster, and so cheerful and persevering in his cast, that Clark and half Berkshire generally looked to him in difficulties. He was by Fitzhardinge Furrier, and Harry Ayris though him so like the old dog in work and shape, that being out of Furriers, he borrowed and bred from him. Statesman, of this year, a very capital hound in chase, also went to Berkeley Castle, but he never got any puppies. The Fitzhardinge Hector was lent them in turn, with especial injunctions from his lordship that he was never to go out in large fields, and in 1853 they entered three-and-twenty by him.

In 1854, among the first litter of Sunderland puppies, came Spangle, who is still doing capital work at Badminton. Boxer and Bobadil, the first of the Bosphoruses, were equal for the Cup in 1856; and in 1857, the great Hercules and Spangle litter carried all before them. There were originally nine, but two died of distemper after they had come in from walk. The symmetry and colour were caught principally from the dam, and the face from Hercules, of whom Hesperus was the

The Hercules Litter.

very image. Honesty was considered better than Harlequin in their classes, and the latter was run hard by Baronet, by Bosphorus; but the judicial decision of the learned Barons, Will Long (who very nearly took a lane flying, the next season on England's Glory), and Joe Maiden, was confirmed on a division of huntsmen, &c., by eleven to eight. So anxious was Mr. Richard Sutton to have Hercules at the Quorn sale, that when he arrived just a few minutes too late, he offered Clark the 210 guineas he had paid for the lot, to get the son of Albion alone. Not a relic of his mealy blue skin and nearly hairless head is preserved; and when we saw him the week before his death, he seemed to have aged very fast since Quorn, but ran in the first flight the same as ever. They worked him for the first time with eighteen couple, and had a capital trial three miles from Appleton Common up to New Bridge, and three back to ground at Tubney Wood. He and Statesman led all the way; Dexter, another of the Quorn lot, did well; but he was always greater in the woodlands than in the open, and Trojan, by Trueman, fat as he was, showed himself a capital line hunter. The Hercules blood has prospered in Mr. Montague's hands; and George Whitemore is especially proud of some bitches by him. The Duke of Beaufort has also two couple to enter; but he died so early in his last season, that there were only four or five litters by him.

The blood bravely held its own again when it came before the Old Berkshire Bench next year in the Bitch Puppy Cup; *The Last Tubney Hound Show.* but still, to quote the impressive *obiter dictum* of Will Long, " *Turn me out Harriet and Sophy, and I don't care which I catch hold of;*" and Joe Maiden was equally troubled in his mind. Three brother-scarlets came in to help, and there we all stood in the yard, that day, Mr. Morrell in the centre, pencil in hand, to take the votes, while a master of hounds, the late

lamented Hunt Secretary and a few old Berkshire
men, some of them cup winners, were grouped about
among the nine-and-a-half couple of entries. Having
once seen Joe Maiden judge hounds, with his hands
folded across his breast, we shall cease to have any
faith in the saying, " That no man was ever so wise as
Chancellor Thurlow looked." Even if Joe heard the
voice of a relative behind him, whom he had not seen
for years, it is even betting that he would not deign to
turn round, till his kennel mind was quite made up.
Robert Tocock was still pale and weak from a crushing
fall ; and when Joe was at his gravest, he kept tapping
his foot for an indefinite period with his stick in despair
of getting a recognition of his sentiments any other
way, and then found that he had been working at the
wooden one. Then there was Will Long, airy and as
stylish as ever, after his seventy years' pilgrimage, with
Jem Hills at his side, still unconsciously replying—
" *Yes, Master !*" as in those great days when with Will
Todd he whipped into him in the Badminton and the
Heythrop. Jem doesn't dwell when he is *In Banco ;*
but with one offhand glance, he just catches the gay
workman of his fancy, and thinks about it no more ;
while Harry Ayris, after a look, about half-measure
between Jem's and Joe's, turns round to consult his
learned brothers, with that quiet shake of his head,
which has been fatal to so many a Berkeley and Cheltenham fox, when hounds drop to hunting, and he falls
to thinking.

Judicial Bearing   The bitches came first, and very soon
of Jem Hills.   all but Sophy by Fleecer, Frantic by
Forester, and Harriet, Harmless, and Helen, by Hercules, were handed to Harris and Pike, outside. " *Put
Frantic and Harmless out !*" was the next injunction
of Mr. Morrell to Clark. Then it was the fair Helen's
turn to go ; but she was after Jem Hills' own heart ;
and when Mr. Morrell resolved himself into a teller,
Jem placed her second. And now the scrutiny of

scrutinies began. One liked Sophy best behind, and another went for Harriet's gay and airy forehand. Another said that " *Sophy could race, and Harriet hunt a fox to death.*" Save and excepting Jem, they shook their heads in such despair at splitting the difference, that Mr. Morrell began to think, that as in Trumpeter's and Rutland's year, there would be a bracket, and two cups to give instead of one. At last, however, the five packed, and Mr. John Aldworth, who got this cup one year with Toilet, just walked into the yard to receive the doleful greeting from Mr. Morrell's lips of " You've just missed it with Sophy." Helen was a good third, so the shade of Hercules was appeased.

Selim by Fleecer, Royal by Greaves's Render, Firebrand by Forester, and Heretic by Hercules were soon the only standers among the same number of dog puppies ; though Jasper by Hercules was recalled for a moment. Firebrand, whose features were a trifle too long for Will Long's fashion-loving eye, had been submitted to a most rigid scrutiny, first with his two feet resting on one brick in the kennel yard floor, and then on separate ones, to see if he was mathematically straight, and was pronounced quite the prizeman of his day. " *Unanimous for Firebrand,*" said Mr. Morrell, when he had gone round, pencil in hand ; and then came the struggle for second. Ayris, Maiden, and Tocock were all for Royal, and the Master of the South Warwickshire, as he stood there—

> " and came for to hear it,
> He werry much applauded the thing they had done."

Long was all for Heretic; and Jem Hills had gone, it was whispered, minutes before, for something else. " *Jem's not with the majority again this time,*" said we to Will. " *Isn't he ?—I know Jem's sort of old ;*" and down went the handle of his hunting whip on to the gay black tan back of Selim by Fleecer, and sure enough it was.

U

Three weeks later those kennels had become a vast chase mart, for the exchange of minds between twenty masters and five-and-thirty huntsmen ; and many a mysterious little knot of three in the park told that a new whip was being engaged. A great fox-hunting era was just about to die out, but there were symptoms of vitality enough about the patriarch Jim Morgan ; and although he was rising seventy-four, they might well ask Clark, why he "*admitted boys into the kennel.*" We care not to dwell upon the woodpecker tap of Mr. Tattersall's hammer, beneath the elm, near the kennels, and the 29½ guinea average for the entered, and the 36 guinea for the un-entered, which it sealed. We must get forward three months.

The new O. B. H. pack had migrated to Oakley, and everything looked very hopeless and drear when we strolled in for the last time to have a look at the old place. The stables from which Memnon, England's Glory, Marlborough, Sir Warwick, Wild Rose, Fisherman, Harkaway, Chesterfield, Bletchington, and Topthorn had been sent on to cover so often, were empty ; and a couple of magnolias near the front door, from which such troops of fox-hunting friends had departed in an evening, and constituted themselves special commissioners to inquire whether the Oxford hacks were as good as when they kept terms, only made the desolation more complete. Even the staunch old chaplain, who not only knew by sight, but had traced and then written out in text-hand, the name and pedigree of every hound of that kennel, to the tenth generation, had fled the spot in despair. The very straw-thatched houses, in which so many scions of Sunderland, Hercules, Hector, and Foreman were nursed, had been taken from that necropolis of an orchard. The Tubney Ghost, which appeared to John Jones, and is popularly supposed, even in its calmer moments, to carry a carving knife, must have absolute sway now ; and it may be that "the voices of the night," cheered on by that spectral sportsman, on Golumpus or Memnon, may be heard at All Hallows Tide, busy among the hazels of Tubney Wood, or running the old line of the Bablock Hythe day.

RAMBLE THE SECOND.

" Held by Diana in due estimation,
Bedeck with a gorse flower the goddess's shrine ;
Throughout the wide range of this blooming creation,
It has but one rival, and that one the vine.
Pluck me then, Bacchus, a cluster, and squeezing it,
Pour the red juice till the goblet o'erflows ;
Then, in the joy of my heart, will I seizing it,
Drink to the land where this Evergreen grows. "

THE Heythrop began, in 1835, with Jem Hills. Jem Hills, who came there from Lord Ducie's, and twenty-five couples, principally Dorimants and Nectars, from Badminton. Jem had been for a considerable time with Colonel Wyndham in Sussex, and many legends of him still linger about Petworth, where he was in for a goodly amount of riding of the Gohanna and Grey Skim hunters. He played in the Sussex eleven for eight seasons, while Bainbridge and Lillywhite flourished, and was selected, from his talented batting, to do battle for 300*l.* against Hampshire, in Sir John Cope's Park. Amid these feats with the willow, he nourished and brought up five cubs from a tea-pot, and he was saddled with a family of six more, in a most remarkable way. They had run a heavy vixen in a small cover, near Eyfold, round and round for nearly an hour and five minutes, till Jem got wearied out, and stationed himself in a ditch to head her. Confiding in his natural gallantry, she jumped into his arms, and he arrived at the kennels with her on the pommel of his saddle.

" Jem's Ditch" at Shillinglee, the seat of Earl Winterton, is also pointed out to this day, and it was there, when they had run their fox for five hours in the large coverts, and for nearly fifty minutes more in an acre spinney, and seemed as far off as ever from killing him, that Jem lay in ambush, and turned him to them by moonlight, at just twenty minutes to ten. Will Staples was once baffled the same way for nearly two hours in an osier bed, quite as small, near the bend of the Severn, which had washed all the soil from the roots ; and it became at last so ridiculous to see the fox trotting after the hounds, and then dodging under the roots, that he had to go in and help them.

The echoes of Jem's key-bugle are also still lingering at Sladeland, and as he played " *Over the hills and far away*," with variations, the hounds sat up and charmed in honour of their favourite musician ; and then, when such *encores* became tedious, with one wave of his hand they would go flying over the brook in a body, and swing themselves round and back, at another.

Fathers of the Heythrop Kennel. When Jem found himself at Heythrop, he set to work to correct the short head and neck and wide chest of the Dorimont and Nectar blood, and used Rutland, Pilot, and Yarborough Plunder. The Pilots had very fine quality; and Harlequin, a grandson of old Pilot, from Heroine, by Fitzhardinge Hector, is now one of the quickest in the kennel. The Plunder bitches were decidedly out of the common, but rather apt to shed their somewhat coarse coats. Rutland Grappler, the sire of the Wynnstay Harold, also did a good deal for the kennel, but he got them rather short. A good deal of Warwickshire Bluecap blood came in the drafts, and Jem sent bitches to the Warwickshire Tarquin, by Belvoir Comus, from Warwickshire Testy. He was a light plain 24-inch hound, and white with yellow spots; but Jim had marked him doing his work over some fallows on Roleright Hills, in 1845,

when the fox went to ground, and determined to have
a slice of him. The nick between him and the Rocket
blood was very great, and Theodore, from Termagant,
was so bred. The Bluecap blood in the Heythrop
came from Mr. Drake's, and they were generally black
tan hounds ; lengthy, but rather heavy-shouldered.
The twenty-five inch Drake Boaster did not disap-
point him, and got all his bitches twenty-two inches,
and with very beautiful forehands, while those by
Vampyre by Beaufort Voucher, on the contrary, were
rather heavy-shouldered, and very apt to knock themselves to pieces over walls ; and Cheshire Chaser,
whose brother Champion did the North Staffordshire
some service, brought the Badsworth Conqueror and
Foljambe Piper blood into the kennel.

The twenty-five inch Roman-headed   Nathan.
Nathan was one of Jem's particulars, and
although he was rather long on the leg, and got his
stock so, he was as low-scented as a harrier, and could
often carry it over fallows or along a road, when
nothing else could touch it, and put the pack to rights
pretty often among the cubs in Wychwood Forest.
He worked him five seasons, and then he went to Mr.
Hillyer's, leaving eight or ten couple of his blood
behind. His science as a road-hunter was such, that
if he had been in the South Warwickshire, Jem would
have no occasion to renew his annual offer to their
huntsmen, beginning with John Jones, to turf over
that piece of the turnpike road which separates the
two hunts near Roleright Hills. Nathan's sons,
Nobleman and Ferryman, are great at a road now,
and on the last day of the 1857-58 season, the former
carried it down one, for a mile-and-a-half. The others
had faith, but would not speak to it ; and Jem trotted
behind, strong in the belief that "*he never told a lie
yet.*" Still he wavered in his allegiance, when a woman,
with a sickly child, sitting under the side of a hedge,
vowed that nothing had passed her way, but Noble-

man knew better, and another nose was added to the Heythrop store.

Old Affable. As a proof of Jem's high esteem, old Nathan was crossed with Affable. This renowned bitch was by Assheton Smith's Ruler, by Harlock's Freeman, and from Beaufort's Artful, but falling blind with the distemper, she was never entered. Ruler came with Jem's baggage in the waggon from Lord Ducie's, and was such a miserable object, that Mr. Smith when he saw him as he was, and what he became, used to declare that no one " ever can know them till they're two." Affable nicked well with the Tarquin and Rocket sort, but her best puppy, Merlin, by Manager by Oakley Factor, wasted early from kennel lameness. She bred forty-five couple in all, and the greater part of two litters from her were entered in one year. Six Affables figure in the Heythrop picture, and their dam was as keen of the sport as any of them. When she got hold of a fox's head, she would tear it in pieces, and go fairly crazy with joy. In lack of nobler game, she would wander away to Woodstock after rabbits for her puppies, crown down on to them, and steadily dig them out. Lord Dillon had her, and sent her home to pup; but she did not admire her change of quarters, and made a well-meant attempt to carry her puppies back to Ditchley. By crossing the brook, and thus avoiding the village, she got four young Plunders safely deposited on the common, and she had carried one on and was leaving it on the steward's door step, when she was discovered. They also say that she was as good as the blind guide on the Eastern Counties line, and that a ladies' maid, who had got lost in the wood coming from Chesbury, would have been left out all night, if she had not met her rabbit-hunting, and submitted to her pilotage.

The Rockets. Rocket, to whom Mystery is now closest allied in blood, was another present at parting, to Jem, from Lord Ducie, who had bred from him and Ranter, through thick and thin. He was by Osbaldeston's Rocket, from Beaufort's Dainty by Dorimont, and Rocket himself was by Lord Vernon's Rallywood, from Baroness, both of which were in the five hundred guinea pack " The Squire" bought from his lordship. Having once been ridden over, he was very shy, and would nip right round the horses at a check to the front. In Lord Ducie's hands he was put to Vigorous, Vanquish, Vanity, and all old Lord Middleton's best blood, going back to Mr. Musters; and he was one of the sixteen couple that came with Jem from the Vale of White Horse, where the blood was still lingering, when Dick Burton left it for Lincolnshire.

Regent was amongst the two Rocket Death of Ranter. and Affable litters of one season, and he greatly delighted Jem in his second, by bringing a drowning fox out of the Charwell, near Ransome Park, retriever-fashion, by the nape of the neck. Like all the Rockets, he was amazingly fond of carrying the head. His own was rather a thick one, like old Affable's, and he was eventually drafted for size. Old Rocket, his sire, was a nice hound, of 23 inches, and invariably got them with more bone than himself. He was stifled in his first season, and then ran to head for six more; and his death was rather a sudden one. He was sitting down in Heythrop Park, during an afternoon stroll with Jem, when he broke a blood vessel, and bled to death on the spot. Oddly enough, his son Ranter died nearly the same way, when he was five years old, in a very hot morning, towards the latter end of cub-hunting. He had run a cub 200 yards into the Ox Copse, on Wychwood Forest, and killed it; when the hounds were counted over he was missing; and it was not until a fortnight after, that he was found lying dead under an oak tree, about a hundred yards beyond where the cub was broken up. He was buried where he fell, and the tree is called, in affectionate remembrance of him, " Ranter's Oak," to this day.

Lifter was a grandson of Rocket's, and strained to Lord Fitzhardinge's kennel on his dam's side. His nose would have delighted his lordship beyond measure, as he would speak to the least touch of a fox, and was in fact one of the very few drag hounds left ; such as they used to boast of in the Holderness in Mr. Hodgson's day, which (as they would have it), feathered at the hedges three hours and ten minutes, after their fox had gone through. He had this peculiarity, that he never would draw a cover, but tried every meuse all round.

Clarendon. Clarendon, by Ranter did as much for the Heythrop as any of Rocket's descendants, and got a great many sandy-coloured hounds. Mr. Morrell used him ; and Conqueror, who was lost on the ice along with Royalist and Pedlar, was by him. It was a miracle how the whole pack escaped that day. They were running across the ice near New Bridge, when it broke, and let the body of the pack through, and then closed and caught the three, while Clark and Will Maiden could give no aid. Clarendon himself went abroad in the drift, as his pace was so tremendous that he could go clean away from the pack, and they were always hunting him and the fox as well. Middleton by Clarendon was, in this respect, still worse than his sire, and Jem lost many a fox through him. He would not throw his tongue till he had got half-a-mile, and then he would try fairly to race his fox to death over the walls.

Tom Hills. Having so often observed Tom Hills on the Epsom hill, in his green coat and top-boots, taking his Derby observations, like an old Surrey general, from the back of Ransley or The Advocate, we determined to view him in his sphere of home usefulness, and sought Garston Hall kennels accordingly. The hall, which boasts of a beautiful cedar, and a well 365 feet deep, is surrounded by a little colony of snug cottages, which make up quite a pleasant village, with Tom as patriarch. The chalk-stone gout has used him rather ill of late ; and he had had also a bad fall, which still makes it difficult for him to raise his left arm to his head. This is by no means the first of his misfortunes, as he has broken both arms, three ribs (by falling on his horn, in the days when they carried them slung), the cup of his elbow in three or four bits, and his blade-bone, as well. Gout, however, bothers him most, and makes his action rather short, but still he gets along as of old when he is once on his pigskin throne. It was with reference to his woes in this way that he said, when we observed that his eyes were rather shut in a photograph, " *Next time I'll have it taken when I've got the gout—that will make me open them fast enough.*" Still we found him very cheery, seated in his arm-chair, which the skin of his once honoured dark chestnut Paddy has lined.

The chairs in the room had all hound-skin cushions, taken from nine of the best of the seven couple of bitches which fell more than a hundred feet down a cutting on the Brighton rail some years ago. Will Long, Mr. Davis, Mr. Haigh (an old master of the pack) ; Squire Waring, with his Kent harriers ; John Ward, with Betsy and Blue Ruin ; Lord Derby's stag-hounds, with Jonathan Griffin on his grey ; Brother Jem (who whipped into him nine years), in the centre of his Heythrop picture ; and the old Surrey Hunt, after Barraud, lent lustre to the walls. Tom, as all the world knows, is in the centre of the latter, on Lounger ; while one of his sons is on Paddy ; and the badger-pye Factor, by Old Surrey Factor out of Dimple, of his most cherished sort, stands close up to Lounger's foot. There was also an enormous fox in a case, but he was not exactly brought to hand in

Tom's usual style, as the hounds flashed over him into
a cover near Godstone, and a farmer found him lying
dead in a furrow next day.

Tom is rising sixty-four, and just entering his
fortieth season as huntsman with his old Surrey pets.
He has been at it with them ever since he was fifteen,
and whipped in for seven seasons to John Cole. Out
of the other forty-two, three were spent behind the
bar ; but he soon took to the scarlet again. Five of
his sons, all trained by himself or Brother Jem, or
both, are in the profession ; and he can say, what
no man ever said before, that three of them—George,
Tom, and Edward (who is with Count Carolli, at
Pesth) are huntsmen, a fourth, Morris, second whip to
her Majesty, and a fifth, Sam, first whip to himself.

The old Surrey country is very full of covers, and
the Godstone side, which requires less wet than the
other, is much the best. Still the hunting is up-hill
work, in more senses than one, as the flints wear out
a pack in no time. At the end of one season they
had only fourteen couple sound, and had to knock
ten couple on the head for hopeless lameness. Tinc-
ture of myrrh is Tom's principal application, and he
finds that the hare-footed hounds stand the flints
much better than the cat-footed ones. Every year
they send out some twenty couple of puppies ; but
the walks are not a land of Goshen, and they seldom
enter more than five or six. John Walker and
Brother Jem have principally come to the rescue with
their drafts, and there are about sixteen couple from
Wynnstay in the kennel now. Mr. Davis also sends
Tom some hounds, when they are not quite fast
enough for his purpose ; but still the Old Surrey line
has been well carried on by their Rummager and
Joker. Warrior, the handsomest son of the latter,
never got a whelp ; but he did infinite service to Tom
in *the* run of his Old Surrey life on the 12th of
February, 1857, with a fox who had already beaten

them twice. The meet was at Nutfield, in the Godstone country, and they found at Old Park, and killed
in the large coverts at Cansion, after crossing the
river five times! The twenty-two miles from point
to point was done in four hours and a-half; and a lad
of the name of Richards, on his pony, stuck to them
all the way. Tom's horse, Advocate, was beat beyond Dry Hill; and then getting on his son Sam's
Doubtful, "the old un" had such a tumble at the
next fence, that to this day they demand of him in
that part of the country, to send a horse and cart to
fill up the hole he made. Be that as it may, Tom
rose from his mother earth like a very Antæus re-
freshed; and as he saw Warrior carry the scent down
a lane into a coppice, he exclaimed, in his unquenched
fervour, to Mr. Ross, "*He's been waiting for us; he
must be owrn now!*"

> "Blest is the eye
> Which dwells between the Severn and the Wye,"

has long been a Gloucestershire saying,   Berkeley Castle.
and we felt the truth of it to the full, as
we climbed, one July evening, to the top of the tower
in Berkeley Park, and looked down as well on that
richly wooded panorama, which was the hunting
ground of the Earl for some half a century. Quite
as keen sporting characters as himself were reared
there. Old Pierce used to sit at his cottage door near
Berkeley, when he could hardly stir, and listen to the
Earl's and Harry Ayris's horns all over the Vale;
and when his lordship passed on his return home,
and stopped, as was his wont, to tell him about the
sport, he was sure to remind him once more, "*I've
heard you and Harry all day—it never goes well with
you, when there's so much duetting.*"

Then there was Jerry Hawkins, who   Jerry Hawkins.
still lives in the print on his thirty-year-
old horse, taking his hat off to cheer Hazard, one of

the few hounds whom the Earl ever had painted. No one loved better to sit at the corner of Barrow Wood, to watch for the vixen, or to swim the Severn from market near Hawe Bridge, and take his chance of fouling the rope. His love of varmint was not 'confined to foxes, but the rats had the unlimited run of his sitting-room, and he knew them all by sight so well, that when Mr. Giles's first whip clipped one over, his house-keeper exclaimed, with her apron to her eyes, that its death was as much as her place was worth, as "master would be sure to miss it."

Earl Fitzhard-inge. The Earl himself did not fancy any dog-hound above twenty-three, and never cared how small the bitches were. He never liked them shy of tongue, and it was no matter if they were straight or coarse, provided their work was only good. "*I don't care for all their looks,*" he was wont to say; "*huntsmen forget to breed hounds for their noses; they're all for looks;—give me the pack that will kill foxes.*" "We musn't forget the old sort," was the maxim he impressed upon Harry to the last, and by that he principally meant the blood which Mr. Corbet and Will Barrow did such wonders with in Warwickshire. He also bought a pack of hounds from Major Bland in Herefordshire, a rough-looking lot, who, like Mr. Corbet's, would hunt a fox and catch him when others couldn't handle him at all. The yellow pied Monitor went back to Major Bland's sort, and Woldsman from the celebrated Beaufort Wanton was one of his best sons. A second cross, between Beaufort Woldsman and their own Delicate produced Desperate, Dissolute, Demon, Dervise, Dalliance, Dinah, and Diligent. The Earl was wont to say of Desperate, that he was the best he ever saw or had, and that with a fair scent, he would not be afraid to take out those seven and catch any fox breathing. Harry Ayris always hung a little to Dinah, but he thought that her daughter Waspish by Fitzhardinge Waterloo

could hunt quite as low a scent. Waspish bred very
few puppies, but among them was a good Melody by
their Manager. Herald by Warwickshire Saffron
from Hyacinth, who goes back to the Desperate sort,
was, along with a daughter of Glider's, the last
hounds the Earl ever saw. They were taken up to
him in his bed-room in his illness, as he was anxious
to have another look at "the old sort," which had
in this instance to be drafted for size, and to judge for
himself as to the blood of Glider, which his friend Sir
Richard Sutton had so ceaselessly pressed upon him.

Lord Fitzhardinge was especially fond   The Herods.
of Chedworth Woods ; and he cared as
little about the colour of his hounds, as he did for
them being "sorty." A thousand guineas would not
have bought his favourite Herod by Hazard by Corbet's Foreman, who was as bare as a Berkshire pig,
and with only a few blue hairs on his sides during the
season, and none at all at the end, except under his
neck. He dates nearly forty years back, and the sort
may be said to have died out in 1833, with the one-
eyed Harlequin, who pulled his neck out of joint,
breaking up his fox, with three or four couple more,
at Tockington. They bred from him one season, and
he left a fine black and tan litter of seven from
Radiant, but not so good as the Desperate lot. Hotspur by Beaufort Regent, from a daughter of another
Harlequin, had also a strong strain of Herod blood
in him, and a head big enough to have satisfied Lord
Hastings, but he got his puppies nice enough in that
point. Both he and his son Hector were very gay and
wonderful drawers, and there was no hound to whom
the Earl trusted more than Hector to get him out of
difficulties. His beautiful tongue pleased him as well;
and he would sit on his horse for half-an-hour to watch
him puzzle out a line of scent.

Harrogate by Fortitude from Hecuba,   Harrogate.
a daughter of Herod, was one of the

same sort, and Mr. Grantley Berkeley loved him quite
as tenderly. He used to amuse Harry Ayris and his
whips, as a puppy, by standing for minutes together
in the kennel, to wind a fox who was tied up near it,
through a hole in the wall ; then racing round and
round a hundred times to feel for the line ; and then
after deciding that the hole was the point, setting off
to test his opinion once more. He was never known
to speak false in the Oakley country or anywhere else,
and he would stop at four cross roads, and wait till
his master or George Carter gave him a sign. He
was given to Carter when he went as huntsman to the
Grafton country, and there he got worn out. After
that he went to Beacon Lodge, and did a little among
the otters, but he was rather unlucky with his stock,
which were often not quite straight.

Warwickshire   Warwickshire Tarquin, who was re-
Tarquin.   commended to the Earl by Jem Hills,
did the kennel some good. They had five couple by
him of one entry, and Tamerlane, Trojan, and Tell-
tale from Garland, of the old sort, were very nice industrious hounds. Tarquin himself was shortish-
necked, and short all together, and his lordship never
fancied him in his work as he did his three sons. Harry
Micklewood.   Ayris has rather an affectionate remembrance of one of the days he was out, as
it was that on which he first happened to ride Micklewood by the Old Sailor, and continued to do so for
ten seasons. His own horse was beat, and he borrowed
the dark chestnut from John Dinnicombe, and when
he landed over his first leap, a hedge on a bank and
ditch, with the hedge from him, he looked back and
cried, " *Thank you, John ! you'll ride Micklewood no
more.*" He originally won his name from the fact of
Mr. Grantley Berkeley having found him out in a
blazing twenty-two minutes from Micklewood Chase,
when seven had a bath in the Rea, but Harry had
never been on him before. Old Ben Chapman used

to admire him wonderfully, and it was his constant saying that "*A man should carry that M icklewood in his eye when he goes to buy anything,*" and "*Mind what you're at; the old horse's ears are forward,*" became as constant a saying in the hunt. But we are forgetting Tarquin, who became stifled at Berkeley, and then went to Wynnstay; where he did not get any puppies. Lord Henry Bentinck's Con- Contest and Comrade. test and Comrade were both crossed with Tarquin bitches to give them more style ; but although Contest could do his work with the pack, Comrade was the perpetual victim of stifle lameness, and never sound for two days together. Among others, they also used Foljambe's Albion, a light-coloured clever hound, as well as Belvoir Roman, and Watchman, with Druid, and the modern Belvoir Rallywood's elder brother Ranter from the Yarborough kennel. John Ward of the Worcestershire had also a rare slice of their Abelard by Hector as a litter of eleven by him from Beaufort Winifred came in, and were all entered with the exception of one, which was too small.

Shropshire is full of old hunting memories, from the time of Tom Moody Shropshire. and Trojan, and when the flag-staff on the grig-clad steeps of Haughmond Hill told that Squire Corbet and Will Barrow had brought back the hounds from Warwickshire for a few weeks in the season. Will Barrow, as his epitaph records, enjoys no more

> "The stirring chase
> Of hounds and foxes striving in the race,"

and sleeps just under the hill from which he plucked so many long-tagged trophies. Those were the days when the Squire had gates four miles round Sundorne, and if he did get to a fence, it was always, "*Please oblige me by turning my horse over; and I'll catch yours*"—but he always forgot. Then there was Sir Richard Puleston, with his curly sterns, who had such a habit of all singling out one hound, and worrying him, that the baronet in vain offered a reward of 200*l.* to any one who would devise a cure. Will Todd did not know of the habit when the forty couple were sold into the Old Berkshire country. They, however, began the very first night at the Kingston Inn kennels, and Will procured a great bell, and rung it, and flogged them, till he almost alarmed the neighbourhood. Next day he kept them out in the yard, and let their unhappy quarry go in and out of the lodging-house as he liked, and they at last got so frightened, that at the first tinkle of the bell, whose rope was at his bed-head, they would stop short in the smallest jar.

Mr. Pelham and his Men. Shropshire has also a keen remembrance of Mr. Pelham, who canvassed Shrewsbury alphabetically. He put his men into white coats with black collars and cuffs, and black velvet breeches; and then, when he had sedulously made them such guys, he would urge his pony for miles out of his road, especially to avoid them. He seems, however, to have kept some eye on them, as he was once, and only once, heard to say, that the hunts-

Ned Bates. man Ned Bates was "mouthy," and that Jacky Tattle, the whip, was "a boy to kill horses." Ned, who is introduced as whip into Mr. Corbet's hunting picture, rode good sixteen stone latterly. He always said "*My Honey*" when he was pleased, or the reverse, and had a nose like a red mulberry. The Rev. Charles Eaton, who was so great over Shropshire or Cheshire for twenty minutes on his scarecrow mare Fair Barbara, once asked him confidentially how much a year on a fair calculation it cost him to keep it painted; but Ned "moved the previous question," and deftly parried the thrust, with —"*Aye! my Honey! if thee'll put thy mare into my stable, I'll bring a blanket off my own bed to kiver her poor bones.*"

The brightest era for Shropshire seems to connect itself insensibly with Will Will Staples and his Whips.
Staples and his two great whips, Jack Wiglesworth
and Tom Flint. The dance at Will's wedding was
quite a county event; and Shropshire men roar yet
over poor Tom's celebrated speech—"*For the honour
you've done me, in proposing my health in my absence—
that's always it, &c.*," when he had never left the room.
Tom Matthews did not hold office under Will, but we
can hardly wonder at the devotion, with which he
always watched for the honour of giving up his horse
in a run to him. This happened seldom enough in
Longwaist's day, who was only once seen resting his
weak crooked knees on a hedge-top, quite unable to
rise at it, while Will kept craftily talking to his hounds,
as if that was an attitude of pure choice on his part,
and not of necessity. The Shifnall men wanted sadly
to back Will and that great raking low-back, against
Moonraker and Mr. Sirdefield, but Will vowed he
could not ride a yard without music.

The Atcham Bridge meet has never The Atcham Bridge Meet.
looked itself, since "the three" were wont
to wait with the hounds in the meadow for Sir Bellingham. We know no spot so rich in hunting history,
even if Jack Mytton had not jumped those rails, with
his arm in a sling. Everything in the scene is so good
of its kind, and the parts so beautifully disposed in
relation to each other, that an artist could make no
alteration for the sake of breadth or effect. The
salmon-haunted Severn, to whose nymphs the Shrewsbury boys have addressed such boundless copies of
iambics and Sapphics, both in Butler's and Kennedy's
time, steals quietly past the osier bed where Will used
to hope he was at home, and on through the massive
iron-grey arches to the sea. A rectory and church,
the red stone of whose Early English tower blends
so gracefully with the ivy which half enwraps it,
shuts out the distant Wrekin; while a herd of dark-

coloured Herefords, for whom the Royal Society has not lived in vain, dot the pastures to the left, and lend life to the deep green mass of Longner's woods behind.

The Hounds of Shropshire.   Large hounds did not suit the small enclosures of Shropshire in those days, and they were given up; but now hounds go over the fence, and do not, as of yore, require three or four jumps to get through them. The Cheshire hounds were, as a general thing, too flying for Will Staples's purpose, but still some of his best hounds were from that blood. Virgin by Cheshire Valiant from Fancy by Lonsdale's Palafox, was good for eight seasons, but she never left Will's heels for the first. In Shawbury Heath she was invaluable, as it was full of gutters two feet deep, covered with ling and grig at the top, and she was the first to find that the fox ran these ditches, and to teach the others to go there. Will got experience of something more than ditches here. He had long noted the old Shawbury Mill dam with a view to a short cut some day, and when he did try his hand at it, he and his horse went in together, and the latter dragged him out as he clung to its tail. Mr. Smith Owen told him to go home and change, but he reappeared in twenty minutes, clad in a farmer's shooting-coat and plaid breeches, and nicked in with his hounds near Wytheford Bridge.

Shropshire Woodman.   If possible he loved Woodman still better than Virgin, and he never had any that would face a Shropshire crowd so well, and go back so resolutely with their hackles up to the place where they last knew of it. Woodman was by Wildboy by Osbaldeston's Wonder from Remnant, and was rather a flat-sided hound under twenty-three. His stock were not big, and most of them tick-marked, and like him, " knew nothing about tiring." Tom Goosey bred from him at Belvoir, and at the time of the madness he went to the Cheshire kennel ; but good

as he was in his work, he did Joe Maiden no good as
a stallion. Shropshire Bluecap, on the contrary,
brought back the Cheshire General blood into the
kennel, and left some very strong short-legged hounds.
Vulcan by Osbaldeston's Vanquisher was a very
favourite hound with Sir Bellingham; and he and
Wildboy, the sire of Woodman, were both puppies in
that draft of both packs, which Sir Bellingham took
from the Squire when he sold him his own on leaving
Quorn. Few hounds were so determined and savage
as Vulcan when he was put out, and on one occasion
when he was running hare, and Joe Maiden, who was
then the baronet's second whip, caught him a heavy
broad-sider for it, he flew at him and bit him right
through his boot and stirrup leather.

And now we pass into Joe's old country, Cheshire Blue-
and those "conservative gorses" whose   cap.
glories the Arley Hall lyrics will not easily let die.
The Tarporley Club had but just made up its mind to
hunt fox, when

     " Bluecap and Wanton taught fox-hounds to scurry,"

and established its renown on Newmarket Heath.
Bluecap was a black-pied twenty-five inch hound, and
was reared at Waverham Wood. He was always at
the head of the pack, and to adopt the words of one
who remembered him when a boy, "We viewed him
with as much veneration as we did Wellington or
Blucher in after-years." Of his daughter Wanton, the
sharer of his triumphs, nothing further is known, except that she was smothered in a fox earth, whereas
Bluecap died in the ordinary course of things in 1772.
The latter was such a hero, that when Cooper the
huntsman used to stop on the turnpike, to see his lad
who was at school at Gorstage Coppy, the boys always
rushed out with a bit of bread for him and the terriers,
and felt quite honoured by his acceptance of it. Again,
at holiday time, Cooper Senior esteemed it the highest

treat he could give Cooper Junior, to let him "*tak Bluecap to lie on the bed with thee, if thou woold.*" His glories were also well diffused through the Potteries, as every Tarporley week Mr. Smith Barry used to send the lad a suit with six china buttons, in front ; and a fox, Bluecap, Wanton, Soundwell, Rockwood, and Old Cooper charging a gate with Cheshire Cheese, engraven thereon.

Cheshire Hounds. Philip Payne left the Cheshire for Badminton after two seasons, to follow the Seventh Duke, whom he had seen out so often when a pupil at Daresbury near Warrington, and then the next huntsman of note was Will Gaff. He carried no horn during his fifteen seasons, and trusted entirely to his wonderful voice. Will Head found the hounds very wild, but very determined ; and full of the blood of—

"Those sons of Old Bedford so prized by George Heron."

This sort was always a great one in Cheshire during that thirty years' mastership, and though they were generally black tan themselves, they went straight back to the red tan Southern Hound. Bedford himself was descended from Meynell's Splendour and Ramper; and Gulliver and Grecian, both were badger pyes and of Bedford lineage. Gulliver was at Heythrop in his thirteenth year, and Jem Hills as well as John Walker bred a great deal from him. His stock were generally dark tan, very high couraged, and as stout as steel, and remarkable for their long sensible-looking heads and large crowns. Victor was another Tact in Finding. of the Bedfords, and quite a fugleman to Joe. He would go a few yards into a cover, and decide at once if there was a fox ; and if there was not, he would sit and triumphantly await the confirmation of his opinion at the huntsman's side. Mr. Villebois' Hannibal, an ambling sulky hound, who never forgave a whip, had the same weird-like tact,

and although Ben Foote was at times so incredulous
that he would try down wind and side wind as well,
he found it was no use wasting time when Hannibal
had said No. He was lent to the Warwickshire for a
week, and the very first time he was taken out, he
went and found his fox instantly, and raced into him
over a country which was equally strange to him.
Two Craven men came to Foote at the kennels a few
days after to tell him of the odd coincidence, and the
likeness of the hound they had seen to their own
Hannibal, and as he had then come back and was
specially drawn for them, they were perfectly bewil-
dered to think how two hounds with precisely the
same marks, should be blessed with precisely the same
bump of "locality."

The Hannibal of the Cheshire was the Cheshire
idol of Joe's heart, but he had to be de- Hannibal.
stroyed in the madness along with Envoy and Bravery.
The latter was by Meynell Ingram's Bertram from
Racket of their capital Nathan blood and quite a little
handmaid to a huntsman. She would hunt her fox
like a beagle, and when they were breaking him up,
she would give just one snack, and then sit up and be
the first to move again. Hannibal was by Cheshire
General, and with immense bone and depth of chest,
and measured good nine inches round the arm ; and
he may well hang up with Bravery, and the renowned
bay Pevorett, in the entrance hall at Wolstanton.
The Heythrop Hannibal did little towards repairing
his loss in after-years, but Lord Hawke's Conqueror,
the Grove Watchman, Heythrop Agent, Shropshire
Bluecap, and Rutland General stopped up such gaps
as even the grand entry of twenty-five couple of
puppies, out of the eighty which came in that spring
from quarters, could not quite fill. The Dapper sort
were all whites, and not such hard runners as the
Craftsman, who were principally white as well, but
too quick and jealous for a less flying country.

Bonny Bell. Wickstead's Harlequin contributed some very good short-legged hounds to Cheshire, and his Bachelor was the sire of Bonny Bell, one of the very fastest that ever huntsman rode to. Unfortunately she had to be drafted in her third season, from having got completely spoilt in a run from Mobberley Wood. She came out with the fox, ran close at his brush four miles over the palings, and across Tatton Park in nine minutes, and killed him. This coursing ruined her, as she could never be got to stoop again, and was always dancing about to get a view. Still, the habit rather amused the late Sir Watkin, and he thus wrote to Lord Delamere, " *Send us all the Bonny Bells you've got—we've such racing; away goes the fox, and then goes Bonny Bell."*

Tom Rance. Sutton's Wildboy and their own Gulliver, Bangor, Manager, Benedict, Watchman, Vagrant, Plunder, Champion, and Rockwood have for some seasons past been the principal sires in the Cheshire kennel, where Tom Rance, who was second horseman for two years to Mr. Gurney, in Norfolk, is now on the threshold of his thirtieth season, as whip. We had never seen Tom till this season, when he requested us to keep a look-out on the towing-path, near Cran Wood, while he watched at the top part of the narrow strip of cover, and as good luck would have it the fox slipped back ; just between us. Then came both to eye and ear, scarcely sixty yards from us, the terrific embodiment of that verse, which has enshrined Tom in all Lancashire and Cheshire hearts—

" Tom Rance has got a single oie, wurth many another's two ;
He held his cap abuv his yed to show he'd had a view ;
Tom's voice was loik th' owd raven's when he skroiked out ' Tally-ho !'
For when the fox had seen Tom's feace, he thoght it toim to go."

Our gratification was so great, that we made an early application for his photograph ; though, alas ! no sun

THOMAS RANCE.

and no pencil, however cunning, can hit him off, as he appeared in that moment of grim extasy.

Joe Maiden has principally clung to his old blood, since he came to the North The North Staffordshire. Staffordshire, and his crack Absolute is by Cheshire Bangor, who goes back to Gulliver from Actress by Shropshire Ajax, who came to the Wolstanton kennels when Mr. Davenport bought Captain Candler's pack. He was the leading hound in that great run of December 17, 1857, when they supposed they changed foxes, and ran for five hours and a half with scarcely a check, through eighteen parishes. A man leaving work at dusk, saw the fox cross the field dead beat, and Absolute knock him over, and struggle with him in a dry ditch, while the body of the hounds were nearly three minutes behind. About a quarter of an hour after that, Mr. Davenport and his son arrived on foot, as both their horses had been ridden to a stand-still, but some one had cut off their hard-earned brush and bolted with it. Joe was not out that day, but he had been reduced to the same straits himself on the memorable February 16, 1832, in the Cheshire country, when his Filho da Puta horse, Milo, *alias* "The Pig," stood still, and was left refreshing himself with a moist clod, while Joe, lame as he was, raced for the brush with Mr. Potts of Chester, who had seized on a horse out of a plough team when his own failed.

Mr. Heron was always very fond of Mr. Meynell's hounds; and it was Mr. Meynell Ingram's. through him that Mr. Meynell Ingram got a good deal of his grandfather's blood (of which Lord Vernon had so much at Sudbury), back to Hoar Cross. When his lordship's hounds were sold at the death of Mr. George Talbot, who had the management, a few couples were retained as a foundation for a small pack, which hunted the Hoar Cross country for three or four seasons; and this was the pack which Mr. Osbaldeston bought for 500 guineas, when he took it

conjointly with the Atherstone. Mr. Meynell Ingram
had hunted hare for several seasons with some small
hounds, bred principally from Lord Vernon's and the
Cheshire, and a few from Quorn. When he succeeded
to the Hoar Cross country, with Old Leedham—who
was once second horseman, and then coachman to Mr.
Meynell—as his huntsman, Fallacy, of the Cheshire
Bluecap, and Nelly, of the Meynell Stormer blood,
were given to him by Mr. Heron; but both of them
were so ill with distemper that they were hardly fit to
bring. He lost Fallacy out cub-hunting on Needwood
Forest Banks; and she went home again, and entered
so well, that Mr. Heron felt it much more of a duty
than a pleasure to write and inform his friend of her
return. Nathan, who became a very popular stallion,
was by Pytchley Abelard from Nelly, one of whose
daughters, Nightshade, had a great litter by Belvoir
Rasselas, which produced three good stallion hounds,
Rummager, Reveller, and Roman, all black tan.
Reveller was a very clever hound, but unfortunately
got poisoned; and Mr. Ingram bred a good deal from
Roman, whose best daughter was Hyacinth. But we
must not forget old Agnes by the Hoar Cross Abelard
from Ringlet by Belvoir Governor. She is fourteen years old, and as her Alaric and Adeline are
right able proxies, she wanders about like a fat Mrs.
Armitage of the kennel, along with Hostile by Sir
Watkin's Admiral, who was making most peaceful
overtures to the haymakers for a share of their supper,
when we first caught a glimpse of the pair. Agnes
has well earned her ease, as she never did wrong, and
would pick out the scent at four roads, when nothing
else could do anything, and even when she was
eleven and quite deaf, she could hunt the line by
herself.

Will Danby.   It is many years since Nimrod set
the clubs and the hunting world in a
roar by his " Tour" anecdotes of the dreams, and

the prayers, and the sayings, and the doings, of
the celebrated Holderness master (whom he irreve-
rently wrote of as "Tommy Hodgson"), and his
equally famous whip, Will Danby. The former has
hung up his horn for years, but Will is just entering upon the fiftieth season of his life in scarlet;
and although the grey hairs may be seen straggling
under his cap, he is a wonderful instance of what a
hardy Yorkshire constitution, good temper, and rigid
temperance can effect for a man in "these degenerate
days." Will is quite a key to Yorkshire hunting history; but tiles have, of later years, become his thorn
in the flesh. "*This draining,*" as he emphatically
observed to us, when we took counsel with him near
the Hurworth kennels, "*is just the ruin of scent; I
wish they'd be done with it; when I was a boy, we could
hunt from morning till night.*" He was born near
Hornby Castle; and the ruling passion with him was
strongly fostered at fourteen, when one of the farm-
houses, included in his father's lease, was converted by
the Duke of Leeds into a kennel for his hounds.
This was the crisis of his fate, and henceforward he
devoted his attention, much more to helping the feeder
to walk the hounds about, than to grounding himself
in the elements of agriculture. His expressed views
on drainage would, in fact, have militated so strongly
against his advancement, that it was well that he
established himself in the good graces of Kit Scaife
the huntsman, and found a more genial outlet for his
energies. When his seven years' probation was over,
some difficulty occurred with the Duke of Cleveland
about foxes, and the hounds were given up. The rare
lot of Pandolpho hunters were sent to the hammer at
Tattersall's, and Kit Scaife, who was always a great
man for kennel condition, took the head of his Grace's
racing stud.

It was a sad pity, as the country was The Duke of
a singularly wild and beautiful one, all Leeds's Country.

dells and ling. They were constantly having runs almost into the heart of Westmoreland, and hounds kept arriving at he kennel all night. In the cover of

> "*Cheerless Understone,*
> *Where cock never crew, and sun never shone,*"

they once divided, and Will had about as much chance of stopping them as a flight of pigeons. After riding wildly in one direction, while Kit went in the other, a shepherd at last halloed to him as if from the clouds on Whiteside, and descended with Bardolph and half a dozen hounds. His account was that they had nearly worried him as well as their fox; but he had summoned courage enough to pick up the brush, and hang it round Bardolph's neck. Of the other run nobody ever knew anything, except that Baronet and his party were found at the mouth of an earth at Masham Moor Heads, thirty miles away.

The Holderness. This wild sort of training, of which the above is a mere sample, and three or four seasons more with the Badsworth and Scarborough, found Will well up to the mark, when Mr. Hodgson took the Holderness, and beckoned him to his side, as first whip and kennel huntsman; and that memorable pair were in their third season, when "Nimrod" arrived at Beverley to watch the proceedings from the back of "Little Shamrock." Few men had such a country to work in, gentlemen and yeomen all fox preservers to a man, and looking on

> "The green gorse in Dringhoe that waves,"

as the most sacred of plants.

Will very narrowly escaped jumping down a coal waste; but the horse's second effort just ·saved him. Jack Robinson. This leap was generally talked of, with one that Jack Robinson, whip to Mr. Bethell of Rise, had taken over Wansforth Lock, some seasons before. He was determined to be with his

hounds, and when Mr. Bethell had in vain remonstra-
ted with him, and saw him coolly turn his cap wrong
side first as a preliminary, he turned his back not to
see him killed. However he got safely over, and at
last died in his bed at Sandbeck, where he hunted
Lord Scarbro's hounds. In later life, he was not the
man (as they say in Yorkshire), " *to burst himself with
tooth watter*"; and six or seven horns of ale in a morning before cub-hunting, for a few seasons, soon
quenched the fire within him. Old Will Smith once
slipped across the Trent, when the hounds were at
Manby, to meet him, one blazing hot August morning,
at Grove. He could neither hear nor see anything of
the hounds, but he espied some one in scarlet at a
wicket-gate, and tore up the ride to enquire. The
horse was quietly grazing ; and the rider, who proved
to be Robinson, was fast asleep. " *Halloo ! old boy*,"
said Will, in his fine cheery tones. " *where are your
hounds ?*" " *Hounds !*" said Jack. " *All right ! how
should I know ? they were here half an hour since—that's
you, Will, is it ? All right ! old fellow—I was just a
bit drowsy*." And so after one or two more thundering claps from Will, to make sure it was " All right,"
the two huntsmen separated, and Will cantered home
again, " *more ashamed than I ever was in my life*."

But we are forgetting Mr. Hodgson Recollections of
and his Will. They hunted four days a Mr. Hodgson.
week with only thirty-six couple of hounds, and killed
thirty-seven brace of foxes ; and towards the close of
another, they hunted nineteen days, and added twenty
noses after splendid runs to their stable array. They
killed them everywhere, and not content with the
intrusion into Sim Templeman's bed-room, they broke
up another in the drawing-room at Sir Clifford Constable's. In short, the housemaids of the East-Riding
never knew where they had them. On one occasion,
Will was seen up to his waist, wading for his fox in
the German Ocean, beneath the crags of Skeleton

Hill. This was the day when Mr. Hodgson, for perhaps the only time in his life, composed a triplet, under evidently a prophetic impulse. They had killed their first fox up a tree near Gransmoor, and he suddenly burst out, as they moved on to draw again with " *Will, I say*—

> "The first we've killed in a tree,
> The second we'll kill in the sea,
> That's the way it will be."

And so the event proved, and Lord Hawke begged the pad to nail for luck on the new kennels at Badsworth. Will wears a trophy at his watch chain to this day, in the shape of the tooth of the Dringhoe fox, which gave them such a run through Nafferton, where they had a slight check, and past Driffield, to Dotteril Whin. He was only a hundred yards ahead of the hounds, within a few fields of the whin, but still they did not view him till Will cracked his whip, and he turned nearly broadside to it for an instant. They ran into him just fifty yards outside the cover, and Colonel Thompson cut a large " H " on the back of one of the trees, for a memorial of that day. An Oustwick Whin fox, which they killed at Little Hatfield, after twelve miles straight, added another to their red-letter days ; and as the present master, and the late Rev. John Bower and Mr. Melford took their fences, stroke for stroke, Aleck Boswell might well say to his companion, as they " crept a bit," to keep near them, " *Look at 'em, Will! no country has three better !*"

Mr. Hodgson's Wind-up. All things come to an end ; and Will shall tell of the wind-up himself. " My last day and last run in Holderness," he writes, " was on May 3rd, 1837. The meet was at Water Priory, the seat of Lord Muncaster. We went twelve miles to cover, and were at him, on and off, for twelve hours under a burning sun, and then pulled him down at

5 p.m. ; and we knew him to be the same fox we had
dusted twice before, on account of one of his thighs
having the appearance of being clipped. So I think
seventeen hours astride of pig-skin in one day made a
very good wind-up of my career in the Holderness."

The next season found Will installed The York and
at White House, within easy distance of   Ainsty.
Bill Scott (who kept a special bottle of raspberry
vinegar for him in the cellarette) as huntsman to the
York and Ainsty. Rosebud and Lollypop were his
favourite nags, and the former carried him for twelve,
and the latter for eleven out of sixteen seasons ; and
Tarquin, Crotchet by Sir Tatton's Climbank, Trouncer
by Hodgson's Vexer, Nestor ; and Triumph, and
Traveller, by Trouncer from Tasty by Trimbush were
among the hounds of his heart, which ran to head
in many a rare thing from Askham Bog, or the Wild
Man.

To be in Will's society, and not learn Trimbush.
about Trimbush, would be drawing him
blank indeed ; and if Mr. Williamson was ever to hear
of it, he would make sure that deponent must have
got hold of the wrong man. Trimbush was by Badsworth Tickler from Yarborough Virgin, and so back
to Osbaldeston's Vanquisher, through nearly as many
V's as there are stiles of that shape near Hurworth.
Will Smith sent him to the Ainsty with a broken arm
and a " beautiful pedigree of five-and-twenty years";
but he never greatly distinguished himself, till he
worked it about half a mile down a road near Shipton-
on-Ouse, which the hares were crossing every instant,
while the rest could hardly feather on the grass.
Both Mr. Lloyd and Will thought he was taking it
too far ; and the former had just said, " *Will! it's
a band or a stallion !*" when he "went through the
hedge like a gun," and killed him soon after. Tom
Carter was a great admirer of his, and sent several
bitches to him, but many of his stock let down their

toes at two years old. He at last became jealous, and
too free with his tongue; and as he deceived Joe
Maiden twice over in the Cheshire, by making a
scent for himself, he soon ceased to use him. From
thence he went to The Sinnington, and so on to Mr.
Hill's; and some of his granddaughters, with their
long dark-coloured heads, are still to be found in
The Hurworth.

Will Danby's Accidents. Twenty-six brace constituted the spoils
of Will's best season with the Ainsty,
which furnished him with the pet run of his life.
They found at Askham Bog, and killed after four
hours and ten minutes near Anghram, in the presence
of only seven or eight out of three hundred; and
some even of that devoted band had to leave their
horses and finish on foot. At the close of the season
of 1852-53, Sir Charles Slingsby became master; and
as he decided to hunt the hounds himself, Will retired
with a testimonial, such as may well make him say,
" *There never was such a well-used man by hunting
gentlemen as I have been.*" As regards accidents, he
has hardly so fair a tale, as, in addition to flesh-rents
innumerable, he has had three thigh-wrenches, and all
his ribs laid bare on the right side up to the breast-
bone. His left arm has been broken once, and his
collar-bone twice; his right shoulder has been put
out; he has had a slight fracture of the skull above
the left eye, in consequence of his horse catching in a
sheep-net; and he also lay for nearly three weeks in
a state of coma, the result of a rheumatic fever, from
swimming a river.

The Hurworth Country. Time has, however, come with healing
wings in each instance, and has left no
trace of these highly varied chances of war; and as
retirement at Acomb was not his *forte*, he became the
huntsman of the Hurworth in '55. With the exception of the country on both sides of the Tees, which
separates Yorkshire and Durham, this hereditary

hunting-ground of the Wilkinson family is of a stiff "up-hill and down-dale character." Still the foxes generally hang to the riverside, which can be reached in half an hour from nearly all the covers, and point away down a good scenting country for Yarm. Their best cover is Fighting Cocks, which was laid down by the present master with 14lbs. of seed to the acre, and includes from eighteen to twenty acres of good gorse, which can bear sifting pretty often during the season. The blood of Hurworth Fury, crossed with that of Badsworth Whynot, is well represented in the kennel by Worker, Woodman, and Wonder; but Buccleuch's Traveller, who came in a picked ten-couple draught, which Mr. Robinson gave John Glover when he re-signed his hounds to Earl Wemyss, has done as much good as anything to them when crossed with the blood of Sir John Cope's Galopade and their Fury. The Galopades were also to be found in those forty-one couples, young and old, which Joe Mason sent off with such sorrow from the station at Bedale to Quorn, and which have for three seasons, more than kept up the glowing *In Memoriam* he pronounced at parting. Ten couple of them are still in kennel, and if the unhappy chop had not occurred, and his lordship had carried out his intention of taking a picked pack for the Gartree Hill fox, which beat him five times one season, we will warrant that Treadwell would not have left either Albert, Ravisher, Ringwood, Reveller, or Chauntress behind. As for the Furies, we quite forget whether Will was speaking of Freeman and Fencer from Fanny, or Tomboy, Trouncer, Terrington, and Trueman from her sister Famous, when he said, " *They tak such pains and have such pluck; they fairly lift a fellow's cap off his head with delight.*" Famous was remarkable in the manner of her death; as she tried to get at her puppies through a small window, and fell into the meat boiler on the other side.

The Badsworth Whynot, who generally got white

Sir Tatton hounds like himself, was by Sir Tatton
Sykes. Sykes's Warrior, who entered himself
his first day, and brought the head home in his
mouth, and about thirty more that season. Splendour (the sire of Warrior and his Brother Wildair),
was perhaps the finest hound Sir Tatton ever bred;
Chalon painted him, and Tom Carter always said that
he despaired of having another like him. He was by
Mr. Hill's Alfred from Lord Middleton's Darling, and
so back through Monson's Duster to Vernon's Victory.
Comrade, who went to Sir Richard Sutton's, was by
him from Charming; and at one time there were
six couple of stallion hounds in the kennel, all by
him, and enough Comrades to make up any pack.
Climback was one of them, and his sons Champion
and Carver were both high wranglers in Sir Tatton's
tripos. Clinker, by Champion from Blowzy, a daughter
of own sister to Bondsman, has been a good deal
used since the present Lord Middleton took to the
hounds: and Mr. Hodgson was wont to say of him
that he would go a hundred miles any day to see
such a workman. He has none of it; but Mr.
Hodgson, as a general thing, did not care about a
little neckcloth, and said "it helps to keep their noses
down."

Sir Tatton, as well as the York and Ainsty, and
Mr. Hill, bred a good deal from Bondsman by Cruiser,
as he liked his deep tongue as well as his work. He
was a rare line hunter, and there was none of that
tiring and skirting which has been fastened by so
many on the blood of Layman, who was the sire of
his dam Bluebell. Cruiser, who was by Musters'
Solomon, and entered in 1852, was always in high
favour at Birdsall; and Mr. Ferneley's art was invoked
to immortalize him. Denmark by Splendour, Pleader,
bred by Lord Yarborough, Trojan, Furrier by Osbaldeston's Flagrant, Walter, and Woldsman, who broke
his shoulder out at quarters, and yet could lead them

in any weather in the meets near home, were also among the Birdsall particulars. Carter hankered after the Fitzwilliam Shiner for years, but he got him nothing good when he did succeed in begging him of Tom Sebright. The cross did not suit, although he had the very flowers of the pack for one or two seasons, and they were rather inclined to be noisy. Viceroy went to the Duke of Buccleuch's; and his son Highflyer, from the Duke's Harriett, has been used to some purpose in Earl Wemyss's kennel. Sir Tatton was always very particular about legs and feet, and his hounds were generally big, with especially great ribs, deep in the brisket, and, as Mr. Conyers and Mr. Marriott used to think, somewhat flat-sided; although oddly enough, it was quite a phrase of Tom Carter's, " Let me see their sides in a line with their thighs."

Mr. Conyers, who took the Lonsdale and Sykes drafts for years, considered the flat sides their great excellence, as they never tired with Jim Morgan in his heavy road work, sometimes twenty-four miles to cover. At times Jem has ridden his hack thirty-three miles from his house to Little Burnfield, had a second breakfast there, and then taken his hounds ten miles to draw. " *We'll stick to the flat uns, Jim, in Essex, whatever they say,*" was his constant remark; " *they'll bear far more fatigue than those square heavy hounds.*" Size was also a great point with Mr. Conyers, and in 1847 he had twenty-five couple of twenty-five-inch hounds; and led by Barmaid, who was nearly as big as any of them, they fairly swept like a hurricane, from scent to view, into their fox over the Roothings. In the wet weather, the bitches were invariably beaten by the dog-hounds. The former had not the necessary stride for the ditches, of which the sides were hollow; and they jumped, as Jim says, " with their hind legs short, another on top of them, and so the ditches were full."

Mr. Conyers.

Y

Wildair by Yarborough Warrior from Fitzwilliam's Willing (whose dam, Julia, ran into her fox alone in Lady Sparrow's park from Brampton Wood, after eleven hours' cub-hunting) was a great hound with Mr. Conyers; and so were Tragedy and Madcap, who would neither of them draw a yard, and Joyful by Justice from Primrose. Justice was drafted by John Ward from the Cambridgeshire kennel at three years old, but he cannot remember what for; and Primrose, like Beauty and Bashful, was of the Lonsdale blood. Beauty goes down to posterity in the portrait with her master; and for her and Bashful, both of whom he bred himself, he refused a hundred guineas from Mr. Assheton Smith. There is a great deal of the old Lonsdale blood in the present Earl's pack at Tring; and it was principally obtained by drafts from Charles Payne.

The Brocklesby.   Will Smith, of the Brocklesby, was laid to rest full twelve years before we ever sallied forth on our summer ramble for " scarlet" incidents, and many a cheery story of man and hound has gone with him. "*Stick to Ranter*" was the last kennel injunction he gave to his son Will, as he lay on his death-bed at Barnoldsby; and it has not been forgotten, either by him, or his brother Tom. He tried several dashing experiments, which many less experienced huntsmen would not have thought of; on one occasion he clipped a hound, and on another he took out a pack of bitches, all in season. "The nose of Yarborough" had lost none of its fame in his hands, but in obedience to the wishes of the late lord the standard was reduced to twenty-three and a-half for dogs, and twenty-two for bitches. The stallion succession goes back to Dover, in 1786, who traced his lineage through Fitzwilliam Ranger. The original Ranter of 1790 was Dover's son from Red Rose, sister to Ringwood, the hound which Stubbs painted. Fitzwilliam Traitor contributed its Truant, in 1797;

then came Ranters and Ringwood in a long black tan line. Reveller and Relish by Rector by Savilles' Rallywood were of Smith's own breeding, and great favourites in 1823. Then there were Druid by Flasher, a son of old Furrier; the grey Trimmer, with his deep note, who found nineteen out of twenty foxes, with the little bitch Prattler always at his side; and Jailer by Sir Tatton Sykes' Monarch, a very clever hound indeed. None of them could carry a scent like him through the steam of a hundred horses on the road; and on one occasion he took it half a mile along the top of a sod wall at Croxby Warren, with the pack on both sides, and his great bushy tan stern waving like a banner, till "the Brocklesby boys" were in raptures.

Will used to say that he always went to Sir Tatton's for ribs, and used his Furrier by Osbaldeston's Flagrant; while Fitz- hardinge's Desperate, Foljambe's Prompter by Hodgson's Valiant, and his Herald by Osbaldeston's Ranter; and the badger pye Cheshire Benedict by Galliard followed in due course. The Quorn Fur- rier also ended his days with him. Mr. Osbaldeston gave him to Lord Yarborough, when he was nine years old; but he was scalded in the back the following year (1830), and, as he failed to get any more puppies, he was put away. There is no picture extant of this patriarch of hounds, and no one at Brocklesby re- members where he was buried. Fairmaid was one of the very last litter by him, and her Dashwood by Yarborough Druid did, along with Foljambe's Albion, and Belvoir Guider, and Chacer, enormous good to the Bramham Moor. At one time or another that kennel-book could show, in the term of its time- honoured toast, full "twenty-five couple" of Dash- woods, principally bitches. The old dog, who came from the Duke of Buccleuch's to the Bramham Moor, was rather ugly and leggy, short in the ribs, and pig-

End of Osbal- deston's Furrier.

Y 2

mouthed; and his stock slightly inherited the last peculiarity, along with very nice necks and shoulders. Ruler was one of the greatest of the Brocklesby kennel cracks, and he came in an odd way. Mr. Foljambe had allowed him to pick one of his best puppies, and, when he inquired about it, Will told him that it always sneezed after feeding; and the consequence was that he sent for it back, and that rich yellow pye by Albion, the very best of his entry, arrived in its stead. Will used also to be perpetually chopping hounds with Sir Richard Sutton; and it was thus that Basilisk by Sir Richard's Ringwood from Bragela came into his hands. He was put to Rosebud, who went back through Rector to Foljambe's Piper, and ran to head in her eleventh season, and Rallywood, Rocket, and Royster were the produce. Never was there a more luckless trio, in one sense of the word. Rocket, a very handsome dog, curiously marked on one side, was kicked and killed in Grimsby Field; Royster fell down a chalk pit in Irby Dales; while Rallywood, after getting his thigh broken, and being used a good deal at Brocklesby, departed, leaving Yarborough Harper, the sire of Wynnstay Royal, behind, and made a new pack for Belvoir. Tom Smith has of late made most use of Nettler by Noble, a son of Ranter from Audible by Foljambe's Albion, and Ruler by Ruler from Victory by Rallywood; and hence the good old sort knows no decay.

The Grove Hounds. Osbaldeston's Ranter was equally the making of Mr. Foljambe's kennel, which had been previously strengthened through Roderick by some plain but very good Richmond hounds. At one time he had twenty-five couple by him, among whom were Stormer, Sparkler, Harbinger, and Herald. Harbinger, who was the most racing of the lot, was given in his prime to Earl Wemyss. Stormer was not clever to look at, but first-rate in his work, and

[margin notes: Brocklesby Stud Hounds.]

did Belvoir great good, especially as a bitch-getter; but for handiness there was nothing to beat Sparkler, and one wave from Mr. Foljambe's hand would send him flying over any double. Tom Carter used to doat on his beautiful appearance and fine ribs; and Lord Henry Bentinck liked nothing better than Conquest from his Comedy. Bonny Lass was another of his rare granddaughters, and ran very forward in her tenth season with her hearing and eye as good as ever, and not a toe down. She was so resolute, that on one occasion she crowned down on to her fox, as it would have done on to a rabbit's nest, and dug and ate him up, with the exception of the head, pads, and brush.

Herald hunted five seasons at Grove, and then went to Lord Ducie's and several other kennels, till at last Lord Henry Bentinck purchased him in a five-couple lot. He delighted Mr. Foljambe most in a run from Babington Springs up to Beverçoats Park, where the hounds came to a check. There was a halloo at the bottom of the park, and Mr. Foljambe blew them away to a fresh fox. Still Herald would not go; and Merry saw him waving his stern, and then collar the hunted one, and kill him in a briar-bush. Mr. Foljambe might well say when Will reached him, with the fox on his saddle, that such a kill was worth a king's ransom. Dick Burton put Herald away when he was nine years old, and the operation very nearly proved fatal to himself. The old dog blew the two drops of prussic acid out on to his face, as he rolled over; and as Dick rubbed it off hastily with his glove, it got slightly smeared on his own lips; and it was not till after he had recovered from a species of fainting-fit, which lasted more than two hours, that he bethought himself of the circumstance.

Comus from Crazy was Herald's best son, and the kennel used him with still greater freedom and success.

He was a wonderfully clever made "Belvoir tan," of about twenty-three-and-a-half inches, and especially great in drawing, and picking out a scent on a cold day. Dick Burton used to say that, with the exception of Rachael by Osbaldeston's Rasselas, whom he brought with him from Lord Ducie's, and who earned his eternal gratitude, with carrying it by herself through more than a hundred horsemen, down the cliff to Riseholme Wood, on his and her maiden day, in Lincolnshire—that there was no nose he could trust to like Comus's.

Comrade, Contest, and Craftsman. He was perfect in his work up to his seventh season, when he died rather suddenly. In 1847 Lord Henry's kennel was half full of Comuses; and it was generally considered a hard-running blood, which required to be crossed with line-hunters. Contest, Craftsman, and Comrade were three very eminent brothers by him from his lordship's Sanguine by Foljambe's Sparkler. Contest was never known to smeuse, but took his gates like a greyhound. Comrade and Craftsman were both better than him in their necks and shoulders; and the latter was given to Sir Watkin Wynne, and got some fifteen couple before he was passed on to the Duke of Beaufort, who has always had a wonderful liking for the sort. At one time his Grace had seven couple in work by the three brothers. John Walker entered seven sisters by the latter from Precious, among which are Curious and Cheerful. Curious was in her turn the dam of Conjuror (by Fitzwilliam Harbinger, a grandson of Yarborough Rallywood), who measures thirty-two inches round the heart, as attested by Lord Berners' bullock-tape. Grappler is also a Craftsman after John Walker's own heart, and he and Conjuror were among "the boys that tickled up the Cheshire fox" from the Rawheads on the last Monday of '58. Some men holloaed at him from the Peckforton Castle Hills; and his death-warrant was signed as he sank into the Vale of Destruction, in a line for Beeston Station, and John Walker called up Cockatoo ; but not sealed till he had given them an hour and five minutes through Harlaston Gorse to Acton, over the finest part of Cheshire. Render, Clasper, and Charon, the latter from a Comus bitch, were all celebrated Contests in the Burton country ; and so were Clansman, Carnage, Candid, and Clarion from Destiny by Driver, a nephew of Herald's. Driver was quite one of Dick Burton's adjutants, and the admiration was remarkably mutual. On one occasion they ran a fox for three hours in Harpwell Gorse as if they would tear it down, and not one hound outside for the last twenty minutes. Driver was the only one missing after they had killed ; and in a few minutes he appeared, with the brush in his mouth, and solemnly laid it at Dick's feet, before the assembled field. Strange to say, he did the same thing over again in the course of the next season's cub-hunting. Contest is in Earl Wemyss's kennel, and his six couple of one-season hounds—more especially Honesty, Heroine, Harbinger, and Highflyer, inheriting as they do his muscular back and loins—are in high favour with his lordship and Will Channing.

The match between Earl Fitzwilliam's and Mr. Meynell's hounds took place in the days of Will Deane, who had come with the hounds from Lord Crewe and Foley's, in Worcestershire. Mr. Meynell brought his ten couple from Kimbolton Castle to the tryst at Hunt's Closes, and the hounds were stopped at the end of forty minutes, when, as Milton tradition has it, Darter and the original Druid, both of them tans, were a good first and second. The Druids were generally dark tans, and Dreadnought was a great hound of the sort. When Tom Sebright succeeded John Clark in 1821, there were a great many blue pied, who ran back to old Glancer. The two sorts united well in Jason, from

Earl Fitz-william's.

whom sprang the celebrated Yarborough Druid. Jason by Genial from Duchess was an old stager when Tom Sebright came, and it was of Genial (who had been killed by a kick from a horse just before), that Lord Lonsdale said, he was the best constitutioned and stoutest hound he ever used.

Milton Stud Hounds. His lordship had also a great many of the Monarch sort. He was by Yarborough's Fairplay from his Vanity, and was entered in 1826, and Tom still loves to tell how he went right away from the body of the hounds near Weston Grove in a great run from Elton's New Closes. The yellow pied Marmion was a son of his, and got his stock with very gay heads and necks, and principally of that colour. He was given to Mr. Foljambe, but died on the kennel bench very soon after he came; and his grandson Marmion by Monarch from Felix, who goes back on his dam's side through Flourish and Finisher to Osbaldeston's Ferryman by Furrier, was used by a great many kennels. The Fatals were also of the Ferryman blood, and Tom thought that nothing nicked better than their cross with the Hermits. John Ward liked the old blood when he whipped into Tom, and the Cambridgeshire kennel in his day was full of Monarchs and Fatals. Marksman, for whom Lord Macclesfield gave 50 guineas at Mr. Henley Greaves' sale, is a fine combination of Marmion with Badsworth Mindful, who goes back, like Badsworth Lubin to Buccleuch's Lexicon. Marplot, the handsomest old hound in the kennel, is all that is left of the sort; and Lord Ducie's Marplot, who made that celebrated jump over the pommel of Lord Portman's saddle, as he stooped to open a gate, did not belong to it, but was of Fitzhardinge blood.

The Shiners have always been very celebrated at Milton. He dates about 1824, and was by the Scarbro' Saladin of the Monson blood, and from Traffic by Yarborough Trimmer. The yellow pied Sports-

THOMAS SEBRIGHT.

man from Faithful by Yarborough Flasher was the
one who did most for the blood, and was particularly
noticed for his beauty. Shiner himself was given by
Lord Fitzwilliam to the Duke of Bedford, at the end
of his sixth season, and not only ran well to head in
the Oakley, but stocked that kennel and the Cambridgeshire to boot. John Walker also dipped into
the sort through Sultan (the sire of Wynnstay Sultan),
and so did Mr. Henley Greaves, who had ten couple
by him from Badsworth Caroline. Lifter and Pleader,
both very dear to Tom, strained back to Drake's
Hector ; and Hermit, who was by Hector from Goldfinch by Yarborough Ganymede, went to the Duke of
Beaufort's, and left several especially excellent daughters behind him.

Badminton paid off his debt to Milton, in the capital
cross between their Flyer and Fitzwilliam Blithesome
by the Yarborough Bluecap, which produced Feudal.
Nearly all this family were rich smutty-faced tans, with
rare shoulders and chests, but perhaps slightly thin
thighs and quarters. Flamer, one of his sons, who
goes back to Osbaldeston's Vanquisher, distinguished
himself greatly two seasons ago, not only by joining
the cry the first day he was taken out, but by bringing
home the head as well. Looking back through the
vista of half a century, perhaps Tom was never quite
so proud of a pupil as when he rode home from
Aversley Wood that day. Ottoman, to whom he has
especially clung of late, is a combination of Yarborough Orator, and Vanity by Belvoir Victor; and
is a lengthy hound, with great bone, and requires
rather an airy style of cross. His shoulders are
not quite so elegant as some, and his bitches are
especially fine, and bigger than his dogs. Eleven
couple have been entered by him at Milton ; and
Wynnstay had a good slice out of him through
Pantomime by their Warrior, who is a grandson of
Yarborough Rosebud.

Mr. Osbaldeston's Entry. Tom Sebright involuntarily sends us back to the days when he whipped in to "The Squire," fifty years ago, on the very first day that glorious rider carried his horn as master, in the Burton country. No master had been better bred to it, as far as strength of character was concerned; and it was told of his mother that, when some one brought her the rumour (during the heat of a ten days' election at York) that her son was hurt out hunting, she said, "*Don't talk to me about my son—he knows how to fall well enough—how goes the poll?*" Tom remembers, as if it was yesterday, that the first run was thirty-two minutes to ground without a check from Eagle Low Wood; and when they had dug down to him, with what delight he turned round and said, "*This is a good beginning, sir; there's a fox a-piece for us in this earth.*" And so having disposed of one, they had two hours and thirty-five minutes with the other; but in spite of four long checks, every horse was beaten to a stand-still. And so we trace the pair on through the South Notts and Atherstone countries, till we find them with Furrier, Rocket, Vaulter, and Vanquisher, and others as good as they, among the pasture lands of Leicestershire. Early in his career, the Squire bred a great deal from Wildboy by Monson's Wonder, who came in the pack which he purchased from his lordship. Vaulter's brother Vigilant by Vernon's Vigilant was the harder runner of the two; but Vaulter was the huntsman's friend, and could put them all to rights on a bad scenting day. Vanquisher was as hard a runner as he was handsome; and, like Furrier, he was eventually given to Lord Yarborough for a stud hound.

Tarquin. Still that most unerring and melodious of finders, the twenty-four inch Tarquin, was Sebright's delight, and two sisters of the same litter were nearly as great. His hind quarters were his plainest part; and he was an odd, short-tempered dog, who bore speaking to so ill, that he and the Squire fell out. Over and over again, the Squire was heard to say to him, "*Ah! Tarquin, if you don't like me, I like you;*" but the proud blood of Trickster by Belvoir Topper steadily refused to make it up. He took no notice of the hounds till after Christmas, but he did no harm; and it was in a fine run from Wragby Woods towards Market Rasen that he suddenly came out, like a shot, from the body of them, and rolled his fox over, single-handed. He especially distinguished himself in the suburbs of Lichfield, when he carried it by himself along nearly three hundred yards of wall, at the bottom of some gardens; and deaf to the shrieks of the women, who rushed frantically at their clothes-lines, to try and rescue some articles at least from the grasp of the scarlet Philistines, marked him for his own between two store pigs in a stye. For six seasons he did his work well; and, in after years, Tom gently laid his remains under a slab, in the path from the huntsman's house at Quorn to the kennel. Then, for the first and last time, did Tom give way to the seductions of verse; and we wish that a tithe of our poets could express their ideas with half the grapple and feeling that he did. A slate was got from the Switheland Pits, and he "furnished copy" to the stone-cutter as follows:—

> "'Tis here my favourite Tarquin lies—
> Turn away sportsmen, and wipe your eyes;
> Not the only favourite in the pack,
> But Tarquin never in work was slack."

Rocket (the sire of Prodigal, and especially great down a road), and Furrier, *Furrier.* were both stud-kings at Quorn in their turn. Furrier was by the Belvoir Saladin, and originally came in a draft from the Duke of Rutland, with whom "The Squire" exchanged very freely. They did not think very highly of him, as his work was not brilliant enough to rub off the impression left by his legs, which had become crooked from being tied up at quarters. It was not, in fact, until February that he came, by a sudden impulse, out of the ruck, with Heedless, another draft bitch, and leading the pack by ten yards, neck and neck, over Garthorpe Lings, brought that renowned fox, "Perpetual Motion," to book at last. He was a black-and-white twenty-four-inch hound, high on the leg, very stout, and a hard runner, but not a great line-hunter. The latter was his sister Frantic's great *forte.* She came in a draft to the Southwold, when at barely three-and-twenty, John Walker commenced his career as huntsman under Mr. Pelham; and she went back to Brocklesby, after she had a litter to their Minister.

The Descendants of Furrier. At one time "The Squire" had forty couple of light and smart, but sadly mute, bitches in the Quorn kennel; and he took at least half of them with him to Northamptonshire, and showed wonderful sport for his first two seasons. In 1831 he had twenty-six couple of them at Brixworth; and there were about ten or twelve couple of them in the seventy which Mr. Harvey Combe bought from him in 1835. Castor, Flasher, and Random were very noted Furrier dogs; and Mr. Parry had eight or nine very choice bitches by them in a draft from Will Todd, who hunted Mr. Combe's for the six seasons they were at Ricksmansworth. The Pilgrims and Rummagers— the one with their long, solemn heads, and the others all gaiety—were among the "Osbaldestons" which clustered round Dick Simpson of the Puckeridge on his rare crooked-kneed Struggles; and knew the cunning notes of that horn, which Will Rose always vowed that he blew to pieces one day, whereas Dick solemnly declares to us that York fell on that side near Reed Wood, and stove it in. There were scarcely seven couple of Castors left when Mr. Combe's pack were put up at Tattersall's, in the July of 1840; and

Malibran, the pink of the bitches, and Melody from Musical (of whom the 1831 Pytchley list merely says, "*Bred by Lord Sondes*") were in the five couple lot, which were bought in for 1360 guineas! Minnie and Merryman were own brother and sister to them, but of different litters; and Mr. Combe had Minnie painted, and would never part with her. Like nearly all the Furrier dogs, Merryman was a splendid jumper; and on one occasion, when Lord Ducie borrowed him for the Vale of White Horse, he got among the stone walls and had all the fun to himself. His lordship gave a long price for Hector simply for the sake of his Ranter blood, as a fork thrust at his quarters had totally lamed him. He also once sent to Jack Shirley, to offer him ten guineas for Castor, who was then nearly worn out; but Sir Richard Sutton had just taken a dislike to him, and had ordered him and Falstaff, another Furrier dog, to be hung a few days before; while Flourisher was retained.

In 1836, the picked twenty couple of Mr. Combe in the pack had a very narrow escape, when Lincolnshire. Sir Richard invited Mr. Combe to have four days in the Burton country. They went down with the boiler in the canal-boat to Leicester, while Will Todd travelled by coach, and a bitch was taken with hydrophobia on the voyage, and bit several of them. It was a melancholy time in Lincolnshire, as they hunted four days and only killed one fox. One Furrier ran away from the pack, and killed a lamb, and they saw him no more. Another was tied temporarily to a carriage-wheel, and gnawed it in two; and at last they had to shoot four couple, get muzzles made for the remainder, and van them back to Cobham. Luckily the trouble stopped there, and the muzzles still hang up in a shed—a sort of memento which Will Todd does not at all need, as he was up three weary nights with them, watching for their jaws to drop.

Will Todd. Will had, however, been pretty well used to hardships, as when he had ridden for five years in London after Lord Scarborough, he helped to take a shipload of horses to Russia, and might have been seen struggling across the ice at Cronstadt, with his portmanteau on his head, to reach a timber ship bound for England. Then followed sixteen years as whip under Philip Payne and Will Long, at Badminton, which he inaugurated by cheeking a fox for a mile and a half on Ramsden Heath, and effectually preventing him from getting into the Forest. The Sixth Duke, who had been watching him with great delight, might well say, "If your young hounds, Philip, enter as well as the new whip, they'll do well." His most favourite recollections with the Furriers, is of a day when they found at Islip Woods, and killed him after an hour in the woodlands. His horse over-reached and split his hoof nearly to the shoe, and when he had got on one of Tilbury's, they found again near Harefield, and came away at a tremendous pace over grass to Batcher Heath, by the corner of Moor Park to Oxey, up to the Marquis of Abercorn's, and then straight to the reservoir on the Edgeware Road. Near the metropolis, Will's horse tired, and Mr. Combe gave him up his chestnut Blunder, and he viewed his fox as he bent back to Harrow, and then got among some flags, beneath where they were building a ball-room. The school lads came out in full force, and rather puzzled the hounds, and he was never found till the next day.

The Oakley Marmions. Merryman was among the four or five couple of Castors which went in the pack to Lord Southampton in 1841. This was the second time his lordship had bought a pack outright, and Ottoman by Pytchley Orpheus, Hannibal, Hesperus, Highflyer, Hercules, and Honesty composed the cream of the Oakley one, which came with Mumford and

George Beers to Quorn when the Marquis of Tavistock gave up his hounds the first time. The latter
four were by the Oakley Hercules, for whom Mr.
Musters had a very strong regard. The pack were
rather unsizeable when they arrived at Quorn, the
dogs large (beginning with the 25-inch Hannibal), and
the bitches light of bone. Six or seven couple of
Marmions by Pytchley Marmion, came along with
them, and it was because Sir Harry Goodricke
thought that Merlin and Marmion of that blood were
soft, that he got rid of the whole pack after the retirement of Lord Southampton (who had bred a good
deal from draft bitches, many of them by, Belvoir
Layman), and replaced them with Mr. Newman"
hounds, which were principally Badminton drafts, and
as wild as hawks. Neither huntsman nor whips
thought that the Marmions were fairly condemned, but
that they were simply rather delicate hounds, with very
fine noses. However, twenty couple were packed off
to Russia, and the rest into all lands. And so ended
one Oakley pack. Never was there a fairer sportsman than its noble master, and he would go so far as
to make his whips stop the hounds to let a sinking
fox get a little farther ahead.

Will Wells's journals, although their Will Wells.
faded ink sorely tests the eyesight, tell
of many a great day with this pack in its early days.
His style of drawing up his remarks is unique, and
he terms the whole—" A Journal of the Operations of
the Oakley Foxhounds, 18—," and heads each entry
as " The Meet at (say) Yardley Chase on Monday as
specified below." The Oakley and the Cross Albans
countries were then united, and in 1811-12 the cub-
hunting began on July 13th, and the season usually
ended on May 4th. Will seems to have been astonished at his own labours, as after recording that
they killed forty-four brace of "foxies" (as he affectionately called them), he adds—" Here ended the

season, comprising a period of nine months and twenty-three days, or 299 days." The Journal seems to record every emotion he felt; occasionally it observes—" Here was a most cheering cry;" and adds, after an unsuccessful lift, " the intelligence was of the falsest kind." On one occasion he seems to have been quite out in his calculations, and he thus took care to acquaint posterity. " And the fox was viewed by Mr. Lee; and the hounds were carried to the spot two minutes after the fox was viewed; and the scent was so very bad, that by tucking the hounds' heads up, they would never once hit off the scent again; nor could one own the scent; not one hound. So we lost our fox by tucking the hounds' heads up to get them near to their fox, after hunting him very pretty for two hours over a pretty country." Still, pretty as this country might have been in his eyes, seeing that he hunted it for four-and-twenty years, the Woore country suited him equally well; and it was there that " the varmint old fellow" was seen in his glory in later years—" Though with scarce a whole bone in his skin;" and ready to break his ribs for the third, and his collar-bone for the eighth time, if he could only get the chance.

Modern Oakley   The best blood in the Oakley kennel
Hounds.   between 1835-46 was from Jasper, an active light-coloured hound of twenty-three inches, while Cottesmore Grecian, from whom he was one or two degrees removed, was said to measure twenty-seven. They sent out a litter of twelve by him in one year, and got them all through the distemper; and when they had drafted the biggest and the smallest, the rest made a very level lot. Jasper came with Phœnix, (a perfect terror to a fox), and Tuneful, in a lot, as a present from the Earl of Lonsdale to the Marquis of Tavistock; and George Beers was especially fond of crossing the Jasper bitches with the Fitzwilliam Monarch and Fatal blood. Prizer, an old-fashioned

broad-nosed hound, also did him great good ; and although he never borrowed him, his was just one of the heads which the late Lord Hastings cast about for so anxiously.

The accompanying illustration, which Lord Hastings. is copied exactly from a little drawing which his lordship once brought down to Will Derry, at the kennel, and which Will has treasured ever since, shows exactly the model head at which his lordship

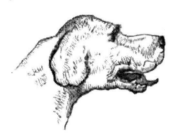

wished to arrive. Sir Harry Goodricke gave him twenty couple of The Quorn, with a very good Fatima, Furrier, and Ferryman, amongst them ; and he set about putting the broad base and heavy lip of the Southern hound upon them. The head of Luther, a Layman hound, which he got from Tom Goosey, just suited him ; and sleepy as he looked, he was always forward when the fox sank. Lancaster from the Cheshire kennel, rather pleased him in this respect ; and so did Royal, whom he got from Mr. Greene of Rolleston. As to foxes' heads, he had also a theory that they should be as big as those of the hounds. These ideas were, however, sadly foiled by having madness in his kennel, all one season, and in six or seven weeks no less than thirteen-and-a-half couple were seized. Will Head first found it out from his boiler, who told him, when he came back from exercise, that Pliant had been very odd with the other

z

hounds, and had just gone to fight Stately, who had puppies. The latter seemed to know instinctively that something was wrong, as they were screaming and scrambling up the wall one upon another, in ghostly terror. As the effects of Pliant's bites, of which she had been very liberal, became more evident, the pack began to play antics, pick up straws, and then try to tear bricks out of the walls ; or go round and round. Their tongues swelled, and their eyes became red, and when they went in to try them with cold broth before hunting, they would often have turned quite black in the night. At last it became so bad, that Will Head simply watched with a twelve foot ash-pole and a noose at the end, and dragged them out, morning after morning, to their doom.

RAMBLE THE THIRD.

"Oh ! who has been in such a scene,
That scene can e'er forget,
In sorrow's mood—in solitude,
That scene will haunt him yet ;
In festal times, in other climes,
He'll think of days so dear,
And take a cup and drain it up,
To saddle, spur, and spear."

Sir Richard Sutton. SIR RICHARD SUTTON swore by the Belvoir and the Yarborough kennels. In Will Smith's day, he was always chopping and changing with him, and sent ten couple of bitches to his cracks each season that he was at Burton. He had also the Rutland draft for many years, and he was wont to say that he always thought his own hounds the first in the world, till he saw the Duke's, every summer. In the Burton country, he had kept his standard rather large, but he got them smaller at last, and never liked to exceed twenty-three inches. His bitches especially were sadly mute, but he used to draw comfort from that, by vowing that it was not a fault, but a beauty; and that as the first few were the only ones that could possibly have the scent, they alone had a right to open. One of his greatest delights, when he was in the Cottesmore country, was to select ten couple, and join packs with the Duke. Osgodby Coppice furnished them a capital day's sport, and another challenge to Lord Forester resulted in such a hard ringing day, that Ben Morgan's horse dropped in Honeypot Lane; and one that had been ridden by the Duke's first whip·died that night. Once too they clashed, and had a capital forty minutes with a head at the end of it; and on another occasion both packs, when Sir Richard was master of the Quorn, met by chance at Owthorpe, and ran out of the Vale to Cotgrave, and killed at Cotgrave Gorse. The Cottesmore Sorcerer (who never got but one litter of two), by Sir Tatton Sykes's Bajazet from Symphony, put them right up a road, and Will Goodall's cheery comment of " *Well done, old Bobtail!*" delighted Sir Richard beyond measure. At these times Sir Richard always said, " *Now, Will, you be huntsman, and I'll whip in to you.*"

The Duke of Beaufort's Potentate His Favourite (whose son Primate, from Beaufort Fatal   Hounds. is the sire of ten and a half of Earl Wemyss's best hounds) took his work with Sir Richard's for a season. His own Potentate was one of six couple by Trueman from Parasol; and Trueman by Belvoir Trueman from Yarborough Pastime, was the very idol of his heart. He not only took him regularly in his carriage to cover, but would never let him go to any meet where there was likely to be a crowd of "thrusting scoundrels." He was a good-looking black and white hound, with a slightly tan face, perhaps a little heavy-shouldered, but with immense power and bone. Being a very remarkable line hunter, he required bitches with plenty of drive, and at one time there were as many as twenty-two couple in the kennel by him. Fifteen and a half couple by him were put up at the first Quorn sale, but the received opinion among huntsmen seems to be that the blood was a little slack with an afternoon fox. His sisters Traffic and Twilight were very good, and he generally got his bitches best and with very great quality. Songstress and Sanguine, from Singwell, were very choice, and Auditor and Albert were among the best of his sons. Sir Richard kept the old dog for seven seasons, and then gave him to Earl Wemyss, who had Albert as well. His lordship had only one left by him; and he died in his possession.

Glider, a little, light, even-made hound of about twenty-one inches, and remarkably good in his work, was another of Sir Richard's tenderest fancies latterly. He was by Lumley's Pontiff from his own Gadfly, and in direct descent from Vine Grampian. He got his stock large, and when he had used him pretty freely, he sent him to Berkeley for a season in exchange for their Albert. Ayris was using him at the time of the first Quorn sale, and in the last letter that Sir Richard wrote to the Earl a few days before his death, he reiterated his favourite maxim, "*Put bitches to my Glider.*" Dairymaid from Dorcas was by him, and formed one of the lot for whom Mr. Richard Sutton gave 200 guineas. Guider by Drake's Duster, from his beautiful bitch Gamesome, was another of his darlings, and so was the hard-running Dexter, and the rare drawer, Hercules, both of whom went to Mr. Morrell's. Then there was Daphne by Dryden (brother to Dexter) from Tuneful, a daughter of Rutland Trouncer, of whose cave exploit we shall tell hereafter; and Ringwood by Bragela by Chaser, a clipping little hound, and very unlike his leggy red sire Charon.

Sir Richard's patience as a huntsman Sir Richard's
was most eminently displayed in the Patience.
great run of twenty miles, from point to point, on
December 27th, 1850. The find was at Cossington
Gorse, and after some very slow hunting over the
Heaths beyond Scorford, they eventually brought
him to hand in four hours at Denton Park. Sir
Richard went home in the Duke's carriage, while the
hounds stopped all night at the Belvoir kennels; and
Will—when he returned from hunting, and found Jack
and his Trueman party—did not fail to dwell, in his
merry style, upon the enormity of running a fox over
the heart of his country, and asking for "grub" and
bed as well; let alone never giving him a chance of
bringing it back to Quorn.

Latterly Sir Richard did not ride with Jack Morgan.
so much nerve: and did not like brooks.
Jack Morgan, on one occasion, rode his horse for him
over Stanton Wyvile Brook, and then carried him
through it on his shoulders; and two years before he
died, he crossed the Smite in the same primitive
fashion, with his bearer fairly up to his hips in mud.
Jack joined Sir Richard from Mr. Mure, and became
his head whip when his brother Ben was made huntsman to the Berwickshire. Before he took to hounds,
he had become pretty well bronzed under the sun of
the tropics, whither he went off at a moment's notice.
He and another man had been put in charge by old
Jim Morgan, of twenty couple of hounds, bull-dogs,
terriers, &c., which were intended for the East. By
the time the voyage from Gravesend to Po.tsmouth
was complete, Jack's travelling companion proved to
be so dull a student, that he forgot the dogs' names as
fast as he learnt them, and as he was haunted with a
vague idea that they would eat him on the voyage,
the captain told Jack to jump on board, and come to
the East. Boy-like, he did so, without having time
even to write to his father, and set to work at once to

build up a place for his pupils in the forecastle. Old Jim bore the suspense like a philosopher ; as he felt an inward assurance that a sharp lad like his Jack had "lit on his legs somewhere." Once at Calcutta he stayed three or four years, and after winning several races on the Arabs, and keeping up his hunting science among tigers and jackals, the present huntsman of the Southwold set foot on English soil once more, and after a few seasons with Mr. Mure took his degree at Cottesmore and Quorn.

Last Days of Sir Richard. Sir Richard delighted most in Mundy's Gorse, Walton Thorns, and Scraptoft ; and in his last three seasons, the latter cover held a fox, which had beaten him at least eight or ten times. On the very Friday before he died the meet was at Barkby Hall, and his three sons, Mr. Banks Wright and the veteran Will Butler, came with him on the drag. The second, or the big pack, was out that day, and Sir Richard rode Shankton and Harkaway. A fox was soon found, which was killed in a drain near Queeniborough ; and then he said, " *Will! there's a good fox lives at Scraptoft: we'll give him a gallop.*" And so they did, ten minutes in cover, and five-and-thirty minutes out, and ran into him near Beeby. " *Jack! it's one of the best days I ever saw. I feel better. I hope I shall meet you at Ratcliffe on Tuesday*"—were the last words he said to his favourite whip, and went up to London immediately after. Tuesday came ; and the Leicestershire field heard the sad news from the lips of the house-steward, just as they were leaving Ratcliffe Hall to draw.

Great Runs with the Duke of Rutland's. Mundy's Gorse and Aylesford Gorse each furnished a rare hour and five minutes, without a check, on the day the Duke of Rutland was invited to come into the Leicestershire country in the interval, after it had lost its lamented chief. Mr. Wood of Market Overton, and Mr. Burbidge of Thorpe Arnold, were the leaders in the first, save and except Will Goodall on Catch-me-who-can. "*Give me the brush, Will,*" said Mr. Wood who had left his horse and run into the field, "*I'm first up.*" "*How can that be when I've got him?*" responded Will ; "*I wouldn't let you have it for a hundred guineas.*" This was on Jan. 9th, 1856, and they killed both their foxes. Well might Will appraise the brush after that fashion, as only once before or since have the Duke's got so far into Leicestershire. On that occasion (March, 1857) they found a fox at Melton Spinney, which left Ranksboro' to the left, through Owston Wood and John O'Gaunt's, and over Tilton Field, to Skeffington, where they ran into him in The Lincolnshire the open. Oddly enough, they had only a Fens. week before made their longest voyage of discovery in-to the uttermost part of Lincolnshire, in a run of two hours and twenty minutes, from Falkinham Gorse. They crossed the Forty Foot river, and killed him near Pinchbeck, and an old woman who had never seen hounds and scarlet before, drove her pig and cow into her sitting room, screamed that the Russians were coming, and put up her shutters, in anticipation of a siege. After receiving a most scorching bene-diction from one of the natives of those wilds, who gasped out that he was "*cutting all the whate up,*" Will left his horse fast in the mud with a tamer native to hold up his head, till ropes could be got, and ran to the end on foot.

The Belvoir annals can furnish runs Remarkable quite as remarkable as that, in a different Kills. degree. In that season of 1854-55, when every spring near the Ropsley kennels was dried up, and when Will had to pay eight shillings for each cartfull of water for the hounds; when he never had but one wet shirt himself, and that on the day of the battle of the Alma ; and when he had not one fall, and killed 110 foxes in 112 days, he had a pair of blazing twenty-five minutes, going on at one time. A brace of foxes went away from the plantations near Beck, and the twenty couple divided to a hound, one fox taking a ring to the right, and the other to the left, and both died honourably within a few yards of each other, close by where they were found. Unlike Captain Macheath, he was enabled in the same year to be happy with both his charmers; as the hounds found a brace at Leadenham Park, came away with them in two bodies, ran parallel, and killed them both, almost to a moment, and within a hundred yards of each other, near the Newark road.

Will Goodall's early career began at the Will Goodall. late Mr. Drake's, where his father still lives; and many and long were the hours he waited outside the House of Commons during the Reform Debates of 1832, when his master was member for Amersham, and the grooms had no covered shed. What stories he could tell of how Ben Foote rated him for stealing away with hounds, and having his first run when he was merely stationed to watch if the fox came out in a rushy corner; and how Griff Lloyd always forgot to pay him the half-crown he agreed on, for carrying him bodily over a brook. He broke in Flounce and Fop, that celebrated brother and sister, for Mr. Tom Drake, for whom he first acted as cover-boy; and after serving four years under Goosey as second whip, he was made the Belvoir huntsman on Tom's resignation in '42. Tom Flint was but too conscious of his one sad failing; and he and Will were such good friends, that he would have cheerfully stopped and whipped in to him, if the Duke had seen fit. Up to that point, the Belvoir hound standard had been twenty-four, but Will reduced it an inch.

Crack Belvoir Jasper, brother to Juniper who went Hounds. back to Mr. Compton's blood; Topper, whom Mr. Shawe brought with him from Sir Thomas Mostyn's, and Saladin, the sire of Furrier, were deemed by Goosey among the fathers of the pack. He also

Engraved by J.B. Hunt from a Photograph
by Bishop of Cheltenham

THE LATE WILL GOODALL.

entered ten couple by Layman, from whom Joe Maiden bred a litter in Cheshire, and liked the sort as much as Tom Carter did. Splendour, sire of the Duke of Grafton's Saffron, and Rockwood were also very great with him, the latter more especially, from his recollections of how he brought home the head on that Goadby Gorse day, whose finish Ferneley's pencil has so well preserved. The run was to Preston Windmill in the Cottesmore country; where Rockwood killed him under a gateway; and as, by the rules of foxhunting, they could not dig, they tied some gorse to a pole, and pushed the fox and Rockwood out together.

Goosey also thought highly of Rasselas by Clinker, who proved himself one of the best stallion-hounds in the kennel; and he was nearly as fond of his sister, Ringlet, from whom the Rutland Stormer was descended. His daughter, Careful, made some wonderful hits in 1839, when she was seven years old; and Mr. Assheton Smith offered Lord Forester 100 guineas for her. Clamorous, another of his daughters, died a very glorious death The Cottam Thorns Day. on the Cottam Thorns day. She was very old at the time, and was only taken out for a treat, when their fox ran the line of Needham Hills, and was killed after four hours in Benington Fen. The Duke and Will were the only two left, and they could hardly raise a trot down the last lane, when they thought they heard them grab him in the next field; but the night was so dark that, after leaving their horses and scrambling through the hedge, they had to feel in their mouths to see if they were correct. Old Clamorous had never worked harder; but apoplexy came on about an hour after feeding, and she lay at full length dead on the bench next morning.

Yarborough Rallywood, who has virtually made the Belvoir kennel what it Rallywood. is, never ran to head, but always got to the end of great runs. He was very long and low; the exact image of the Ringwood that Stubbs painted for Brocklesby, and with somewhat round quarters, which made him rather the harrier, and although good twenty-three, he was mean to those who like a big hound. In fact, he was quite a *multum in parvo*, and Will thus summed up his merits in the last sentence of the last letter he ever wrote us: "He was *the lowest* dog I ever saw in my life, with the largest fore rib, combined with a beautiful neck and shoulders, and a pleasing intelligent countenance." Old Will Smith wanted the Belvoir Grappler, and said "*I'll give you anything in the kennel for him,*" and Will selected Rallywood, in spite of his broken thigh. This exchange was never made, owing to Smith's untimely death, and Grappler died at Belvoir; but the negotiations were renewed with young Will Smith, and he sent Rallywood, by whom he had at one time about fourteen couple of working hounds, and got Trouncer in exchange, and then Raglan by Rustic, whom he liked no better. Will was so fond of his prize, when he at last got hold of it, that fifty-three couple of his puppies, from ten couple of "the very best stuff" in the kennel, were sent out in the second season. He came to Belvoir in 1851, at nine years old, and was worked a whole season, and when he died in 1853, he found a fitting necropolis in the centre of a flower plot, in Will's garden; and a red-currant tree now blooms over his remains.

Rallywood's Descendants. Clinker and Chaser were the first of his get, and raced in their eighth season like greyhounds. Their immense pace they inherited from their dam Caroline, whose dam Toilet added to this quality the knack of being able to go just as fast or as long, in or out of condition. Caroline once found a fox in the woodlands by herself, and went away before the whole pack. Not a hound could catch or gain a yard on her, and she at last ran bang into him alone. Rallywood, Sailor, and Lucifer have been the last great immediate descendants of him ; and Comely and Clara by Lucifer from Cautious by Craftsman were two of John Walker's "dearies"; but Comely lost her foot by a stub, in cub-hunting, and it mortified and dropped off, and they only saved her to have one litter by Yarborough Nettler. Pyramid, the victim of a somewhat similar misfortune, we saw wandering about the Wynnstay paddock ; but in her case the fox curled round, when she seized it, and bit her hamstring clean in two. Lucifer was a tremendous runner all his time, and especially remarkable as a puppy, and Lucifer and before he ever came in from quarters, he Lictor. would regularly appear at the meet, and run with the hounds.   He was quartered at Hose, and on one occasion he was going with his master to Melton Market, when he espied the Duke's second horseman, and on second thoughts went with him to Piper Hole. They found at Clawson Thorns, and had an excellent run with a kill, and Lucifer well up.   Just as they were going to draw again, he took right off with a hare, and they lost him, till they had hunted their next fox nearly up to Lord Harboro's park, when he was seen racing to meet them, among hosts of hares. The pack were stopped, as usual, at this point ; and when he had taken a turn at a deer, in Croxton Park, coming back, he had his supper at Belvoir, and was sent home.

This was also the habit of his brother Lictor when he was at walk at Clawson.   He would sometimes join Will, and then a day or two after, by way of a change, he would be seen remarkably busy with Sir Richard Sutton's.   He once joined the Quorn at Holwell Mouth, and they killed their fox in the woods, close by Belvoir Castle.   Sir Richard and Lord Rosslyn had arranged to take the draft that season, and the former was so pleased with Lictor's work, that he said to Jack Morgan, "*Get off, Jack, and see if he's straight; if he is I'll have him, if I get first pick."* Jack shook his head after the inspection, and said, " *He'll never come to Quorn, Sir Richard;"* and so it proved, as Will Goodall worked him six seasons, and then Lord Henry's, Sir Watkin's, and Mr. Devonport's kennels used him. It was always said that he carried the scent across some dry fallows that day, near Clawson Thorns, and Will never failed to point him out to Jack when he came to the kennel, with— " *There, my lad, that's the dog that killed your fox for you; you wont have him; I'll keep him to show me the road into some of your country."*

Trouncer.   The Pytchley bred a good deal from Trouncer by Trimmer, who was one of the most intelligent hounds that ever drew a cover. One day the Duke's had had a capital run from Croxton Park, and they then went for an afternoon fox to Melton Spinney, and ran up wind, twelve miles, to Belvoir. Will was left alone when he got there, and he had quite lost the hounds, after vainly trying to track them on the rides. The present Lord Scarborough and Mr. Drummond were the first to come down from the Castle, when they heard his horn; and then Trouncer opened in reply on the top of Blackberry Hill. When Will spoke to him, he cantered away and waved his stern, and looked over his shoulder at him, to bring him along till he guided him to a cave, under the hill, where a fire had been lighted for tea parties in summer. There were the pack as black as sweeps, from their vain efforts to get up the chimney after the fox; and Will had to dislodge it as he could. All Trouncer's descendants were full at head, and one of them, Destitute by Sutton's Dryden, from Tuneful, one December night, when it was almost dark, jumped the Croxton Park wall with the body of the hounds, and turning to the left, while the whole of the others flashed to the right, killed her fox by herself. Dryden did the kennel great good, especially with Daphne and Dowager, who in a run when, as Will's diary has it, "Guider, Trusty, and Notary were making hits all day over the plough," raced clean out of the pack, and into their fox about fifty yards a-head of everything, after a blazing hour from Humby Wood, and killed him by themselves, two fields from Newton Gorse. Since they got so well set up with Rallywoods, the Belvoir have used but very few stallions from other kennels. Warwickshire Saffron did little for them; but Foljambe's Duster and Finder answered well, and they have the Drake Duster blood in perfection through Songstress and Guider, by whom, at one time, they had three couple of stallions, of whom Gamester was among the foremost.

Like his sire, who ran seven seasons, Belvoir Comus. Grappler was a great finder, and so was Comus, whose stock have been the most persevering of line hunters. There was such a run on him at the kennel, when he was in his zenith, that for nearly a month Will's great bed, which was popularly supposed to be able to contain three huntsmen with ease, and four at a pinch, was never empty, as no less than 60 couple of bitches were sent to him and his compeers. He is a remarkably large wiry dog, by Champion by Fitzwilliam Shiner, from Barmaid, with a beautiful forehand, though his roach back rather spoils him. Champion was unusually clear-winded, and it made very little difference to him if he had been in kennel a month. The Brocklesby, Lord Henry's, and Mr. Foljambe's, all had Comus, and Mr. Davenport has since used him. His dam Barmaid was always in high favour with Will Goodall. In her first season, she was so inveterately fond of hare, that she was all but condemned. However, as good luck would have it, the fox was lost after a capital run at Sir Thomas Whichcote's, amid hundreds of hares; they came to a check, and all passed ᴜᴀᴇ smeuse but her. She stopped and flew the hedge into the field, and spoke; and little as he believed her, she at last seemed so determined, that Will backed her over three fields. Not another hound spoke up to that point; but the cry began in the third field; the trot merged into a gallop; they raced into their fox after three miles, and the credit and life of the future dam of Comus was saved.

Will Goodall's Diary. Two long December evenings we spent with Will Goodall at Belvoir, to look over his diary, and have a little chat about the collection of materials for this chapter. He went with us heart and soul, when he heard it sketched out; gave us what he called "the cream of my hunting fun;" and there are, in fact, few pages in which we do not recognise some story or remark that we owe to him. Still there would have been many more, but for his peculiar dislike to speak of any run, however great it might be, without a head at the end. It was dismissed into the abyss of Time, as not worth remembering. Writing seemed his delight; and instead of preserving them in print, he actually copied out the whole of the price-lists of the hounds at the Quorn sales, to which he felt far too sad to go. His correspondence with other huntsmen was enormous; and in the Exhibition year he visited sixteen kennels, and never got to Hyde Park at all. He loved these outings, but still he was glad to get home; and watching his bees by the hour, and playing with his boys at cricket, were his chief summer pleasures. Croxton Races he enjoyed amazingly; and as usual he came to his wife for a handful of silver, for his friends amongst the yokels, who generally expected a glass of ale, if he had not caught them heading foxes or giving false halloos during the season. They used always to be on the look-out for him, as he kept the course with his whips, and many a joke passed between them There was a great story against one of them for hi avarice. Will had marked him down during the year for something ; and as he was one of the "good boys" that day, and kept behind the cords so well, he was honoured with half-a-crown. He positively grumbled ; and Will, in his pleasant way, said, " *Well, give it me back !*' and the man, thinking, from the tone, that it was to be exchanged for a crown, did so, and off Will rode with it, and taught him a lesson which his comrades did not forget to keep alive. He was rather amused this year with five of the Farmers' Plate horses getting distanced, and made a note of it in his Hunting Diary along with Zuyder Zee's victory. Two or three more days' hunting followed, and then the last one, when they met at Belvoir.

His phraseology was very unique and expressive; and " *screamed over the fallows,*" " *raced into him and eat him,*" " *a blazing hour,*" " *blew him up in the open,*" &c., were great expressions with him, and very characteristic of the ceaseless energy of the man. His diary, which will, we trust, be printed, is a very remarkable work—quite as much for the little comments on man, horse, and hound throughout it, as for its vivid description of the sport itself. Passing events are interspersed here and there. We find the death of "my much respected friend John Ashbourn" chronicled near Mr. Assheton Smith's ; and the marriage of a first-flight Meltonian is not forgotten. He never failed to see what every hound was doing, and at night a little cross was put above each of their names for every good hit they had made. When it was something out of the common, they had a note as well. For instance, " Lucy made a famous hit at Williford, and won her fox ;" " Belle showed great superiority of nose ;" and "Wishful beat the whole pack, and, racing out of it, caught the fox." Wishful, however, catches it herself in a widely different sense from his pen that self-same season ; and we find it down against her in black and white that she " and

Willing behaved very ill, running hare most obstinately in Easton Wood." There is also a word of condolence " for poor old Trusty, who never got away from Irnham Wood, and missed it altogether." He tells, too, how on one occasion he "had eleven and a-half couple of stallions out ;" how "George and Jem both got into Lenton Brook ;" how "Knipton gave me a terrible fall, jumping into a blind grip (no fault of his) ;" and how he had to whip off at night, "leaving him to give us another good run, and die, I hope, honourably in the open."

The closing entry was as follows—

"On Wednesday, April 6th, we met at Belvoir. Found our first fox in Barkston Wood ; run ringing about the hills with a very bad scent for two hours, when the hounds began to improve, getting off a vixen which had laid up her cubs. On to an old dog-fox. They set to like business ; and after running him hard for an hour-and-half, they forced him out over the Doghorse pasture—a ring over Musson's farm, and back to the wood. Away again, the same ring, in view of the hounds to cover in a large drain, which Comely was soon in, and drove him out ; and they killed him most handsomely in the open, after being engaged from first finding in the morning for four hours—thus ending one of the worst seasons on record. A hot sunny day like June, wind South, glass very low, and the ploughs as dry and hard as iron, the hedges and trees all as green as in the middle of summer, and a great many nests of young birds already hatched. Leverets and cubs are very forward ; indeed, such a forward spring has never been known by the oldest inhabitant.

Hounds out *this*, the last day—

Barbara	Racket	Caroline	Captive	Charlotte
Duchess	Redrose	Rival	Careless	Hostess
Lenity	Rally	Redwing	Dulcet	Ruin
Lively	Comely	Sempstress	Gertrude	Bonnylass
Furious	Famous	Chorus	Gracious	Norah
Wanton	Rachel	Comedy	Clara	Novelty
Willing	Destitute	Waspish		[16½ couple].

I rode a horse of Markwell's on trial, but did not like him. Second, Knipton ; third, Tom Chambers, on Staunton's horse.

Times out, 101 ; foxes killed, 56."

His Death. A bad fall from the first of the three horses near the Reeded House, when he lay for full a minute on his horn, which he invariably carried in his breast for convenience, or a cold which had been lingering about him, laid him low at last, just at daybreak, on the third anniversary of that very May-day on which the Hunt had presented him with its memorable tribute, and the Grantham inn had rung again with the chorus, " *Bill Goodall is the boy !*" They took his horn to his bedside some days before he died, and he showed them exactly how he fell; and half-sitting up, took it with all the animation of health, as if it revived him to lay hold of it again. He had only once risen from his bed during his ten days' illness, and that was to show Lord Henry Bentinck his young Rallywoods of the third generation in the new entry. As if with a sort of melancholy prescience that it was not to be, he often said how he " should love to see them at two-years-old ;" but they only swelled that strange mournful requiem for him which arose from the kennel, and fairly thrilled through the mourners as the hearse moved away. He lies not many paces from Tom Goosey, just within the church-yard gate at Knipton, and under the shade of that bold chain of woodlands in which his cheery voice had been heard, early and late, for seventeen seasons. By all, from " *my kind Lord Duke,*" as he called him, when his Grace bent over him to bid him farewell, down to the humblest labourer, for whom he always had some pleasant greeting or other, his memory will ever be cherished. Among his brother huntsmen he had long lived down all jealousy, and they freely accorded to him that high position which he had so fairly won both in the field and the kennel, and which he so un-assumingly maintained. Those who knew more of his inner life, or saw him on his death-bed, could trace to its true source that consistently gentle firmness which made him all-powerful in managing a cloud of horse-men ; and it would be well if many who love the sport as dearly as he did, would ponder, now that he is gone,

over the great and striking lesson which his life taught,
and which his fame sealed.

Mr. John Warde.   And so leaving Belvoir, we get back
once more to Northamptonshire. Fifty
years ago, Mr. John Warde, with Jem Butler and his
son Will (so renowned in after years with the Badsworth and Mr. Foljambe's), might have been seen at
Sywell Wood, and if a rate was heard, it was certain
to be at the expense of a Charon, or a Cerberus, a
Solomon, or some other mythological or scriptural
name. Cerberus went back to Mr. Lee Anthony's
Clothier; and the wisdom of Solomon was extended
over twenty-six inches. Philip Payne never liked Mr.
Warde's hounds, and thought them loose and weak-
loined. None could stoop better to a scent, but they
had no drive about them; and fine as the bitches
looked, they were rather too heavy, and lost action
very early; looking, so Will Butler used to say, "*good
seven, when they were four.*"

The Lambton   His hounds in the Craven country
Hounds.   afterwards were of a very different stamp,
and it was from his Jasper, Prodigal, and President,
that the Lambton pack principally sprang. Under
Winter, in 1828, the latter were in their glory, and
Sedgefield had become quite a Melton of the North;
but at last they were bred in and in, till there was no
music left, and huntsmen began to speak of their legs
from a mere tobacco-pipe point of view. Mr. Lambton
would never let them be pressed, or allow any one, if
he could help it, to be in the same field with them,
and hence they fared very ill in Leicestershire with
Lord Suffield, though their pace was tremendous when
they did get away. Three thousand guineas were
given by his lordship for 58¼ couple of old, and 20
couple of young hounds, and Mr. David Robertson
got 47½ of them for 750 guineas. In Northumberland,
Charles Treadwell got a chance with them at last, and
increased his "nose" score from 32 brace to 44½ brace

in four seasons. For three weeks in the wild weather they could not kill a fox, except by chopping, and then they went out twenty-one days, and killed twenty-two foxes in succession.

The days of Dick Knight, who spurned the lapstone and the awl at Roade, for the horn and spurs, are spoken of elsewhere; and for the pleasant era of Lord Althorp's mastership, we have those The Althorp quaint vellum-backed volumes of the late ᴱʳᵃ· Charles King's to fall back upon. It is well known that Charles offered to ride, dance, play the fiddle, and hunt a pack of hounds, against any man in the Midland counties; and to these he might have added a fifth accomplishment, namely, keep a diary.

In those days they had a much wider range of Pytchley country, and generally began on July 26th, and hunted up to the 3rd or 4th of May. No day closed without his putting down the list of the hounds, with observations. And very varied they are. " Gouty shown symptoms of tongue"—" Syren rather noisy"—" Plunder noisy at the fences"—" Glider (Fitzwilliam) ran a hare to Byfield, and back to Charwelton Spinneys." Then after the cheering announcement that " the young hounds joined in the cry," it is candidly stated that they ran a cur and two greyhounds half a mile down a lane. On November 18th, 1816, there was "still corn standing in Kilsby field;" and not long after " Young F." is gibbeted, as having " dug out a fox, and sold him in Kettering Market."

Crick had its origin about that time, Crick. from the fact of a fox having been found in a hedge-row, and being killed after a severe run in Oxfordshire. When the cover had been made, they went to it once a fortnight, and the horses were prepared as if for a Derby. The fields were not so large then, and the foxes better, and in fact there has not been a great thing from it since the fifty minutes to Naseby Reservoir in Mr. George Payne's day. Very fearful were Charles King's troubles, forty years ago, when he got among the "Crick thrusters;" and well might he, in the bitterness of his heart, record at night, "The day being bad, and the horsemen mad, drove the hounds mad, so we made mad work of it, and lost a brace of foxes."

No keener souls than Lord Althorp and Sir Charles Knightley ever watched the work of hounds, and they were seldom away from the kennel for nine months in the year. Once they rode over there from Pytchley in a deep snow, and took fifty couple out; and Lord Althorp always spoke fondly of it, even when politics and shorthorns had deadened his heart to his first great love, and said that he "should never forget the beautiful music of Sywell Wood." His lordship reduced his standard by crossing with Mr. Assheton Smith's, for whose use he sometimes paid Tom Wingfield 25*l.* a year; and besides Champion and Pontiff, he was especially fond of their Saladin. It was on Nov. 10th, 1817, that he got the fall, from which he never really recovered, in the course of a two hours' run from Brampton Wood; and then the reins departed for a season into Sir Charles's hands; and he found himself with fifty couple, principally by Ottoman, Orpheus, and New Forest Justice.

Badger Hunting. Two years before there had been some six couple by Outlaw, who was bred by Mr. Lee Anthony in the Oakley country. The old dog was light of tongue, and straight-necked, and could not turn with his fox; but to those who, like Will Butler, made it

> " Their delight on a *cloudy* night,
>   In the season of the year,"

to go badger-hunting, he was worth his weight in gold. The Pytchley spinneys were full of them; so much so, that shortly after reading in the diary that " we found old Bobtail not ripe for running, and killed him," there occurs an entry, "Sept. 19th, 1818, dug Brampton Wood fox out, and found five badgers in one drain." Scarcely any are left now; and one of those few is transplanted to the Brocklesby country to act as an architect of earths.

Mr. Assheton Smith's Denmark was a most wonderful dog for badgers, and very **Badgers.** soon learnt, under Jack Shirley's tuition, that the bridge of the nose and the brisket were the only vulnerable points. The majority of hounds do not enjoy it like a fox, and never know what to make of it as it runs through the low cover, or faces them with its back against a tree. Sherwood Forest used to be very full of them, and so was "the Dukery." Mr. Lumley Savile's hounds, which then hunted these parts, came across them so frequently, that they learnt to "unbutton a jack-badger's jacket just like a rabbit." On one occasion, when the earths had been more than usually well stopped, they took forty couple into Winkbourne Hills and Acrine Brale, and were home again before nine, with three foxes and four badgers for the hunting journal. The music that morning was like "a peal of church-bells"; and when the hounds got back to kennel, they looked as if they had been inside a dead horse.

Mr. Savile's pack were a very rough-looking lot; but still Mr. Musters fancied **Mr. Musters.** their Rallywood and Regent, and bred extensively from them in 1820. The Nottinghamshire Squire was very fond of small bitches, from twenty-one to twenty-two inches, and began his breeding principally from Lord Yarborough and the Duke of Rutland's Saladin, whom Mr. Shawe always said was his best. Saladin's daughter Proserpine was the dam of the celebrated Pilot (by Rutland Rasselas), who came to Mr. Musters in a draft, and became *the* hound of his heart. Knowing him to be peculiar in his habits, especially in drawing a cover, he would never let him be spoken to, and they would hear his peculiar yapping note right away by himself, when nothing else would speak.

He did not get clever dog-hounds, but Mr. Musters had twenty couple of Pilot bitches by him when he gave up the Pytchley. According to his contract, he proposed to leave another twenty couple for the country, when he finished in the April of '27 ; but "The Squire" would not deign to accept them. Mr. Musters continued to breed from Lord Yarborough ; and with some eight-and-twenty couple of hounds in his kennel, Bunney Park to draw, and Baronet to ride, he was as happy as a boy to the last, and brought his eighteen brace a season to hand. His dog pack were about twenty-three-and-a-half in height, and as steady as they could be ; but the bitch pack were rather wild. Nine couple of the best were selected for the latest picture that was painted of them, with himself on Baronet ; and poor Markwell on a brown mare, and Humphrey Pierce on a chestnut sire, were the servants who were grouped on the canvas with that undisputed king of gentlemen-huntsmen.

Lord Chester-   When Lord Chesterfield had the
field.   Pytchley country, with Will Derby as huntsman, he bred considerably from Belvoir Rasselas and Splendour. The latter had come to Brixworth as a draft hound through Mr. Errington, from whom his lordship bought the pack ; and like Pilot, he drew by himself, and was a great hound for going through gorse. Tyrant by Sir Richard Sutton's Woldsman was, however, the pet of his lordship's fancy, and when he had done with him he gave him to Sir Tatton. On one occasion they found a brace of foxes in an osier-bed at Misterton, and all save him went to the one who broke on the Lutterworth side ; but his lordship had the hounds stopped, and put to the fox which Tyrant brought out by himself ; and they killed it, after a great run, near Flecknoe.

Mr. Tilbury, with a truly prophetic eye, asked Sir

Francis Goodricke the name of his horse that morning; and on being told that it was "Patent Lever," he rejoined—"*Mind they don't make a stop-watch of him before they're done.*" And sure enough the baronet was glad to stop at Walton's Holt, four miles off the finish. There were other runs as great in that short but merry Northamptonshire reign, and none greater than that from Kelmarsh to Stoke. On this memorable day, Mr. Stubbs on Baronet and Will Derry on a grey, were both in Loatland Brook together, forming the most impressive of tableaux. Baronet had jumped short, and was scrambling out with his own rider on his back, and the weight of Will and his grey to boot. Lord Chesterfield got well over lower down, on Marmion; they just heard him say, "*I'm so glad Will's in the brook,*" but they never caught him till they killed, five miles away. Perhaps the fastest forty minutes was when his lordship was on Claxton, and Will was tearing away on a chestnut mare after losing his stirrups in Creaton Brook. They found at Berrydale, away past Cottesbrook Cow Pasture, leaving Spratton on the right, and close by Merry Tom (whose bones were never found till they were dug up at the stile where he died, by the Harborough Railway navvies), to Pitsford across the turnpike to Boughton Green, and ran into him on Moulton Lings. Their longest runs were with a Long Ould fox, which they had to bequeath to Mr. Tom Smith. In the first run with him the hounds were stopped at Earls Barton, after running twenty-five miles; and in the second, at Kettering, after twenty miles. Mr. Smith always thought that he ran him to Lamport one day, and chopped him the next.

Mr. George Payne, who bought fifteen couple at Mr. Greene's sale, bred very few hounds, as he did not like to spare his best bitches, and the kennel which ranked Destiny and Dainty by Sir Tatton's Dragon from Quorn Gainsome among its

The Pytchley.

best, was principally kept up by the drafts from Lord
Henry Bentinck's. When the late Lord Alford succeeded him, he had a large draft from the Duke of
Rutland's; but since then they have bred their own,
and principally used the Belvoir and Fitzwilliam
stallions. Barrister, that mightiest of jumpers, by Fitzwilliam Bluecap, has been the sire of many very good
hounds; but still the Pillager blood has been the chief
stay to Charles Payne. Pillager ran six seasons, and
never had a whip except to put him from the trough;
and at present there are twenty couple, principally tan
hounds, related to him. He was by Juggler by Lonsdale Senator from Playful (an own sister to Burton
Contest), whom Mr. Payne got along with Prophetess
in a draft. Helicon, Hotspur, and Prosper have been
all great Pillager dogs, and Pliant by Pillager especially distinguished herself in a run of thirty-five minutes
from Lord Spencer's cover to Sulby Reservoir. The
fox ran alongside it, and then dashed in midway, and
while the other hounds all got to the middle, and cast
themselves right and left, she was the only one that
crossed at once, and got half a mile past Sulby Hall,
towards Marston Hills, before the body of hounds
could get on terms with her. The fox, however, was
so washed that they never enjoyed it after.

Twelve Hours in Geddington Chace. Pillager died rather suddenly in his
sixth season, and hence Will Goodall,
who rather fancied him, never got a
chance. It was inflammation of the liver and not a
hard day, which killed him, but he went through one
calculated to kill a dozen packs. This was early in
August, 1853, and the scene a twenty-five acre plantation near Geddington Chace, close by the high road
from Kettering to Stamford. They found at a quarter
past five, and after being at it three hours with their
first fox, changed on to a shabby little vixen, who
slipped like a witch through the briars and sedge; and
when she had been headed three times, fairly defied

the dog pack to make her break. During the whole day they only threw up twice, and Charles Payne went in and cast them across it. For four hours they expected to kill every minute, but all in vain, and Lord Hopetoun and Captain Newland rode home, quite tired out at three. A sort of *cordon* of country people was drawn up in one corner, but she slipped through their legs, over and over again, and even when the second whip had been despatched to Brigstocke for four couple of the best bitches, and they had tried their best for another hour, she was as lively and inexhaustible in her dodges as ever. Pillager and Helicon (who was then a mere puppy), ran with the bitches to the last, and not only went home with their sterns up, but were the first off the benches in the morning. Every hound was stripped bare in his breast and fore-legs; Jasper and his sister Joyful dropped beaten on the road; and Charles Payne was so anxious about them all, that he went to see them twice after feeding.

The Pytchley country has always been celebrated for its foxes, but unfortunately *Pytchley Foxes.* there has been a sad craven habit of running them with greyhounds, and one man is known to have killed eleven in one year. In Mr. Musters's mastership, the Sulby Gorse fox was as renowned as the Gartree Hill one in Mr. Osbaldeston's, at Quorn. They both finished on the same day in their two countries, and as each had determined to have a turn at their old foe, Mr. Musters offered to back himself for 5*l.* to kill his fox, against "The Squire" killing his. He went out of the gorse at the first crack of the whip, past Bosworth, and leaving Theddingworth on the right, to Laughton Hills, where a man stood at the head of the earths. Bending rather more towards Sibbertoft, he ran the same line back again, and near Theddingworth they viewed him in a large pasture. "*There he goes,*" said Mr. Musters; "*they shan't say I killed him unhand-*

some." In this spirit he wouldn't lift his hounds a
yard ; and a flock of sheep bringing them to a check,
his fox got 'a field ahead, and though they once spoke
to it on the road between Harboro' and Welford, they
never could hunt him afterwards. " The Hunsbury Hill
Devil" was another of Mr. Musters's " difficulties" for
three seasons ; and generally took off by Wootten and
Delapre. On the last occasion, Will Derry tried to
head him at a gate ; but he would stop for no one,
and led them right through Brayfield Furze and
Yardley Chase nearly to Olney Bridge, where they
lost him. They gave him such a dusting that day,
that he appeared no more at Hunsbury Hill, which
had then some capital lying, and it was thought that
the dark-coloured fox which George Carter killed with
the Duke of Grafton's next day, travelling in the direction of Newport, must have been the old Pytchley hero
in banishment.

Foreign Foxes. The importation of foxes has increased
to a very great extent, and it is said that
in one year about a thousand were in Leadenhall
market. The supply comes principally from Holland.
It does not do to enquire where all of them come
from, but it is certain that Essex is fearfully stripped,
and Norfolk as well. A great many have come from
Scotland, and Ireland has of late become rather an
importing than an exporting country.

The largest order ever executed, was for a celebrated
ex-master of hounds in one of the Southern countries.
Philip Castang, the well-known Leadenhall dealer, had
an unlimited commission to stock the country, and in
three weeks, by writing to Holland, France, Germany,
and Scotland, he got together about seventy-five
brace, dogs or vixens, just as they chanced to come,
small ones at twelve and sixpence, and large at fifteen
shillings. As it was a remarkably good order, and he
did not wish to give time to have it limited by post,
he divided them into fourteen lots, and packed them

off on the six heavy coaches, beginning at six in the morning, and finishing off at 8 p.m., with two boxes on the top of the mail, so that cubs kept arriving at The Squire's, all day and night as well. That gentleman was considerably astonished at his agent's activity; but he sent a cheque, and simply said that he should require no more. However, so many of them preferred the better lying of the adjacent country, that several more went down in subsequent seasons.

Foxes are not so plentiful on the Continent as they once were; but still the French peasants who dig them out in the sandy districts between Boulogne and Paris, are seldom allowed more for them than a couple of francs and a dinner. The original French fox had a very long narrow head, and was rather long in the leg, and not so bright in colour as the English fox, but now there is hardly any difference between them. Russian foxes are blacker than ours, and Tom Goosey had a very favourite one, which used to live on a slab in his garden, and now confers lustre in death along with Mr. Lorraine Smith's hunt sketches, on the Belvoir Inn parlour. The Canadian foxes are very like our own ; and an octogenarian ex-master of the Montreal hounds assures us that when he used to hunt them with his twelve couple, in covers about forty miles by twelve, they would perpetually head back when they had run six miles in it, as if they did not like to venture into a strange country. The German foxes are grey in the muzzle, and, like the Dutch ones, have a more bluff countenance, and a bull head. They arrive with rabbit cargoes from Ostend, and at times from Rotterdam in cattle-boats. French foxes come over less punished than they used to do, when the communication was slower ; but as masters of steamers will not take them as freight, they import them in small egg-boats, ten or so in a box, with some plucks for provender.

(side note) Foreign Foxes.

Turning-down Foxes. We believe that " Frenchmen " were first imported before the Revolution · by some of the *noblesse* who had been guests at Althorp, but Dick Knight never thought much of them. In the first year of his Pytchley mastership, Lord Alford imported six brace of the largest Scotch ones he could procure. Three brace were turned down at Cottesbrook, but they were not found for two seasons, and Charles Payne could never account for more than three brace altogether either by brush or hearsay. This was not the first time that turned-down foxes have mysteriously disappeared. The last day that Sir Bellingham Graham was in the Pytchley country, he got thirteen foxes down from Herring's, and kept them in a straw place all night. The meet was at Lamport, and they drew every wood for miles round ; but to the sad disappointment of an enormous field, they were all blank.

Some large Sardinian foxes were once turned down at Belvoir, but they thought nothing of Blackberry Hill, and did little else but prowl, wolf fashion, about the houses. Sir Harry Goodricke was as unlucky with the three brace of Russian foxes which were sent him from Count Matuzevich. They were shaggy, rather long on the leg, and small headed, and took their feed regularly all summer at John O'Gaunt's ; but when the season came, they had absconded, and they never could get the slightest glimpse, or trace the faintest cross, of them. The Count also sent a few to Mr. Greene, and one or two of them showed good sport. Captain White sent a former Quorn master some very good ones from Derbyshire, which he kept in training, when cubs, in a barn, by the aid of a terrier and a four-in-hand whip. No pupils could have turned out better, two of them especially, which ran the same line from Peatling Gorse, nearly to Shankton Holt, where the Captain was up both times, and recognised them by his private " broad arrow."

Mr. Horlock also introduced some forty brace of Holland foxes, very lengthy, "with ears like donkeys," and very thick brushes. They had nothing of the phlegmatic character of their country of dykes about them, and were nearly as good as his Cliffe Wood fox, which was found three or four times a season for four seasons, and went as straight as a line each time for Rookeley. Harry Ayris also ran one for four or five seasons from .Haselton Grove to Iford, and he will have it that Jem Hills brought him back past Haselton Grove to Chedworth Woods.

It has always been a saying in the Heythrop, "*better by half shoot a child than kill a fox*," but alas! one of the finest of them was once found drowning in a trap, and his stuffed remains are in Jem Hill's parlour as a warning to evil doers. The Brewin are the largest forest foxes, and have very long legs, and a great deal of white about them. Sometimes it comes out very prominently in a particular year, and extends to stockings up to the knee. "The Forester" was one of the best of his clan, and for three seasons he defied Jem's wiles, but the last day of the 1856-57 season from Oddingly Ashes was fatal to him, and he was headed at the earths near the Cider Wells, after an hour and a quarter, and killed. Jem got two or three very red Irishmen, but they did not like his look at all, and, on further consideration, decided to emigrate, nobody knew where.

It has always been a joke of Jem's against Harry Ayris that his foxes are "of the squirrel sort;" but seeing that Jem's own have become so terrified of him, that they have lately felt compelled to reside in the trees at Middle Aston Gardens, thirty feet from the ground, we do not expect that he can throw a stone at the Berkeley foxes again, fond as they have always been of climbing. The Shropshire foxes had once the same habit;

The Heythrop Foxes.

Tree Climbers.

and in Mr. Smyth Owen's time they found three in one tree at Barton-on-Sales, one of which ran down the inside of the trunk. The Cantlop fox always resided in a tree, and Jack Wiglesworth knew almost to a yard where to go to, to whip him down. For five or six seasons, he was always lost near Cantlop Mill, as he went between the mill wheel and the mill, and ran his line back when they were casting forward for Eaton Maskett. The miller honourably kept his secret, but he was worried at last with a trap round his foot, and the country people said that he lifted up the earth, when he was buried, and mourned for him, as an old county worthy with a vested right in a mill.

Whaddon Chase has produced some rare bob-tails; and the Brocklesby had their "Bobby," but without a brush at all, and of five years' honest standing before hounds, when they ran into him at last. Probably they would not have done it then, if a footman, who commanded too good a view of the tree of refuge from his pantry window, had not dishonourably peached. The Wing fox was also of great renown, but he fairly beat Mr. Selby Lowndes after some great runs in the second season. They had a check near Cresslow, and lost him in Mr. Drake's country, and they never found him more. Joe Maiden had also several fierce tussles with "The Tiger," who looked like one, as his dark-whiskered form swept out of Huxley Gorse for three seasons. He got quite tired of Joe's assaults at last, and after giving them sixteen miles with two checks through Stapleford Gorse, Tarvin Delamere, and Piele Decoy, he was viewed for the last time under Tarvin Church, and never came back from the Forest.

Many great foxes retire from an ungrateful country at last, in this fashion, after they have beaten both huntsmen and hounds. Charles Tredwell had a light-coloured friend of this kind, whom he generally found for five seasons at Colthorp br Marston Whin, and

drove into the York and Ainsty. The most beautiful
fox that ever came to London, is said to have been
one which was trapped in a Norfolk warren; and
perhaps the biggest ever seen in Yorkshire was
one killed in Will Danby's time, in a thirty-five
minutes from Skipworth Common to Barlow Village. Foxes might well prosper in Holderness, as
on more than one occasion old James Stavely, who
was a sort of amateur guardian of Hatfield Whin, did
not scruple to square his good wife with a new gown
or a work-box, and then kill her chickens for the cubs,
out of pure philanthropy. He argued that it was better
for the interests of sport that he should give them her
chickens, than that they should eat their own dam, as
cubs in some few instances, one of them in Oldwick
Wood, have been known to do if she can bring them
no food. His heart fairly bled with sympathy
when he heard of the boast of the Cottam Warren
guardian, that he had killed eighty brace of Sir Tatton's
in two years, and that the more foxes Tom Carter
brought through it the better, as he was "sure to have
them as they come back." The Sledmere Whin fox
fell into nobler hands, as Mr. Foljambe brought him
back as the best trophy of his brief visit with his
hounds to that country. He was as handsome a fox
as was ever killed in Yorkshire, with white pads,
throat, and breast, and white up to the hocks and
under the belly, and his head, we believe, still hangs
in the entrance hall at Osberton.

Will Long had also a celebrated piebald friend, who
was known as "Old Bald," for three or four seasons,
and was then wantonly shot. They were never done
seeing his white face and neck going as straight as a
line from Toxley; and the veteran Will Baker used
regularly to say, "*I've got Old Bald for you again.*"
On one occasion he jumped up by the side of a pond
near the cover, and the delight of the old sportsman
was so great, that he set off when he had gasped out

"*Blessed ! if it ain't Old Bald,*" and rode like distraction as he never did before or since. Ropsley Rise had also its " Old Piebald," but Will Goodall gave him such tremendous drillings, always down wind, for six seasons, that he turned quite grey with trouble at last. His home was the woodlands, which he would never leave, and many of the woodmen said they remembered him for nearly eleven years. His fur was like fringe, and his skin was as thick again as it ought to have been, when they grabbed him at last ; and as they could hardly pull him to pieces, Will considered that it would be best to skin him, and to have a cap made out of it, which could defy Time.

A Farewell. But we have fairly run from scent to view, and our note-book, the companion of so many pleasant days, is thrown, blotted and helpless, into the waste-basket at last. After wandering with it, according to Bradshaw and the sign-posts, nearly three thousand leagues, we may well feel glad it is gone ; and it must go hard with us indeed before we buy its little marble-backed successor, and make a sporting Ulysses of ourselves again. We have left few nooks of real " Silk" or "Scarlet" interest unexplored, from the pleasant meadows

> " Where Greta trips with twinkling feet
> To join the statelier Tees,"

down to the glades of the New Forest and the haunts of the White Collars. In *Nimrod's* day, the Turf, the Chase, and the Road were as inseparable as the "Three Legs of Man" on the Manxman's shield. The memory of "The Road," with " Sir Harry Peyton's greys, Lord Sefton's white-legged chestnuts, Annesley's roans, Fitzroy Stanhope's dark-browns, Dolphin's pies, Russell's speedy bays, Barry's whites, Lord Harborough's fast little browns,"* and all the

---

* Sketches by Whiz.

other crack turns-out of the Twickenham Club, has its one modern Recorder; and it required no little hardihood on our own parts to determine not to sever The Turf and The Chase.

We would never have intermeddled with the latter, if the most subtle of tempters had not suddenly appeared in the form of Dick Christian. It was nothing but the bewitching conversation of that ancient fossil of a man, which made us disregard all red-tape precedents, and dash at the subject "for better for worse," and trust to luck and labour to pull us through.

If a gig-coalition had not been proposed, Dick's like of extreme Leicester usefulness, spent in "*ketching 'em up, and making 'em go,*" with those lank, weird-like fingers, would have been infallibly a sealed book to hunting generations to come; and hence if the "Scarlet" chapter to which it gave birth, is not strictly orthodox, we must suffer as unwilling martyrs to literature together.

THE END.

CPSIA information can be obtained at www.ICGtesting.com
Printed in the USA
244483LV00014B/85/P